Omar Massalha

TOWARDS THE
LONG-PROMISED PEACE

Saqi Books

British Library Cataloguing-in-Publication Data
A catalogue record for this book is available from the
British Library

ISBN 0 86356 057 1 (Hb)
ISBN 0 86356 065 2 (Pbk)

© Editions Albin Michel S.A. – Paris 1992

This edition first published 1994 by
Saqi Books
26 Westbourne Grove
London W2 5RH

Typeset by Group E, London

Contents

Contents

Contents

Acknowledgements

I wish to thank all those who have contributed to this book, especially Mr. Ahmed Derradji, a jurist and member of the Bureau of the International Association of Democratic Jurists (IADJ), for his valuable co-operation. I extend my most heartfelt thanks to the following eminent jurists and experts in international law whose thoughts made the legal part of this work possible: Mme. Monique Chemillier Gendreau at the Université de Paris VII; Mr. Badr Kasmé, Docteur en Droit, Licencié ès-Lettres; Mlle. Marie-Claude Dock, Docteur d'Etat en Droit; and M. Alain Pellet, Professor at the Université de Paris X, Nanterre and at the Institut d'Etudes Politiques de Paris and Member of the United Nations International Law Commission.

I should also like to express my thanks to my friend, Nicholas Gregory, for his important contribution to the production of the English version of this book.

May I also thank Mme. Scouarn, Mlle. Khadra and the Palestinian Graphics Centre.

Doing the Unthinkable[1]

'Welcome to this great occasion of history and hope'. Thus did US President Bill Clinton open the signing ceremony for the Declaration of Principles on Self-Government in the occupied Palestinian territories on Monday 13 September 1993 at the White House (see Appendix 11): Yitzhak Rabin was on his right and Yasser Arafat on his left. The most inconceivable encounter in modern history unfolded on the White House lawn before 3,000 guests.

The first official Israeli-Palestinian agreement, dubbed 'Gaza–Jericho First', was signed by Shimon Peres, the Israeli Foreign Minister, and Mahmoud Abbas (Abu Mazen), head of the PLO's Department of Arab and International Relations, in a ceremony marked by the same magnanimity with which Rabin and Peres addressed the Palestinian people in their official speeches.

Immediately after the signing of the agreement, at 11.43 Washington time and under the protective gaze of a radiant President Clinton, Arafat and Rabin shook hands in an expansive gesture which shattered the most deep-rooted of all the psychological taboos that had separated Palestinians and Israelis. In the process, two incompatible dreams evaporated: Greater Israel and Greater Palestine. Henceforth the political destinies of the two leaders would be strangely intertwined.

The previous three rounds[2] of bilateral Israeli-Palestinian negotiations in Washington had made disappointingly little headway. Israel had made one

9

minor procedural concession: it 'turned a blind eye' to the fact that the members of the Palestinian delegation declared that they were official PLO negotiators, following an ostensible 'dispute' between themselves and PLO headquarters in Tunis over Arafat's apparent complaisance towards Israel's official proposals. In an attempt to make progress, however, Arafat and the Rabin–Peres team had already opted for a strategy of secret contacts while continuing to send their delegations to Washington. Moreover, the Clinton administration had also sensed that the talks at the State Department were likely to be irretrievably deadlocked and had begun to look favourably upon the efforts of its friends to find alternative solutions to the impasse.

All in all, 14 secret meetings between Israeli and PLO negotiators were held in Norway in the space of 8 months; all but 3 of the meetings took place in the 4 months prior to the White House ceremony. The first such encounter took place from 20 to 22 January 1993 at Borregaard, south of Oslo. The Palestinians present were Ahmad Krayy (Abu Alaa), Director-General of the PLO's Economic Department; and Hassan Asfur, an aide to Abu Mazen. The Israelis were Yair Hirschfeld, a professor of history; his assistant, Professor Ron Pundik; Yoel Zinger, Legal Adviser; and Uri Savir, Director-General of the Foreign Ministry. Acting as go-betweens on the Norwegian side were Foreign Minister Johann Jörgen Holst and his wife, Marianne Heiberg; Secretary of State Jan Egeland; and the Director of the Institute for Applied Social Research (FAFO), Terde Rod Larsen.

The Americans, though aware of the secret contacts, seemed unaware of their seriousness until, in August 1993, Foreign Secretary Warren Christopher embarked on a Middle East tour to provide the final impetus for agreement on the 'Gaza–Jericho First' plan to be concluded in Oslo on 20 August. The Oslo document bore the initials U.S. (Uri Savir) and A.K. (Ahmad Krayy).

Mutual Recognition

It was not until the night of 8–9 September 1993 that agreement was reached between Krayy and Savir on mutual recognition: the Oslo negotiations culminated in the drafting of two letters of recognition at the Hotel Bristol in Paris, in the presence of Norwegian Foreign Minister Holst. On 9 September, in Tunis, Yasser Arafat put his signature to recognition of the state of Israel (see Appendix 10). Far more than the Gaza–Jericho agreement, this spectacular mutual recognition marked a historic turning-point.

The youth of the *intifada* could rightly claim to have been the driving force behind this recognition since, in fighting against the occupier—not Israel itself—they, more than anyone, had forced an awareness on the people of Israel of the harsh reality of the Palestinians' lot. Israel's decision to recognize the PLO was also motivated by the threefold crisis—financial, military and political—engulfing the organization and which had made it less threatening and more conciliatory to the Jewish state. Rabin had furthermore been obliged to acknowledge that the Palestinian negotiators in Washington were not empowered to make any substantial decisions without prior clearance from Tunis. Moreover, time was on the side of the fundamentalists, Hamas and Islamic Jihad, if there were no diplomatic moves. Their repeated and bloody attacks on Israeli soldiers and civilians had only highlighted the need to bolster the PLO as a force for moderation and a counterpoint to violence. Rabin could also act in the knowledge that he had received a mandate from the Israeli electorate during the 1992 general elections, thus encouraging his move towards this dramatic reconciliation.

This mandate was, however, conditional on a swift conclusion of a peace agreement with the Palestinians in particular and the Arabs in general. Since Rabin had set himself a nine-month deadline for an agreement on Palestinian self-rule, time was running out and his dilemma was about to be compounded by the imminent collapse of his coalition: the religious party Shas had announced its intention of leaving the government if one of its two ministers were found guilty of corruption. (The Supreme Court duly recorded a 'guilty' verdict only days before the Washington ceremony, prompting Shas to abstain in the subsequent Knesset vote which supported the peace agreement.)

At this point, it is necessary to stress the crucial importance of another reconciliation, both personal and political, between the perennial rivals for the Labour Party leadership: Yitzhak Rabin and his Foreign Minister, Shimon Peres. Rabin's endorsement of Peres' secret diplomacy imposed a formidable partnership on the Israeli domestic political scene: it boosted public support for the agreement with the PLO and was in stark contrast with a Likud opposition disconcerted by the speed of events and bedevilled by persistent friction between its glib, lightweight new leader, Benjamin Netanyahu, and the more experienced Ariel Sharon and David Levy.

The Palestinians, and Arafat in particular, were faced with a daunting choice: increasingly beleaguered, they had little option but to accept an encouraging preliminary agreement in the hope that it would contain the seeds of a much more advantageous final settlement five years later. It was precisely the lack of any credible alternative put forward by Arafat's opponents that made their objections so futile.

It was an economically straitened and morally chastened Israel and a disintegrating PLO, therefore, that finally moved towards the inevitable step of mutual recognition—secure in the knowledge that the peoples they represented were too wearied by war to object.

This seismic change in the Middle East enabled Israel to emerge from its regional and economic isolation and the PLO, for the first time, to give a piece of land to its people. Furthermore, it implied acceptance of the notion of shared land and held out the hope of mutual prosperity. The Palestinians thereby accepted that Israel would live in peace on land which, in 1948, had been two-thirds Palestinian-populated. The Israelis, for their part, agreed to the establishment of an autonomous Palestine at the expense of what might have been Greater Israel. After a century of bloody confrontations and 50 years of war, the Palestinians were no longer refusing to accept the legitimacy of Jewish settlement in Palestine, and the Israeli immigrants were finally recognizing the existence of the Palestinian people and its national rights—when both sides had previously believed that victory over the enemy should be total and that their opponents' fate should be exclusion or exile. Those who had dared speak of compromise had been branded as traitors to their respective causes. Arafat and Rabin had now signed out of existence an era of reciprocal exclusion through the act of mutual recognition.

By reconciling the competing rights to the land of the two nations, they had reconciled two peoples, ending decades of conflict, suffering, humiliation and hatred, and ushering in a new era of peace. The day after the White House ceremony, Jordan joined the peace process by signing, at the State Department, an agreement with Israel on the agenda for future negotiations.

The Washington agreements and the historic handshake between Arafat and Rabin sent a tremor through the Middle East, triggering a powerful tectonic shift in attitudes in both Israel and the occupied territories. Immense hopes were born, though the process which had been set in motion was fragile and complex. Its future—as well as that of Arafat himself—would be determined in Gaza. Many obstacles remained since almost all the most difficult issues had not yet been negotiated. The Israeli-Palestinian *agreement* might become the blueprint for a potential Israeli-Palestinian *alliance,* whose foundations would be essentially economic. The main enemies of such an outcome would be the diehards on both sides: Israeli and Palestinian extremists, moved by a messianic obscurantism and bent on perpetuating their own versions of a 'Holy War'.

The agreement would not only involve a freeze on new Israeli settlements and on expulsions of Palestinians; it would also rid the Israeli-Arab state of war of its *raison d'être*. If the pilot areas of Gaza and Jericho proved a success, autonomy would be extended, after negotiations, to the remainder of the occupied territories. The agreement was very vague, however, on a number of 'grey areas': the number of members who would sit on the future autonomous council; control over the Allenby Bridge; the limits of Jericho; the currency; the modalities of the Israeli troop withdrawal; and the question of whether the inhabitants of East Jerusalem could be elected in the polls to be held in the occupied territories for the council. These were just some of the points still to be settled in future negotiations on the implementation of the agreement.

Furthermore, all the 'sensitive' areas from Israel's point of view—final status of the occupied territories, refugees, Jerusalem, settlements, among others—were to be deferred to the negotiations on a final settlement. Until then, external security, the settlements and foreign affairs were to remain the sole preserve of Israel. The Palestinians would initially have to content themselves with their own police force and courts, which begged the question of how they would respond if an Israeli settler were to attack a Palestinian.

Israel had certainly negotiated from a position of strength and had yielded little or nothing on the key issues. However, both parties had decided that to try to resolve all the problems *before* signing an accord would be fruitless and would inevitably result in deadlock; they doubtless concluded that the most profitable way of overcoming such obstacles would be a 'leap of faith' and mutual recognition in the hope that the *symbolism* of public recognition would engender the goodwill and dynamism required to tackle the problems of *substance*.

In the process which had now been set in motion, the Palestinians could discern the makings of a Palestinian state. Since autonomy was to be a transitional phase, it was only logical that the next phase would be self-determination. Moreover, the Washington agreement provided for the establishment of *territorial* autonomy (whereas the Camp David Accords had only spoken of the autonomy of *people*), thus planting the seeds of a Palestinian state and discarding the Israeli Labour Party's much-touted 'Jordanian option'.

In assessing the agreement, however, one should not limit the evaluation to a book-keeping exercise. While the concessions made were admittedly assymetrical, Israel had none the less conceded the Palestinian people's legitimacy on land now to be shared between both Israelis and Palestinians.

The Timetable

The Washington agreement stipulated the following calendar:

13 October 1993   Entry into force

13 December 1993   Agreement on the Israeli army's with-
                                   drawal from the Jericho area and the
                                   Gaza Strip

13 December 1993—April 1994   First phase of the five-year transitional
                                   period

(In the period following the entry into force of the agreement and Israel's
withdrawal from Jericho and Gaza, authority would start to be transferred
to the Palestinians for education and culture, health, social affairs, direct
taxation and tourism.)

13 April 1994   Completion of the Israeli withdrawal
                                   from Jericho and Gaza

13 July 1994   Deadline for direct elections to the self-
                                   governing council

13 December 1995–13 April 1996   Start of negotiations on the final status
                                   of the West Bank and Gaza Strip,
                                   covering: Jerusalem, refugees, settle-
                                   ments, security arrangements, borders,
                                   and relations with neighbouring states

13 December 1998–13 April 1999   Entry into force of the permanent status
                                   of the West Bank and Gaza Strip

According to the timetable for implementation of the Israeli-Palestinian
Declaration of Principles on Self-Government, the PLO and Israel agreed
that the Palestine Liberation Army—renamed the High Committee for
Palestinian National Security—would be responsible for law and order in
Jericho and Gaza after the Israeli army had withdrawn. President Arafat had
recently ordered a restructuring of units for this purpose. It was also agreed
that Arafat would go to Jericho and/or Gaza in December 1993 or January
1994. Even at the time of the White House ceremony, it was possible to

14

imagine the tumult that such an arrival would arouse among the Palestinian population. For the first time, they would be welcoming back their legitimate leader to their homeland. The atmosphere among the Palestinians had already swung from apprehension at the first announcement of the agreement in Norway to an explosion of hope when the accord was finally signed in Washington. It was probable that Arafat's return would have at least as profound an impact on the Palestinians—and on the Israelis—as the Rabin–Arafat handshake.

Reactions to the Agreement

In general, the agreement provoked enthusiasm in the West, satisfaction in Asia, Latin America, Africa and Eastern Europe, reticence in Israel, a feeling of acquiescence among the Palestinians, and measured support in the Arab states. Conversely, the Middle East's fundamentalists and left-wing extremists expressed their violent opposition to the agreement.

The Palestinian opposition compared Arafat to Marshal Pétain, accusing him of wilfully undermining the PLO's institutions by provoking an artificial financial crisis in order to sap the morale of the organization's cadres and cajole them into accepting the autonomy agreement. Naif Hawatmeh, the DFLP leader, felt that the agreement had no legitimacy and called for a referendum and elections to a new Palestine National Council. None the less, the PLO Executive Committee grudgingly approved the agreement and a majority of Central Council members seemed certain to endorse it at their next session. In gaining acceptance of the agreement, however, Arafat had alienated several friends as well as his enemies: even prior to the announcement in Norway, leading moderates and centrists were resigning, including the PLO chief in Lebanon, Shafiq al-Hout, and the influential poet, Mahmoud Darwish. The most visible opponent of the agreement, after it had become public, was none other than Arafat's Foreign Minister and chief lieutenant, Farouq Kaddoumi, who refused to go to sign the document in Washington. (He later retracted his opposition in view of the imperative of national unity.)

The Lebanese Hizbollah condemned the agreement and Iran considered it to be a surrender by the PLO leader. The accord caught Amman and Damascus unawares. They had previously been in a position of relative strength at the Washington negotiations, but the 'Gaza–Jericho First' deal put them on the defensive. Syria, Lebanon and Jordan all complained that they had known nothing of the secret Israeli-Palestinian negotiations, when the Palestinians had pledged not to sign a separate peace which might create splits in Arab ranks. President Assad of Syria and King Hussein of Jordan both accused the PLO leader of going it alone as Sadat had done. Syrian, Lebanese and Jordanian displeasure went far beyond a matter of protocol, however. In Lebanon, the agreement triggered a wave of fear and anxiety as it did not clearly address the fate of the Palestinian refugees provisionally settled in the country since 1948. Furthermore, the Lebanese were afraid that Tel Aviv would replace the Beirut of the 1960s as a commercial and financial centre for tourism and services.

In Jordan, the Arafat–Rabin handshake was perceived as a threat; King Hussein was concerned at the prospect that lasting peace might raise hopes that would then be difficult to fulfil and merely end in frustration. Saddled with an enormous foreign debt and high unemployment, his country was no longer willing to manage others' crises. To compound Jordan's disquiet, the Washington agreement virtually ruled out the 'Jordanian option': there was little chance of a Jordanian-Palestinian confederation now that the Israeli Labour Party had apparently abandoned its traditional support for this idea by promoting the renaissance of a distinct Palestinian identity. Not only was Jordan no longer the logical heir to the PLO, but the US administration had abruptly decided to shore up Arafat's position as a bulwark against the Islamists. It was even conceivable that Jordan might be threatened by absorption into Palestine since the agreement might foster a powerful Israeli-Palestinian economic force to the detriment of Amman. Ever since 1967 the West Bank had been living under a *de facto* Israeli-Jordanian condominium, covering currency, education, civil administration, the Holy Places and the Islamic *waqfs*. This condominium, or jointly exercised 'right' to sovereignty over the West Bank, was now doomed. Jordan also feared a brain drain and a flight of capital to the new Palestinian entity, a process which would provoke a grave economic and financial crisis in the Hashemite Kingdom.

Syria's reservations stemmed from its traditional policy of seeking to obtain the best possible conditions for an Israel withdrawal from the Golan. Damascus had always wanted to be the 'godfather' of any agreement with Israel. It now feared isolation and the loss of its status as a privileged negotiator. The Israeli-Palestinian agreement did indeed constrain Syria's room for manoeuvre although President Assad would still exert pressure, through his many assets, to ensure that the Palestinians did not sign any final peace agreement with Israel before he did.

As far as the other Arab states were concerned, the Arab League Council of Ministers met in Cairo in September 1993 and decided to express only lukewarm support for the agreement, owing to criticism by Syria, Lebanon, Libya, Iraq and Sudan. In its final communiqué, it merely declared that the Israeli-Palestinian accord was 'a first step of some importance on the road to realizing the principle of the exchange of land for peace'.

The United States reaction was of particular interest. After years of vehement opposition to the PLO, and especially its Chairman, the importance of the US volte-face could scarcely be underestimated. In deciding to 'rehabilitate' Yasser Arafat and to burnish his image as a 'man of peace', the most pro-Israeli of US administrations had apparently forgiven a leader who was supposed to have irrevocably burnt his boats with the Americans during the Gulf War. Among the many unforgettable scenes that marked Arafat's stay in Washington, few could match the sight of the PLO leader dining with the 'high priests' (Michel, Moyniman and others) of the Jewish lobby in the Senate—'Israeli-occupied territory', in the memorable words of Pat Buchanan.

Economic and Political Consequences

The PLO's Economic Department estimated that $10–12 billion would be needed over seven years to revitalize the West Bank and Gaza Strip. According to a World Bank report, $3 billion would be required for a ten-year programme of reconstruction of the Palestinian infrastructure; a further $2.5 billion should come from privately financed initiatives.

President Clinton was to convene a donors' meeting in Washington at the beginning of October 1993 at which the US, Japan, the EC and the Gulf states, as well as Israeli and Palestinian experts, would attempt to organize funding for Palestinian self-government. The US was offering an annual financial contribution of $100 million over five years, while the EC pledged $600 million over the same period. The Scandinavian countries would contribute $140 million and the Japanese an annual $100 million for nine years. The still reticent Gulf states had not yet decided the amount of funding they would provide.

There would be a need, in any event, for capital and know-how from the Palestinian and Arab diaspora since the private sector would have to be the driving force behind long-term development and employment. Clearly, tangible improvements in the daily lives of the Palestinians would be the best guarantee of the success of the all-too-fragile process of reconciliation and, in turn, of the task of establishing peace and stability in the Middle East. The West Bank and Gaza would need an annual growth rate of 30–50 per cent to gain real autonomy from Israel. Anything less would amount to replacing the occupying soldier by an exploitative economic overload. Such an outcome would also mean that national tensions had merely been replaced by social ones.

Furthermore, if the Palestinians were to help to establish, maintain and consolidate peace in the region, they would require true independence and political neutrality, where the Israelis sought real security. Indeed, the existence of a neutral Palestinian state, such as we have outlined earlier, would be the most reliable safeguard of peace and prosperity. The Palestinian-Israeli-Jordanian confederation advocated by Shimon Peres might then follow, but it would necessarily have to be preceded by the creation of a sovereign and neutral Palestinian state. Abba Eban, one of Peres' predecessors at the Israeli Foreign Ministry, recognized the importance of nationhood: he spoke in favour of a community of sovereign states on the lines of the EC as a more promising alternative than confederation. Above all, it was vital that the Palestinians avoid the débâcle that occurred in Algeria after the Evian Agreements with de Gaulle's France—a *coup d'état* and the blinkered, destructive anti-Westernism that followed it.

Palestine would need to be democratic and secular; capable of overcoming its divisions, regionalism and thirst for revenge; and open to Israel and the wider world. This implied that both the Israelis and the Palestinians should swiftly bury their pain and resentment, learning to forgive so that life might triumph over death and love over hate. With their common roots in Canaanite civilization, they would have to join forces to build an area of democracy and prosperity. The risks involved were enormous—peace had many determined, fanatical and armed enemies—and many questions had been left unanswered, but the agreement was a step in the right direction. The gradual nature of its implementation would necessarily make it a slow, lengthy, delicate operation with its attendant risks and potential disasters, and the Palestinians could not tackle it alone. Its success was, therefore, an international responsibility.

The Washington signing ceremony had created a new drive towards peace. The international community now knew that it should act speedily in various ways to maintain the momentum. The Rabin government was also expected to follow up the agreement quickly with a series of goodwill gestures towards the Palestinians such as the early release of political prisoners, the prohibition of the torture of detainees, an end to repression and the swift return of the remaining deportees at Marj-Ezzohour in south Lebanon (189 of them had already been allowed back on 9 September 1993). Above all, Israel would have to begin serious negotiations with the PLO on the real problems. Failure to do so would only strengthen the hand of the PLO's extremist opponents.

First, the Jerusalem taboo had to be broken. If the Israelis and Palestinians had agreed to share the land, it was difficult to see why the Holy City—sacred to all Abraham's children of the three monotheistic faiths—

should be excluded. It ought now to be possible to envisage co-sovereignty for Jerusalem as a dual capital with, perhaps at a local level, a single municipal council. The Holy Places might then be afforded a special status and be safeguarded by international guarantees.

A solution also needed to be found to the question of the Israeli settlements in the occupied territories. Israel and the PLO would have to work together to solve this problem in a way that met the requirements of justice and legality without triggering a civil war or, worse, open conflict between Israel and an independent Palestine. The Israeli government would first have to recognize the illegality of the settlements constructed under its predecessors; the Palestinians should then avoid an attitude of vindictiveness towards the probably small number of settlers who would want to continue living as an isolated minority in an independent Palestinian state. Such magnanimity would be a fine example of the Palestinians' traditional tolerance and would present a welcome contrast with the repugnant phenomenon of 'ethnic cleansing' practised in the former Yugoslavia.

To give hope to the Palestinian refugees who had fled their homeland in 1948, the Israeli government could seek to redress the injustice visited upon them by recognizing at least the principle of their theoretical right of return. As an interim token of goodwill, these refugees might be accorded the right to visit their ancestral home in Israel. An equitable solution to the refugee problem would have two advantages for Israel itself. First, it would allow the most talented intellectuals, technicians and cadres of the Palestinian diaspora to bring back to the region the skills and experience they had acquired abroad in order to boost the Palestinian economy and promote political stability. Second, by granting the broad masses of Palestinian refugees the chance to revisit their childhood homes, Israel would defuse much of that explosive resentment which had made such a powerful contribution to the violence and terrorism of recent decades.

As for the PLO, it would now have to carry out a thorough revision of its charter and its programmes. The transfer from Tunis to Jericho, and the transition from being a government-in-exile to becoming a provisional self-governing authority, would amount to an immense political and organizational challenge for the PLO, but would also present an unprecedented opportunity to update and reform its methods of operating, thereby promoting democracy and creating unity in the Palestinian movement. Such a consolidation would be imperative in order to meet the enormous risks posed by the 13 September agreement.

The Israeli and Palestinian change of heart could now change the course of Middle East history. The Arab states could at last strike a balance between their traditional Islamic identity and the demands of modernization, building on the examples of Indonesia and Morocco. Regional development had been hampered by conflict for half a century; the Israeli-Palestinian peace now made the idea of a regional 'common market' seem feasible. The projects were already spilling forth from their long-neglected drawers: international experts had for years been drawing new roads, airports, railways, deep-water ports, electricity grids and waterworks on their maps of the Middle East. The reconstruction of Palestine would be the first stage in this colossal endeavour.

Ultimately, the aim would be to achieve long-term stability and prosperity in the region through the creation of some sort of large-scale Middle East economic community. An Israeli-Palestinian-Jordanian confederation might well prove to be the nucleus of such an economic community and, as Shimon Peres indicated, be the best guarantor of its constituents' security. This 'common market', in turn, might then expand to take in the Arab Mashreq and Maghreb, the countries of the Economic Co-operation Organization,[3] especially Turkey, Iran and Pakistan, and even some of the sub-Saharan countries. Crucially, each of these member states would retain its own identity, sovereignty and special characteristics, while working for the establishment of a common economic ideal that would be open to the outside world.

In conclusion, the successful development of economic and political co-operation between Israel and an independent Palestine would make everything possible. The future political stability of many of the world's areas of conflict can best be secured through economic prosperity, not military muscle. However, if the full potential of such co-operation is to be achieved in the Middle East, the 'change of heart' mentioned in this book, and which seems to be dawning as these words are written, must be taken to its logical conclusion: the Israelis must accept all the implications of the historic reconciliation with the Palestinians and their aspirations. By granting full *potential independence* to the Palestinians, Israel would be encouraging an accompanying *economic interdependence* which can only benefit both nations and both peoples.

8 October 1993

Foreword

The stubborn and varied nature—political, strategic, legal, as well as religious—of the Palestinian-Israeli and Arab-Israeli conflict has kept it at the forefront of the concerns of all who strive for global peace.

The commencement of the Middle East peace conference in Madrid on 30 October 1991 was a landmark in the history of the process to resolve this long-standing conflict. And it was pleasantly symbolic that Spain, for eight centuries the cradle of the unique confluence of the three revealed religions and of the three civilizations which stamped their identity on the Mediterranean—'our common sea'—should have been chosen to host this encounter of rekindled hopes.

Indeed, it is with the Madrid conference that Omar Massalha, previously the Permanent Observer of Palestine to UNESCO, opens his book dedicated to the yearning of Palestinians and Israelis for the promise of peace.

Two qualities stand out in this lucid and well-documented work. First, it provides a profound insight into a dauntingly complex conflict, explained in a way that takes us all the way back through its many ramifications to its source. The author's historical overview elucidates the various aspects of a confrontation fraught with symbolism and emotion—factors that mark this conflict out from others which all too regrettably continue to mar peaceful coexistence between peoples and nations across the globe.

The second and, in my view, fundamental characteristic of this study is the manifest honesty and moderation with which it addresses the most controversial dimensions of the conflict, especially in the legal sphere. Devoid of the shibboleths and invective, the bias and rewriting of history, which for so long have bedevilled approaches to this subject, Massalha displays a restraint that is all the more laudable for eschewing the partisanship to which his official duties may have driven him in favour of the measured and dignified tone of the academic. While not purporting to observe the impartiality of an uncommitted bystander—inconceivable in such instances for any human undertaking, however sincere—the author presents a serious and rigorous treatise which will enlighten not only the specialist but also all those who honestly seek to comprehend the intricacies of their history and thus better serve the ideal of peace.

Endeavours such as these are a necessary prelude to a productive dialogue between this conflict's two antagonists, and give voice to the hope that in the most promised of lands—witness to the dawning of the three founding faiths and of the great values of our age—its peoples may tomorrow see their dreams and actions converge and the tree of peace and life flourish anew.

Federico Mayor
Director-General of UNESCO
Spring 1993

Part I
The Middle East Peace Conference

1
Madrid: The Launch of the Peace Process

At last, after nearly half a century of talking without listening while exchanging nothing but gunfire, Arabs, Palestinians and Israelis have sat down face-to-face, perhaps driven more by outside pressure than desire, to engage in a dialogue of peace. The Madrid conference, officially called the Middle East peace conference, lasted three days in plenary session (30 October–1 November 1991) with scarcely two days of meetings for the bilateral negotiations between the Israelis and the Palestinians and Jordanians; the Israelis and the Syrians; and the Israelis and the Lebanese (3–4 November 1991). It marked, without doubt, a historic turning-point in the Middle East, and perhaps in the world. As an event, it ranked with the toppling of the Berlin Wall on 9 November 1989.

Several taboos were broken: the wall, or psychological barrier, was brought down and Arabs, Palestinians and Israelis met together in the same room in the Madrid Royal Palace. They listened, spoke and responded to each other. In Madrid, therefore, Israel obtained its 'psychological recognition' by the Arab countries: the first, essential stage towards diplomatic recognition. Madrid, in the eyes of international public opinion, established the legitimacy of Palestinian national aspirations and demands by virtue of the fact that the Palestinians participated as full partners and interlocutors.

The choice of Madrid was no accident. Indeed, the emotional legacy of the past was enormous but also ambivalent in its symbols. Arabs and Jews lived together in Spain from the eighth to the fifteenth century. It was the age of their cultural and scientific splendour and of Judaeo-Arab fraternity, as witnessed by the great Arab philosopher, Averroes (Ibn Rushd: b. Cordoba, 1126; d. Marrakesh, 1198), and his Jewish disciple, Maimonides (Mosheh Ben Maymon, b. Cordoba, 1135; d. Cairo, 1204). At the same time, however, Madrid, and thus Spain, revived in the collective Judaeo-Arab memory the trauma of their expulsion in 1492 and of the Inquisition by the overzealous Catholic Kings. By a strange quirk of fate, five centuries after these events, Spain played host to Arabs and Jews in order to establish peace among them in their own region.

Several times since their birth, the three monotheistic religions had fought and then become reconciled whenever they mixed religion with politics. After 638 the Muslims reconciled the Christians and Jews in Jerusalem, thus enabling them to live together. In Andalusia, this role was performed for some time by the Jews, in settling differences between the Christians and Muslims. At the Madrid peace conference, it was the turn of the Christians to reconcile Jews and Muslims by promoting peace between them. To Jews and Arabs, Andalusia symbolized a 'Paradise Lost'. Would the choice of Madrid help them to break free from their ambivalent feelings towards Andalusia, and lay to rest their illusions of domination and their nostalgia for times past, so that they might rid themselves of a similar vision of domination in the future, and thus acknowledge that a profound change had taken place in the world? They would, albeit perhaps to varying degrees, all thereby be adopting a new mind-set in order to find a fresh, constructive vision and to make peace among themselves in the region. As Michel Jobert, the former French Foreign Minister, said, 'It is high time to stop conceiving of tomorrow as though it were yesterday.' In other words, would the Arabs and Jews be ready to make the concessions required for the negotiations to achieve peace? Would they see Madrid as a bridge linking all the peoples of the Mediterranean—Madrid, designated cultural capital of the Europe of tomorrow and of the second Renaissance, and the capital of a country which was to host the 1992 Olympic Games in Barcelona and the Universal Exposition in Seville? Would they heed Jefferson's appeal of 1 August 1816 in which he stated, 'I prefer the dreams of the future to the history of the past'? Or that of Abraham Lincoln: 'I don't know who my grandfather was; I am much more concerned to know what his grandson will be'? Does one not find in such words the message of the Spanish people, so enthusiastically and proudly hosting this Middle East peace conference in their capital?

The choice of Madrid surprised everybody. The decision was announced on 18 October 1991 at a joint press conference held by the American Secretary of State James Baker and the Soviet Foreign Minister Boris Pankin in Jerusalem, the city of symbols, the very capital of all the children of Abraham's faith: Jews, Christians and Muslims. Just as the choice of Madrid was highly symbolic, so also was the Holy City of Jerusalem, where it was declared that the Middle East peace conference would open on 30 October 1991 in Madrid, in the presence of Presidents George Bush and Mikhail Gorbachev. In issuing the invitations, the co-sponsors presented Israel, Syria and the PLO with a fait accompli: Israel had preferred the *status quo*, Syria an international conference, and the PLO full participation as a partner (only to be—at least officially—completely excluded). The three parties were compelled to make up their minds, since none of them wanted to shoulder the grave responsibility of thwarting the Americans' endeavours.

Since the occupation of Jerusalem by General Allenby on 9 December 1917—some five weeks after the Balfour Declaration of 2 November of that year—every attempt at reconciliation or peace in Palestine had failed. By 1991, however, the international climate had improved, with the settlement of local or regional conflicts across the globe: in Afghanistan, Namibia, Nicaragua, South Africa, Angola, Eritrea and Cambodia, among others. This situation, together with James Baker's ability to take advantage of such propitious circumstances, enabled the Americans to apply their procedural formula, setting in motion once again a peace process which had been dogged by failure (the most recent example being the election mechanism for the occupied Palestinian territories).

Three factors led to the success of American diplomacy. First was the end of the Cold War (owing to the ideological, political and economic collapse of the former Soviet Union, which had been allied with the Arabs), followed by the USSR's declining interest in the Middle East and the ensuing unrivalled supremacy of the US, Israel's ally and by now the sole superpower (a factor which forced Syria to abandon its policy of strategic parity with Israel). Second was the 1991 Gulf War which, by destroying Iraq's military strength, neutralized the military option against Israel for the foreseeable future—although this war made the US politically and morally beholden to its Arab allies in the anti-Iraqi coalition to make a 'sincere effort' to relaunch the peace process after the conflict had ended. And third was the strategy of open-mindedness and unilateral concessions pursued by the PLO since 1988, in line with the realistic objectives of the *intifada*.

Taking these factors into account, as well as Israel's intransigence, especially Shamir's stubborn refusal to accept the principle of 'land for peace', the US administration had to maintain its credibility in order not to be accused of a policy of 'double standards' in the region. Seeking rapid progress, for reasons both of domestic politics (helping in George Bush's re-election) and of foreign policy (facilitating a *pax americana* in the Middle

East), Baker stressed form over substance: he concentrated on finding a procedural formula acceptable to Israel, the PLO and the Arab countries, in the absence of even a modicum of agreement among them on substance. True to its maximalist, power-based policy and its rationale of force, Israel imposed its own conditions, so that procedure took on extreme importance. 'Every detail will become fundamental,'[1] wrote Michel Jobert in this connection.

Syria, Jordan and Lebanon all participated in the conference, with recognition of Israel held back as a bargaining chip. The Palestinians, by accepting 'autonomy' as a transitional stage, placed themselves in a minimalist negotiating position, thus restricting their room for manoeuvre; they therefore chose a strategy which contrasted with Israel's maximalist stance of denying that the Palestinians had any right to their own land. The USSR, for its part, pledged to follow the US strategy. As for the European Community, it decided not only 'to do nothing which might hamper American diplomacy',[2] but also to support the Americans' efforts. For Egypt and the Gulf states, their decision to take part in the conference was not a sovereign one. It was a sign more of their dependence on Washington than of their policy of moderation or resignation. The United Nations' attendance at the conference was only token and the UN was not entitled to speak. The countries of the Arab Maghreb Union participated as observers at the request of both the Americans and the Palestinians.

In accepting the American formula, the parties concerned allowed the US and USSR to co-sponsor the Madrid conference, with the European Community, the Gulf Co-operation Council, Egypt, Saudi Arabia and an observer representing the UN Secretary-General also attending. In a compromise agreed on by all the parties, James Baker thus managed to convene a conference which came half-way between the Israeli demand for a regional conference and the European-Soviet-Arab demand for an international one. This formula was designed to enable the conference subsequently to involve the UN Security Council in endorsing any agreed peace settlement.

To gain a better grasp of the stakes involved and the complexity of the situation which had made the Baker approach necessary, and to understand its origins and points of reference, we will refer briefly to the failures to achieve peace in the Middle East and at the evolution of US policy there.

Missed Opportunities

The Balfour Declaration of 1917 was a turning-point in Palestine's history.

From that declaration to this day, the country's destiny has been played out beyond its borders: in London until 1947–48, then in New York and Washington. Before international factors intervened in determining Palestine's fate, Jews and Arabs had lived side by side in an atmosphere of tolerance, friendship and co-operation from Marrakesh to Baghdad, in Algiers, Tunis, Cairo, Jerusalem, Beirut and Damascus, not forgetting Yemen.

The first half of this century saw the emergence of an international dimension which took several forms: promises, secret agreements, Commissions of Inquiry and White Papers among others. It also witnessed the failure of the manifold forms of Palestinian resistance: national congresses, petitions, strikes, riots and outbreaks of violence, followed by the first Arab-Israeli War of 1947–48 (see Part II). After the 1947 UN General Assembly resolution which partitioned Palestine into two states, one Arab and one Jewish (Resolution 181(II)), and the end of the British mandate on 14 May 1948, Count Bernadotte and his aide, the French colonel, André Sérot, were the first to lose their lives in the quest for Palestinian-Israeli peace when they were murdered by the terrorist Stern Gang of Yitzhak Shamir on 17 September 1948. Through Resolution 194 (III) of 11 December 1948, the United Nations requested that a Conciliation Commission composed of members from the United States, France and Turkey continue Count Bernadotte's efforts to seek a negotiated and peaceful settlement, based on Resolution 181 (i.e. the Partition Resolution).

This commission organized two conferences in Lausanne (1949) and Paris (1951), but both failed because of Israel's demand that the basis for the negotiations should be the 1948–49 demarcation lines and not the 1947 Partition Resolution. The Arabs refused to recognize Israel's *fait accompli* and no real negotiation was possible. The Palestinians were completely absent from these UN efforts. The Conciliation Commission proposed the settlement of most of the Palestinian refugees in the Arab countries, a sharing of the waters of the River Jordan, a regional development plan, a free port at Haifa for Jordan and a few minor Israeli withdrawals from Palestinian territory conquered in 1948–49. The Arab states and Israel rejected the commission's proposals. The failure of the two conferences marked the end of the UN's attempts to give effect to the Palestine Partition Resolution.

The United States had been involved in Palestinian-Israeli affairs since 1919, when President Wilson asked the Allies at the Versailles peace conference to send the King-Crane fact-finding mission to the area. The mission's report had proposed a radical change in the Zionist programme in the Palestinian people's favour. However, in the 1940s, the US supported

Jewish immigration into Palestine. As for the American position in the UN Conciliation Commission, it was spelt out in a letter of 29 May 1949, conveyed to the Israeli government by Ambassador James G. McDonald,[3] in which President Truman expressed his disappointment at Israel's intransigent position at the Lausanne conference. He described Israel's rejection of any territorial compromise and of any settlement of the refugee question on the basis of Resolutions 181 and 194 as dangerous for peace in the Middle East. He did not, however, take any specific measures to force Israel to comply with the two resolutions.

Eisenhower was the first US President to exert pressure on Israel. After the tripartite (Franco-Anglo-Israeli) aggression against Nasser's Egypt in 1956 (the Suez War), he demanded, in a televised speech on 20 February 1957, that Israel withdraw from the territories it had occupied (Sinai and the Gaza Strip), or it would be subjected to sanctions. In this resounding speech, Eisenhower stressed the role of the United Nations in guaranteeing justice based on respect for international law, in the belief that 'peace and justice' were two sides of the same coin. He also pledged to seek just solutions to the problems of the Middle East region which would accord with international law.[4]

The Suez crisis set the seal on Nasser's leadership of the Arab world. France and Britain lost their traditional positions as regional powers. What ensued, however, was the beginning of direct confrontation in the Middle East between the Americans and the Soviets. This new and important element would make the Palestinians the principal losers and victims of great-power rivalry.

American policy on the Arab-Israeli conflict began to shift in the middle of the 1960s[5] under the administration of President Lyndon B. Johnson, who had previously led the Jewish lobby in Congress. It entailed financial and military aid, strategic co-operation, American vetoes in the Security Council in support of Israel, and systematic voting with Israel at the UN General Assembly. In short, Israel became almost a fifty-first American state and a forward base against the Soviet Union, which had become the ally of the Arabs. This American policy, begun by Johnson, was continued and strengthened under the administrations of Presidents Nixon, Ford and Carter, and reached its peak under Ronald Reagan. Subsequently, the end of the Cold War and the collapse of the Eastern bloc brought the Bush administration round to a more balanced policy, perhaps inspired by that of Eisenhower.

In this new situation, marked moreover by the consequences of the 1991 Gulf War, Israel's strategic importance lost ground to the need to preserve oil interests in the region and to strike a political balance, which necessarily required a just settlement of the Palestinian problem. Otherwise, this problem might spawn political or religious extremists, who would pose a serious threat to the stability of the Arab regimes and to the interests of the United States.

The period from 1957 to 1967 was characterized by the absence of any initiatives to resolve the Arab-Israeli conflict with the exception of the 1965 initiative of the Tunisian President, Habib Bourguiba, which advocated the partition of Palestine into two states in accordance with the 1947 UN resolution—an initiative rejected by Israel, the Palestinians and the Arab states alike. It was only after the 1967 Arab-Israeli War that the Security Council intervened by adopting, on 22 November 1967, Resolution 242 (see Appendix 4), which decreed 'the withdrawal of Israeli armed forces from territories occupied in the recent conflict'. The UN Secretary-General then designated the Swedish Ambassador, Dr Gunnar Jarring, as his mediator 'to proceed to the Middle East to establish and maintain contacts with the states concerned in order to promote agreement and assist efforts to achieve a peaceful and accepted settlement'. The first Jarring mission to the Middle East in 1968 failed, following Israel's refusal to withdraw fully from the occupied territories.

At the same time, General de Gaulle presented a draft settlement based on the commitment of the Big Four (the United States, the Soviet Union, France and Britain) to work for the implementation of Resolution 242. President Johnson expressed reservations about the French proposals. The four-party discussions took place at the UN but were to no avail, owing to the Americans' lack of support. The failures of the Jarring mission and the French plan led to the outbreak of a war of attrition between Israel and Egypt, beginning in March 1969.

On 9 December 1969 the US Secretary of State, William Rogers, announced a two-track settlement plan: an Israeli-Egyptian element, involving Israeli withdrawal from Sinai, demilitarized zones and true peace between the two countries; and an Israeli-Jordanian one, involving Israeli withdrawal from the West Bank, which would become totally demilitarized. Israel rejected the plan because of the Israeli-Jordanian element, while Egypt accepted it as a basis for negotiations. On 19 June 1970 Rogers put forward a second plan to halt the dangerous drift. This plan proposed a three-month cease-fire, the acceptance by all the parties of Resolution 242 and the resumption of the Jarring mission.

On 23 July 1970, the anniversary of the 1952 Egyptian revolution, Nasser announced his acceptance of the Rogers Plan; Jordan followed suit three days later. On 1 August Israel, in its turn, accepted the second Rogers Plan, and Jarring resumed his mediation on 6 September. The Palestinians rejected both Rogers Plans, as they had rejected Resolution 242, since they felt that they ignored the existence of the Palestinian people and its national rights, reducing the problem to a mere question of refugees. Nasser supported the Palestinians by stating, on several occasions, that Egypt, in accepting Resolution 242, was only seeking to erase the aftermath of the Israeli aggression of June 1967, while the Palestinians were entitled to refuse both Resolution 242 and the Rogers Plan since they denied the existence of the Palestinian people and its national rights.

Two serious events caused the Rogers Plan to founder: the Jordano-Palestinian War of 15–27 September 1970 ('Black September') and the death of Gamal Abdel Nasser on 28 September of the same year. Nasser had had two options: one military (the 'Granite Plan') and the other political (the Rogers Plan). President Sadat would later say that Nasser's choice before his death had been the second option, that of peace. After these two events, Israel became the pillar of American policy in the Middle East. The period between Nasser's death and the October 1973 War was one of 'neither war nor peace'.

Jarring abandoned his mission in 1972 after several fruitless attempts at settling the Arab-Israeli conflict. The United Nations thus failed to secure implementation of Resolution 242 on Israeli withdrawal from the Arab territories occupied in 1967, just as it had earlier failed to apply the Partition Resolution (181) of 1947. Both failures may perhaps be explained by the statement of the then Israeli Defence Minister, General Moshe Dayan, on the 1967 War:

> Our fathers had reached the borders assigned by the Partition Plan. The generation of the Six-Day War enabled the borders to be extended to Suez, the Jordan and the Golan, but it is not over yet. After this, there will be new cease-fire lines.[6]

At an international meeting of parliamentarians in Cairo in February 1970, Bertrand Russell pointed out that, in pursuit of its policy of the *fait accompli*, Israel had periodically resorted to violence to extend its borders, with each new conquest becoming the point of departure for the negotiations it then offered while it wilfully ignored the injustices created by its previous aggression.[7]

During this period of phoney war, three new factors came into play. First, Kissinger, who was hostile to the Rogers Plan, took up the Middle East question and advocated a policy of stalemate in order to neutralize the Soviet Union in the region and to force the Arab countries of the Mashreq to turn to the United States to break the deadlock. Second, President Sadat caused a major stir when he decided, on 18 July 1972, to expel the Soviet Union's military advisers from Egypt. And, third, the oil-producing countries took control of the international oil market. These three decisive factors, to which should be added the October 1973 War and the first 'oil shock', freed the logjam in the Middle East. Before the end of hostilities (which had begun on 6 October 1973), the Security Council adopted Resolution 338 on 22 October 1973—originally a joint US-Soviet text. It stipulated the following:

The Security Council:
1. Calls upon all parties to the present fighting to cease all fighting and to terminate all military activity immediately, no later than 12 hours after the movement of the adoption of this decision, in the positions they now occupy.
2. Calls upon the parties concerned to start immediately after the cease-fire the implementation of Security Council Resolution 242 (1967) in all of its parts.
3. Decides that, immediately and concurrently with the cease-fire, negotiations shall start between the parties concerned, under appropriate auspices, aimed at establishing a just and durable peace in the Middle East.

Resolution 338 was immediately accepted by Egypt, followed by Syria and Israel. Kissinger went to the Middle East to prepare the Geneva conference in order to promote the implementation of the resolution. The conference opened in Geneva on 21 December 1973, under the auspices of the United States and the Soviet Union. Syria boycotted the first session; the Palestinians had not been invited to participate. In two days of proceedings, each party rigidly expressed its position. The only decision taken at this first session was the creation of a technical military committee to discuss disengagement.

On 18 January 1974 an agreement was signed by Egypt and Israel for the disengagement of their forces along the Suez Canal front. On 31 May 1974 a similar agreement was signed by Israel and Syria. (Both agreements were signed in Geneva.) On 4 September 1975 a second Egyptian-Israeli disengagement agreement was signed after Israel had received a set of American commitments in return, comprising: military and economic assistance, oil, diplomatic support, co-ordination on the issue of the Geneva conference to ensure that the negotiations were conducted on a bilateral basis, a refusal to negotiate with or to recognize the PLO so long as it did not recognize Israel's right to exist and refused to accept Resolutions 242 and 338, and the rejection of Palestinian participation at the Geneva conference. These Israeli conditions, accepted by the Americans, blocked the peace process which had been set in train in Geneva.

The first signs of a change in the American attitude to the Palestinians, and hence of a new US policy, began to emerge when Senator Fulbright[8] became the first American official to recognize the rights of the Palestinians as a people. Joseph Sisco,[9] Assistant Secretary of State for the Near East, was the first leading American official to advocate recognition of a Palestinian entity. It was not until the inauguration of President Carter in 1977, however, that an American president for the first time recognized 'the legitimate rights of the Palestinian people'.

Carter took two initiatives to resolve the Arab-Israeli conflict, based on three vital issues: peace, borders and the fate of the Palestinians. On 1 October 1977, at his instigation, the Americans and Soviets published a joint communiqué calling for a comprehensive settlement at the Geneva conference, which was to resume in December at the latest. The text of the communiqué called for the withdrawal of Israeli armed forces from the territories occupied as a result of the 1967 conflict, and a solution to the Palestinian question which would include guarantees of the Palestinian people's legitimate rights. The two superpowers pledged to guarantee the international borders subsequently to be determined in a comprehensive settlement. In the communiqué, they invited the Palestinians' representatives, for the first time, to take part in the Geneva conference.

The Palestinians and the Arab countries welcomed this declaration, whereas Israel, the American Jewish lobby and the American conservative right (because of its hostility to any agreement with the Soviets on these problems) exerted unprecedented political pressure on President Carter. Yielding to this pressure, Carter retreated, in a US-Israeli 'working paper' in which he reneged on his commitments. Sadat's visit to Jerusalem on 19 November 1977 finally dashed the hopes vested in this conference, which never reconvened.

The Camp David Conference

American policy took a new turn after the failure of the Geneva conference when President Carter invited the Israeli Prime Minister, Menachem Begin, and the Egyptian President, Anwar Sadat, to participate in a summit at the US President's residence at Camp David. This conference lasted from 5 to 17 September 1978, with Carter playing the main role as intermediary. On the basis of Resolution 242, the three leaders adopted framework accords purporting to be a 'comprehensive settlement' of the Arab-Israeli conflict. In fact, they constituted a separate peace treaty concluded between Egypt and Israel: Egypt gradually recovered the Sinai and Israel obtained full diplomatic recognition from Egypt.

The Israeli-Egyptian Treaty was signed on 26 March 1979 (see Appendix 6). The negotiations on Palestinian autonomy or, more precisely, on 'the modalities for establishing the elected self-governing authority' in the West Bank and Gaza, began on 25 May 1979. Israel put forward its own interpretation of the Palestinian section of the Camp David Accords:

> The Israeli Military Authority would remain the source of any authority devolved to the administrative council; land and water resources, security and public order would remain under Israel's control; the settlement policy would be continued.[10]

Egypt rejected Israel's claims while putting forward its own interpretation: autonomy was a transitional phase to ensure the transfer of power to the Palestinians as a step towards sovereign independence.

On 30 July 1980 Israel annexed East Jerusalem. President Sadat responded by suspending the talks on Palestinian autonomy, after eight fruitless negotiating sessions. The Palestinian section of the Camp David Accords—a document entitled 'Framework for Middle East Peace'—is but a new version of the Begin Plan of 28 December 1977 (see Appendix 5). The Palestinians rejected all the provisions pertaining to autonomy. Indeed, they considered that these accords did not bind them in any way since they were not party to them. Xavier Baron has written in this connection:

> As was the case sixty years earlier with the Balfour Declaration, the Palestinians were confronted with decisions which would determine their destiny without their being consulted and without their being given the chance to decide freely on their future . . . The Camp David Accords not only afford them merely a secondary role but, perhaps more seriously, divide them into categories, each of which is promised—potentially—a different solution: there are those from the West Bank and Gaza; those of 1948; the 'refugees'; and lastly those from East Jerusalem, who are completely forgotten. The fragmentation of the Palestinian people is enshrined in the text.[11]

For George Corm, the Camp David Accords were a treaty favouring Israel:

More seriously, the accords are an updated version of the Balfour Declaration. Egypt and Israel alone effectively dispose of the vestiges of Palestine, the West Bank and Gaza, while inviting a third government, also non-Palestinian—that of Jordan—to join future negotiations on the legal status of these territories; a status which the agreement leaves undetermined for a period of five years, enabling the Israelis to maintain their claims of sovereignty over the West Bank and Gaza.

For the Israelis, Palestinian autonomy means the administrative autonomy of the inhabitants, as the accords only provide for an autonomous authority; the text even specifies in brackets 'administrative council'. None of this either closely or remotely resembles a blueprint allowing the collective will of a people to be sovereignly exercised. Menachem Begin, furthermore, had Jimmy Carter make quite clear, in a letter annexed to the accords, that for the Israeli government, the expression 'West Bank' is 'interpreted and understood' as 'Judaea and Samaria', the biblical terms upon which Israel bases its legal claims. In the same letter, the American President specified that he had taken good note of the fact that the expressions 'Palestinians' and 'Palestinian people' were and would be interpreted by the Israeli party as 'Palestinian Arabs'. The nuance is a major one: it maintains and sets the seal on the Zionist fiction according to which there is no such thing as the Palestinian people; one, that is, which is able to express collectively an autonomous political will.[12]

With these accords, Israel neutralized any action Egypt could take in the region, thus enabling it to muster all its strength to eliminate the PLO and the Palestinian resistance. It launched three attacks against the Palestinians in 1978 and in 1981–82, the last of which succeeded in forcing the PLO's cadres and fighters to leave Lebanon. These conflicts pointed up the real problem, that of Palestine, because its protagonists were exclusively Palestinians, and it was on that problem therefore that the subsequent peace initiatives would focus.

The International Conference

The return to a political and diplomatic stalemate in the region, as a result of the failed Geneva conference and the separate Israeli-Egyptian Accords, was to give rise to a new initiative, this time from Europe. Thanks to the active role played by France, the European Community began slowly but surely to involve itself in Middle East matters.

Madrid: The Launch of the Peace Process

On 13 June 1980 in Venice, the EC adopted a declaration intended to serve as the basis for a peaceful solution in the Middle East. The declaration listed the political elements conducive to breaking the prevailing deadlock: Israeli withdrawal in accordance with Resolution 242; the Palestinian people's exercise of their right to self-determination; involvement of the PLO in any peace settlement; and a halt to the establishment of Jewish settlements in the occupied territories, which were deemed illegal and a threat to peace.

President Mitterrand, during his 1982 visit to Israel, tried to mediate on the basis of the principle that there should be two peoples and two states on the land of British-mandated Palestine. He found no common language with the Israeli Likud leaders, who spoke to him in terms quite unlike those used by Labour: an Israeli withdrawal from the West Bank was not negotiable—no longer for 'security' reasons, as was the case in Labour's time, but because of the 'historic rights' of the Jewish people.

On 7 September 1983 an international conference on the question of Palestine was held in Geneva under the auspices of the UN. Its recommendations on the mechanism to resolve the Palestinian question were adopted by the UN General Assembly on 13 December 1983 (Resolution 38/58C), which invited the UN Secretary-General, in consultation with the Security Council, to convene an international conference on the Middle East to seek a settlement of the Israeli-Palestinian/Arab conflict on the basis of UN resolutions. On 12 December 1985 General Assembly Resolution 40/96 restated the call for an international conference to be convened. On 23 February 1987 the European Community supported the idea of the international conference as the most appropriate means of resolving the Arab-Israeli conflict. The United States, however, opposed the convening of such a conference, feeling that the time was not yet right. During his visit to Cairo in February 1987, however, the Israeli Prime Minister, Labour's Shimon Peres, announced his acceptance of the idea of an international conference as an 'umbrella' for direct negotiations with the Arab countries.

During the 1982 Israeli siege of Beirut, Pierre Mendès France (the former French Prime Minister), Nahum Goldmann (the former President of the World Jewish Congress) and Philip Klutznick (the former American Commerce Secretary) published in *Le Monde* of 3 July 1982 a declaration in the form of a peace initiative: it called for an Israeli-Palestinian solution, based on mutual recognition, which would guarantee the exercising by the Palestinian people of their right to self-determination and ensure peaceful Israeli-Palestinian coexistence. Although the PLO welcomed this initiative, it was rejected by the Israeli government.

On 7 August 1981 Crown Prince Fahd of Saudi Arabia had put forward a Middle East peace plan based on the relevant UN resolutions. When first submitted to the Arab Summit in Fez on 25 November 1981, the plan did not receive unanimous backing. The second Fez Summit of 9 September 1982, however, approved it after amendment (see Appendix 8). Israel rejected both versions of the plan. In July 1986 King Hassan II of Morocco invited Shimon Peres to Ifran to discuss the Fez Plan with him. The talks came to nothing. On 1 September 1982 US President Reagan announced a peace plan (see Appendix 7), based on principles which effectively restated the Camp David Accords: recognition of the full autonomy of the Palestinians, allowing them to run their own affairs for five years; a halt to the establishment of settlements in the West Bank and Gaza; and autonomy of these territories in association with Jordan after the five-year transition period—in other words, after negotiations establishing the principle of 'land for peace'.

The 'Jordanian Option'

The attempts to resolve the Palestinian question by means of the 'Jordanian option' go back to 1948, when Britain imposed the partition of Palestine between Israel and Jordan, thus applying the UN Partition Resolution in its own way by excluding the Palestinians, whereas the resolution actually provided for the creation of two states, one Palestinian, the other Israeli.

After the 1967 War, it was Israel which proposed involving Jordan in a resolution of the Palestinian question. On 15 March 1972 King Hussein of Jordan proposed the creation of a United Arab Kingdom encompassing Jordan and the West Bank. This proposal was rejected by the PLO. The King put forward a second plan on 22 June 1977 for the creation of a federation; then, in 1983, he suggested a confederation as a half-way house between the Fez Plan and the 1982 Reagan Plan. Both these plans were also rejected by the PLO.

On 11 February 1985, however, the PLO and Jordan concluded an agreement based on the 'land for peace' principle and the self-determination of the Palestinian people in an Arab confederation of two states, Jordanian and Palestinian. This agreement was to have allowed a joint initiative to be relaunched as a basis for negotiations between Israel and a joint Jordano-Palestinian delegation. Along the same lines as the Fahd Plan, it amounted to implicit recognition of Resolution 242 by the PLO. Several PLO factions expressed reservations about this agreement and the 1985 hijack of the Italian cruise ship, *Achille Lauro*, was intended to torpedo this Jordano-Palestinian peace initiative.

The negotiations did not take place. Jordan held the PLO responsible for this situation because of the latter's refusal explicitly to accept Resolution 242 and its implications. On 19 February 1986 King Hussein announced that he could no longer continue political co-ordination with the PLO and, on 7 July of that year, ordered that the PLO's offices in Jordan be closed.

Palestinian Peace Initiatives

In July 1967 Farouq Kaddoumi, head of the PLO Political Department, proposed the setting-up of a Palestinian state in the West Bank and Gaza.[13] This was rejected both by his organization and by Israel, the latter for four reasons: the creation of a Palestinian state would imply recognition of the Palestinian people's existence; a Palestinian state would demand Jerusalem as its capital; Israel would no longer be able to annex West Bank lands on the pretext of border 'adjustments'; and Israel feared that the Palestinian state would make territorial claims against Israel.

At the fifth session of the Palestine National Council (PNC) in February 1969, the PLO proposed to Israel that a joint, secular, democratic state be created in Palestine. The plan was deemed to be utopian and was rejected. In 1974 Yasser Arafat restated the proposal for a joint, secular, democratic state at the UN General Assembly.

The 1988 Palestinian peace initiative, which led to the proclamation of the state of Palestine in the West Bank and Gaza, alongside Israel, and which stemmed from a change in the PLO's strategy, was a watershed in the Israeli-Palestinian/Arab conflict. The PLO exploited the new situation created by the *intifada* to adopt a policy of openness and realism. On 13 December 1988, at the UN General Assembly in Geneva, the President of Palestine presented the three points of the Palestinian initiative:

(i)   there should be a meeting of the preparatory committee of the international conference on the basis of the 1986 Gorbachev-Mitterrand initiative;

(ii) the occupied territories should provisionally be placed under UN trusteeship; and

(iii) there should be a comprehensive settlement between Israel, Palestine and the Arab countries on the basis of Security Council Resolutions 242 and 338.

At the end of his speech to the General Assembly, Arafat appealed to the Israelis:

I ask Israel's leaders to come here so that we can make peace . . . away from the threat of new wars, whose only fuel would be our children and your children . . . Come, let us make peace, the peace of the brave, away from the arrogance of force and the weapons of destruction, away from the occupation of tyranny, humiliation, slaughter and torture.

At a press conference the following day, Arafat stated that the PLO renounced terrorism, that it recognized Israel's right to exist and that it accepted Resolutions 242 and 338 (the three conditions which the United States had pledged to Israel ever since 1975, after a secret accord reached between Kissinger and Israel when the second agreement on the disengagement of Egyptian and Israeli forces in Sinai was signed). On 14 December 1988 US Secretary of State George Shultz announced that the United States had decided to 'begin a substantive dialogue with the PLO'; the first US-Palestinian meeting took place two days later.

This dialogue, conducted in Tunis, was suspended in June 1990 following the attempted landing of commandos belonging to Abul-Abbas' Popular Liberation Front (PLF; a pro-Iraqi organization) on the beach at Tel Aviv in May 1990, an action designed to wreck the dialogue. Some four months previously, the 'substantive dialogue' had been transferred from Tunis to Cairo, where it had become indirect and been conducted through Egypt, so that negotiations might be held 'in better conditions' on the Shamir, Mubarak and Baker Peace Plans, which the Palestinian peace initiative had triggered. The progress made by Baker contributed to the resumption of the US-Palestinian dialogue through Palestinian interlocutors from the occupied territories, acting with the authorization of the PLO leadership in Tunis.

The Shamir Plan

To counterbalance the positive impact of the Palestinian initiative, which had put pressure on the Israeli government, Shamir grudgingly presented a 'peace plan' of his own in April 1989. It was adopted by the Israeli government on 14 May 1989. This plan, which reiterated the main points of the Camp David Accords, proposed elections in ten constituencies for the ten members of the 'autonomous council' which was to negotiate interim autonomy status for a five-year period. At the end of three years of autonomy, the discussions on final status were to start. Palestinians residing outside Gaza and the West Bank, as well as those from East Jerusalem, were to be excluded from the vote. The establishment of Jewish settlements in the occupied territories was to continue, as was the maintenance of the occupation until this autonomy status entered into force. Lastly, no negotiations would take place until the *intifada* ended.

In accepting the Shamir Plan, Baker announced, on 22 May 1989, that he was as opposed to annexation or permanent Israeli control of the occupied Palestinian territories as he was to the establishment of an independent Palestinian state. In August 1989 Egypt's President Mubarak put forward a ten-point plan in the form of questions or requests for clarification on the Shamir Plan. Israel immediately issued an official rejection of the Egyptian plan.

The Baker Plan

In December 1989 James Baker presented a five-point plan, which was a synthesis of Shamir's five points and Mubarak's ten:

(i)   a dialogue between an Israeli delegation and a Palestinian delegation would be held in Cairo;

(ii)   Egypt's only responsibility would be to consult with the parties concerned;

(iii) the list of members of the Palestinian delegation should meet Israeli demands;

(iv)   Israel would participate in the discussions on the basis of the Shamir Plan and the Palestinians would be free to express their views on the negotiations and Shamir's draft election plan; and

(v)   a tripartite meeting of the Israeli, Egyptian and American Foreign Ministers would be held in Washington in order to create the right conditions for a constructive Palestinian-Israeli dialogue in Cairo.

On 9 March 1990 Likud responded to the Baker Plan by only accepting part of it and agreeing to begin talks provided that the Palestinians of East Jerusalem were excluded and that the PLO did not interfere in these talks. Shimon Peres, on the other hand, announced his acceptance of the plan as it stood. This issue caused the break-up of the Israeli National Unity government of Labour and Likud.

On 11 June 1990 Shamir formed a new government with the ultra-nationalist and ultra-religious extreme right. It set new conditions for the Cairo discussions with the Palestinians:

(i)   the Palestinians should accept limitation of the negotiations to a discussion of the autonomy set out in the Camp David Accords;

(ii)   the Arab countries should make a gesture to Israel before it would
        agree to negotiate with the Palestinians; and
(iii)   consideration of Arab-Israeli relations should precede the discussions
        on the Palestinian question.

On 13 June 1990 Baker, exasperated at such recalcitrance, reacted to
these new Israeli conditions by stating, 'Our number is 1-202-456-1414.
When you're serious about peace, call us.' In a letter to President Bush on
27 June 1990, Shamir restated his position on the continued establishment of
Jewish settlements in the occupied territories, and on the exclusion of the
PLO, and his opposition to participation by Palestinian exiles or inhabitants
of East Jerusalem in a possible Palestinian delegation. Furthermore, he
swore to Likud officials that he would never give the Arabs an inch of land,
even if it were necessary to make the negotiations drag on for ten years.
Baker's response to the intransigence of the extreme right-wing Israeli
government was perceived by the Palestinians as US disengagement from the
search for a solution to the Palestinian problem, as had been the case with
all previous American administrations.

Internally, the increased repression of the *intifada*, the threats to transfer
the Palestinian population to Jordan, and the arrival in Israel, *en masse*, of
Soviet Jews in order to settle the occupied West Bank strengthened the
feeling among some leading Palestinian officials that the Palestinian peace
initiative had foundered and that the option of armed struggle should now be
given serious consideration. The situation was merely compounded by the
threats of war which loomed over the Gulf at the start of the summer of
1990, after Saddam Hussein's statements at the Baghdad Arab Summit of
28–30 May 1990 in which he had denounced the economic threats which, he
said, were directed at Iraq by Kuwait, and called upon the Arab countries to
take up the military option against Israel again in order to liberate the Holy
City of Jerusalem. The Palestinian leaders were faced with an explosive
situation which constrained their freedom of manoeuvre and which offered
no way out of the stranglehold.

On 2 August 1990 Kuwait was occupied by Iraq. On 10 August an
Extraordinary Arab Summit was held in Cairo. Arafat put forward a plan to
settle the crisis peacefully by creating a Good Offices Committee, which
would comprise five Arab heads of state, to ensure that Iraq withdrew from
Kuwait and that the disputes which had arisen between the two countries
were settled by peaceful means. The plan failed because of the opposition of
a majority of Arab states, which instead condemned Iraq and called for
external intervention. The PLO abstained from supporting this decision, thus
expressing its objection to resorting to forces foreign to the region to settle

disputes between Arab countries. This stand was deliberately misconstrued as PLO approval of the occupation of Kuwait. It was actually the natural reaction of a people subjected to an occupation marked by fierce repression.[14] The Palestinians' refusal to join or to support the anti-Iraqi coalition caused a rift between the PLO and the coalition's members.

After Saddam Hussein's defeat, the PLO faced hostility in the region, which hampered the resumption of efforts to seek a solution to the Palestinian question.[15] In 1992 *Ramses*,[16] the annual global economic and strategic report of the French Institute of International Relations (IFRI), accused the PLO of taking Iraq's side:

> The PLO leadership, by choosing to side with Iraq—the Arab power which was going to revive the military option *vis-à-vis* Israel—thus suggested that it renounced its peace strategy. The PLO's resultant loss of credibility in Western eyes and in those of a number of Arab countries is a serious setback which the Palestinian authorities are anxious to put right, as a priority, so that they can recover their previous international diplomatic position.[17]

The 1991 Gulf War, while upsetting the balance of forces in the region, further highlighted the vital need for a settlement of the Palestinian problem, which might otherwise engender another conflict. Realizing this imperative, the American administration decided to resume its efforts to push forward the frequently disrupted diplomatic process, this time in very changed circumstances.

2
The US Initiative

Aware of the new decisive and exclusive role of the United States in the Middle East following the Gulf War, President George Bush promptly explained how his administration intended to resolve the security issues in the region and settle the Arab-Israeli conflict so as to ensure that this monopoly did not become a burden. He believed in a sort of a *pax universalis*, in other words a *pax americana*, and felt that American plans for the Middle East fitted in with the attainment of a somewhat vague and nebulous 'new world order'. On 6 March 1991 the US President announced a Middle East peace initiative to Congress, stating determinedly that:

> The time has come to put an end to the Arab-Israeli conflict . . . A comprehensive peace [in the Middle East] must be grounded in UN Security Council Resolutions 242 and 338 and the principle of territory for peace . . . elaborated to provide for Israel's security and recognition, and at the same time for legitimate Palestinian political rights.[1]

Drawing lessons from the Gulf War, he stated that, in modern times, geography was no longer a guarantee of security and that this security could not be ensured by military force. He asked his Secretary of State, James Baker, to give priority consideration to the Israeli-Palestinian/Arab question and to work for the implementation of the American initiative in order to achieve Middle East peace.

Two days after Bush's speech, James Baker set out on his first tour of the Middle East. On 12 March 1991 he met ten leading Palestinian figures from the occupied territories at the residence of the US Consul-General in Jerusalem. The PLO gave its authorization for this meeting; it was the first time that a Palestinian delegation had met a US Secretary of State.

On 8 April 1991 Baker began his second Middle East tour. He secured Israeli agreement to the holding of a regional conference, but it was accompanied by a series of conditions and guarantees. According to Israeli military radio, Shamir presented nine points (agreed upon by Israel and the United States at the end of this tour) to his cabinet on 11 April 1991:

(i)   the two countries accepted the principle of a regional conference, under the auspices of the United States and the USSR, leading to direct negotiations between Israel and the Arab states;

(ii)   the two countries accepted that the final aim of the peace process could not be the creation of a Palestinian state;

(iii)   the composition of the delegation of Palestinian personalities from the West Bank and the Gaza Strip should be determined in agreement with Israel;

(iv)   the United States did not demand the presence in this delegation of Palestinians from East Jerusalem (annexed by Israel in 1980) or of Palestinians previously expelled by Israel;

(v)   Israel refused any dialogue with the PLO and the United States would not resume its dialogue with it;

(vi)   the two countries agreed that there was no single interpretation of UN Security Council Resolution 242, with the United States recognizing Israel's right to have its own interpretation (the English version of the resolution refers to Israeli withdrawal 'from territories' while the French version speaks of withdrawal 'from the territories' occupied in 1967);

(vii)   Resolution 242 would be the subject of negotiations between Israel and its Arab counterparts in the final phase of the process;

(viii)   the first phase of the negotiations would deal with the status of self-government in the West Bank and the Gaza Strip, and, at the end of three years of such a regime, negotiations should begin on the final status of these two regions; and

(ix)   the USSR should re-establish diplomatic relations (severed in 1967) with Israel and accept the principles of the peace process in order to be party to the regional conference.[2]

These terms, which were equivalent to preconditions for the holding of the regional conference and which the United States apparently accepted, were reminiscent of the conditions which Israel set out to Kissinger in 1975 in return for its withdrawal from Sinai.

On 14 April 1991 Yasser Arafat rejected the convening of a regional conference, fearing that, in a situation marked by a balance of forces in Israel's favour, such a formula would bypass a settlement of the Palestinian question. He did, however, restate the PLO's agreement to an international conference. During Baker's fifth tour to the Middle East from 18 to 22 July 1991, President Mubarak proposed a lifting of the Arab economic boycott of Israel in exchange for a freeze on Jewish settlements in the occupied territories, as already requested by the Group of Seven Industrialized Countries at their London summit. Israel refused the proposal, and thus Washington's wish for 'confidence-building measures' to improve the climate did not meet with a favourable Israeli response.

On 31 July 1991, at the end of the US-Soviet Summit in Moscow, a joint communiqué announced that it had been agreed by Presidents Bush and Gorbachev that a Middle East conference would be held in October at a place yet to be agreed. This joint communiqué specified:

> President Bush and President Gorbachev reaffirm their commitment to promote peace and genuine reconciliation among the Arab states, Israel and the Palestinians. They believe there is a historic opportunity now to launch a process that can lead to a just and enduring peace and to a comprehensive settlement in the Middle East. They share the strong conviction that this historic opportunity must not be lost.[3]

They recognized that peace could not be imposed but would only result from direct negotiations between the parties. The United States and the Soviet Union pledged to do their utmost to promote and sustain the peace process. As co-sponsors, they would seek to convene a peace conference in October of that year that would launch the bilateral and multilateral negotiations, with the invitations sent out at least ten days before the start of the conference. In the meantime, US Secretary of State James Baker and Soviet Foreign Minister Alexandr Bessmertnykh would continue to work with the parties to prepare for the conference.

On the very next day, Baker began his sixth tour of the Middle East. The communiqué was satisfactory to, and accepted by, Israel. The Palestinians in their turn, anxious not to obstruct the US initiative, gave their agreement in principle, but it was, none the less, accompanied by many conditions and guarantees.

It was during his seventh tour (16–20 September 1991) that the US

Secretary of State handed 'letters of assurance' to the concerned parties, on the modalities of the conference which they could all accept. In these letters, the United States made pledges to each party which did not contradict those given to the others and which would not jeopardize the chances of the conference going ahead. It thus respected the principle of refraining from making conflicting commitments and from creating a situation which would prompt one party or another to refuse to participate in the peace conference.

In the 'letter of assurance' given to Israel, Washington pledged not to work for the creation of a Palestinian state while, at the same time, stating its hostility to the continuance of Israeli occupation of the Palestinian territories and the Golan. Further, it restated its opposition to the division of Jerusalem, in the belief that its final status would be fixed at a later stage in the negotiations. Lastly, the United States accepted that there were different interpretations of Resolution 242,[4] which would enable Israel to present its own subjective interpretation.

In the Palestinians' 'letter of assurance', the American administration reaffirmed the position set out in President Bush's 6 March speech and in the Baker Plan on the concept of interim self-government with limited jurisdiction, as provided for in the Camp David Accords (see Appendix 6). Furthermore, the letter asserted the Palestinians' right to choose their own delegation and to broach any question of concern to them at the conference. The letter did not mention the Palestinian people's right to self-determination, or the question of halting Jewish settlements in the interim period, or what the future 'final status' of the occupied Palestinian territories might be.

In its 'letter of assurance' to Syria, Washington recalled that it did not recognize Israel's annexation of the Golan in 1981. As for Jordan's 'letter of assurance', it stated that the conference would be convened on the basis of UN Resolutions 242 (1967) and 338 (1973), which required that Israel withdrew from the territories it had occupied in 1967.

In these 'letters of assurance', the US administration specified its position on the questions which concerned each party. All its pledges merely reflected its Middle East policy.

Israel's Intransigence

At the end of eight months of faltering discussions on procedural questions, the American Secretary of State had not managed to shift significantly Israel's stance of before the Gulf War. Baker had denounced this position on 13 June 1990 when he said that Israel was 'not serious', yet it had now become the 'serious' starting-point for the negotiations! Israel's intransigence, which Baker was thus accepting, conflicted, however, with the majority opinion of the Israeli public which, because of the *intifada*, was moving in increasing numbers towards favouring territorial compromise in return for peace, according to opinion polls published in the Israeli press.[5]

The hardening of the Israeli government's position primarily reflected Likud's revisionist ideology, or selfish nationalism, which ignores the human suffering it engenders. This chauvinism was bolstered by the presence in the coalition government of the ultra-religious and ultra-nationalist extreme right, whose political manifestos call in unambiguous terms for the deportation to the Arab countries or the West of all Palestinians, both those in the territories occupied in 1967 and even those in Israel! This increased rigidity also reflected a tactic intended to gain time, in order to integrate the Soviet Jews and overturn the demographic situation in the occupied territories in the Jews' favour, thereby developing the policy of *faits accomplis* (pursued ever since the Zionist movement first established a Jewish settlement on the Palestinians' land at the end of the last century) to create an irreversible situation.

Such intransigence was also intended to enable Israel to make the fewest possible concessions at the peace conference negotiations. The Shamir government wanted the conference to be a 'Camp David mark II' in order to normalize relations with the Arab world. On 7 October 1991, speaking in the Knesset (Parliament), Shamir set four Israeli conditions for his government's participation in the conference:

(i)   The Palestinian delegation should be incorporated into the Jordanian delegation and its members should be approved beforehand by Israel (which meant they should not be members of the PLO, Palestinians from East Jerusalem or delegates from the Palestinian diaspora). Israel threatened to withdraw from the conference if the Palestinian delegation was chosen by the PLO or spoke for it. This diktat was rejected by the Palestinians on the grounds that one does not choose one's adversary and that Israel must recognize the existence of the Palestinian people.

(ii)   There was to be no self-determination for the Palestinian people, no independent Palestinian state and no settlement of the final status of Jerusalem.

(iii) The conference sponsors would have no power to influence the course of the negotiations. By virtue of this condition, Israel was actually seeking to meet in separate face-to-face negotiations with the Arabs—so as to bypass the resolutions of the United Nations, international law and possible pressure from the Americans. (The Arab countries were aware of their weakness but, none the less, rejected the notion of an Israeli diktat and called for the intervention of a mediator in the event of deadlock at the negotiations. For them, the ability to resort to American mediation was an important factor in neutralizing Israel's military superiority.)

(iv)   The peace conference should be an 'umbrella' allowing direct, bilateral and separate negotiations to be conducted, according to the 'Rhodes formula' and leading to contractual peace agreements based on the autonomy of population and not of land (in keeping with the Camp David Accords, which treat the Palestinians as a minority and not as a people, and with Israel's interpretation of Security Council Resolution 242).

Shamir also announced his agreement to multilateral, regional meetings to discuss matters of common interest, such as water, the environment, refugees and economic development. In short, through these conditions, Shamir was proposing the establishment of a *pax hebraica* in the region: Israel was offering the Arabs peace and, in return, the Arabs would give up the territories that Israel was occupying!

The Aims of the Arabs and Palestinians

The Arab countries' 1982 Fez Plan (see Appendix 8) was a common point of reference in determining their policy on the Palestinian question and their attitude towards Israel. The 1991 Gulf War drastically affected the consistent development of this policy. The Arab world's inability to resolve the Iraq-Kuwait conflict, which was purely Arab in its origins, and the fact that certain Arab countries called on foreign protectors to settle it had two major adverse consequences: the loss of the Arab Mashreq's political independence and the rise to pre-eminence of the United States since, as a result, the Americans became the key player in the Middle East game and in the Arab/Palestinian-Israeli conflict.

Taking these factors as well as global changes into consideration, the Arab world agreed to become involved in the peace process proposed by the Americans. The Arab peoples were passive bystanders in this crucial process, the outcome of which would soon determine whether they would enjoy socio-economic and democratic development or suffer the sort of grave political instability that could already be discerned. In the course of his many trips to the Middle East, James Baker managed to persuade the Arab countries to accept the compromise conference which he was advocating (instead of the international conference they were demanding, to be sponsored by the five permanent members of the UN Security Council and in which the PLO would participate as a full partner). However, notwithstanding the unreciprocated concessions the Arab countries had made, their position remained unchanged on the following points:

(i)   Israel's withdrawal from the occupied territories, upon completion of the negotiations, on the basis of Security Council Resolutions 242 and 338;

(ii)   a halt to, or freeze on, Jewish settlements in the occupied territories; and

(iii) the satisfaction of the Palestinian people's national rights, which would entail the creation of an independent state.

On 24 October 1991 the Arab countries bordering Israel, the PLO, Saudi Arabia (as representative of the Gulf Co-operation Council) and Morocco (representing the Arab Maghreb Union) decided, in Damascus, to consult regularly during the bilateral and multilateral negotiations in order to adopt a common Arab position as the talks with Israel proceeded; a co-ordination committee was set up for this purpose. Jordan reaffirmed the policy it had followed with respect to the Palestinians since 31 July 1988. It considered its disengagement from the West Bank to be final and irreversible, and would do nothing about Palestine without the prior agreement of the PLO. As for the Jordano-Palestinian delegation, Jordan considered that it was for the Palestinians to choose whether to go alone into negotiations with Israel or to be incorporated in a joint delegation, for which it would be the exclusive prerogative of the PLO to designate its Palestinian members. Syria refused to make concessions of substance. It did, however, agree to yield on matters of form. It relinquished its idea of the international conference under UN auspices as well as the creation of a joint Arab delegation by acquiescing in the principle of bilateral, direct and separate negotiations as advocated by Israel.

The Minimalist Palestinian Position

Since it began on 1 January 1965, the Palestinian resistance, which was incorporated into the PLO in 1968, has not been an unmitigated success; it has endured several setbacks, some serious. Mistakes or abuses were committed by some of its leaders or its factions, especially in Jordan and

Lebanon, while elsewhere they carried out terrorist attacks. On each occasion, however, Israel's response was out of all proportion to the initial act: a massacre for a terrorist attack, an aerial bombardment for a shoot-out, a bullet for a stone, a court conviction for an opinion. Such inordinate reprisals are part of a deliberate policy of seizing on any pretext to attain other objectives than penalizing the act committed, since too many of Israel's interests of state are incompatible with the existence of an independent Palestinian state.

This Holy Land of Palestine is a victim twice-over of geo-ideological factors. Its neighbours are small peoples who aspire to greatness at Palestine's expense because of their retrograde and nostalgic ideologies: Greater Israel (according to the myth of Solomon), Greater Jordan (according to the 'Bilad al-Sham' ideology of Arab revolution, propounded by Sherif Hussein of Mecca) and Greater Syria (according to the ideology of the Syrian Nationalist Party of Antoine Saadé, inspired by the Belgian priest, Lammens). The PLO leadership, aware of this blurring of myth and reality in the Middle East, has adopted a policy of ambiguity, which Arafat dubbed *la-am* (from the two Arabic words for 'yes' and 'no') which could mean either 'yes and no' or 'neither yes nor no'!

This tussle with the Arab countries has not always worked in favour of the Palestinians, who have wanted both to assert their independence and to oblige the other regimes at the same time. The most serious failure of this policy was at the Cairo Arab Summit of 10 August 1990, when the Arab regimes demanded that the Palestinians adopt a clear-cut stand and take sides during the Gulf crisis. The Palestinians, believing in the virtues of mediation, ended up displeasing both belligerents. On the one hand, the PLO refused to become integrated into the Iraqi camp, rejecting Iraq's three requests for the formation of a Palestinian militia in Kuwait, the opening of a second front against Israel in south Lebanon, and the organization of terrorist strikes against the coalition allies' interests around the world. On the other, it refused to join the coalition camp, partly because of its hostility to foreign interference in the Arab countries' internal affairs and partly because of political factors within the PLO itself. The allies considered those who did not belong to their camp to be hostile, and therefore penalized the PLO and the Palestinian people. In Kuwait, this meant pogroms and witch-hunts against the Palestinians; in the Gulf states, it meant a freeze on relations with the PLO; and in the West, it meant the PLO's 'disqualification'. It was, therefore, a case of 'might is right'.

While the Gulf War weakened the PLO as an institution, its role and function as mobilizer of the Palestinians' hearts and minds emerged unscathed, if not enhanced. Learning the lessons of the Gulf War and taking account of the profound changes in the world which had made the United States the only remaining superpower as the twentieth century neared its end, the PLO leadership decided to discard its costly policy of ambiguity. Given President Bush's 6 March 1991 speech and Baker's ensuing trips to the region in search of Middle East peace, the PLO felt this was an opportunity not to be missed.

In support of US efforts, it convened the twentieth session of the Palestine National Council (PNC) in Algiers from 23 to 28 September 1991. The PNC adopted a political declaration which set out principles to be respected and objectives to be attained. It mandated the PLO Executive Committee, albeit with a degree of leeway, to negotiate the terms of Palestinian participation at the peace conference, on the understanding that the final decision would rest with the PLO Central Council, an intermediate body between the PNC and the PLO Executive Committee (see Part IV). For the first time since the PLO's creation in 1964, the PNC adopted a decision by vote instead of by consensus: 256 for, 68 against, with 12 abstentions. Two Palestinian organizations boycotted this session of the council: the Islamic fundamentalist movement, Hamas, and the 'Salvation Front' (a coalition of pro-Syrian factions), which was hostile to any concessions or political compromise.

In its declaration, the PNC stated the following principles and objectives:

(i)   the conference to meet on the basis of UN Resolutions 242 and 338 (in other words, according to the 'land for peace' principle);

(ii)   the recognition of the Palestinian people's national rights, especially the right to self-determination and sovereign independence;

(iii)   the refugees' right of return;

(iv)   Israel's commitment to withdraw from East Jerusalem;

(v)   an immediate halt to the establishment of Jewish settlements in the occupied Palestinian territories, especially in East Jerusalem;

(vi)   the dismantling of the Jewish settlements illegally established in the occupied Palestinian territories;

(vii) PLO designation of the Palestinian representatives at the peace conference without external interference, and permission for them to refer back to the PLO; and

(viii) guarantees of the links between the various stages towards a final settlement, of the Palestinians' sovereignty over land and water during the transitional phase, and of their autonomy in managing social, economic, cultural and political affairs.

In this political declaration, the PLO for the first time accepted the principle of a joint Jordano-Palestinian delegation, provided that the Palestinian component was on an equal footing with the Jordanian one, and that, like the other invited parties, it received a separate invitation. On the night of 17 to 18 October 1991 the PLO Central Council consented to the formation of a joint Jordano-Palestinian delegation to the peace conference. It left it to the Executive Committee to proceed with the composition of its Palestinian component. This decision was also adopted by vote. Georges Habash's Popular Front for the Liberation of Palestine (PFLP), Naif Hawatmeh's Democratic Front for the Liberation of Palestine (DFLP) and the pro-Iraqi Arab Liberation Front (ALF) voted against.

On 19 October 1991 an International Conference in Support of the Islamic Revolution in Palestine opened in Tehran. It issued an anticipatory condemnation of the Madrid conference, to which Yasser Arafat reacted by denouncing Iranian interference in Palestinian internal affairs.

The acceptance of autonomy as a transitional phase and the elevation of Palestinians from the occupied territories to the forefront of the Madrid negotiations were two fresh and major concessions by the PLO—with no quid pro quo—intended to remove hurdles obstructing the convening of the peace conference. It chose from 'the interior' 14 official delegates and 4 alternatives to be led by Dr Haidar Abdel Shafi from Gaza. Two other delegations, comprising politicians and experts who had been vetoed by Israel, were also present in Madrid to advise the official delegation authorized to negotiate with Israel. These were the Steering Committee of advisers, whose leader and spokeswoman were Faisal al-Husseini and Hanan Ashrawi, respectively, and a second, unofficial delegation headed by Nabil Sha'ath, Arafat's adviser. Contact between Arafat and the Palestinian delegations in Madrid was maintained by direct telephone link. In effect, Yasser Arafat was present in Madrid in all but person.

By adopting this policy of setting minimal conditions, the Palestinians hoped to reap the expected rewards. What they insistently demanded, in return for their concession of accepting autonomy as a transitional phase, was a halt to Jewish settlements in the occupied Palestinian territories, thus preventing Israel from exploiting the time required for negotiation and the autonomy period by continuing its 'Israelization' of these territories and from making the potential outcome of the negotiations essentially meaningless. The continuing Palestinian participation in the bilateral negotiations would depend, to a large extent, on this neutralization of the time factor.

Baker's Crucial Role

The new international situation, Bush's determination, Palestinian moderation and Baker's tenacity were the necessary, albeit insufficient, conditions for a process to be launched which might produce peace, harmonious coexistence and co-operation in a region previously racked by war, antagonism and the ensuing suffering. In an attempt to tackle a complex situation of 50 years' standing which had now become deadlocked, the US Secretary of State employed a new method. This was no continuation of Kissinger's 'small steps', nor of Carter's Camp David. On the basis of the American policy of 'constructive ambiguity', Baker managed with great skill to sidestep the obstacles by reducing the conflict to a procedural problem; all questions of substance would be discussed in the course of the conference itself.

His eight regional tours in as many months focused mainly on haggling over the modalities and procedural aspects of the conference. Each time he arrived in Israel, he was 'welcomed' with new settlements. This led him to point out, on 22 May 1991, that only 35 per cent of the occupied territories had escaped Israeli expropriation and that there was 'no greater obstacle to peace than settlements',[6] which, he added, were not only continuing to be built without let-up but were actually being accelerated. The Palestinians reacted to this accelerated settlement activity by saying that 'Israeli bulldozers are moving faster than Baker's plane.'

President Bush was unable to obtain an assurance from Shamir that the $10 billion that Israel wished to borrow from American banks to finance the settlement of Jews would not be used to colonize the occupied territories. He decided, on 6 September 1991, to ask the US Congress to delay consideration of the Israeli request for loan guarantees for 120 days. He was concerned not to jeopardize the peace conference since, as he recalled, the settlements issue would largely determine whether there would be war or peace in the Middle East. Not wanting to impose a solution, the US administration decided to act as a catalyst—'offering encouragement, advice, recommendations, proposals and opinions to assist the peace process', in Baker's words.

On 18 October 1991 the USSR resumed diplomatic relations with Israel, thus enabling letters of invitation to the Middle East peace conference to be sent by the United States and USSR to the interested parties, including the Palestinians. Before the deadline for answering expired, all the parties had responded affirmatively. The key points in the invitation were as follows:

After extensive consultations with Palestinians, Arab states and Israel, the

United States and the Soviet Union believe that an historic opportunity exists to advance the prospects for genuine peace throughout the region. The United States and the Soviet Union are prepared to assist the parties to achieve a just, lasting and comprehensive peace settlement, through direct negotiations along two tracks, between Israel and the Arab states, and between Israel and the Palestinians, based on United Nations Security Council Resolutions 242 and 338. The objective of this process is real peace.

Toward that end, the President of the United States and the President of the USSR invite you to a peace conference, which their countries will co-sponsor, followed immediately by direct negotiations. The conference will be convened in Madrid on 30 October 1991. President Bush and President Gorbachev request your acceptance of this invitation no later than 6.00 p.m., Washington time, 23 October 1991, in order to ensure proper organization and preparation of the conference.

Direct bilateral negotiations will begin four days after the opening of the conference. Those parties who wish to attend multilateral negotiations will convene two weeks after the opening of the conference to organize those negotiations. The co-sponsors believe that those negotiations should focus on region-wide issues such as arms control and regional security, water, refugee issues, environment, economic development and other subjects of mutual interest.

The conference will have no power to impose solutions on the parties or veto agreements reached by them. It will have no authority to make decisions for the parties and no ability to vote on issues or results. The conference can reconvene only with the consent of all the parties.

With respect to negotiations between Israel and Palestinians who are part of the joint Jordano-Palestinian delegation, negotiations will be conducted in phases, beginning with talks on interim self-government arrangements. These talks will be conducted with the objective of reaching agreement within one year. Once agreed, the interim self-government arrangements will last for a period of five years. Beginning the third year of the period of interim self-government arrangements, negotiations will take place on permanent status. These permanent status negotiations, and the negotiations between Israel and the Arab states, will take place on the basis of Resolutions 242 and 338.

The co-sponsors believe that this process offers the promise of ending decades of confrontation and conflict and the hope of a lasting peace. Thus, the co-sponsors hope that the parties will approach these negotiations in a spirit of goodwill and mutual respect. In this way, the peace process can begin to break down the mutual suspicions and mistrust that perpetuate the conflict and allow the parties to begin to resolve their differences. Indeed, only through such a process can real peace and reconciliation among the Arab states, Israel and the Palestinians be achieved. And only through this process can the peoples of the Middle East attain the peace and security they richly deserve.[7]

The Plenary Meetings

The peace conference was officially opened at the Royal Palace in Madrid on Wednesday 30 October 1991, in front of 4,665 accredited journalists and on television screens throughout the world. 'The Arabs' and Israelis' Appointment with History', proclaimed one Lebanese newspaper headline. During the opening ceremony, after the welcoming speech by the Spanish Prime Minister, Felipe Gonzalez, President George Bush took the floor. He spelt out the aims of the conference as follows:

> We come to Madrid on a mission of hope, to begin work on a just, lasting and comprehensive settlement to the conflict in the Middle East . . . we seek peace, real peace.

This peace, in his view, should be predicated on security for Israel and justice for the Palestinians. In the absence of justice, there would be neither legitimacy nor stability. He added:

> We believe territorial compromise is essential for peace . . . what we envision is a process of direct negotiations proceeding along two tracks: one between Israel and the Arab states, the other between Israel and the Palestinians. Negotiations are to be conducted on the basis of UN Security Council Resolutions 242 and 338.

The President went on to say that the Israeli-Palestinian negotiations would comprise several phases, and be conducted on the basis of the provisions of the Camp David Accords on autonomy:

> beginning with talks on interim self-government arrangements. Once agreed, interim self-government arrangements will last for five years; beginning the third year, negotiations will commence on permanent status. No one can say with any precision what the end result will be; in our view, something must be developed, something acceptable to Israel, the Palestinians and Jordan, that gives the Palestinian people meaningful

control over their own lives and fate, and provides for the acceptance and security of Israel.[8]

Bush also stated that the multilateral negotiations would deal with problems common to the peoples of the Middle East, such as arms control, refugees, water and economic development. He concluded his speech with the words, 'There will be disagreement and criticism, setbacks—who knows?—possibly interruptions . . . Peace need not be a dream. Peace is possible.'

President Gorbachev, in his opening address to the conference, stated, 'Durable peace means the fulfilment of and respect for the rights of the Palestinian people.' The Dutch Foreign Minister, Hans van den Broek, speaking on behalf of the European Community, recalled the principles which would guide the 12 throughout the peace conference negotiating process: Resolutions 242 and 338, 'land for peace', secure and recognized borders, and the exercise by the Palestinian people of their right to self-determination. Still speaking on behalf of the 12, he called for a freeze on Israeli settlements in the occupied territories and an end to the Arab boycott of Israel. The Egyptian Foreign Minister, Amr Moussa, recalled his country's traditional position, and stated that the Palestinians should be treated as a nation.

On 31 October 1991, the second day of the plenary session of the Madrid conference, the floor was taken by the Israeli Prime Minister, the Jordanian Foreign Minister, the head of the Palestinian delegation, the Lebanese Foreign Minister, and the Syrian Foreign Minister, in that order and each speaking for 45 minutes. Each speaker gave his own version of the conflict and expressed his opening position. Each of the belligerents, on both sides of the conflict, had determined its priorities on the basis of its own policies. For Shamir, this meant peace first, with the other items to follow. For the Arabs, it meant withdrawal from the occupied territories first, and then peace.

Shamir's view was that it would be 'regrettable if the talks focus primarily and exclusively on territory. It is the quickest way to an impasse.' He proposed to the Arabs 'peace for peace', after a lengthy and subjective recollection of history.

In his speech, Kamal Abu-Jaber, the Jordanian Foreign Minister, set out the principles of the Arab Peace Plan, adopted by the Arab Summit in Fez, Morocco, in 1983. He was also adamant in his assertion that 'Jordan has never been Palestine and never will be.'

The head of the Palestinian delegation, Dr Haidar Abdel Shafi, made the moving speech of a humanist and realist. Addressing the Israeli people, he stated, 'We are willing to live side by side on the land,' indicating that a future of peace would be rich in promise. Abdel Shafi recalled the 1988 Palestinian peace initiative, based on a solution to the conflict by means of the creation of the two states of Israel and Palestine. He went on to say that peace and co-operation would come if there was a resolution of the refugee and Jerusalem problems. He asked Israel to halt immediately 'all settlement activity and land confiscation',[9] so that the Palestinians could trust in its good faith, since 'peace cannot be waged while Palestinian land is confiscated and the status of the occupied territories is being decided each day by Israeli bulldozers and barbed wire'. Abdel Shafi made clear that the Palestinians were ready to accept the proposal for a transitional stage, so long as the interim arrangements did not turn out to be permanent. Finally, he asked for the occupied territories to be placed under international trusteeship, pending a final settlement.

The Lebanese Foreign Minister, Fares Boueiz, insisted on the implementation of Security Council Resolution 425 (1978) on the withdrawal of Israeli armed forces from south Lebanon. He also warned against any attempt to resolve the Palestinian problem by settling some of the Palestinian refugees in Lebanon, which would upset Lebanon's delicate demographic balance.

The conference's last speaker on 31 October 1991 was the Syrian Foreign Minister, Farouq al-Shara. His main points were: the refusal to recognize the Palestinian people's right to self-determination had led them to feel that 'resorting to violence is the only valid means of obtaining this right'; 'peace and the usurpation of other people's land are incompatible'; 'UN Resolutions 242 and 338 should be implemented without any haggling'; and 'international public opinion is more aware than ever, especially since the Gulf War, that one cannot accept double standards in our time, that the principles of international law, and not of the jungle, must be respected, and that the resolutions of the United Nations, and not brute force, should be applied'.[10]

The third day of the conference was given over to the exercise of Israel and the Arab states' rights of reply. Each party defended its position and criticized the excesses of the other side. The Israelis were unyielding, and so were the Arabs. The day was marked, above all, by a vitriolic stand-off between Syria and Israel. The dispute dismayed Baker and forced him to spell out the American concept of a compromise order of priorities between the Arab position and that of Israel:

Land, peace and security are inseparable elements in the search for a comprehensive settlement . . . Peace by itself is unachievable without a territorial solution and security . . . A territorial solution by itself will not resolve the conflict without there also being peace and security . . . Security by itself is impossible to achieve without a territorial solution and peace.[11]

Finally, Baker appealed to the negotiating parties, 'Don't wait for the other side to start; each of you needs to get off the mark quickly.'

It seems that Baker, who is credited with setting the negotiations in motion, was a firm believer in group dynamics or group psychotherapy, and thought that bringing Israelis and Arabs together would have a positive effect, gradually ridding the two sides of their fears, prejudices and taboos, and of their distorted and distorting perceptions of each other.

The agenda of the conference's second phase, after that of the plenary session, included the date and venue of subsequent meetings. Despite deliberating for two days, the parties took their leave without having agreed on either.

A Bilateral Dialogue of the Deaf

In Madrid and Washington, the bilateral negotiations between the parties to the conflict had not even started. They were still the object of a battle of wills. First, there was a dispute over the nature of these bilateral negotiations. The Arabs insisted that the sponsors should be present to help the parties, whereas Israel wanted an exclusively 'one-on-one' format, which would give them greater leeway in dealing with UN Resolutions 242 and 338, and demanded separate negotiations reminiscent of those at Rhodes, and at Mena House at the foot of the Pyramids. But was this a dispute between the advocates of an international conference on the one hand, and those who demanded direct negotiations on the other, or was it simply a typical negotiating scenario with each side seeking to secure a favourable starting position?

The Shamir government's tactics of intransigence and defiance continued between Madrid and Washington: new settlements were created in the occupied territories, settlers occupied more Palestinian houses in East Jerusalem, and on 11 November 1991 the Knesset adopted a new resolution stipulating that the annexed Syrian Golan was not negotiable. Yitzhak Shamir made more statements hostile to territorial concessions and to the creation of a Palestinian state. His government authorized Jewish settlers in the occupied territories to form an armed militia to enforce its writ even in Palestinian villages. Moreover, on 2 January 1992, a new Israeli budget was adopted which provided for the construction of 5,000 new housing units in the occupied territories. On the same day, the Israeli government decided to expel 12 Palestinians, after the murder of a Jewish settler. To crown it all, Shamir threatened to call an early general election in order to paralyse the bilateral negotiations.

Conversely, at its fifth congress, the Israeli Labour Party adopted a resolution, on 21 November 1991, supporting the repeal of the Israeli law which prohibited contacts with the PLO—an offence punishable by imprisonment. This was a moral victory for the gaoled Israeli pacifist, Abie Nathan, who had met Yasser Arafat in defiance of this law. The Labour Party for the first time recognized the 'national rights' of the Palestinians, while refraining, however, from going a step further by recognizing the Palestinian people's right to self-determination. It further proposed a one-year settlement freeze in the occupied territories, except in Jerusalem and the Jordan Valley (Allon Plan).

On 10 November 1991 Arafat, who had asked Palestinians to back their delegation in Madrid, encouraged the creation of 'political committees' in the occupied territories to support the peace process. That month, he stated, 'The *intifada* will last until the end of the occupation. This unarmed revolt will continue in waves until the Palestinian flag is raised over the churches and mosques of Jerusalem.'

Three weeks after Madrid, no agreement had been reached between the Arabs and Israelis on the date and venue for the bilateral negotiations to resume. On 22 November 1991 the United States presented the parties with a *fait accompli* by proposing Washington as the place and 4 December 1991 as the date for the second phase of the peace conference, which in Madrid had spawned three separate fora. These fora were, therefore, due to reconvene at senior official level. On the Arab/Palestinian side, the delegates were: Abdel Salam Majali, the head of the Jordanian and Jordano-Palestinian delegation; Haidar Abdel Shafi, the head of the Palestinian delegation; Muwaffaq al-Allaf, the head of the Syrian delegation; and Souhail Shammas, the head of the Lebanese delegation. On Israel's side, Elyakim Rubenstein was responsible for negotiations with the Jordano-Palestinian delegation; Yossi Ben Aharon led the team in the talks with Syria; and Yossi Haddas and Uri Lubrani were assigned to the negotiations with Lebanon. Israel accepted Washington as the venue for the negotiations, but rejected the date of 4 December, and instead proposed 9 December for the resumption of the bilateral talks.

The American administration suggested that Israel and the Palestinians should prepare an 'autonomy model' for the occupied territories, while deferring to a later date the question of the authority to be entrusted with running it. Baker suggested that, whenever a problem concerning the Palestinians was discussed, 'the majority of the members of the Jordano-Palestinian delegation should be Palestinians, with a certain Jordanian presence, and vice versa'.[12] The Arab countries accepted the place and date proposed by the Americans. The Palestinians, Jordanians, Syrians and Lebanese arrived in Washington for the resumption of talks with the Israelis on 4 December 1991, but the Israelis kept to their own schedule, and for several days conducted an 'empty chair' policy. The Arabs then proposed 10 December for the talks, since Israel's date of 9 December marked the anniversary of the *intifada*.

The second round of the bilateral negotiations of the peace conference, lasting from 10 to 18 December 1991, became deadlocked. The only agreement reached was that the negotiations should be resumed on 7 January 1992, in the US Federal capital. The procedural battle prevented the Israeli-Palestinian negotiations from taking place. The Israeli-Syrian and Israeli-Lebanese talks took place in the rooms prepared for this purpose, on different floors of the US State Department. The Israeli-Jordano-Palestinian forum, provided for by the Madrid conference, was confined to a corridor, since the three parties refused to enter the room reserved for them, there being no agreement on the meeting's modalities. The Palestinians and Jordanians wished to split into two delegations, but the Israelis refused one-on-one talks with the Palestinians so as not to recognize the Palestinians' separate identity. This conflicting order of priorities brought the Israeli-Arab bilateral negotiations down to a discussion of procedural issues and a trading of mutual recriminations, with a refusal to discuss matters of substance.

It was now for Washington to bring these positions closer as it alone was responsible for the peace process, following the break-up of the Soviet Union. The American administration could not impose its arbitration since it had pledged to Israel not to do so, except at the request of both the Israelis and the Arabs. Hanan Ashrawi accused the Israelis of wishing to 'dictate their conditions'. She asked Washington to intervene and to play an active part in the negotiations, as its passivity was contributing to, if not encouraging, Israeli intransigence. Indeed, neutrality between the victim and the oppressor was tantamount to support for the latter. The Syrians, for their part, accused Israel of not wishing to talk about exchanging 'land for peace', while the Israelis accused them of refusing to talk about a peace treaty.

In the first week of December 1991, just prior to the resumption of the bilateral negotiations in Washington, the United States and the former Soviet Union had announced that the third phase of the peace conference—the multilateral negotiations on regional problems in the Middle East (arms control, water, refugees, environment, economic co-operation, etc.)—would begin in Moscow on 28 and 29 January 1992. Syria and the PLO declared that they would not take part in this third phase until meaningful progress had been made in the second—bilateral—phase of the negotiations.

On 21 and 22 December 1991 Kazakhstan's capital, Alma-Ata, hosted a summit meeting of the leaders of the republics of the former Soviet Union—with the exception of Georgia, which did not participate. The summit sealed Mikhail Gorbachev's final eclipse by Boris Yeltsin, the President of the Russian Federation, who had foiled the attempted coup d'état of 19–21 August 1991. The meeting proclaimed the creation of the Commonwealth of Independent States and the demise of the Union of Soviet Socialist Republics. President Gorbachev announced his resignation on Christmas Day, bringing the Soviet Union to its official end, therefore, on 25 December 1991. Russia took the Soviet Union's seat on the UN Security Council and its place as co-sponsor of the Middle East peace conference.

Faced with this extraordinary end-of-year unheaval and wishing to gain a better grasp of the repercussions and implications of the USSR's demise, Yasser Arafat began a lengthy tour of the Asian Communist countries and the countries bordering the former USSR, as well as Kazakhstan, in the second half of December 1991. Farouq Kaddoumi, his Foreign Minister, convened a meeting in Geneva (21–22 December 1991) of Palestinian representatives accredited to the EC countries, for an exchange of views on the new international political developments and their future consequences for the Palestinian question. Kaddoumi called on his representatives to take appropriate steps to express the Palestinians' wish that the European Community take on the role of co-chairing the peace conference with the Americans and Russians. Kaddoumi—his name derives from Cadmos, brother of the Canaanite princess, Europè, from whom the continent of Europe takes its name—also enjoined his representatives to work in the spirit of building a 'common Euro-Arab home'. They were to support the initiatives already taken by the Mediterranean countries to contribute to the establishment of a new ethical and political order, founded on justice, solidarity and co-operation, in what seemed to be an impending era of peace as the twentieth century drew to a close.

Following the Israeli government's decision of 2 January 1992 to expel 12 Palestinians from the occupied territories, the Palestinian, Jordanian, Syrian and Lebanese delegations decided to mark their protest by deferring their journeys to Washington for the resumption of the bilateral Arab-Israeli negotiations. The Israelis arrived in the American capital for the planned meeting of 7 January, but this time it was the Arabs who temporarily practised an 'empty chair' policy.

The US Initiative

At the PLO's request, the Security Council met on 6 January 1992 and adopted Resolution 726, which firmly condemned Israel's decision to expel the 12 Palestinians and asked it to reverse its decision. The Arab parties were satisfied with the Security Council vote and, after the PLO had directed a concerted approach, they decided to resume bilateral talks with the Israeli delegation, beginning on 13 January 1992.

Thus the Palestinians', Jordanians' and Israelis' acceptance of Baker's compromise proposal put an end to the 'corridor diplomacy' which had marked the December 1991 meetings, enabling the second round of bilateral Jordano-Palestinian-Israeli negotiations to proceed in Washington. This compromise meant that the composition of the Jordano-Palestinian delegations negotiating with the Israeli delegation would vary, depending on the particular subject under discussion: nine Palestinians and two Jordanians when dealing with Palestinian issues; nine Jordanians and two Palestinians for matters pertaining to the Jordanians. This third round of the bilateral negotiations inaugurated in Madrid began in Washington on 13 January 1992 and ended on 16 January without any agreement on procedure, with the parties confining their discussions to setting an agenda. Seasoned observers were expecting this sort of development since it reflected the gulf separating the position of the Israelis from that of the Palestinians.

The first stumbling-block was that of Jewish settlements in the occupied territories. Whereas the Palestinians viewed this problem as a major obstacle to a discussion on peace and on the territories' future so long as the settlements continued, the Israeli delegation made it known that they did not intend to discuss it. They also refused to discuss the autonomy plan presented to them by the Palestinians on 14 January. This plan was predicated on the commonly accepted principle that autonomy enshrines the free exercise of part of the sovereignty of a population, through that population's representatives, over the territories it inhabits and which are recognized as belonging to it. The plan provided for the withdrawal from these territories of Israeli troops and their replacement by United Nations forces, and the creation of a Palestinian Interim Self-Governing Authority to comprise a legislative assembly of 180 representatives elected under international supervision, an executive council of 20 members and a judiciary. It stated that:

> The aim of the interim self-government is to ensure a peaceful and orderly transfer of authority from Israel to the Palestinians and to create the right conditions for negotiations on the final status of the occupied Palestinian territories.

The Palestinians saw this agreement as a five-year transitional phase, which should culminate in Palestine's sovereign independence.

Subject to this proviso, the Palestinians' acceptance of autonomy was a major concession on their part and one which they agreed to only as a temporary measure to overcome the hurdles and ensure the success of the negotiations, in which their hopes of peace were vested. They considered it a stop-gap solution which would lead to the eventual fulfilment of their main demand: the exercise of their right to self-determination.

The Israelis' notion of autonomy was the very antithesis of the Palestinian position. For them, it was to mean only limited autonomy, covering persons and not territory; the outcome of the interim phase was intended to sanction the application to the Palestinians of a status reducing them from a nation to a mere minority, with no right to sovereignty over, or legal and historical tie to, their territory, which would then be deemed to be an integral part of Israel. The simple mention of the autonomy question led, on 19 January 1992, to the withdrawal from the Israeli coalition government of two extreme right-wing parties, Tehiya and Moledet, who held three and two Knesset seats respectively. The government thereby lost its parliamentary majority.

The Multilateral Negotiations in Moscow

As agreed in Madrid, the two co-sponsors issued invitations on 14 January 1992, during the second Washington round, to some 30 countries to participate in the multilateral negotiations on co-operation in the Middle East region, to be held on 28 and 29 January. Invited to these negotiations were Israel, all the Arab countries (except Iraq and Libya), Turkey, China (after it re-established diplomatic relations with Israel on 24 January 1992), India (which re-established diplomatic relations with Israel on 29 January 1992), Japan, Canada, the European Community and the European Free Trade Association. Of the 30 or more countries invited, however, only 22 actually attended the Moscow conference; notable absentees included Syria, Lebanon and the Palestinians.

Faithful to its previously expressed stand, Syria, with the support of Lebanon and the PLO, refused to attend the negotiations, considering them to be premature, given the lack of substantial progress in the bilateral talks. Syria understandably felt that negotiations could not begin on the framework and subject matter of true co-operation in the Middle East without a previous settlement of the Palestinian question and the conflicts between Israel and the Arab states in the region. In the logical view of the Syrians, enemies cannot co-operate while they are still at war: co-operation is the product of peace, which presupposes the prior eradication of both the conflict and its causes.

The Israeli concept of the multilateral negotiations, contrary to what would seem logical, was predicated on the principle that co-operation settles conflicts. Even if one were to accept such reasoning, the impression left by Israel's behaviour since the opening of the Madrid conference was that it had in fact sought to retain the occupied territories, secure peace and recognition, and become a key partner in every field in the Middle East and Gulf region, without itself having to give any ground.

The Palestinians, for their part, felt it was essential to expand their delegation to include representatives from East Jerusalem and what is dubbed the 'diaspora' (in other words, Palestinians from outside the occupied territories), especially the refugees, whose plight and fate were to be one of the subjects of the multilateral negotiations. To show their goodwill and to avoid being rebuked for practising an 'empty chair' policy, the Palestinian delegation nevertheless went to Moscow on 26 January.

The two co-sponsors expressed understanding for the Palestinian approach but felt that it was not possible to depart from the framework that had already been decided on for representation (known as the 'Madrid formula') without Israel's agreement—this was tantamount to a rejection of the Palestinian proposal. The Palestinians put forward a second proposal whereby they would agree to adhere to the 'Madrid formula' provided that the representatives of the diaspora and East Jerusalem could take part in the deliberations of the working groups to be set up. While approving this proposal, Baker again indicated that it required the consent of Israel, which continued categorically to withhold it, even for the negotiations on the refugee problem. This only confirmed what had been said earlier by Hanan Ashrawi, the spokeswoman of the Palestinian delegation: 'If Israel has problems with the Palestinians from Jerusalem or the diaspora, it doesn't mean that the world must adopt the Israeli point of view.' Thus, the co-sponsors acknowledged an Israeli right of veto, to be used or withheld at will, even on questions to be dealt with at the multilateral negotiations on which all the participants had extended agreement except Israel. Israel also objected to the UN Secretary-General's participation in the negotiations.

In such circumstances, the Palestinian negotiators could not afford to risk 'going it alone' in disregard of the feelings of the Palestinians both inside and outside the occupied territories and of the complexity of the new problems they now faced. They therefore refused to take part in the Moscow negotiations. Israel could not hide its satisfaction at 'getting what it expected', in the words of its Foreign Minister, which, to him, meant Israel's recognition by some ten Arab countries by virtue of their having engaged in negotiations with his country.

The Moscow multilateral negotiations, whose purpose was limited, led to the creation of the structures and timetable for future meetings. Thus, working groups were set up on the following subjects:

(i)   *the environment*, to meet in Tokyo on 15 May 1992, with Japan as co-ordinator;

(ii)   *security and arms control*, to meet in Washington on 13–15 May 1992, with Russia and the US as co-ordinators;

(iii) *refugees*, to meet on 13–15 May 1992, with Canada as co-ordinator;

(iv)   *economic development*, to be co-ordinated by the European Community and to meet on 11 and 12 May 1992 (its decisions requiring adoption by consensus); and

(v)   *water resources*, to meet in Vienna on 12–15 May 1992, and to be co-ordinated by the United States.

All these groups were to be accountable to a steering committee chaired by the US which should 'ensure continuity in the peace process, oversee the multilateral negotiations and suggest new fields of activity'. This steering committee comprised the following members: US, Russia, EC, Saudi Arabia (Gulf Co-operation Council), Tunisia (Arab Maghreb Union), Egypt and the parties to the conflict. Some Arab countries proposed the creation of another three working groups to deal with Jerusalem, human rights and health. This proposal was forwarded to the steering committee for consideration.

What conclusions can be drawn from the climate in which the first multilateral negotiating round took place, from the incidents it provoked and from the disappointment it bred? First, when comparing the media coverage in Moscow with that in Madrid, one can readily appreciate that the multilateral talks were conducted in a deep gloom befitting the icy Russian winter. The media non-event was compounded by the partial political failure of these preliminary negotiations, owing to the absence of three of the major protagonists—Palestine, Syria and Lebanon—which were the only Arab countries in the region whose territory was either partly or wholly occupied. How could one imagine co-operation and peace without them or, for that matter, counter to their interests? The Arab peoples experienced nothing but frustration and disenchantment as a consequence of this first encounter.

Conversely, Israel, and Shamir in particular, had every reason to take heart from this initial outcome, which bolstered Israel's extremist position. It enabled Shamir, furthermore, to present himself during the Israeli election campaign as the 'architect of peace' and of a 'Greater Israel' at the same time.

Bush could claim that he had kept his promise to the American public that he would unstintingly pursue the peace process. As for the Palestinians, they remained more wedded than ever to their position of meaningful participation, according to their flexible and practical proposal, in all the working groups. Moscow could draw satisfaction from having hosted the conference, which had helped to establish Russia as the former Soviet Union's successor in tackling, albeit timidly, the problems of the Middle East. As far as the European Community, China and Japan were concerned, it was still too early to gauge the scale of their future role in establishing stability, peace and co-operation in the region. Their participation in the negotiations none the less set the seal on their entrance as players in the peace process arena.

3
The Process Itself Becomes the Main Issue

By the end of eight sessions[1] of bilateral discussions, no meaningful progress had been made. Yet none of the parties involved in the talks had dropped out so as not to be held responsible for deadlock in a region whose wounds were festering out of control. It was the Americans, because of their singularly influential position, who closed off any alternative to the peace process and who also compelled all the parties to continue to participate. This American paramountcy also managed ostensibly to keep in motion the multilateral negotiations begun in Moscow on 28–29 January 1992, followed by two sessions in the spring and summer of the same year. The fourth multilateral session, scheduled for February 1993, was postponed owing to Israel's expulsion of 413 Palestinians to south Lebanon on 17 December 1992.

These multilateral discussions had been little more than a forum for exchanging views and were intended more to involve the rich industrialized countries and the Gulf states in the subsequent funding required to foster the normalization of Israeli-Arab relations, should the present peace process succeed. Washington saw this process as an ideal means of justifying its intervention and military presence in the Middle East, especially the Gulf, thereby ensuring 'regional security', arms control, economic development and political change throughout the entire area. These aims were of a piece with a global strategy of securing a *pax americana* through a stability predicated upon a freer, more secure and more prosperous Middle East. This strategy also sought to pave the way for Israel's integration in the region for the sake of its own interests and security, but also in order to lighten the burden that Israel's protection placed on the Americans themselves.

The enormous gulf which separated the various parties made peace a distant prospect but, since a new Arab-Israeli war seemed scarcely conceivable for the time being, this state of expectancy, of neither war nor peace, had enabled the process gradually to take the place reserved for a true peace. The process had become the main issue, not least because everyone believed there were advantages to be drawn from this inconclusive transitional phase.

The Fourth Bilateral Session

Just before the fourth session (24 February–4 March 1992), a series of Israeli provocations soured the atmosphere between the Arabs and Israelis: the leader of Hizbollah was assassinated, four members of the Palestinian delegation were arrested, and there were raids and incursions into south Lebanon. As a 'consolation' to the Arabs, James Baker chose 24 February 1992, the day when the bilateral negotiations resumed in Washington, to present to Congress his position on American aid to Israel: this made the granting of the $10 billion in loan guarantees conditional upon a halt to all further Israeli building in the Palestinian territories occupied in 1967, except where construction work had already begun. The next day, George Bush endorsed his Secretary of State's stand. The Shamir government replied on 17 March 1992 by rejecting the Americans' terms; Israel withdrew its request for loan guarantees so that it could pursue its settlement policy free from any constraints.

As for the Israeli-Palestinian talks, no one had been expecting any tangible results since the main aim was to keep the wheels of the peace process in motion, if only in formal terms. Both parties had exchanged their plans for administration of the occupied territories during the interim period. The Israeli version was presented to the Palestinian delegation on 2 March 1992 in the form of a ten-page working paper that used the term 'interim arrangement' instead of the 'self-government' referred to in the Camp David Accords. It stipulated that administrative authority would be 'delegated', not 'tranferred', to the Palestinians in the following areas: law enforcement, administrative affairs, agriculture, education and culture, budget and taxation, health, industry, trade, tourism, local policing for criminal matters, local transport and communications, municipal affairs and religious affairs. The plan would allow Israelis to continue to settle in the occupied territories and Israel would retain its exclusive right to deal with security matters in all aspects: external, internal and in the field of public order. It constituted a back-sliding on the Camp David proposals for autonomy and threatened to turn the Palestinians into 'civil servants of their own occupation' while they were consulted on economic and social issues. Shamir's government thus sought to put an end to the *intifada*, secure the continuation of settlements and maintain Israel's control over the occupied territories in order to claim Israeli sovereignty over them at the end of the interim period.

The Palestinians rejected the Israeli paper and, on 3 March 1992, presented their own 14-page document containing a detailed plan for self-government which covered the interim arrangements to be made in the occupied territories and, more particularly, the establishment of the Palestinian Interim Self-Governing Authority (PISGA). The Palestinian autonomy plan, which had been first conveyed to the Israeli delegation on 14 January 1992 at the third round of the bilateral negotiations, had been split into three parts: the basic concepts and detailed programme of the PISGA, preliminary measures for the interim phase, and election modalities. The Israelis rejected the proposals *en bloc*.

The US administration blamed the Palestinian delegation for being unrealistic at the talks. It suggested that they focus on specific proposals rather than present general schemes that were part of an overall plan to establish a Palestinian state to which both Israel and the administration were hostile. As the session closed on 4 March 1992, the Arab delegations made clear their disappointment with the stalemate and lack of progress at the talks. The Americans, however, viewed the fact that the Israelis and Palestinians had actually exchanged proposals and were continuing to talk as a success in itself.

The Fifth Session

When the contents of the Israeli 'working paper', presented to the Palestinians on 15 March 1992 at the fourth negotiating round, became known, 117 members of the Palestine National Council sent a memorandum to the PLO leadership calling for a suspension of the talks until the PLO was officially represented at them. This protest movement evaporated after Arafat's plane crashed in the Libyan desert in April 1992: during the 15 hours that Arafat was missing, it became obvious what a key figure he was in the peace process. The negotiations with the Israelis duly resumed in Washington on 27 April for a period of four days.

In the course of this session, the Israeli delegation put forward its plan for municipal elections as a step towards the establishment of administrative autonomy. The Palestinian delegation rejected the proposal and called for legislative elections instead. When the session ended, the Israelis and Arabs gave diametrically opposed assessments, the former seeing it as the 'first real working meeting' while the Palestinians, Syrians and Lebanese could detect nothing more than deadlock. There was, however, significant progress in the Israeli-Jordanian talks.

Israeli insistence on moving the negotiations from Washington to another capital, preferably in the Middle East, was finally rewarded at this session: in May 1992 Rome was chosen as the next venue for the bilateral Arab-Israeli talks.

The Sixth Session

The Palestinian negotiators, whose right to participate in the peace talks was rooted in their allegiance to the PLO, discreetly sent representatives to the Palestine Central Council (PCC) meeting held in Tunis from 7 to 10 May 1992. The meeting had been postponed from 9 April owing to Yasser Arafat's convalescence from the aircraft crash. At the close of this regular PCC session, the council restated its commitment to the 1988 Palestinian peace initiative (set forth at the 19th session of the Palestine National Council) as the basis for the Palestinians' position in the peace process; the ultimate aim remained the establishment of a Palestinian state with Jerusalem as its capital. The PCC stressed that a halt to settlements was the key to the entire peace process and made clear that it viewed the interim phase as simply a stepping-stone to outright independence: a stage in which the occupation would disappear, all occupying forces would be withdrawn and the Palestinian people would democratically exercise its right to elect its own representatives to a Legislative Assembly, thus permitting the formation of a provisional Palestinian government in the independent state's capital, Jerusalem.

As for Israel's proposal for municipal elections, tabled at the fifth negotiating round, the PCC judged that such a ballot should only take place after the Legislative Assembly had been elected and authority had been transferred to the Palestinians. Furthermore, municipal elections should be held in accordance with Palestinian, not Israeli, law. No decision was taken on whether the Palestinians should attend the sixth session of the bilateral negotiations.

The major new factor in the Middle East after the fifth round of talks was the victory of Labour over Likud in the Israeli general elections of 23 June 1992. Labour improved its position from the 40 seats it had taken in 1988 to 44; Likud dropped from 39 seats to 32; the left-wing Meretz bloc (comprising the Retz, Shinui and Mapam movements) increased its representation from 10 to 12 seats; on the far right, Tsomet quadrupled the 4 seats it had taken in 1988, and Moledet added 1 seat to its previous 2; the religious parties shared 16 seats (Mafdal 6, Shas 6 and the Torah 4); the Democratic Front (Hadash-Communist) with 3 seats, and the Arab Democratic Party with 2, completed the picture. Rabin's Labour Party joined forces with Meretz and Shas to form the new government, which duly won a vote of confidence in the Knesset on 13 July 1992.

Three days later, Rabin called a halt to the 'political' settlements in the occupied territories, prompting an appreciative James Baker (who arrived in Israel on 19 July) to extend his agreement in principle to the granting of the loan guarantees so long denied the government of Yitzhak Shamir. (Official approval for the $10 billion was given by President Bush on 11 August during Rabin's visit to Bush's Maine home in Kennebunkport.) Baker also managed to convince Rabin that he should give priority to the negotiations with Syria. The combination of American pressure and Hosni Mubarak's pleading during Rabin's visit to Egypt on 21 July led the Israeli leader to change his priorities (although throughout the election campaign he had placed emphasis on the paramount need for a settlement with the Palestinians).

In a television interview with the US network PBS on 14 August 1992, Rabin expressed his opposition to the trial municipal elections proposed by Likud, and suggested instead that elections be held in the occupied territories in April–May 1993 for the 'Palestinian Administrative Council' to be responsible for the transitional period referred to in the Camp David Accords. The date 1 December was to be the deadline for agreement on the modalities of these elections and 1 February 1993 was to be the deadline for determining the areas of life to be managed by the Palestinians. It was a plan which retreated significantly from the manifesto Labour had adopted at its fifth congress.

Meretz (Rabin's coalition partners) for its part proposed Israeli withdrawal from virtually all the occupied Arab territories. It introduced into its manifesto the term 'Palestinian state' instead of 'Palestinian entity'. It also accepted PLO participation in the peace talks at some later stage and continued to advocate self-determination for the Palestinian people. It none the less opposed the right of Palestinian refugees to return to Palestine. Meretz, comprising three left-wing parties, stressed the importance of human rights in its joint platform. It drew up a ten-point plan addressing the grievances of the Palestinians of Israeli nationality who live in Israel proper, such as the need to abolish their segregated status in civil and political life, to establish equality in municipal budgets between Arabs and Jews, and to achieve parity in appointments to high public office. Shas, the Sephardic religious party, was the third component of the Rabin government. Although, as 'Haredi', they are ultra-orthodox, they do not espouse the chauvinist nationalism dear to the 'Mafdal', the National Religious Party.

Rabin's attitude to the peace process was marked by a different style, approach and set of priorities from his Likud predecessor. Whereas Shamir had pursued a policy of wilful prevarication, in which his only concession to the US initiative had been to go to Madrid and his main aim had been to impose acceptance of the territorial *status quo* on the Arabs, Rabin set about creating a fresh climate with a number of confidence-building measures and placatory gestures that might improve Israel's image abroad and convince the international community, especially the Arabs, of his good faith.

Thus he drastically reduced state subsidies and credit for 'political' settlements; froze the construction of roads in the occupied territories; decided to return East Jerusalem houses confiscated and occupied by Israeli settlers to their Palestinian owners; peacefully defused the siege of al-Najah University of 15–17 July 1992; and reopened Faisal Husseini's Arab Studies Centre on 30 July after it had been closed for four years.

The *Revue d'Etudes Palestiniennes*,[2] quoting Israeli press sources, reported that Rabin had suggested that Husseini turn the centre into a permanent headquarters for the Palestinian delegation to the peace talks. Subsequently, in the summer of 1992, part of the building housing the centre duly became the delegation's headquarters, known as 'Orient House'. In a gesture to the European Community, the Rabin government granted diplomatic status to the EC's representative in the occupied territories responsible for economic and humanitarian assistance to the Palestinians, Thomas Dupla, though until July 1992 he continued to operate out of Brussels after being appointed nine months earlier.

For the first time, an Israeli leader criticized Israel's obsession with seeing itself as an isolated Jewish state surrounded by enemies. Speaking at the 32nd World Jewish Congress in West Jerusalem on 30 July 1992, Rabin appealed to Jews to change their mentality and rid themselves of this feeling of isolation from which they had, in his words, suffered for almost half a century. His Education and Culture Minister, Shulamit Aloni, had levelled even harsher criticism at this Israeli syndrome in an interview with *Haaretz* 13 days earlier:

> It is no secret to anyone that our educational system relies on knee-jerks and develops neither personal thought nor a critical mind. In fact, the authorities brainwash children from nursery school on. At the tenderest

age, they are taught to imbue thenselves with a clan-like mentality and fear of the outside world and the wicked goyim. Always hearing that we are victims and martyrs makes us think that we are always right, and any criticism and self-criticism become futile. I intend to fight this indoctrination. Children must learn, firstly at play, that there is always a choice to be made between various options; may they then learn to check their sources and to compare books which put forward differing opinions. If I were a teacher of religion, I would endeavour to understand with the pupils the intentions that lie behind the narrator's style, the time, the social context and the beliefs of his milieu.[3]

Further conciliatory gestures were made on 23 August 1992, on the eve of the sixth negotiating session: the release of some 800 Palestinian prisoners who had served two-thirds of their sentences; permission to reopen houses which had been boarded up and streets which had been blocked off for more than five years as retaliation and collective punishment by the Israeli army; and authorization for Palestinians over the age of 50 from the occupied territories to enter Israel without prior permission. When the talks resumed on 24 August, Israel cancelled an expulsion order on 11 Palestinians, but it refused to abolish the practice altogether, even though it breaches the 4th Geneva Convention.

At a meeting in Damascus on 20 August, the Syrian, Lebanese, Jordanian and Palestinian Foreign Ministers agreed to Arab participation in the month-long sixth session. The Israelis retained the same negotiators, except that Itamar Rabinovitch, a moderate historian close to Shimon Peres, replaced the fervent advocate of a 'Greater Israel', Yossi Ben Aharon, in the talks with the Syrians. Appointed on 1 August, Rabinovitch took a new approach, offering a different style and a measured, constructive tone to his Syrian counterparts and implying that Israel would be ready to withdraw partially from the occupied Golan Heights in pursuance of Security Council Resolution 242.

For the first time since Madrid, the Syrian delegation presented a written paper to the Israelis on 3 September. What the head of the Syrian delegation, Allaf, called an *aide-mémoire* was not made public, but it apparently for the first time made explicit reference to the possibility of Syria's signing a peace treaty with Israel. Indeed on 23 September at the opening of the UN General Assembly in New York, Farouq al-Shara, the Syrian Foreign Minister, stated that Syria was ready for 'full peace' with Israel in return for a 'full withdrawal' from the occupied Golan and gave assurances of the 'undoubted sincerity' of his government. Thus, the new term 'full peace' replaced that of 'comprehensive peace' previously used in Syrian political discourse.

The Process Itself Becomes the Main Issue

A number of leaks indicate that this easing of the logjam was the result of an American offer covering three main points:

(i)   Israel would accept the principle of an exchange, if only partial, of 'land for peace' and its government would ask the Knesset to agree to repeal the 1981 law which annexed the Golan;

(ii) Syria would withdraw its forces deployed around the Golan and would participate in the multilateral negotiations; and

(iii) talks would begin on a phased withdrawal of forces and a parallel phased normalization of relations.

US or multinational troops would be deployed in the demilitarized areas of withdrawal and could only be removed with the consent of both belligerents. It should be noted that the document which Israel presented to the Syrian delegation at this session made no mention of the word 'withdrawal'.

Meanwhile, the Jordanian delegation felt able to assert that the draft agenda proposed by their Israeli counterparts, in its letter and its spirit, constituted a new beginning. The Lebanese, however, still came up against Israel's refusal even to contemplate ending the occupation of the 850 km of their territory it held. Again Israel omitted to use the term 'withdrawal' and justified the occupation on grounds of security.

As for the Palestinian delegation, they were forced to arrive a day late, owing to the humiliating administrative harrassment of 5 of their 28 members. At the session, they received a working paper in which Israel detailed all the conditions involved in the transfer of 'administrative responsibility' in some 15 spheres. The only novelty in the proposal, compared to that of Shamir, was acceptance of a Palestinian police force and a readiness to envisage joint Israeli-Palestinian control of land and water resources. The paper also pledged to allow the holding of elections in the occupied Palestinian territories for an Administrative Council of 15 members, but this fell a long way short of the Palestinians' demand for a 180-member Legislative Assembly. Indeed, Rabin's proposals were viewed as little more than a reformulation of Shamir's policy. The Palestinian negotiators called in vain for Israel to reaffirm the applicability of Resolution 242 to the Israeli-Palestinian conflict prior to any agreement on an agenda and prior to any discussion on the interim period of self-government, and in their turn presented their own 10-point paper on the transitional phase and self-government arrangements.

The Seventh Session

A week before the seventh session of the bilateral negotiations (21 October–18 November 1992), the Palestine Central Council met for three days in Tunis. In its final communiqué, it reaffirmed previous PCC and PNC decisions, rejected Rabin's distinction between 'political' and 'security' settlements, and stressed the importance of an increased European contribution to Middle East peace and stability and, more particularly, of more meaningful European participation in the peace process. The council also called for Japanese, Chinese and Canadian involvement in the process. Furthermore, the question of Jerusalem was given high priority.

The Israeli delegation in the talks with Syria for the first time presented a paper mentioning withdrawal from the Golan, on 22 October 1992. Israel advocated a separate settlement of the conflict with Syria, calling for a peace treaty that would not be contingent upon progress elsewhere in the talks with the Palestinians, Jordanians and Lebanese.

None the less, with US presidential elections on 3 November looming, the Israelis and Jordanians reached agreement, a year after the Madrid conference, on the details of their agenda; the document listed security, sharing of water resources, territorial issues, refugees and bilateral co-operation, and stated that their ultimate objective was a 'peace treaty'. No progress was made, however, with the Palestinians or the Lebanese.

Reflecting on the modest achievements of the seventh session, the Assistant US Secretary of State for the region, Edward Djerejian, declared on 19 November 1992 that there had been no 'spectacular breakthrough', but that the parties remained committed to the search for a peaceful settlement.

The Eighth Session

The eighth bilateral negotiating session (held in Washington from 7 to 17 December 1992) was intended to maintain the momentum of the peace process during the US presidential interregnum. As both Arabs and Israelis awaited Bill Clinton's official assumption of power, the President-elect declared his opposition to any delay or slowing-down of the talks. Whcn the discussions resumed, the Israelis proposed a form of administrative autonomy to the Lebanese for the occupied southern strip of the country; this was rejected out-of-hand, as the Lebanese demanded full compliance with Security Council Resolution 425.

As for the Palestinians, the Israelis continued to speak only of the establishment of an interim autonomous authority and not of its final status, let alone of the requirements of Resolution 242, which the Israelis continued to keep off the agenda. The Palestinian delegation, now limited to four members, proceeded to boycott the fifth meeting of the session. The other Arab delegations scaled down their own attendance in solidarity, as a result of Israel's decision to expel 413 Palestinians to south Lebanon. This act was to have more serious consequences than simply spoiling President Bush's farewells to the negotiating delegations.

The Clinton Administration in the US

Bill Clinton's election had nothing to do with his foreign policy stance, least of all on the Middle East, and everything to do with a widespread sense of weariness and frustration among the American electorate with his predecessor's economic policy. Furthermore, the vigorous, innovative, albeit financially extravagant, campaign fought by the independent Ross Perot helped to produce a far-from-convincing majority for the Democrats in which Clinton scored the lowest percentage of votes for a winning candidate in decades. His victory signified, therefore, a rejection of George Bush and the Republicans more than the triumph of his own ideas. His achievement, none the less, was to perceive a certain 'wind of change' in the country and to turn it to his advantage.

If foreign policy played any role at all, it stemmed the 'haemorrhaging' of support for Bush, who was able to contrast his own stature as a proven international statesman with the manifest inexperience and ignorance of his younger rival, thus playing on voters' fears of how any future international crisis might be tackled. These misgivings apart, however, the electorate saw fit to return the first Democrat candidate since Jimmy Carter left the White House 12 years earlier.

Clinton had largely restricted his campaign to the major domestic issues—the economy, the budget deficit and health care—to the virtual exclusion of international affairs, except where they might influence the national economy: for example, the impact of NAFTA (the North American Free Trade Agreement) on the domestic jobs' market, and the looming trade war with Europe and Japan owing to disagreements in the Uruguay Round of GATT. The only international problems to catch his attention were the carnage in Bosnia (thanks largely to his running-mate's rapport with the Bosnian Foreign Minister, Haris Silajdzic) and the imminent arrival of thousands of Haitian refugees fleeing the military dictatorship which had ousted the democratically elected Father Aristide. The Madrid peace process received scant attention: Clinton expressed broad support for the peace talks and for their continuation. He nevertheless made little effort to conceal his sympathy for Israel's position, not only to attract Jewish votes but also because of the close ties between his campaign team and the pro-Israel lobbies, especially AIPAC (the American-Israel Public Affairs Committee). More worrying still was his support for Israel's request for the $10 million in loan guarantees, at a time when Shamir's position on settlements was at its most intransigent, and for the recognition of Jerusalem as the undivided capital of Israel. One should also take account here of the importance of Clinton's choice as running-mate, Albert Gore. The Tennessee senator had been conspicuously zealous in his support for Israeli policies during his own campaign for the Democrat nomination four years earlier when he had lost to Michael Dukakis, the Massachusetts governor who was subsequently trounced by George Bush.

Whether Clinton's stance on the Middle East was sincere or opportunist, he succeeded in taking a disproportionate share of the Jewish vote from an incumbent President and especially Secretary of State who had been depicted by some sections of the press as 'anti-Israeli' and even 'anti-semitic'. The Palestinians and Arabs in general had virtually taken Bush's re-election for granted and had drawn comfort from the belief that Baker would soon be back at the helm of US foreign policy. Clinton's victory, therefore, came as a shock, not least because leading Palestinian negotiators had openly 'campaigned' for Bush and had thus gravely undermined their position with the Democrats.

This setback was exacerbated by Clinton's nominations for the key posts at the State Department and in his National Security Council. To replace Baker at State, he nominated Warren Christopher, a former senior Carter administration official who had been closely involved in the Camp David Accords and was co-chairman of the Clinton transition team in the months between the election and the inauguration. Christopher had been the target of some hostility among leaders of the pro-Israel lobby who had even written to Clinton, asking him not to appoint Christopher because he was 'Carter's man and Carter was no friend of Israel'. To reconcile the lobby to the subsequent appointment of Christopher (in itself a victory for Israel since his main rival for the post had been Lee Hamilton, the House of Representatives' foreign affairs committee chairman, who was reputed to be more responsive to the Palestinians), Clinton proceeded to staff the upper ranks of the State Department and National Security Council with policy analysts known for their pro-Israeli and Zionist views. Thus, Baker's Middle East policy chief, Dennis Ross, was replaced by Samuel Lewis, a former US ambassador to Tel Aviv and a Jew who was close to the Israeli leadership. As deputy to his new National Security Adviser, Anthony Lake, Clinton appointed Sandy Berger—of similar political vintage to Lewis—and, as their principal analyst on the Middle East, he chose Martin Indyk, an Australian academic who had only recently been naturalized as a US citizen and who was known for his anti-Palestinian bias and judged by certain Israeli press commentators to be 'more Zionist than Shamir'.

Thus, in wishing to focus on domestic priorities as well as to conceal his ignorance of foreign policy—in this instance, the issues at stake in the Madrid peace process—Clinton had simply delegated responsibility for Middle East policy to some of the most fervently anti-Palestinian members of the foreign policy establishment. He thereby guaranteed an Israeli stranglehold on the new administration's policies just when US impartiality was more vital than ever.

The changes in personnel were promptly reflected in a policy shift. Rabin's first visit to the new President was conspicuously cordial, the Israeli Prime Minister's views were met with deep understanding, and it became clear that the US would henceforth refrain from exerting any meaningful pressure on Israel, unlike the previous administration's attempts to present at least a semblance of impartiality and balance. The Americans' strategic agreements with Israel on security co-operation were renewed with unquestioning alacrity, and Christopher caved in to Rabin's determination to disobey Resolution 799 by agreeing to a deal that patently breached the resolution's demands for a speedy return of all the deportees. Indeed, Clinton repeatedly commended Rabin's 'forthcoming' attitude, and chose to step up the pressure on the Arab states to put an end to their economic boycott of Israel rather than persuade the latter to make serious concessions on the deportees and on settlements.

This all demonstrated that the new administration, while advocating the continuation of a peace process which had been tilted against the Arabs and especially the Palestinians from the outset, had departed sufficiently from the tenuous impartiality of Baker's approach to render the entire process irretrievably advantageous to Israel at the Arabs' expense. In inheriting a process devised and set in train by others, Clinton had at the same time forsaken the position of 'honest broker' and pursued an approach more reminiscent of Ronald Reagan.

Four years before Clinton's election, the black civil rights advocate, the Reverend Jesse Jackson, had demanded and obtained a debate on the Palestinian question at the Democrat Party Convention, in return for his own withdrawal from the presidential race. By focusing exclusively on the governing party ever since then, the Palestinians and their allies in the United States had thereby squandered a valuable opportunity to build up a constituency of support in the party that was to take power in 1993. It was an already-established belief that Israeli intransigence—be it that of Shamir, Rabin, Peres or whoever—on the major questions of substance would remain unshakeable without robust political intervention from the United States. Such intervention seemed more unlikely than ever after Clinton's election. If Washington could not bend Israel to the demands of Resolution 799, what hope was there of compelling it to meet the altogether more onerous requirements of Resolution 242?

In the meantime, continued involvement in the peace process was discrediting the PLO still further among its own constituency, depleting its already dwindling support in the occupied territories; Syria and Lebanon were aware of their reduced chances of recovering lost territory since Israel could shirk its obligations to the Security Council with such ease and impunity; and the Arabs' leaders, particularly Yasser Arafat, were having to confront the widespread and growing suspicion that the peace process would bring the Palestinians nothing better than a negotiated political suicide if no meaningful and immediate progress were made once the peace talks resumed.

The Deportees

On 18 December 1992, the day after Israel's expulsion of 413 Palestinians, the UN Security Council unanimously adopted Resolution 799, which:

> Strongly condemns the action taken by Israel, the occupying power, to deport hundreds of Palestinian civilians, and expresses its firm opposition to any such deportation by Israel;
> Reaffirms the applicability of the 4th Geneva Convention of 12 August 1949 to all the Palestinian territories occupied by Israel since 1967, including Jerusalem; and
> Demands that Israel, the occupying power, ensure the safe and immediate return to the occupied territories of all those deported.

The council did not, however, lay down a precise timetable for Israel to repatriate the deportees, nor did it recommend sanctions if Israel refused to comply. Indeed, Chapter 7 of the UN charter, under which punitive action may be invoked, has never been mentioned in any resolution dealing with Israel.

Rabin's action placed the PLO in an untenable position *vis-à-vis* its own people. It made it impossible for the organization to instruct its negotiators to resume public discussions with an Israeli delegation whose government had not only violated international conventions, resolutions and law but had, above all, reawoken the Palestinians' greatest fear: the nightmare of 1948, when whole towns and villages of Palestinians were driven *en masse* out of their homeland.

Of the 413 deportees 16 were expelled by mistake. Israel stated that these were individuals accused of a variety of crimes ranging from simply belonging to the Islamic movement to incitement to violence, and who had been serving sentences in Israeli gaols. They were the only deportees legally authorized to return to the occupied territories. The remaining deportees had been charged with no offence and had been the subject of no judicial proceedings, yet they were compelled by Israel to languish in a 'no man's land' between Israeli and Lebanese lines for a period due to last two years. Their 'removal' took place in the middle of winter and they were forced to live in makeshift shelters with minimal resources, in conditions of extreme cold, rain and snow, since the Lebanese army had refused to allow them past their lines on government instructions. Beirut was determined to prevent, at whatever cost, the entry of these Palestinians into that part of Lebanese territory under its control.

In an attempt to secure implementation of Resolution 799, the UN Secretary-General, Boutros Boutros Ghali, dispatched two special envoys, James Jonah and Chinmaya Gharekhan, to Israel at the end of December 1992 and at the start of January 1993 respectively. Both representatives returned empty-handed. In a report to the Security Council on 25 January 1993, the Secretary-General recommended that 'all necessary measures' be taken to ensure that Israel complied with the resolution calling for the immediate return of the Palestinian deportees. Israel rejected the report as 'biased' and further refused to accept Boutros Ghali's proposal to establish a UN mechanism to monitor the situation in the occupied Palestinian territories. The next day, Ismat Abdel-Meguid, the Secretary-General of the Arab League, reacted to Israel's refusal to comply with Resolution 799 by stating, 'It is high time that the Security Council understood that the policy of double standards can no longer be pursued.'[4]

On 28 January 1993 the seven judges of the highest legal body in Israel, the Supreme Court, unanimously turned down the appeal made on behalf of the deportees. It went on, however, to rule that 'collective' expulsion orders were illegal, thus allowing each of the men to be heard individually if they wished to seek redress in one of the 14 military commissions specially set up for the purpose. The requests would have to be made in writing, however. The court further decreed that the individual expulsion orders issued on 17 December 1992 against the 413 Palestinians were valid. This ruling created a legal precedent and it showed to what extent Israeli justice functioned differently depending on whether Israelis or Palestinians were being tried. *Le Monde*'s special correspondent, Patrice Claude, summed up the dichotomy thus:

> Independent, liberal and marked by the best traditions of Western law for the Israelis, based on the principle of the presumption of innocence and the Anglo-Saxon practice of habeas corpus, the judicial authority looks for all the world like a mere recording studio for the wishes of the political and military authorities when it is Palestinians that are involved.[5]

Israeli lawyers specializing in the defence of human rights responded to the Supreme Court's decision by lamenting the fact that, in Israel, 'justice stops at the Green Line'. However, to gain a better understanding of why the court did not take a stand on the substance of the deportation question but only on the expediency of immediately repatriating the deportees, one must go back to October 1979, when, in a watershed ruling, the court called for the dismantling of the Jewish settlement of Elon Mareh, created in the occupied territories by the Gush Emunim movement, on the grounds that it was not warranted by any requirements of security.

To obviate recourse to the Supreme Court, it was therefore decided that a special jurisdiction be set up, whereby the role of the court would be supplanted by military appeals committees or military commissions, whose members would be military men appointed solely by the Israeli regional commander. These commissions, in practice, simply support the policy of the occupying military and civilian authorities towards the Palestinians: human rights violations, confiscation of land, and construction of settlements.

On 1 February 1993 a US-Israeli agreement was announced which provided for the immediate return of 101 of the Palestinian deportees, the halving of the two-year period of exile for the remainder, and the right of humanitarian organizations to provide aid by air. The US pledged to block any binding decision against Israel in international fora and not to demand further conciliatory steps from the Israelis, regardless of the position taken by the Arabs and of the US's responsibility for ensuring a resumption of the peace talks. This 'deal' between Clinton and Rabin was fiercely criticized by Likud, who saw it as a capitulation. It was rejected out-of-hand by the deportees themselves, the PLO and the Arab countries, who demanded full compliance with Resolution 799 which had called for the immediate return of all those deported. Israel was thus spared a showdown with the Security Council while not complying with the requirements of its resolution. Warren Christopher, the new US Secretary of State, said that further UN action was 'unnecessary', and the EC followed the US line by refraining from scaling down its co-operation with Israel. On 12 February 1993 the Security Council endorsed the American approach by agreeing on a statement which hailed Israel's decision on a partial return of the deportees as a 'step in the right direction'.

The Arab countries' priority was to prevent Hamas from having a 'veto' over negotiations to which it was, in any case, hostile. The Palestinian negotiators, for their part, were risking all their credibility among the Palestinian people in general so long as Israel escaped condemnation and continued to employ such repressive measures in the occupied territories. The head of the negotiating delegation, Haidar Abdel Shafi, made it known that he would take no part in discussions with Israel while it refused to comply with Resolution 799.

Through a variety of messages and intermediaries, the Palestinians asked the US to pressure Israel to halt its bloody repression, repatriate the deportees and improve living conditions in the occupied Palestinian territories. From 17 to 25 February 1993 Christopher toured the Middle East in an attempt to put the peace process back on track. It was clear to him that an immediate settlement of the deportation issue was not viewed by the Arab countries as an absolute precondition for a resumption of talks. The PLO, however, indicated that it might accept a phased return of the deportees over a period of six months or an Israeli commitment to put an end to the practice once and for all. The deportees themselves continued to demand an immediate return *en bloc* unless Israel pledged to rule out any further deportations. Rabin, for his part, deemed the matter 'closed' and did not envisage making any further gestures.

During his Middle East tour, Christopher restated the Clinton administration's commitment to continuing George Bush's policy of peace talks, democratization and control over the proliferation of non-conventional weapons. He also stressed Washington's wish to be a 'full partner' in the peace process, promising that it would be more active than in the past. Given the clear reluctance of the new administration to exert any meaningful pressure on Israel, however, such renewed vigour promised to be a double-edged sword for the Arabs since it would likely portend nothing more than stronger arm-twisting for them and more sophisticated window-dressing of ostensible Israeli 'concessions'. Moreover, in the spring of 1993, the charge of 'double standards' seemed more valid than ever. As Washington continued to vacillate over the horrifying crimes of 'ethnic cleansing' and systematic rape[6] inflicted on Bosnia's Muslims by the Christian Serbs and Croats, its quiescence on the Palestinian deportee question and on the ever-worsening repression in the occupied territories stood in stark contrast to the robust response to Iraq's invasion of Kuwait, its weapons programmes and treatment of minorities. Not surprisingly, the appeal of fundamentalism among the Arab and Muslim masses continued to increase as a result.

The Ninth Session

The ninth session was held from 27 April to 13 May. To break the deadlock, the new US administration seemed ready to accept the six proposals made by the Palestinians on 25 February 1993. Israel, however, rejected them. They would have meant that the US would guarantee that Israel would no longer resort to deportation and that Israel would establish 'arrangements' for the return of the 413 deportees, accept the return of a number of Palestinians expelled between 1967 and 1987, pledge to continue the peace talks on the basis of Resolutions 242 and 338, and accept that the two resolutions' provisions on withdrawal from the occupied territories applied to East Jerusalem.

On 10 March, in their capacity as co-sponsors of the peace process, the Russian Foreign Minister, Andrei Kozyrev, and US Secretary of State, Warren Christopher, sent out invitations to the Arabs and Israelis to resume the bilateral negotiations in Washington from 20 April to 6 May 1993. The Palestinian delegation refused to take possession of the letter of invitation from the US Consul-General in East Jerusalem, Molly Williamson, because the deportee question had not been resolved.

The invitations to the multilateral negotiations, initially scheduled for 9 February 1993, were sent out at the same time. The five commissions were due to meet for a third round of talks in successive sessions spanning one month: the Commission on Water (27–29 April 1993) in Geneva; the Commission on Economic Development (4–5 May) in Rome; the Commission on Refugees (11–13 May) in Oslo; the Commission on Arms Control (17–20 May) in Washington; and the Commission on the Environment (24–25 May) in Tokyo. These working bodies, set up after the Moscow conference, had already held two sessions in the spring and autumn of 1992. Israel had boycotted the first sessions of two of these commissions—on economic development (11–12 May 1992 in Brussels) and on refugees (13–15 May in Ottawa)—because the Shamir government objected to the presence of representatives from the diaspora in the Palestinian delegation. The Rabin government reversed this policy before the second sessions, on condition that the Palestinians were not from the PLO, the PNC or from East Jerusalem, and that Resolution 194 of the Security Council, which dealt with the right to return of Palestinian refugees, was not raised in the talks. This resulted in the exclusion of the Palestinians' chief negotiators in the two commissions concerned since they were both members of the PNC. In addition to opening the door to the participation of Palestinians from the diaspora, the Israelis also allowed the UN to take full part in the meetings.

Work in the other three commissions proceeded normally, if uneventfully. The European Community's involvement, together with that of Japan, Canada and the Gulf states, was intended to encourage the belligerents to make concessions in return for the promise of economic and financial assistance. Moreover, since the US had borne the cost of financing the Camp David process alone, it hoped to share the financial burden this time with other affluent countries. The exercise was substantially undermined, however, by the boycott of Syria and Lebanon, which refused to participate until tangible progress had been made in the bilateral negotiations. The Israelis viewed the multilateral talks as essentially a means of easing some of the pressure in the bilateral negotiations by normalizing relations with the Arab world without having to make any real concessions. For the Palestinians, there was the consolation of having obtained the representation of their diaspora in one area at least of the peace process.

The bilateral negotiations, however, had ground to a halt owing to the absence of any agreement between Israel and the Palestinians on the basic principles and nature of the proposed self-government. The gap between the two sides on the question of transitional autonomy was wide: Israel did not want autonomy to become an embryonic form of Palestinian statehood, preferring intead to grant the Palestinians a flag without a state, whereas the Palestinians sought to obtain in this transitional period the state, albeit temporarily without a flag.

At the end of eight sessions of bilateral talks, no significant advance had been made. In the occupied territories themselves, no far-reaching 'confidence-building measures' to facilitate the negotiations had been adopted and no steps had been taken to create the conditions which might curb the violence. This was, above all, what prompted the Palestinians to decline the invitation they were offered by the peace process co-sponsors on 10 March.

Two days later, Muhammad Nazzal, Hamas' representative in Jordan, significantly expressed—for the first time since the movement was founded—the fundamentalists' readiness to accept, as an intermediate step, 'the establishment of a Palestinian state in the West Bank and Gaza Strip'.[7] The statement was directly connected to the tragic turn of events in the occupied territories, especially in Gaza (where increasing numbers of leading Israelis were calling for a unilateral Israeli withdrawal): violence, reprisals, bloody confrontation, extreme manifestations of rage and hysteria, particularly by settlers, leading to curfews, and ultimately the sealing-off of the Gaza Strip at the beginning of March and of the whole of the West Bank towards the end of the same month.

It had been an eventful spring: Rabin had paid his first visit to President Clinton on 15 March; Ezer Weizman had been elected by the Knesset to replace Chaim Herzog as the seventh President of Israel on 24 March (taking office on 13 May); and Benjamin Netanyahu, Israel's chief spokesman at the Madrid conference, had succeeded Yitzhak Shamir as Likud leader the next day. Netanyahu had survived a campaign to discredit him by openly admitting that accusations of private indiscretions were true. He was thus free to stand as Likud candidate for the premiership in 1996, now that a new law (passed on 18 March 1992), which provided for the election of the Prime Minister by universal suffrage, would come into effect at the 1996 general elections.

On 26 and 27 March Faisal Husseini headed a large Palestinian delegation at a meeting in Washington with Secretary of State Christopher, while on 6 April the Egyptian President, Hosni Mubarak, met President Clinton for the first time, in Washington. Christopher emerged from this encounter to announce that if the Palestinians were to reverse their decision not to attend the ninth negotiating session, 'positive things' would happen. Certain US circles implied, moreover, that Israel was ready to take steps to improve the Palestinians' conditions in the occupied territories and to make new proposals upon resumption of the talks, provided of course that the Palestinians turned up.

On 9 April the Israelis announced that they would allow Faisal Husseini to move from the Palestinian negotiators' steering committee into the delegation proper. The significance of this gesture was open to conjecture, but the Palestinians viewed it as betokening a gradual recognition of the PLO's role in the talks and of the possibility of a future discussion of the status of Jerusalem. Furthermore, according to US officials, Israel was apparently countenancing the return of a number of Palestinians expelled between 1967 and 1987, the easing of the tax burden on Palestinians and the provision of new facilities for those wishing to invest in the occupied territories.

On 13 April Arafat and Mubarak met in Cairo for important discussions prior to the latter's meeting the next day, in Ismailiya, with Prime Minister Rabin. Mubarak impressed upon Rabin the urgent need to lift the blockade in the occupied territories and pleaded with his Israeli guest to make some goodwill gestures to the Palestinians.

Two days later, there began the most important series of inter-Arab meetings since the start of the year. Of particular significance was Arafat's visit to Syrian President Assad in Latakia. On 19 April, after four days of meetings in Damascus and Cairo,[8] the Foreign Ministers of Syria, Lebanon, Jordan, Palestine and Egypt decided, in the Syrian capital, to request the postponement of the ninth session, originally scheduled to resume on 20 April. Two days later, the same ministers agreed to a resumption of the talks on 27 April. The new US administration, for whom this would be the first session under its auspices, followed up this announcement by reaffirming the basic premises of the peace process and its opposition in principle to deportation. Warren Christopher himself publicly restated the validity of Resolutions 242 and 338 as the foundations of the peace process, declaring that this meant 'land for peace', the realization of the Palestinian people's legitimate political rights and security for all the parties.

The next day, Yitzhak Rabin published a communiqué in which he recalled that the deportation of over 400 Palestinians did not constitute a 'precedent' and had been an 'exceptional' measure—the implication being that there would be no further deportations. Israel had already accepted that Faisal Husseini could become the official head of the Palestinian negotiating delegation.

Peace by Consent or Peace by Negotiation?

Three major developments in the Middle East followed the end of the Cold War and the USSR's consequent decline as a superpower: the massive influx of Soviet Jews into Israel, Syria's rapprochement with the West and Iraq's invasion of Kuwait. The 1991 Gulf War and the new US-Soviet *détente* led to the collapse of the Arab Rejection Front which for years had been trying, in a variety of ways, to forestall the advent of a *pax americana* in the Middle East. Today, however, to paraphrase Anwar Sadat, the Americans hold 99 per cent of the cards in the region.

The Madrid conference was the first tangible result of the end of the Cold War, providing a fresh boost to US aims in the Middle East: stability to protect its oil and strategic interests, and security for Israel through a peace settlement and the normalization of Israeli-Arab relations, thus easing the burden of US economic and military aid ($4 billion a year)—especially now that Israel had lost its strategic value as a bulwark against the Soviet Union. It was the new political climate born of the Gulf War that the Americans immediately exploited in order to frame the Middle East negotiating process in the manner that became known as the 'Madrid formula'.

The Arabs and Israelis had conflicting views about how the problems between them should be tackled, however, and little progress had been made up to May 1993 in narrowing the gap. The Syrians' priority was to liberate the Golan within a comprehensive Arab-Israeli peace, while the Lebanese sought to negotiate the restoration of their sovereignty over all their territory. The Palestinians wanted freedom and independence; the Jordanians' aim was stability and equilibrium.

Israel, facing the prospect of a nuclearized Middle East in the course of the next decade, pursued a policy of trying to rid itself of the administrative burden of governing the Palestinian people without impairing its military supremacy or its purported right to settle Jews in the occupied territories. By engaging in secret contacts with the Arabs, both in the region and in European capitals, Israel had aroused feelings of rivalry among the Palestinians, Syrians and Jordanians as to the possible benefits each could derive from peace talks, as well as mutual suspicion since each Arab party feared Israel would strike separate deals with each of the others at that party's expense. None of the parties perceives 'common interests' in this process and given such contradictions, one may reasonably ask whether the United States has the will or the capability to create such 'common interests' so that peace can be freely consented to by all the participants, without its having to be imposed from outside.

The Palestinians spurn the notion that there can be convergence or community of their interests with those of Israel so long as they have no certainty that Israel's intentions are sincere and that it has discarded the aim of dominating them. This desire of the Palestinians to avoid being subjugated, indeed, remains true regardless of whichever country may wish to keep them in thrall. The 'Madrid formula' was therefore flawed from the outset since its basis was the notion of 'common interests'—a diplomatic term which only takes into account arrangements between states, and not between a state and a people deprived of its right to self-determination, independence, and the creation of its own sovereign state.

The Palestinians also view the 'autonomy' currently on offer to be an anachronistic concept inherited from the Cold War—just like that of 'federation' or 'confederation'—when the aim was to avoid the creation in the Middle East of a Cuba-style Palestinian state. Furthermore, autonomy is not conducive to stability. On the contrary, it can only prolong the risk of conflict and perpetuate the rivalry among the surrounding states, who may seek to share the spoils of the Palestinians and their land in order better to control them and keep them in the sort of dependence that prevailed before 1948. The very notion of 'autonomy' rests on a misconception, as though the West Bank and Gaza Strip were simply 'disputed' and not 'occupied' territories; hence each party's designs on them.

Two fundamental questions need to be answered: is autonomy

practicable? and will the Palestinian people accept it? For the Palestinians have developed a deep-seated collective feeling of being victims, subjected to a historic injustice. From being a majority, they have overnight become a minority in their own country, or else refugees scattered across the diaspora. They also feel that the Arabs have failed to rescue them—indeed, that they have often exploited their distress—and that the West, particularly the United States, has supported an Israel which has continued to deny the Palestinians their most elementary human rights. Regardless of where they are and what social, economic, cultural and political disparities distinguish them, the Palestinians are profoundly conscious of their unity. None of them accepts the idea that they can be divided into 'Palestinians of the interior' and 'Palestinians from outside'.

The PLO considered the rescue of the Palestinian people to be its paramount priority, which explains why it accepted the 'two state' solution, whereas the fundamentalists and more radical nationalists felt that the liberation of the land should take precedence. Palestinian pragmatism produced a third path by combining the two approaches at the 1988 session of the Palestine National Council, when it proclaimed the establishment of a Palestinian state on part of historical Palestine in order to save the Palestinian people from the twin dangers of assimilation and dispersion and to put an end to the tragic plight of the refugees, both under occupation and in exile.

The Palestinians also fear the possible conclusion of separate Arab-Israeli deals which would deprive them of any leverage whatsoever and thus render their situation hopeless. They view the 'transitional autonomy' as though it were an embryonic state which would become independent in due course. This explains why they have studied so painstakingly every single component of the proposed autonomy to see to what extent it might be consistent with their aspirations to statehood. Indeed, their support for Jordan's involvement in the Palestinian cause is contingent upon a consistent Jordanian commitment to a Palestinian state. Conversely, Israel's insistence on a role for Jordan, on the basis of the autonomy stipulated in the Camp David Accords, amounts to recognition of Jordan's supposed right to interfere in certain areas of Palestinian affairs. The accords were intended to restore Jordan's influence over the Palestinians and especially to restrain the Palestinian nationalist tendency. Ultimately, they were to grant Jordan outright sovereignty or integration with a Palestinian entity (through the transfer of competence in certain areas to the Palestinians, the joint competence of Israel, Jordan and the Palestinians in other areas, and the maintenance of Israeli control over the remainder).

It is doubtful whether Jordan, surrounded as it is by competing or hostile countries, has the capability to act as 'Big Brother' to the Palestinians, whether in economic, demographic or cultural terms. Rather, there is good reason to fear that such a development would be susceptible to political exploitation by extremists and would run the risk of open conflict between the Palestinians, resentful of their dependence, and their Jordanian masters.

The whole concept of autonomy was devised by Menachem Begin, who had drawn on Jabotinsky's ideas—in turn, strongly influenced by the Ottoman system of the *millet*. Moshe Dayan's conception of autonomy, at the end of the 1960s, was supposed to leave the Arabs to their own devices, but under Israeli military domination, with the presence of Jewish settlers ensconced in their midst. This design was skilfully concealed behind a specious acknowledgement of the Palestinians' right to determine their own fate, but not that of Israel—the ideological 'Greater Israel'.

The Israelis are also prone to erratic changes of attitude, depending on whether they argue from the standpoint of victims or oppressors, causing them to convey conflicting views. As individuals, they prefer to live apart from the Palestinians, but they oppose both the creation of a Palestinian state and Jordanian control of the occupied territories. Yet they also oppose annexation of these lands for fear that such a move would create a binational state. Most Israelis support retaining control of the occupied territories but reject the absorption of the Palestinians; hence their desire to continue controlling the occupied territories but at the least possible cost. In 1989 Yitzhak Rabin had sought to revive the concept of autonomy; he was effectively the instigator of the Shamir initiative to divest Israel of administrative responsibility for the Palestinian population without prejudicing Israeli military control or Jewish settlement in the Palestinian territories occupied after 1967.

There is a further contradiction in Israel's position: while seeking immediate peace with the Arab states, it wishes to defer peace with the Palestinians on the pretext that a transitional stage is needed to create a climate conducive to such a peace. Yet it is well known that the enmity between Syria and Israel is no less fierce than that between the Palestinians and Israel—as any cursory reading of the Israeli press would demonstrate.

It is interesting to ask why most Israelis, on both the left and the right, oppose both a Palestinian state and the PLO, and prefer to deal with Jordan. From Labour's point of view, a Palestinian state would endanger Israel's security, whereas Likud fears such an outcome because it would jeopardize the realization of its dream of a 'Greater Israel'. Likud's reasoning precludes any meaningful dialogue since this concept of a 'Greater Israel' stems from recent Zionist ideology and is devoid of any historical, geographical, demographic or religious foundation. The legitimacy of Labour's misgivings is also highly questionable since they have been largely superseded by events, now that the Cold War has ended.

Indeed, why should the future Palestinian state not be a 'Middle Eastern Costa Rica', instead of another 'Cuba'? Why not promote the idea of negotiating a neutral Palestinian state, thus ruling out its use as a launch-pad for attacks on Israel and creating a buffer state which would bolster Israel's security as the new state entered into agreements of non-aggression and good-neighbourliness with Israel, Jordan, Egypt and Syria? Such agreements would also be buttressed by international commitments underwriting the Palestinian state's neutrality. The Arab states might pledge to refrain from using neutral Palestine as a political tool in their disputes, and Palestine would give an undertaking not to serve as a base for fomenting disorder in Israel and Jordan, by prohibiting the use of Palestinians residing in those countries as political pawns. In return, the neutral Palestinian state would be entitled to expect a commitment from its neighbours not to attack it or to interfere in its internal affairs, while the guarantors of its neutrality would provide for its protection by means of multinational forces.

The Palestinian state must seek a solution which would enable it to acquire regional and international credibility while avoiding a position of dependence on any other country. As a parliamentary, neutral democracy, such a state would be a model of moderation, stability, pluralism, tolerance and coexistence between the followers of the three monotheistic faiths. It would also be a haven for Christians fleeing persecution elsewhere in the region.

The state would also have to address economic problems by pursuing the 'diplomacy of development' in order to attract foreign investment and assistance. While accession to or even association with the European Community is a remote prospect—at least initially—it would seem prudent to build upon the idea of creating a regional Benelux-like grouping, comprising the smaller but intellectually rich countries of the area. Economic policy should be the linchpin of Palestine's foreign policy, but it would require stability and moderation if other governments were to be encouraged to provide assistance and promote joint ventures. There would, therefore, be no better way of guaranteeing the Palestinian state's security than a policy of neutrality *vis-à-vis* its stronger neighbours, given this imperative of stability for the country's construction.

For Israel, acceptance of a neutral Palestinian state would be a surer way of guaranteeing its own security than any number of illusory 'security zones' or settlements of Jewish citizens on and within Palestine's borders. Such an acceptance would convince the Palestinians that the Israelis were sincere and had foresworn a policy of domination. Such a change in Israel's outlook would unquestionably induce the two parties to engage in real diplomacy for peace, to the advantage of both, and on a healthy basis at that.

This sort of relationship cannot be achieved through the autonomy arrangement. In the event of an agreement to permit the creation of a neutral Palestinian state, however, peace might act as a catalyst for a new climate to be achieved with the Syrians, Lebanese and Jordanians as well, prompting all the parties to negotiate in good faith to determine the areas where their interests converged and where solutions could be found to their differences.

Lastly, such a change in Israel's position, with its concomitant change in the 'Madrid formula', would only enhance the conviction of the negotiating parties that nothing could be gained from a peace artificially imposed from outside and that their interests would best be served by arriving at peace of their own free will and by common consent.

Until now, the leading Israeli parties, Labour included, have aimed, at best, to impose their own solution on the Palestinians, ruling out any idea of an independent state, and deciding, if things went awry, to conduct an exercise in 'damage limitation'. Yet solutions cannot be imposed, as history will testify. There is no place in the Middle East for either a *pax americana* or a *pax hebraica*. The Israelis must realize that their interests would be more secure if they put an end to the decades of occupation. A change of heart to a position consistent with genuine peace, and based on an acknowledgement of their Palestinian neighbours, would pave the way to wide-ranging co-operation in the Middle East—a region that is rich in natural and human resources and which needs all its inhabitants to work together for peace and economic development.

This recognition of the Palestinians as a people with equal rights and as potential partners would not be without precedent in modern history: the independence granted to Algeria and to Namibia, de Klerk's recognition of South Africa's black majority and the radical shift Gorbachev wrought in the USSR's relations with the countries of Eastern Europe bear clear witness to how the world can and must change.

Part II
Historical Overview

4

Palestine from its Origins to the Nineteenth Century

Palestine lies at a point linking Africa, Asia and Europe, and this strategic location was to determine much of its history. It was a thoroughfare, a corridor in constant use, and at the same time, it was coveted by the great empires of Egypt and the Middle East, the crossroads of the trade routes coming from Egypt, Mesopotamia and the Aegean. It was for that reason that the Great Powers, fascinated by its position, always attempted to control or dominate Palestine or, at least, to draw it into their sphere of influence. In the course of its history, Palestine was to be sometimes the theatre of wars instigated by other powers, and at other times an area of peace where different cultures, religions and civilizations existed side by side. Such periods were the consequences of wars of expansion and conquest by the neighbouring empires, or else of their division and weakness which enabled Palestine to emerge from the night of terror to resume its true vocation as a bridge linking the ancient countries of three continents.

Palestine's role and its developing culture and trade gained strength in the periods of peace between Mesopotamia and Egypt. At such times it became a channel for busy exchanges between those countries and a forum for dialogue between civilizations—this being one reason why the Canaanites were the first to invent the alphabet, which was the next natural stage of development after the scripts of the Sumerians and the Egyptians.

The history of Palestine has been shaped not only by wars, population shifts and the mutual influence of the various civilizations of the large region in which it is situated. Another equally important factor affecting its destiny is its geography. Although Palestine covers a small area in comparison with some other countries, nature has endowed it with a varied climate ranging from the temperate to the tropical and a varied topography that includes mountains, plains, valleys and desert. Their distinctiveness lent each of these four regions a degree of self-sufficiency, which explains how they came to acquire 'city-state' political systems geared to their geographical peculiarities.

In Egypt and Mesopotamia, the Nile, the Tigris and the Euphrates were determining factors in the economic and political systems, giving rise to the establishment of centralized states which controlled the distribution of the wealth derived from those rivers and the safety of the population of the entire region. Palestine, however, did not have to establish a centralized state, owing to the existence of the Jordan, which flowed through just one of its four regions. That left room for a confederation of city-states in the periods when the country's star was in the ascendant, and especially during the millennia of the Canaanites, who laid the foundations of Palestine's history.

Jerusalem was the perfect model of a city-state. According to Palestinian legends, it was built some 3,000 years before the birth of Christ by the goddess Anath for the worship of Salem, the Canaanite god of the evening star (Venus): hence the name of the city (Uru-Salem, *uru* meaning 'city' in Canaanite). Jerusalem possessed all the features of a genuine metropolitan city: combining all four types of climate, it lay at a strategic meeting-point, commanding the traffic from south to north and west to east. Its position on impregnable heights made it nothing short of a fortress.

Jerusalem's political organization and system inspired the Canaanite Kings to forge these city-states into a confederation or unified state. The lifespan of that state was wholly dependent on external factors: reaching its apogee when the neighbouring empires succumbed to decadence and division, it fell apart when they recovered their full strength and invaded the country. The Palestinian state thus tended to suffer an eclipse rather than complete destruction when it came under the sovereignty of Egypt or Mesopotamia. At a later period this was also the fate of the Kingdom of David and Solomon, which split into two states— Israel and Judaea—both of which became vassals of Egypt or Mesopotamia.

Throughout its long history, Palestine has witnessed foreign invasions, occupations and the battles of great conquerors: Thutmose III, Necho, Sargon II, Nebuchadnezzar, Cambyses, Alexander, Antiochus, Pompey, Vespasian, Titus, Ibn al-As, Ibn al-Walid, Saladin, Richard Lionheart, Napoleon, Ibrahim Pasha, Allenby, etc. The invaders of Palestine settled only in the towns and at strategic points in order to control trade routes while exploiting the population: the sole exceptions were the Crusaders and the Zionists, who replaced one population by another.

The history of Palestine has always been written by its conquerors, who shaped it in their own image and in accordance with their own conception of past, future and current events. Although it is difficult to convey an accurate picture, the Bible, the findings of archaeological investigations and the recorded deeds and traces left by the invaders none the less provide valuable source material with which to write the history of Palestine. At all events, that history should be written by the Palestinians themselves. But whatever their nature, all the sources point towards generally accepted conclusions: that Palestine has always, within living memory, been a meeting-place of civilizations, of the three monotheistic religions and of cultures, with an established tendency towards pluralism, tolerance and peace. Palestine's geostrategic position predestined it for that noble and generous calling and made it the source of a message for all humanity.

The French writer Paul Valéry once said:

> History is the most dangerous product ever synthesized by the chemistry of the intellect . . . It is the stuff of dreams. It intoxicates peoples, implanting false memories . . . leading them into delusions of grandeur or persecution, and makes nations bitter, arrogant, insufferable and vain.[1]

Having before us this vast panorama, which is difficult to define too minutely without betraying history, and bearing in mind Valéry's apposite remarks, we shall first look into the past and then attempt to glimpse the future of the Palestinian people, while emphasizing the point that they have suffered the greatest injustice of our time after the tragedy of the holocaust of the Jewish people in Europe.

Although history is now subjected to the rigour of scientific analysis in the search for truth, the fact remains that the human contribution, a determining factor, can by no means be relegated to the background without overturning all the annals of history that time has stamped with its indelible seal. This survey will extend from prehistory to modern times, bearing in mind that traces of the earliest human activity have been found in Palestine. Francis Hours writes that:

> The first signs of human activity in the Near East date back about one million years. The most important evidence is to be found in the valley of the Jordan at Ubeiddiya, where several strata date back to the Old Acheulian . . . In Palestine, *homo sapiens (qafzeh)*[2] emerged as early as

the end of the Middle Palaeolithic. The second half of the last pluvial from 40,000 BC saw the development of new tools with the Upper Palaeolithic and the spread of a human type similar to ourselves.[3]

Jacques Cauvin states that 'the countries of the Levant were experimenting with cereal cultivation in the eighth millennium. Emmer was domesticated in the valley of the Jordan at Jericho during Pre-Pottery Neolithic A.'[4]

According to the *Grand Atlas Universalis de l'Archéologie* and the *Grand Atlas de l'Histoire Mondiale*, Palestine played a part not only in the birth of agriculture but also in sedentarization, the invention of the alphabet and the development of architecture. These processes may be traced over a period of some 10,000 years, between 14000 and 3500 BC.

In Early Bronze Age II, towards the start of the third millennium BC, Palestine reached an advanced stage of centralization with the production and distribution of agricultural surpluses. Historians consider this period, with its new economic, social and political order, to be the beginning of history in Palestine. The origins of human life in Palestine are thus lost in the mists of time. 'Galilee man' and 'Carmel man' were already *sapiens* when their European contemporaries were Neanderthals. Carbon-14 dating places the Natufian civilization in Palestine between 10000 and 8000 BC and the Ghassulian civilization at around 3600 BC. It was during this last period that a real craft industry emerged in Palestine. Knowledge of these two civilizations is still limited. Current, and possibly future, research will help to develop it.

The Canaanites

Around 3200 BC, a new civilization termed Canaanite made its appearance throughout Palestine. It was more sedentary and agrarian than its predecessors and developed what were in effect towns. The country's agricultural surplus provided an opening for trade links with its neighbours. These techno-economic structures signalled the transition from prehistory to history.

The Canaanite civilization flourished, unifying Palestine and Syria, from Gaza to Ugarit and Ebla, through a single language, culture and religion until about the thirteenth century BC, according to Martin Noth:

We therefore find in urban Syria-Palestine during the Bronze Age a civilization deeply attached to the soil. It gradually developed and changed within that area until around 1200 BC, when it fell into decline, collapsed and disappeared, without leaving any precise clue as to the causes of its downfall.[5]

It should be noted that other highly regarded authors do not share this hastily formed judgement regarding the 'disappearance of the Canaanite civilization'. E.M. Laperrousaz gives what he considers to be the real reasons for its decline, namely, external factors:

The depredations of the Egyptians together with the havoc wrought by semi-nomadic bands were certainly responsible for Palestine's decline during that period compared with the situation at the end of the Middle Bronze Age before the Hyksos were expelled from Egypt.[6]

[He also writes:] Although the missions by the Israelites in the thirteenth century and by the Sea Peoples in the early twelfth century ended the Canaanite period in Palestine, Canaanite city-states controlled the valleys and plains of northern Palestine for a further two centuries. The Canaanites emerged with new vitality under the name 'Phoenicians', and participated with Israel in forging the Palestinian civilization of the Iron Age.[7]

H.E. Del Medico writes, 'In spite of the country's conquest, it was Canaanite history that continued until Assyrian rule in the reign of the sovereigns of Judah and Israel.'[8] The Canaanite civilization was formed through the intermingling of different groups that settled in the country. Besides the Canaanites, who were in the majority, other minority groups were composed of Amorites, Aramaeans, Nabataeans, Hebrews or Indo-Aryans, together with the Hurrians, the Hittites or the Sea Peoples such as the Philistines.

During the Early Bronze Age (3100–2200), the Canaanites fell within the sphere of influence of Mesopotamia. Around 2000 BC, Egyptian influence was predominant in Palestine. The Egyptian Prince Sinuhe gives the following description of a flourishing country around the second millennium BC: 'There were figs and grapes, and more wine than water. Honey was abundant, olives plentiful and all kinds of fruit grew on the trees.'[9] Sedentary farmers and stockbreeders, the Canaanites were also traders and diplomats. They played a prominent role in cultural exchanges, as evidenced by archaeological discoveries. They were also renowned for their creativity and practical flair: inventors and propagators of a written alphabet, producers and exporters of war chariots, builders of mighty fortresses (Gezer, Jericho, Megiddo, Taanach and Lakish) and of underground hydraulic piping. The

Canaanite civilization was so strong that it swiftly assimilated the Transcaucasian immigrants who arrived *c*. 2600 BC.

Around 2000 BC the Amorite attacks, spanning several centuries, annihilated Palestine's Early Bronze Age civilization. Urban life disintegrated and the fortresses were destroyed (Hazor, Megiddo, Beisan and Jericho). During the Middle Bronze Age (1800–1500 BC), the Canaanites built new fortresses and there was a full-scale renaissance. The Ras Shamra tablets show that the agrarian deities Hadad, El, Ba'al, Anath, Salem, Saher, Aliyan, Dagon, Yamm and Mot[10] were worshipped in Palestine, which signals a further stage in the settled way of life and in agriculture.

In approximately 1500 BC new conquerors, this time Aryans, arrived in Palestine. Known as the Hurrians, they strengthened the feudal order and imposed their suzerainty. However, according to Roger Garaudy, 'they were assimilated by the Canaanite civilization'. He adds that the Hurrian hegemony in Palestine was short-lived: the Pharaoh Thutmose III (on coming to power in 1468) marched on Gaza and defeated the coalition of Palestinian princes in Megiddo. 'Palestine had become a province of Egypt. Its princes were vassals of the Pharoah.'[11]

Garaudy summarizes the ensuing developments as follows. In about 1370 BC, the King of the Hittites from Syria succeeded in replacing Egyptian overlordship by exploiting the quarrels among Palestinian princes. In 1286 BC Ramses II tried to resume control of Palestine, but the peace concluded with the Hittites committed them to pacify Palestine. In the late thirteenth century BC the Hebrews infiltrated Palestine from the deserts of Arabia and the eastern plateaux. And in the early twelfth century, the Sea Peoples (the Philistines) disembarked on the coast and conquered western Palestine.

A new chapter in the history of Palestine began. Before embarking on it, it may be useful to assess the achievements of the Canaanite civilization. The foregoing summary has already given us an overview of the social structures of Canaanite society, a feudal society of farmers and traders situated at the crossroads of the ancient Babylonian, Egyptian and Mycenaean civilizations, of its political, commercial and cultural links with its neighbours and of the mixed cultural and ethnic elements of which it was composed. As a meeting-place and a transit route for conquerors, merchandise and ideas, Palestine's syncretic future was preordained.

As well as helping to invent the alphabet, the Canaanites acquired a reputation for sculpture and purple dyeing. The background to the latter skill is an interesting story. The Canaanites discovered the product from which they extracted the dye in the purple molluscs at Acre and sold it to the Greeks, who used it to dye clothes. It is the same dye that cardinals and bishops have used since those distant times to give their robes a distinctive colour. The Greeks, on catching sight of the Canaanites from their shores, used to call them the 'phoenixes', a word of Greek origin meaning purple. This accounts for the fact that the Canaanites living on the coast of Lebanon and Palestine became known as the Phoenicians, and when Saint Augustine asked peasants in Carthage whether they were of Phoenician origin, they replied that they were Canaanites—'We are Chanani.'[12]

A further noteworthy achievement of the Canaanites was in the field of human spirituality. The Canaanite Bible of Ugarit consists of poems recording the oral traditions of the Canaanites at different periods in their history. These documents found at Ras Shamra also furnish proof of the remarkable cultural unity of Palestine from Gaza to Ebla. The god El (Lat in pre-Islamic Arabia?) of the Canaanites became the Hebrew Elohim and the Arab Allah. The heirs of El are Ba'al and his sister Anath (Manat in pre-Islamic Arabia?). His equivalent in Egypt is Aton. The Canaanite Bible, which cannot be isolated from the Middle Eastern cultural heritage as a whole, gives some indication of the Canaanite legacy, which was of considerable importance.[13]

> Words, expressions and whole sentences from the Hebrew Bible suddenly cropped up in these writings from the fourteenth century BC. Would the Ugaritic tablets reveal the whole Canaanite background to the Old Testament, a possibility that had long been predicted by certain scholars and historians?[14]

However, prior to the encounter between the Canaanite religion, which began to develop in the third millennium, and the Hebrew religion of the twelfth century, it should be noted that in the former, a religion of farmers, the divine was revealed essentially through nature whereas, in the religion of the Hebrew nomads, the divine revealed itself through history. The Canaanite gods are gods of the fertility of the soil; the gods of the nomads are guarantors of this historical continuity of the tribes and their values.[15]

We have already shown how Palestine's geo-strategic position laid the country open to invasion and conquest by neighbouring empires, events that exerted an outside influence on the stability of the economic and political organization of Palestine. But these external factors were not the only source of instability. Others, which we shall call internal factors, also played a role, although their impact was less marked. They mostly made their appearance following a weakening of internal authority owing to dissension or conflict among local chiefs.

On the alert for these events, the nomads infiltrated Palestine from the south and east through the desert, and settled around the towns, waiting for the right moment to attack the farmers and seize their crops. But this was inevitably associated with a tendency to choose a settled way of life, and many of these nomads from outside Palestine eventually became sedentarized.

The Canaanites' capacity for assimilation facilitated this trend, which contributed to the intermingling of cultural, religious, social and linguistic elements and also had economic and demographic consequences. This phenomenon, which was cyclical in the history of Palestine, has been admirably described by Henry Laurens in his book, *Le Grand Jeu*.[16] Such an analysis makes it easier to put into perspective the history of the Hebrews in Palestine at the time of the Canaanites.

It was between 1300 and 1100 BC that the Hebrews began to enter Palestine, settling in the east in a semi-desert area, while the Philistines arrived from the west, settling in the rich and fertile area along the Mediterranean coast.

The Hebrews

An analysis of biblical texts, which are the only source of the ancient history of the Hebrews in Palestine, shows that they arrived from Egypt about 1300 BC, under the leadership of Joshua, either as a result of gradual infiltration or through wars of conquest and extermination.

E.M. Laperrousaz, in his article in the *Encyclopaedia Universalis*, states:

The Bible is the only source of detailed information we have on the arrival and settlement of the Israelites in Canaan: the first five books (Genesis, Exodus, Leviticus, Numbers and Deuteronomy, which are collectively known as the Pentateuch by the Christians and the Torah, i.e. the 'Law', by the Jews, since they believe that those writings contain the commandments that the Hebrews, through Moses, received from their god, Yahweh, on Mount Sinai, after their flight from Egypt, as a condition of his 'covenant' with them) give an account of the origins of the world and of the origins and wanderings of the Hebrews until their arrival on the banks of the River Jordan—in short, the prehistory of the 'chosen people'. The following books (Joshua, Judges, Samuel, Kings, Chronicles, Ezra and Nehemiah) narrate the history of this people from their arrival in Canaan until their return from exile in the time of the Persians. The Bible includes many other books, such as those bearing the names of prophets or those which, such as Psalms, Proverbs, the Song of Solomon and Ecclesiastes, are works of a more philosophical or literary nature.

Unfortunately, these books, which bear signs of having drawn, with varying degrees of skill, on several traditions belonging to different periods and sources, were not written according to criteria recognized by modern historians.

Whenever possible, it is essential to test and check the information that they provide against archaeological or other data.[17]

As we have noted, Palestine already had a very long history and a civilization that was original for its syncretism. It was a flourishing country which is described in Deuteronomy (VIII, 7–9) as:

> a good land, a land of brooks of water, of fountains and depths that spring out of valleys and hills; a land of wheat, and barley, and vines, and fig trees, and pomegranates; a land of oil, olive and honey; a land wherein thou shall eat bread without scarceness, thou shall not lack any thing in it; a land whose stones are iron, and out of whose hills thou mayest dig brass.

About 1000 BC David, a member of the tribe of Judah, but at the head of Philistine mercenaries, succeeded in conquering the Canaanite city of Jerusalem. This was regarded as neutral territory unaffected by the rivalries existing between the tribes of Israel, which had formed a city-state in the north-east of Palestine, following the example of the Canaanites, and the tribes of Judah, which had settled in the south-east and were also organized as a city-state. The strategic position of Jerusalem enabled David to control these tribes, although the city itself continued to be inhabited by the Canaanite population. David established his kingdom by uniting these two city-states with other, non-Hebrew peoples. Ruth, his grandmother, was a Moabite, while his son, Solomon, who succeeded him on the throne, was born to a Hittite woman. After the death of Solomon in about 926 BC, the kingdom of David, which had lasted only 73 years, broke up, and the situation prior to David was restored. As far as the Hebrews were concerned, they re-established their city-states: Israel in the north-east and Judah in the south-east.

When the King of Israel decided to end his vassalage to Assyria and become instead the vassal of Egypt (II Kings XVII, 4), he refused to pay tribute to Assyria and entered into relations with Egypt. It was then, in 722 BC, that the Assyrian army captured the king and the city-state, which ceased to exist. The city-state of Judah survived, however, paying tribute as a vassal to the King of Assyria.

The Pharaoh Necho (609–583 BC) occupied Palestine at the beginning of his reign, but Egyptian domination did not last and the Pharaoh was defeated in 605 by the King of Babylon (Jeremiah XLVI, 2). The King of Judah, Sedecias, made the same mistake as the King of Israel and also shifted his allegiance, since he thought that Egypt was more powerful than Mesopotamia.

In 587 BC the army of Nebuchadnezzar conquered Jerusalem and destroyed it, including the Temple of Solomon which was the prototype of Canaanite temples (according to the Bible, it was King Hiram I [969–935 BC] who sent the materials and the architects needed to build this temple). The city-state of Judah, in turn, ceased to exist and its leading citizens were exiled to Babylon. When Cyrus, King of the Persians, captured Babylon, he gave permission for the exiles to return.

In the second century BC the Maccabeans, under Roman occupation, established a Hasmonean dynasty of vassal kings. In 63 BC Pompey conquered Palestine, which then became a vassal kingdom of the Romans.

It was in Palestine that Jesus lived; the Church was subsequently founded there and Palestine then became the Holy Land of the Christians. The Jewish vassal state was destroyed by Titus in AD 70 and after the Bar Kochba rising, which was crushed in 135, the Jews lost their political independence. Some of them formed a religious community in Palestine, while others were converted to Christianity like the rest of the population. From the second century onwards, Palestine was a Roman province separate from Syria, and gradually it became Christian.

This history of the Hebrews, based on what is written in the Bible, presents a major historical problem, stemming from the fact that no archaeological or documentary evidence has so far been found to substantiate the biblical account and provide historical confirmation. Father de Vaux, though believing in the historical truth of the Bible, recognizes, like all other historians, that there is nowhere to be found 'any explicit allusion to the Hebrew patriarchs, to the sojourn in Egypt, to the exodus, or even to the conquest of Canaan, and it is very doubtful whether the silence will ever be broken by new texts'.[18]

Kathleen Kenyon states:

One of the major difficulties in establishing the chronology of the entry of the Israelites is that at no point in a single site can one say that the material evidence shows that a new people had arrived . . . It must be accepted that all the Israelite groups arrived as essentially nomadic people . . . , and that when they settled down they took over the equipment of their predecessors in the land . . . The culture of Palestine was essentially Canaanite.[19]

Another writer, W.F. Albright, believes that, at the time of the first confrontations between the Canaanites and the Hebrews, the followers of Yahweh and the followers of El rejected one another's gods, but then the Hebrews, as they settled in Canaan, identified their god with those of the indigenous inhabitants: they even adopted his name, El (God); in the plural, Elohim.[20] Like several other authors, Roger Garaudy maintains that:

The Hebrews, during their settlement in Canaan, gave up their Aramaic dialect and adopted instead the 'language of Canaan', as is stated in Isaiah (XIX, 18); from the Canaanites these nomads learned the written alphabet, which enabled them, in the tenth century, to make the transition from oral tradition to the written word.

The Hebrew nomads also learned farming techniques from the Canaanites, and their way of life became increasingly similar, the more so as the number of mixed marriages rose.[21]

Garaudy goes on to state that:

As the Hebrew nomads settled on the land, their religious beliefs became more and more impregnated with the worship of Ba'al practised by the sedentary Canaanites. This religious assimilation is closely bound up with political assimilation. The Hebrews wanted Gideon to found a hereditary monarchy, such as already existed among other peoples (Judges VIII, 22). Gideon refused the offer to become king, while continuing to combat the followers of Ba'al.[22]

During this period, the organization of communities in the region into small groups of peoples and tribes was, in the eyes of the latter, inevitably accompanied by religious beliefs inspired by gods who made promises to their subjects in the form of myths. This acted as a means of cementing together the members of a social group by providing them with a hierarchical structure, a belief, an ideal and a means of protection.

However, the fact that these gods called for the destruction of those groups who stood apart from those claiming to have received an exclusive message conflicts, on the face of it, with the basic principles of any spiritual and moral system. Furthermore, this exclusivity appears even more irrational when one people or tribe claims that the promise is intended only for them and excludes any other community. The choice of the social group receiving such a promise must necessarily rest on arbitrary and subjective criteria.

If we take into account the fact that these gods and the accompanying beliefs only took root in a restricted local area, doubts are bound to arise as to the value and truth of these messages and promises. The universal monotheistic revealed religions do not advocate exclusiveness or discrimination as revealed from on high. On the contrary, they are open to all peoples without distinction. To base historical claims on such messages or promises would seem to be irrational. According to the Torah, the Hebrews were promised the land of Canaan by Yahweh, provided that they obeyed the divine law. At the stage of social development reached in this period in the Fertile Crescent, virtually all the peoples of this region received from their gods promises similar to those made to the Jewish people. The same was true of the Canaanites: 'the presence of Ba'al at any place guaranteed the rights of the owner to the land'.[23] The Hittites believed that it was the goddess Arinna who had established 'the frontiers of the country'.

In Palestine, a land of cultural and ethnic cross-fertilization, the religion of the Torah, which had been exclusively embodied in tribal ways of life, attained the status of a universal religion. It represented the advent of prophetic faith, a true transmutation of values and spiritualization of primitive belief. The promise no longer concerned the ownership of a land, but announced a Kingdom of God extending to the whole of the universe in the peace and harmony of its peoples: 'Lift up a standard for the people . . . Behold the Lord hath proclaimed unto the end of the world' (Isaiah LXII, 10–11); 'For, behold, I create new heavens and a new earth: and the former shall not be remembered nor come into mind' (Isaiah LXV, 17); 'And all nations shall flow into it' (Isaiah II, 2); 'And they shall beat their swords into ploughshares, and their spears into pruning hooks: nation shall not lift up sword against nation, neither shall they learn war any more' (Isaiah II, 4).[24]

In Palestine, with the revelation of Judaism, beliefs moved from tribal to universal application, something which had not occurred previously in Egypt or in Mesopotamia. This development, thanks to the prophets of Israel, represents the first of the three pillars of the faith of Abraham. It is the main contribution of the Hebrews to the spiritual heritage of the human race.

The Philistines

In the early twelfth century BC the Sea Peoples, or Philistines, came from the Aegean, Greece, Asia Minor and possibly Crete. They succeeded in settling in the rich, fertile coastal plain which stretches from Gaza to Mount Carmel.

From their name, the Romans derived the geographical name, Palestine. It is therefore to this people that Palestine owes its name. Unlike the Hebrews, who were able to maintain their settlement for 13 centuries, occupying as they did an area that was not subjugated by invaders as it was made up of desert and the austere mountains of south-eastern Palestine, the Philistines, in the plain, had the disadvantage of having settled in an area that was difficult to defend and open to invasion.

To our knowledge, no document of specifically Philistine origin has yet been discovered. According to the Bible, the Hebrews and Philistines fought for several centuries over the region through which the 1949 armistice demarcation line was drawn between Israel and the Palestinian occupied territories.

In the nineteenth and twentieth centuries, extensive excavation work was conducted in Palestine for archaeological, theological and political reasons. The excavations were organized with specific ends in view, to the detriment of research on other aspects of the Canaanite civilization.

The history of the Philistines, and more especially the contribution they made to that civilization, have not been the subject of any major archaeological excavations, apart from the discovery of pottery and sarcophagi; hence the need for specialists to include this objective in their future activities. Consequently, after the eighth century BC, all trace of the Philistines as a distinct entity seems to have been lost.

Other historical data are still missing, such as the attitude and role of the Canaanites with regard to the conflicts between the Hebrews and Philistines, the contribution made by the Philistines to the Canaanite civilization, and whether the Philistines were absorbed by the Canaanites or left Palestine, and, in the latter case, which regions they chose as their destination. All these unanswered questions call for a sustained effort in the field of scientific archaeological research.

Palestine during the Graeco-Roman and Muslim Eras[25]

The period from the eighth to the sixth century BC saw a decline in the Egyptian and Mesopotamian Empires, which were supplanted by the Persian and Greek Empires. The geopolitical position of Palestine—an ideal strategic corridor into Egypt—once again drew the new empires like a magnet. Persian domination over Palestine was to last from 539 to 533 BC. In 332 or 331 BC Alexander the Great conquered Palestine, which thus fell under Greek domination. Alexander's successors, the Ptolemies of Egypt and the Seleucids of Syria, then fought for control over Palestine, which alternated between being a province of the Ptolemies and a province of the Seleucids. The Seleucid King Antiochus IV (Ephiphanes) (175–163 BC) hellenized Palestine. In 63 BC Pompey conquered Palestine and turned it into a Roman province.

In the fourth century AD the Romans divided Palestine into four provinces. When the Roman Empire adopted Christianity, three centuries after the ascension (for the Muslims) or crucifixion (for the Christians) of Jesus of Nazareth, Palestine, now under Byzantine occupation, began to attract pilgrims and became a place where many chose to lead a reclusive life. Among the ever-increasing number of churches, Constantine built the Church of the Holy Sepulchre in Jerusalem. His mother, Helen, in turn had churches built on the Mount of Olives and in Bethlehem. A.S. Rappoport describes this Palestinian spiritual development as follows: 'Palestine became the land of saints and anchorites, monks and monasteries, nuns and convents, basilicas and relics.'[26]

The evolution of beliefs in Palestine thus passed from the Canaanite Ba'al, through the Hebrew Yahweh, to the monotheist faith of the prophets of Israel. With Jesus, a new change in the concept of God occurred: whereas the grandeur of Ba'al and Yahweh was expressed in the power of a state or a king, with Jesus it took the form of poverty and a total lack of material power. This was the God of the New Covenant.

The Palestinian Christians refused to regard Jesus as God, since monotheism excludes the Trinity such as it was formulated by the Graeco-Roman Church. Unlike other groups, they did not believe in the divinity of Christ. The Palestinian Christians belonged to the school of thought considered 'heretical' by Byzantium, through their membership of the Arian, Nestorian or Monophysite sects, which had not accepted the doctrine of the Trinity. The Byzantine Emperors persecuted Palestinian Jews and so-called 'heretical' Palestinian Christians alike. This explains why the Palestinians offered no resistance when the Persians occupied Palestine for the third time in 614.

In 629 the Byzantine Emperor reconquered Palestine and the persecution of those who rejected the Christian dogma of the empire was resumed. The intolerance of the Byzantine Emperors, the presence of Arabs in Palestine (Nabataean, Ghassanid and others) from before the Christian era and the similarities between Islam, Judaism and Palestinian Christianity made Muslim penetration into Palestine an easy step and, for the people, a form of 'liberation'.

In 638, under the Caliph Omar (634–44), Palestine was conquered by the Arabs, or rather by Islam, which amounted to a corollary of the Judaism and Christianity already revealed in Palestine. God said to the Prophet

Muhammad in the Quran:

> Say: We believe in God, in what has been revealed to us, and in what was revealed to Abraham, Ismael, Isaac, Jacob and the tribes. We believe in what was given to Moses and Jesus, and in what was given to the prophets by their Lord. We make no distinction amongst them, and we surrender ourselves to God. [Quran II, 136 and III, 84]

This new religion brought peace and prosperity to Palestine for several centuries. Jerusalem became a Holy City for the Muslims as it was already for the Jews and Christians. The Prophet Muhammad is said to have been transported from Mecca to Jerusalem, and thence to have ascended into heaven from the 'Rock' of the esplanade of the al-Aqsa Mosque. For some believers, this ascension by night was only a vision; for others, Muhammad really did go up to heaven. Al-Aqsa is mentioned in the first verse of the sura known as 'The Night Journey':

> Glory be to Him who carried his servant by night from the Sacred Temple of Mecca [al-Masjid al-Haram] to the further Temple of Jerusalem [al-Masjid al-Aqsa] whose surroundings We have blessed, that We might show him our signs. God hears all and observes all. [Quran XVII]

During the hegira, Muslims, like Jews, turned towards Jerusalem when they prayed. It was in Jerusalem in 660 that Mu'awiyah was proclaimed founder and Caliph of the Umayyad dynasty. In 691 Caliph Abd al-Malik built the Dome of the Rock, symbol of the unity and continuity of the faith of Abraham: Jewish, Christian and Muslim. Abd al-Malik's son, al-Walid, built the al-Aqsa Mosque. The majority of Palestinian Jews and Christians were converted to Islam.

After the conquest, by order of the Caliph Omar, those who were loyal to their earlier faith were treated with great tolerance, except under the reign of the Fatimids of Cairo. In 1009 the Fatimid Caliph al-Hakim (996–1021) ordered the Holy Sepulchre to be pulled down. But, with few exceptions, neither Jews nor Christians were persecuted in Palestine or in any Muslim lands. The majority of the Palestinians were Arabized and Islamized and played an active part in the political, cultural, economic and religious life of the Muslim Empire of the Umayyads and Abbasids. Many governors, ministers, scientists, poets, writers, architects, doctors and theologians were of Palestinian origin.[27]

The peace and prosperity that Palestine enjoyed during the Islamic era from the seventh to the tenth century were interrupted by foreign invasions, and these coincided with the decline of the Muslim Empire. In 950 the invasion came from Byzantium, and from 1071 to 1096 Palestine was invaded by the Seljuks. The third invasion, which turned Palestine into the theatre of constant warfare, was that of the Crusades, beginning in 1096. Jerusalem was taken by storm by Godefroy de Bouillon and a Christian kingdom was established in Jerusalem. The Crusaders deliberately made Palestine an enclave, and there they lived, as a foreign body or an outpost of the West, holding sway with the arms and funds collected in the West by the Church.

After two centuries of occupation (1096–1291) characterized by a succession of wars against the Palestinians and the Arabs, the Crusaders were driven out and the last of them left Palestine, in 1291, by sea from the port of Acre. Two events accelerated the eviction of the Crusaders from Palestine: the withdrawal of all support by the West and the battle of Hittin (1187) under Saladin's leadership.[28]

The Mamelukes were the first to benefit from the end of the Crusades. After the reign of the Ayyubids, the Bahri Mamelukes held Palestine under their sway from 1250 to 1382. The Burji Mamelukes followed them from 1382 to 1516, when the Ottomans invaded Palestine. The Mameluke period was the cultural 'golden age' of Palestine, which had already begun with the Ayyubids (1187–1247). Science and literature flourished, under the generous patronage of the Ayyubid and Mameluke sultans and kings. Teaching establishments sprang up throughout the land; building, farming, crafts and trade all flourished. During this period, pilgrims of the three monotheistic religions poured into Jerusalem, and the city acquired the facilities needed for their comfort and safety.

Jerusalem was also a great cultural centre. Most of the religious sciences, literary and other, ranging from the exegesis of the Quran, the *hadith*, law, Quranic readings, theology, mysticism, grammar, rhetoric, literature and poetry, to history, mathematics and logic, were taught in Palestine, particularly in specialized *madrassas*, of which there were more than 40 in Jerusalem.

A large part of al-Hanbali's book *Uns al-Jalil*[29] deals with the work of restoration, decoration and construction carried out with a view to embellishing and enlarging the Dome of the Rock and al-Aqsa Mosque. It also deals with the mausoleums, *zawiyas*, *madrassas*, *ribats*, *torbets*, citadels and other monuments built in Jerusalem during the Mameluke period. Al-Hanbali gives the biographies of nearly 440 scientists, legal advisers, *qadis*, preachers and teachers of the Holy City of Jerusalem and a list of major works written in Palestine during this period of its history.

Ottoman Palestine

Towards the end of their reign, the Mamelukes went into decline and their authority began to wane. They levied increasingly heavy taxes which the Palestinians could no longer afford to pay. The Palestinians' position worsened considerably as a result of the repression to which they were subjected and the plague of 1513 which wiped out part of the population. As a result, they were incapable of resisting the Ottoman invasion in 1516.

In 1517 Selim I incorporated Palestine into the Ottoman Empire by turning it into a province divided into six districts (Ajlun, Lajun, Nablus, Jerusalem, Safad and Gaza). Palestine enjoyed peace and prosperity for several centuries, particularly under the reign of Suleiman the Magnificent, who built the ramparts of Jerusalem. Suleiman recognized the right of François I, King of France, to protect the Christians who were followers of Rome in Palestine and throughout the empire, while leaving intact the supremacy of those of the Greek Orthodox persuasion, especially in Jerusalem. In 1774, under the terms of the Treaty of Küçük-Kaynarca, Russia secured the right to protect the Orthodox Christians of Palestine and the Ottoman Empire. In 1808 it also obtained the right to protect the Christian Holy Places in Jerusalem.

Russia's right was contested by Louis-Napoleon Bonaparte, who himself claimed the right to protect the Christian Holy Places in Palestine. The Crimean War (1854–5) was followed by the Treaty of Paris on 30 March 1856, which brought to an end the conflict between the Roman and Orthodox Christians and resulted in a return to the *status quo ante* with regard to the Holy Places. This position was confirmed at the Congress of Berlin in 1878.

By virtue of its geographical position, Palestine enjoyed a strong economy and thriving trade throughout the sixteenth and seventeenth centuries. From the seventeenth century onwards, France established sound economic bases in Palestine. External factors, however, once again had a destabilizing effect. Rivalry among the European powers led to friction among Christians in Palestine, a factor that was subsequently exploited in order to justify European intervention in the nineteenth century, leading to the establishment of trading colonies and consulates.

By way of internal factors, several outbreaks of social unrest and frequent revolts against Ottoman domination took place, brought about by the excessively high taxation and levies which the empire imposed and which overwhelmed the Palestinian peasantry. The most significant revolt took place at the turn of the sixteenth century: it was instigated by the Lebanese Prince Fakhr al-Din, who took control of the districts of Safad, Nablus and Ajlun and the northern part of Palestine in addition to Lebanon. This

Christian Druze prince was executed by Sultan Murad IV in 1634.

In 1749 the Palestinian Prince Daher Omar created a Palestinian principality, with Safad as its capital. It encompassed the whole of Galilee, Ajlun and the coastal plain as far as Jaffa. Omar was crushed in 1775 by Ahmad Pasha al-Djazzar, in accordance with the mission assigned to him by the Ottoman Sultan to put an end to the independence of Palestine. Al-Djazzar settled in Acre, where he reigned as an independent despot for some 20 years over all of northern and central Palestine, while maintaining links with the Ottoman Sultan. When Bonaparte invaded Palestine in February 1799, he was driven back by al-Djazzar with the help of a British naval expeditionary force. Bonaparte's defeat outside Acre brought his Middle Eastern campaign to an end.

During the first half of the nineteenth century, Muhammad Ali of Egypt sent his son, Ibrahim Pasha, to occupy the two neighbouring provinces of the Ottoman Empire, Palestine and Syria; he succeeded in doing so in the summer of 1832. Britain subsequently encouraged the Ottoman Sultan to take up arms against Muhammad Ali in order to recover Syria and Palestine, despite the support given him by France. For that purpose, the European powers, backed by the British navy, formed a coalition against Muhammad Ali, who admitted defeat and returned Syria (in November 1840) and Palestine (in July 1841) to the Ottoman Sultan.

These events must be seen within an overall geo-political strategy in the region. Britain and the European coalition feared Muhammad Ali who, thanks to France's help, had built Egypt up into a military power, a power which would have to be reckoned with, while the Ottoman Empire was showing signs of weakness. Having encouraged and helped the Ottoman Sultan to take up arms against Muhammad Ali, who was forced to capitulate, Britain and all the European powers joined in the conflict even before their ultimatum to Muhammad Ali had expired. They forced him to accept the Treaty of London of 1840,[30] which stipulated the restitution of Syria and Palestine to the Ottoman Sultan and obliged Muhammad Ali to remain within the territorial limits of Egypt.

One cannot but draw a parallel between this conflict and the ambitions which prompted it on the one hand, and the Gulf War of January 1991 on the other. In strategic terms, what was at stake was identical: in the first case, freedom to ply the trade-route to India; in the second, the unhindered supply of oil, especially to the United States and Europe—not to mention other political and military considerations. Robert Mantran writes:

During the period that extended from the Ottoman conquest until the end of the nineteenth century, the population of Palestine comprised a majority of Muslims, a sizeable minority of Christians, a smaller minority of Druzes and a handful of Jews; most of these Jews lived in the towns along the coast, while a few lived in Jerusalem . . .

The Zionist movement took charge of emigration to Palestine from 1880 onwards by collecting the funds and by beginning to purchase plots of lands in that country; in accordance with his pan-Islamic policy, however, Sultan Abdulhamid II showed no sympathy for such immigration and endeavoured to restrain it, without, however, being able to oppose it effectively . . .

A little later, after 1908, the government of Young Turks, of which a number of Ottoman Jews were members, encouraged Jewish immigration into Palestine, in opposition to the Arab nationalists, or at least did nothing to limit it; it has been estimated that the Jewish population of Palestine rose from approximately 20,000 people in 1880 to 50,000 in 1900 and 80,000 in 1914.[31]

Seeking to explain this change, Burhan Ghalioun attributes the causes to the fact that the Ataturk regime shifted its policy of alliance with the Arabs to one of closer relations with Europe, which it adopted as a model in all fields. In this regard, he writes:

The Young Turks began their nationalist revolution through a coup d'état in 1908 and adopted a resolutely pro-Western stance, developed an aggressive pan-Turanian nationalism, and abandoned the alliance with the Arabs, subsequently confirmed through the abolition of the caliphate (1924).[32]

The Palestinians were full citizens, enjoyed the same rights and were bound by the same obligations as the Turks. Civil rights were affirmed in the Ottoman constitution of 1908, which acknowledged the right of the Palestinians to take part in politics. In the parliamentary elections of 1908, several Palestinian deputies were accordingly elected to represent Palestine. In the parliamentary elections of 1913, Palestine was represented by ten or so elected members, three of whom represented the constituency of Jerusalem (Faidi Alami, Said Husseini and Ragheb Nashashibi).[33]

Under the Ottoman Empire in the late nineteenth century, the prosperity and wealth of Palestine in the cultural, social, economic and agricultural fields were a fact of life described by Europeans in accounts of their travels. Within the 28,000 sq. km which make up the surface area of Palestine, and with a population of approximately 800,000, there were some 1,000 villages or flourishing towns. Jaffa, for example, was well known for the production of cotton, olives, grapes and particularly oranges, which were very popular in the West (40,000 crates of oranges were exported to Europe in November 1889). Haifa and Acre were well known as ports, Nablus for its production of olive oil and soap, Ramallah, Hebron and Majdal for their textile, leather and glassware industries and Gaza for its pottery and olive presses. Jerusalem was described as a major trading and craft centre, particularly for leather, mother-of-pearl, and wooden religious artefacts.

In their reports, European diplomats described Palestine as a vast expanse of cornfields, varying types of vegetation, lemon groves and fruit orchards of all kinds, watered in part by means of irrigation systems. There were also numerous industries and teaching and cultural institutions (newspapers, publishers and cultural activities). The road and rail network was the essential vector for this economic activity. A French firm of building contractors, whose head office was in Paris, had built the railway line from Jaffa to Jerusalem. The building of roads and railways had also been undertaken by other British and American companies.

One may, therefore, say that this brief survey of the political, economic, social and cultural history of Palestine shows, as Michel Mourre puts it, that:

> The biblical history of Palestine, to which the development of the Judaeo-Christian religion has given a high profile, would not seem, however, to have been more than a brief episode when set against the vast backdrop of Palestine's past.[34]

This continuous historical process bears a strange resemblance to a pendulum: from the east, between 4000 and 400 BC, came waves of immigration by the Canaanites, Amorites and other invaders from Mesopotamia; while from the west, from the early twelfth century BC, there was a flow of immigration by the Sea Peoples—the Philistines—and, from the fourth century onwards, by Greek, Roman and Byzantine invaders. After 1,000 years or so, the pendulum swung again from east to west with the Arab conquest at the beginning of the seventh century BC, and so on.

The Palestinians are thus the descendants of the indigenous Canaanite peoples who were the majority group, of the Amorites, Ammonites, Moabites, Edomites and Aramaeans, who had lived in the country for at least 5,000 years, and of the Hebrews and Philistines, as well as of the invaders who occupied or dominated Palestine such as the Babylonians, Hittites and Egyptians, who were succeeded by the Persians, Greeks, Romans, Arabs, Crusaders and Turks. The Palestinians of today are not descended only from the Arabs. Their Arab identity is much more of a cultural than an ethnic phenomenon. Henry Laurens sums up this particular

114

aspect of contemporary Palestinian identity as follows:

> The Arabs have been present in Palestine for many centuries: well before the birth of Christ, they were nomads and caravan traders along the Jordan Valley. The earliest Arab states appeared in Transjordan, the largest being Petra, and, during the Byzantine period, the Christian emirate of the Ghassanids.
>
> Islam was to spread quickly and went hand in hand with Arabization, through the integration of the new converts into the conquering Arab tribes and their adoption of the conquerors' genealogy. This Islamization was not total, and, in the twentieth century, approximately 10 per cent of Arabs were still Christians, predominantly Greek Orthodox, who claimed to be the descendants of the Christian Arabs from before the advent of Islam. Linguistic and cultural Arabization, on the other hand, was complete.[35]

The unique geo-strategic position of Palestine, situated as it was between the sea and the desert and at the meeting-point of three continents, helped to make it a testing-ground for integration and assimilation and the inter-mingling of human groups of the most diverse origins. What matters in terms of the universal civilization of humanity is not so much the succession of historical periods but rather the contribution that Palestine has made to civilization on account of its exceptional position, which rightly prompted Chairman Yasser Arafat to say how proud all Palestinians were to be natives of this Holy Land, as it was the land of the Prophets.[36]

This mix of Semitic, Aryan and Indo-European ethnic groups and of different civilizations, religions and cultures has nurtured a multifaceted society whose various component groups have achieved unity in diversity through a spirit of tolerance which has led to mutual understanding among them. This tolerance, which is the very antithesis of exclusiveness, has enabled the various social and ethnic groups to preserve their own identities. An illustration of this is to be found in the Armenian community, which has lived in Jerusalem and Palestine since the fifth century and has kept its cultural identity, language and traditions intact, while being proud to be Palestinian. After the massacre of which they were the victims in 1915, Armenians in large numbers found refuge in Palestine. The causes of the repeated and sometimes protracted wars and rebellions which have occurred in this region do not lie in the society itself but in the ambition, greed, rivalry and vengefulness of the expansionist powers.

Despite the toll in human misery and material deprivation bequeathed by these conflicts, their only long-term consequence has been to lessen the ill-feeling among the Palestinians and to give a strengthened sense of belonging to a society with a preordained destiny. Exclusiveness was an attitude adopted by only a few groups, who were more attached to temporal than to spiritual values such as harmony, tolerance, equality and fraternity.

Such were the lives of these peoples, with their hopes and their despair, their joys and their sorrows, but, in spite of successive invasions, they never lost their individuality. Modern history, however, particularly since the beginning of the twentieth century, has been ruthless to Palestine and the Palestinians. Their fate was, once again, to be profoundly altered against their will and over their heads, while the swing of the pendulum continued—this time influenced not only by geo-strategic factors but by international political motives leading to the creation of spheres of influence and settlements in furtherance of a policy of expansion and domination.

From Religious Zionism to Political Zionism

Fleeing from persecution and the intolerance of the Inquisition in fifteenth-century Spain, Jews and Arabs found a safe haven in Palestine. Other Jews immigrated to Palestine after the massacre of 300,000 Jews in Poland by Bohdan Chmielicki's Cossacks in 1648, the pogroms organized by the Russian tsars from 1882 and the Dreyfus affair in France (1894–1906).

Palestine, a country of tolerance and of ethnic and religious pluralism, allowed them to settle on its soil unopposed. Nor did it take any action against religious Zionism, which began a tradition of pilgrimage to the Holy Land and led to the establishment of Jewish religious communities in Jerusalem, Safad and Tiberias. Religious Zionism had no political programme and did not aspire to seize power in Palestine. Its sole aim was to create a spiritual focus for the Jewish faith and Jewish culture. The leading proponents of this form of Zionism in the nineteenth century were the group known as the 'Lovers of Zion'.

There was no hostility to religious Zionism in Palestine. Its devotees were well received. Mixed marriages and the Zionists' economic, social and cultural activities provide evidence of their integration into the Palestinian community. Today's PLO leadership includes several Palestinians descended from mixed marriages of this kind.

While religious Zionism was well received, however, political Zionism was not. From the outset, it met with opposition and hostility from the Palestinian people. Its political programme was viewed by the Palestinians as seeking at all costs to attract Jews from all over the world to Palestine, driving out the Palestinians in order to establish a Jewish state in the heart of the Arab world on the ruins of Palestine. Political Zionism reduced the Old Testament to a political manifesto, a development that was a sad reminder to the Palestinians and Arabs of the Christian political Zionism preached by Pope Urban II in 1095, which had led to the Crusades.

This political Zionism disregards the very existence of the Palestinian people and their presence in their own country for 5,000 years—they are not mentioned even once in Herzl's *The Jewish State* (1896) or in the resolutions of the Congress of the World Zionist Organization. To justify its political existence, the movement for political Zionism claimed that there was a geographical and historical vacuum and that Palestine was 'a land without people for a people without a land'. We shall see later that this denial of the other, which made Palestine out to be a historical and geographical 'desert', is at the root of the tragedy of the Palestinian people and of the injustice it has suffered for approximately one century. This moral and physical assault on the Palestinian people diverted Palestine from its calling as the land of God's revelations, made it the victim of a new form of colonialism and turned it into a permanent battlefield.

For the West, the emergence of this political movement was in line with the thrust of nineteenth-century history and could be explained by the persecution of the Jews in Europe and the resurgence of nationalism and colonialism. These factors enabled the Zionist movement to convince the West of the 'legitimacy' of its aspirations and claims regarding the establishment in the land of Palestine of a Jewish nationalist state that would be 'an outpost of civilization as opposed to barbarism'.[37]

The movement also exploited Christian Zionism, which helped it to gather strength and support. According to Henry Laurens:

> This idea of return was supported by Anglo-Saxon Protestants, who interpreted certain verses of Saint John's Apocalypse as meaning that the fulfilment of the prophecies, that is to say the Last Judgement, could take place only when the whole Jewish people had been reunited in the Holy Land prior to their collective conversion to Christianity. This school of thought, now known as Christian Zionism, was very influential in English and American ruling circles in the nineteenth century.[38]

For the Jews, the founder of political Zionism was Theodor Herzl (1860–1904), author of *The Jewish State*, whose principles began to be put into practice in Basle in 1897 with the holding of the first World Zionist Congress. Herzl and his Zionist movement subsequently turned religious Zionism into political Zionism, exploiting religion for political ends through a selective and sectarian reading of the Bible and of Jewish tradition.

Substituting nationalism for Judaism, they built their political platform on the themes of 'chosen people', 'covenant' and 'promised' land, thus draining those great general principles of their real substance, which precluded exclusiveness, privilege and a claim to superiority. The 'chosen people', as interpreted by the Zionist movement, excluded the Palestinian people. Yet God does not discriminate among his creatures.

In addition, the Zionist movement turned the 'promise' into a privilege and a title deed to the land. It dismissed with contempt the faith that venerated membership of the community of Abraham, casually forgetting Ismail, Abraham's eldest son, although he belonged to the same stock. As for the 'promised land' and the 'covenant', whereby the God of the Hebrews, Yahweh (son of the Canaanite God El), offered a country in return for submission to divine law, these should, as already noted, be seen in the context of the evolution of human societies at that time and in that region. Other societies—Canaanite, Egyptian, Mesopotamian, Hittite, etc.—had received similar promises from their gods and concluded similar covenants. The Hebrews were not exceptional in that respect.

Are there not grounds for drawing a comparison between the drift of the Zionist movement from the religious into the secular sphere, thus breaking God's laws, and the Hebrew people's transgressions in the past, frequently denounced by their own prophets, when they failed to comply with the conditions attached to the 'promise' and the 'covenant', namely, submission to divine law?

With the coming of Christ, God announced to the whole of mankind a 'New Covenant' to replace the old and promised them His kingdom, which must therefore be a heavenly and not an earthly kingdom.

In exploiting religion for political ends, the founders of Zionism, like subsequent Israeli leaders, chose 'the doctors who killed the prophets', thus focusing on Joshua's account of the massacres of the Canaanites rather than on the anathemas and curses of Jeremiah or Micah, and thereby fore-shadowing and justifying the massacres of Palestinians. Emphasis was also placed on the racially discriminatory laws of Esdras rather than on the universalist messianism of Ezekiel and Isaiah or on Abraham and Moses.

Moreover, the founders of Zionism did not hesitate to highlight Jewish claims to have exceptional qualities and their proclivity to conquest and domination, instead of stressing universalism, which did not isolate the Jewish people from other people since it guaranteed the Jews in Palestine unity with the other Eastern components of the faith of Abraham: its Christian and Muslim components. The Zionist movement's definition of Judaism, whose messianic and universalist character was deliberately neglected, was severely criticized and rejected by the majority of Jews.

Walter Laqueur, summarizing their criticism, has written:

The case against Zionism was, very briefly, that as a secularist movement it was incompatible with the religious character of Judaism; as a political movement it was inconsistent with the spiritual emphasis in Judaism; as a nationalist movement it was out of keeping with the universalist character of Judaism; and it was a threat to the welfare of Jews as it confused gentiles in their thinking about Jews and thus imperilled their status.[39]

Politically, the founders of Zionism used the most abject means to attain their ends, subscribing to the view that 'the end justifies the means'. For example, they sought to co-operate with Nazis, Fascists and anti-semites to make their dream come true: to force Jews to leave their countries of origin in order to build a 'Greater Israel'. Ralph Schoenmann, denouncing this shameful behaviour, wrote:

Theodor Herzl approached none other than Count von Plehve, the instigator of the worst pogroms in Russia—the pogroms of Kishinev—with the following proposition: 'Help me to reach the land [Palestine] sooner and the revolt [against tsarist rule] will end'.[40]

This anti-Zionist Jewish writer also accused the Zionist Stern Gang of having sought to conclude a military pact with Nazism. He wrote:

On 11 January 1941 Avraham Stern proposed a formal military pact between the National Military Organization (NMO), of which Yitzhak Shamir, the former Prime Minister of Israel, was a prominent leader, and the Nazi Third Reich. This proposal became known as the Ankara document, having been discovered after the war in the files of the German Embassy in Turkey.[41]

The Israeli newspaper *Yediot Aharonot* of 4 February 1983 also revealed that Shamir's Stern Gang had collaborated with the government of the Nazi Third Reich. The 19 August 1983 issue of the Israeli weekly *Hotam* confirmed the existence of the 'Ankara document', which was signed by Stern and Yitzhak Shamir (who then went by the name of Yazernitsky). Moreover, when Shamir was arrested by the British in December 1941, the charge against him was 'terrorism and collaboration with the Nazi enemy'.[42]

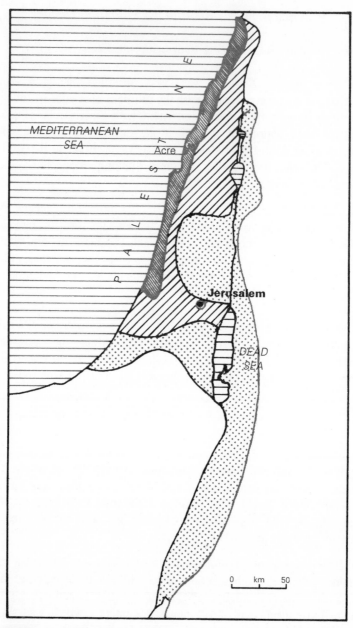

MEDITERRANEAN
SEA

Acre

PALESTINE

Jerusalem

DEAD
SEA

0   km   50

 Frontiers of the kingdom in 1191, following an agreement between Saladin and Richard Lionheart

 Frontiers of the kingdom following the agreement between King al-Kamel and the Germanic Emperor Frederick II (1229)

 Frontiers reached by the Kingdom of the Crusades before 1187

Map1. The Kingdom of the Crusaders (1099–1291)

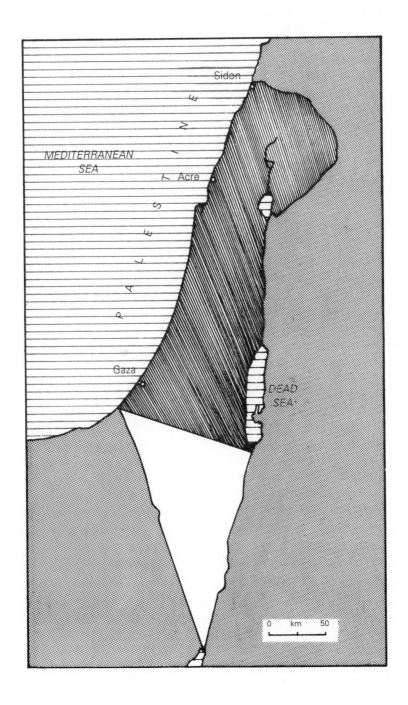

Map 2. The Palestinian Principality of Daher Omar

5
Zionism in Action and the Palestinian Reaction

At the first World Jewish Congress, the members of the Zionist movement realized that their dream of establishing a Jewish homeland in Palestine could not be fulfilled unless they approached European governments to enlist their support. In his address to the first Zionist Congress in Basle in 1897, Max Nordau described the aim of Zionism as follows:

> Zionism aims at the creation of a home for the Jewish people in Palestine to be secured by public law. To that end, the Congress envisages the following: . . . Preparatory moves towards obtaining such governmental consent as will be necessary to the achievement of the aims of Zionism.[1]

Theodor Herzl approached Kaiser Wilhelm II with that end in view in 1898, proposing that Palestine be made 'a society guaranteed by a charter and placed under Germany's protection'.[2] The Kaiser having declined, Herzl tried in 1900 to win Britain over to his cause, but again met with a refusal. In 1901 Herzl had a meeting with the Ottoman Sultan, Abdulhamid II, to obtain his support for the project, but the talks ended in failure. The pattern was repeated in 1903, when Herzl met von Plehve, the Russian Minister of the Interior. A meeting with Pope Pius X, in 1904, proved equally unsuccessful.

Following this series of failures, Herzl abandoned his project in Palestine and turned his attention to Cyprus, Argentina and other countries as possible locations for the establishment of a Jewish state. During this period of prospecting, Austen Chamberlain proposed to the Zionists, in 1903, the creation of a Jewish state in Uganda. The proposal was submitted to the sixth World Jewish Congress by Herzl and defended by him. The congress approved it by 295 votes, with 177 (mainly Russian) delegates voting against. This decision marked the first split in the Zionist movement, seriously weakening its authority. Britain went back on its offer shortly after the congress, having granted Uganda to other white settlers. After his failure to find an alternative to Palestine, Herzl returned to his original plan.

On 3 July 1904 this phase came to an end with the death of Herzl, who left behind a divided and weakened movement which declined until 2 November 1917. On that date, Sir Arthur James Balfour, then British Foreign Secretary, made a declaration in the form of a letter addressed to Lord Walter Rothschild, a British citizen and vice-chairman of the organization representing British Jews. The letter is reproduced in full below:

Dear Lord Rothschild,

I have much pleasure in conveying to you, on behalf of His Majesty's Government, the following declaration of sympathy with Jewish Zionist aspirations, which has been submitted to, and approved by, the Cabinet:

'His Majesty's Government view with favour the establishment in Palestine of a national home for the Jewish people, and will use their best endeavours to facilitate the achievement of this object, it being clearly understood that nothing shall be done which may prejudice the civil and religious rights of existing non-Jewish communities in Palestine, or the rights and political status enjoyed by Jews in any other country.'

I should be grateful if you would bring this declaration to the knowledge of the Zionist Federation.

Yours sincerely,

(signed)

Arthur James Balfour.[3]

In law, this declaration is null and void, since it concerns a territory over which Britain had no jurisdiction allowing it to determine the territory's future. Nor is it in any sense an agreement between states, since the person to whom the letter is addressed is simply a British citizen. The Palestinian community alone had the right freely to determine its destiny.

The Balfour Declaration, whose real motives will be analysed later, caused splits in the community in Palestine when its chief components, Christians, Muslims and Jews, had been living together peacefully and considered that they shared the same hardships and the same destiny. The declaration sanctioned the division of this community for colonial ends, causing political, religious, social and cultural tension and serious consequences which are at the root of the current tragedy faced by this community, whose members belong to the three great monotheistic religions and are the direct descendants of Abraham.

This move, corrupt in a legal as well as a moral sense, on the part of a great colonial power that was later to establish its mandate over Palestine, lies at the heart of the great injustice of the twentieth century of which the whole Palestinian people were to be the victims. George Corm has written that, through this document, the British government was presuming to determine the future of Palestine, over which it had no legal or actual sovereignty, for the sake of a religious community, the Jews, who almost all lived outside that country.[4] He adds that the text—which claimed to respect rights and justice—made an astonishing reference to the Arabs, who constituted 91 per cent of the population, as 'non-Jewish communities in Palestine', and decreed that their 'civil and religious rights' should not be infringed. Yet not a word was said about the political rights of these strange 'non-Jewish communities', the Palestinian people, which the declaration refused to name, but to which it denied any possibility of a collective existence by depriving them forthwith of all political rights.[5]

This political volte-face by Britain during the First World War marked a radical departure from its previous policy, which had been marked by a deep distrust of Zionism. The change was partly due to speculation about the possible fall of the Ottoman Empire and to British fears about what might happen if France moved into Palestine. Such a move would create common borders between Palestine and Egypt at a time when the latter was a British protectorate, and this would threaten British interests, especially the security of those interests and the use of the Suez Canal.

To ensure the success of its policy, Britain contacted the Sherif of Mecca, Hussein ibn Ali, who agreed to help Britain defeat the Ottoman Empire in exchange for the creation of a great Arab state. This agreement was the subject of ten letters sent by Hussein to Sir Henry McMahon, the British High Commissioner in Cairo, between July 1915 and February 1916.

However, almost at the same time, starting on 21 October 1915, the British began secret talks with France that led, in May 1916, to a compromise dividing up the Middle East between France, which was given Syria, Lebanon and northern Palestine, and Britain, which received Iraq, Jordan and the rest of Palestine. This Sykes-Picot Agreement was only another instance of deception on the part of Britain, just as it had deceived Herzl by going back on its offer to the Zionist movement to establish a

Jewish national home in Uganda.

This time, the victims of the deception were to be both Sherif Hussein ibn Ali and France. To the former—through a tendentious interpretation of the agreement resulting from the negotiations with McMahon—Britain claimed that Palestine was not part of the great Arab state to which it had promised independence. As for France, it could no longer capitalize on the Sykes-Picot Agreement, since Britain violated its undertakings after its victory over the Turks following the war which started in Palestine in March 1917 under the leadership of General Allenby, and which ended in October 1918 with the occupation of Gaza, Haifa and Jerusalem, where Allenby established a military administration. So it was that Britain, playing its own version of poker at the expense of the Palestinian people, promised Palestine to everybody: to Sherif Hussein with the creation of a great Arab state; to France, even if only in part, following the Sykes-Picot Agreement; and finally to Zionist Jews through the Balfour Declaration.

None the less, there was still hope for an understanding between Jews and Arabs that might preserve peace in the region and avoid the trap set for them by the British with the complicity of the Zionist movement. Thus, on 3 January 1919, Weizmann and Emir Faisal, son of Sherif Hussein, signed an agreement drawn up by Colonel T.E. Lawrence whereby Jewish immigrants would be given the opportunity to settle in Palestine. The agreement did not tackle the issue of the future status of Palestine, which was due to be resolved at the Versailles peace conference. However, the conference, which opened on 18 January 1919, discussed the matter on the basis of the Balfour Declaration, thus dismissing the promises made to Sherif Hussein ibn Ali following his exchange of letters with McMahon, despite the personal intervention of Emir Faisal at the peace conference. This time, Britain's duplicity was sanctioned by the major powers.

In a reversal of the situation, and after Syria, including Lebanon and Palestine, had been declared independent in Damascus by the Arab nationalists in March 1920, with Faisal as King, serious incidents broke out between Arabs and Jews, especially in Jerusalem.

In addition, disagreement arose between Britain and France; the latter, referring to the Sykes-Picot Agreement, refused to allow the settlement of Jewish immigrants in Palestine, over which France should have authority. However, in August 1920, the two powers concluded the Treaty of Sèvres, whereby France and Britain were granted mandates over Syria and Palestine respectively—with a view to the implementation of the Balfour Declaration in the latter case. The same legal and political arguments demonstrating the illegality of the Balfour Declaration also apply to this provision of the Treaty of Sèvres.

So it was that, just after the end of the First World War, the fate of Palestine and its people continued to fluctuate at the whim of political ambitions, rivalries and tensions between European powers, which had previously sought a safe route to India, and which now had oil or strategic/ military interests—or both—to safeguard. All the political and economic conditions were right for the Palestinians to react violently to the implementation of the Zionist movement's plan, and to offer patriotic resistance. In addition to the deteriorating political situation in the country, the Zionist settlements both aggravated the economic situation and posed a serious threat to the Palestinians, who found themselves the victims of expropriations or illegal purchases of their land.

When, in 1886, some of the *effendis* (mostly feudal rulers of non-Palestinian origin) first sold land belonging to two villages in the Jaffa region to the Zionist movement, serious clashes took place when the peasants were expelled from their land. According to Ralph Schoenmann:

> When the settlers at Petah Tikvah sought to push the peasants off the land, in 1886, they met with organized resistance, but Jewish workers in neighbouring villages and communities were wholly unaffected. In fact, until the Balfour Declaration of 1917, the Palestinian response to Zionist settlements was unwisely tolerant. There was no organized hatred of Jews in Palestine.[6]

However, the *effendis* were not the only ones to sell Palestinian land to the Zionist movement. According to Neville Mandel:

> In some instances, lands were sold by the government to the Jews because the peasants were unable to pay their taxes, and on other occasions the peasants fell victims to usurers who in turn sold the land to the Jewish immigrants.[7]

None the less, whatever the illegality of these transactions may have been, it should be stressed that the surface area of the land sold to the Jews was not more than 5.6 per cent of the total area of Palestine. By now, the Palestinians no longer viewed political Zionism as representing people seeking a place of refuge, but as a plan aimed at eliminating the Palestinians in order to set up a Jewish state.

General Clayton, the head of the Arab Bureau in Cairo and responsible for political affairs, wrote to his superiors in London about the effects of the Balfour Declaration. He commented that the policy which was enunciated in clause No. 4 (regarding Jewish settlement in Palestine) would meet with strong opposition from both Christian and Muslim Arabs, who had shown distrust of the lengths to which H.M. Government were prepared to go as a consequence of Balfour's announcement to the Zionists.[8]

The British government sent a commission to Palestine, led by Weizmann and with W. Ormsby-Gore as liaison officer, to follow up the Balfour Declaration. This sparked off violent reactions among the Palestinians, who saw this new initiative as proof of an irreversible resolve to put the declaration into effect. As a result, they set up joint Muslim-Christian Committees to thwart the plan, which became their prime target. The reports that Clayton and Ormsby-Gore sent to London left their determination in no doubt.[9] A secret service report stated that the political consequences of the commission's visit had not so far been positive. Christians and Muslims did not feel any easier in their minds about their future, and still feared for their rights if the Zionists' aspirations were realized: they were going ahead in forming committees to look after their own interests.[10]

However, while organizing against the Zionist plan, the Palestinians had not closed all doors. In reply to Weizmann's Jaffa speech of 8 May 1918, the spokesman for political and religious leaders there said that both Muslims and Christians should treat their Jewish compatriots as they treated one another, so long as the Jews regarded and respected the rights of those two religions, thus confirming their words with deeds.[11]

Weizmann wrote to Balfour opposing the request that Palestinians be involved in the work of the convention responsible for settling the country's problems. He claimed that the democratic system was not workable in this instance, on the grounds that it did not take into account 'the superiority of the Jew to the Arab, the fundamental qualitative difference between Arab and Jew'.[12]

The Muslim-Christian Committee in Jaffa paid tribute to the President of the United States, Woodrow Wilson, for his declaration of 14 July 1918 on the right to 'national self-determination'. The committee emphasized the Arab nature of Palestine, saying:

If the country be the pretext, we should hasten to say that the country as well as the inhabitants are Arab. If numbers be the pretext, it should not be forgotten that the Arabs are 30 times more numerous than the Jews. If majority of the land be the pretext, the Jews must be warned that the portion they possess in Palestine is nothing more than 1/500 of the land belonging to Muslims and Christians. Is it for the language? Then it is well known that the language of the country is pure Arabic.[13]

The Palestinian conference, held in Jerusalem from 27 January to 10

February 1919, sent the Versailles peace conference a manifesto in which it stressed the indivisible nature of the Arab people of Palestine and the invalidity of all agreements impairing the sovereignty of the Palestinian people, by virtue of the principle upheld by President Wilson. Britain did not reply to this memorandum, and its failure to react was partly responsible for exacerbating ill-feeling and fomenting demonstrations, disturbances and violence. The British government's attitude is further illustrated by a letter to the Prime Minister from Balfour, who was then Foreign Secretary:

> The weak point of our position, of course, is that in the case of Palestine we deliberately and rightly decline to accept the principles of self-determination. If the present inhabitants were consulted they would unquestionably give an anti-Jewish verdict. Our justification for our policy is that we regard Palestine as being absolutely exceptional, that we consider the question of the Jews outside Palestine as one of world importance.[14]

The Palestinian attack of 1 March 1918 on two Jewish settlements on the Syrian border and the rioting that followed between 4 and 10 April, during which 9 people died and 242 were injured according to official figures, were significant indicators of the country's state of ferment. In February 1920 the Palestinians rebelled, initially using peaceful means such as meetings, protest motions, petitions, demonstrations and strikes. Hajj Amin al-Husseini played a leading role in this unrest. On 25 April the San Remo conference designated Britain as the mandatory power over Palestine. In 1921 the Palestinians attempted to organize a general revolt, only to discover, on 24 July 1922, that the League of Nations had confirmed the British mandate over Palestine. Contrary to Articles 20 and 22 of the Covenant of the League of Nations, none of the 28 articles of the mandate took the rights or claims of the Palestinian people into consideration. The Balfour Declaration, however, was officially endorsed and the Council of the League of Nations entrusted its implementation to the mandatory power.

Britain opened wide the doors of Palestine to Jewish immigration. From 1922 to 1927 the Jewish population accordingly rose from 84,000 to 415,000, and the amount of land purchased or confiscated from Palestinians increased from 79,000 to 200,000 hectares. Every conceivable concession —for the most part economic, and more particularly industrial and agricultural—was granted to the Zionists. In contrast to their attitude towards the Palestinians, the British authorized the Zionists to possess weapons. In a word, they made it easy for Zionist organizations to set up a state within the state.

Zionism in Action and the Palestinian Reaction

The first phase of Palestinian resistance to Britain's policy, which permitted an influx of Zionist immigrants into Palestine and dispossessed the Palestinians of their lands, was essentially a peasants' revolt: in 1929 there were a growing number of violent riots against the British and clashes with settlers, followed by urban uprisings, especially in Jaffa, Nablus, Tiberias, Safad, Haifa, Hebron and Jerusalem. Unreasonably harsh repressive measures were applied by the mandatory power against the Palestinians alone, supposedly to 'restore order': hangings, mass arrests, curfews, banning of the Palestinian press and several other penalties, while no action was taken against the Zionists, who enjoyed total impunity.

The deteriorating situation in Palestine forced the British government to send out a commission of inquiry to make appropriate recommendations. The Johnson-Croesbies Commission recommended an urgent halt to the Zionists' policy of intensive settlement. Faced with a popular uprising that they could not pacify or repress, the British were forced to try to put an end to the riots by satisfying certain Palestinian demands through the publication of a White Paper in 1930. In the White Paper, Britain decided to block Jewish immigration and encourage the employment of Palestinians. Under Zionist pressure, the British came to question the paper, however, and it was speedily withdrawn.

The Palestinians then reacted by organizing themselves into a fully fledged anti-Zionist, anti-British and anti-feudal popular revolution, led initially by Izzeddin al-Qassam. He fell, gun in hand, while fighting the British, on 19 November 1935. From 1936 to 1939 there was an all-out insurrection in Palestine, starting with a general strike from 21 April to 11 October 1936, the longest general strike in history. This was a revolt by the Palestinian peasants against British repression and the expropriation of one third of their arable land. It took the form of civil disobedience and armed insurrection. The British imposed martial law on 30 July 1936, and a vast campaign of repression was unleashed, involving murders, executions, expulsions, mass arrests and the demolition of houses.

Faced with the Palestinian uprising, the British began to turn to the Zionists for support. They prohibited the Palestinians from possessing weapons, at the same time preventing Arab countries from supplying them with weapons to defend themselves, while Zionist military and paramilitary organizations continued to receive arms from the British and from Europe. As the situation became ever more alarming, the British government tried to find a way of accommodating both the Zionists and the Arabs while safeguarding their own interests. With the support of the League of Nations, Britain convened a conference in London on 8 February 1939, with the aim of securing the agreement of both parties to the partition of Palestine. The conference failed because of British attempts to favour their Zionist allies.

On the eve of the Second World War, the British government issued a second White Paper on 17 May 1939.[15] It envisaged the establishment within ten years of an independent Palestinian state and the limitation of Jewish immigration to 75,000 persons a year for the following five years. It also stated that no further Jewish immigration should be authorized unless the Arabs of Palestine consented! The paper also provided for a restriction on land purchases by Jews. Satisfied with the White Paper, the Palestinians ended their revolt against the British, as they were advised to do by the Arab countries of the region.

The Mufti of Jerusalem, Hajj Amin al-Husseini, who was suspicious of the British, was forced into exile in Iraq after an Anglo-Zionist attempt on his life. He rejected the White Paper because the British were negotiating directly with the Arab governments and not with the Palestinians and were acceding only partially to the demands of the Palestinian people. Britain's second occupation of Iraq forced the Mufti to take refuge in Nazi Germany. The Mufti's stand in favour of the Third Reich was a political statement against the British, with a view to securing the independence of Palestine. We find here the same motives as those which prompted the Zionist Stern Gang, with Friedman, Yellin-Mor and Yitzhak Shamir, to offer Nazi Germany an alliance against the British with a view to establishing a Jewish state in Palestine. This was obviously a fundamental miscalculation and a reprehensible position. Despite the calls for a revolt put out by Nazi Germany during the Second World War, not only did the Palestinians not respond, but 12,500 of them joined the British forces against the Nazis.

Although Britain tried to put the 1939 White Paper into effect, the Zionist organizations fought it and frustrated its implementation. The Jewish Agency then set about organizing illegal Jewish immigration. The British attempted a blockade of the Palestinian coast and several tragic incidents occurred: ships transporting refugees were wrecked; disaster befell the *Exodus* in July 1947; and the *Patria*, which was taking Jewish refugees from Nazi Germany to Mauritius, was scuttled in 1940 off the Palestinian coast during its stopover in Haifa as a result of terrorist acts by the Haganah—252 Jewish refugees and all the British crew were killed.

In the 1930s a serious politico-ideological rift developed in the Zionist Organization in Palestine (the Jewish Agency and its military wing, the Haganah). In 1937 it split into two groups: the workers' movement led by David Ben-Gurion, head of the Jewish Agency's Executive Bureau; and the right-wing group headed by Jabotinsky, a Haganah dissident who founded Etzel (Irgun Zvei Leumi). This 'national military organization', known as revisionist Zionism, was itself to split in 1939, after the death of Jabotinsky, into two organizations: Irgun headed by Menachem Begin, and Lehi (Lohmei Heruth Israel) led by Abraham Stern. The latter, a Polish Jew, was killed in 1942 and was replaced by a triumvirate of Eldad, Snab and Yellin-Mor. Yitzhak Shamir was placed in charge of military operations. These splits in the movement spelled the end of its unity. Ben-Gurion's organization ceased to co-operate with the British in protest against the White Paper, while the other two groups resorted to acts of terrorism.

The Stern Gang organized a series of attacks against British troops in Palestine. Within a very short time, Irgun, in turn, resorted to terrorism. Stern's most spectacular action was the murder of Lord Moyne on 6 November 1944 in Cairo, while Irgun blew up the King David Hotel in Jerusalem on 22 July 1946, killing 92 civilians and military personnel and wounding hundreds of others. The two revisionist organizations committed various terrorist acts, including sabotage of communications networks, hostage-taking, parcel bombs sent to Europe, car bombs and executions of prisoners.

The British authorities retaliated by imposing on the Zionist organizations, as of 1945, the same emergency laws as they had previously applied to the Palestinians between 1936 and 1939—much the same as those enforced today by Israel in the occupied Palestinian territories. Ben-Gurion's Haganah followed Irgun and Lehi's lead in resorting to terrorism from October 1945 onwards. The other response by the Zionists to the second White Paper, similar to their reaction to the first White Paper in 1930, was to step up the establishment of Jewish colonies for ideological and military—and not economic and demographic—purposes. This was in line with their policy of establishing *faits accomplis* and their strategy of establishing Jewish settlements throughout Palestinian territory, especially near the borders with neighbouring Arab countries in order to justify their territorial claims in the event of partition and, in the event of war, to use them as forward bases. Even the design of the buildings was governed by military considerations and not urban or architectural criteria. We find the same policies and approaches after 1967 in the occupied West Bank and Gaza.

British support for the Zionist organizations under the mandate was proving inadequate in the eyes of these organizations; they sought to go beyond the framework of the mandate, which provided for the creation of a 'Jewish national home', and move towards the establishment of a 'Jewish state'. This situation, encouraged by President Truman, led to a showdown between the Zionist organizations and Britain, which remained anxious to safeguard its position *vis-à-vis* the Arab countries. This confrontation culminated in the battle waged by the Zionists to eliminate British influence, purporting to be a 'colonized people' struggling for liberation after having themselves exercised colonial power.

The Tunisian author Ghazi Mabrouk has this to say on the subject:

> Britain, which had played the part of protector of Zionism and of the 'home country', saw the Zionist settlers turning against it, as Rhodesia did before becoming Zimbabwe. The battle waged by the Zionists against the British, which had all the hallmarks of a 'war of independence', represented a break between the settlers and their administering power. It was the victory of one form of colonialism over another, at the expense of the Palestinian people, who might as well not have existed.[16]

When the official Vatican paper *L'Osservatore Romano* of 28 May 1948 wrote, 'Zionism is not the Israel of the Bible. It is that of the Balfour Declaration and of its times,'[17] it was viewing Zionism as a political movement inspired by the major events of the nineteenth century, the century which saw the emergence of nationalism and colonialism.

Meanwhile, on 12 May 1942, Ben-Gurion pushed through what came to be known as the Biltmore Programme at a meeting of representatives of the Zionist movement at the Biltmore Hotel in New York. The programme, endorsed on 22 May 1945 by the Jewish Agency, dropped the reference to a 'Jewish national home' in Palestine, and referred instead to a 'Jewish Commonwealth'—a Jewish state ruling over the whole of Palestine. On the subject of what amounted to a metamorphosis of Zionism, i.e. the Biltmore watershed, Migeon and Jolly wrote:

> The participants unanimously adopted a resolution known as the Biltmore Programme. They demanded, among other things: the immediate issuing of 100,000 entry visas to Palestine; the control of immigration by the Jewish Agency; the abolition of restrictions on land sales; and the establishment of a Jewish state as soon as a Jewish majority was attained in Palestine.[18]

The Biltmore Programme, which for the first time openly stated the objectives of the Zionist movement, was later endorsed by Truman, who was to espouse the Zionist cause. Biltmore marked the beginning of the supremacy of chauvinist political Zionism over universalist religious Zionism.

Many Palestinians regard the PLO charter as a Palestinian reaction, and a very belated one at that, to the Biltmore Programme, for Palestine has, since ancient times, been part not only of the Jewish religious heritage, but also of the Christian and Muslim religious heritage. In their view, the PLO charter envisages the establishment in Palestine of a secular and democratic state in which Jews, Christians and Muslims would be equitably represented.

From 1943 onwards, the United States began its direct involvement in the Palestine question, an involvement encouraged by the American Congress, whose sympathies already lay with Zionism. In July 1945 President Truman exerted unprecedented public pressure on the British to persuade them to grant 100,000 Jews permission to immigrate into Palestine. Britain refused, however, invoking the need to take account of the legitimate interests of the Palestinians and their firm opposition to any such immigration.

Ernest Bevin, the British Foreign Secretary, then proposed to Truman, by way of a solution, the formation of a joint Anglo-American Committee of Inquiry to investigate the situation of Jews in Europe and look into the possibility of their emigrating to Palestine. The joint (Morrison-Grady) Committee recommended in its report, published on 1 May 1946, that Jewish immigration into Palestine be facilitated, chiefly by dividing Palestine into a number of provinces, with an extension of the British mandate or its replacement by a United Nations trusteeship and the annulment of most of the British White Paper—which had taken the interests of the Palestinians into consideration. The committee's proposals were rejected by both the Zionists and the Palestinians.[19]

All these proposals conceal an obvious fact: both during and after the Second World War, European and American leaders created obstacles to the influx of Jews fleeing from Nazism and hoping to settle in their countries. Hence the policy of encouraging Jewish immigration into Palestine, whose people had nothing whatsoever to do with the holocaust. Displaying a curious contempt for the Palestinians and denying them the same rights as any other people, the governments of Europe and the United States, turning history upside down, rushed headlong into a project to make the Palestinian people—the victims of their policy—suffer the consequences of the holocaust by allowing the Jews to settle in Palestine. In complicity with the Zionist organizations, whose creation they encouraged, these governments turned the Jewish victims into aggressors against the Palestinians and the Arab peoples.

The British government took into consideration the recommendation of its War Office's General Staff, set out in a memorandum in 1918: 'The creation of a Jewish buffer state in Palestine, even if the state itself is weak, is strategically desirable for Britain.'[20] After creating all the necessary conditions to achieve this aim, Britain concealed its real intentions by pretending to be faced with a choice between two conflicting situations: applying the Balfour Declaration and safeguarding the interests of its Arab policy in the region. Finally compelled to make a choice, under pressure of events that we have already described in detail, Britain decided as a last resort to turn over the Palestine file to the United Nations on 18 February 1947, announcing its intention to relinquish its mandate on 14 May 1948. Pontius Pilate could not have done better!

The End of the British Mandate

Laurens describes the situation in Palestine in the wake of the Second World War as follows:

> During the whole period 1945–1947, the Palestinian Arab population remained calm as violence escalated between the British and the Zionists. The political split was wider than ever. The hardliners joined forces behind the Mufti, while some left-wing groups that had recently emerged in urban areas tried to reach a compromise with the Zionists. Ben-Gurion was opposed to any negotiations that might lead to a two-nation Palestine. The adversaries of [Hajj Amin al-]Husseini turned to King Abdallah of Transjordan, who viewed the Palestinian affair as a way of implementing the first stage of his project for a Greater Syria. He secretly confirmed to the Zionist authorities his project for far-reaching Jewish autonomy in his great Arab kingdom. More pragmatically, he put forward the idea in 1946 of a friendly partition of Palestine between Zionists and Jordanians. Although contacts between the King and the representatives of the Jewish Agency were maintained, no agreement was reached. The Mufti and the Arab states were suspicious of Abdallah's intentions and decided to oppose them by every means at their disposal.[21]

Shortly before the end of the Second World War, the representatives of the independent Arab states met in Alexandria, Egypt, on 25 September 1944, to adopt a common Arab policy that would safeguard their national interests. Palestine, which had not yet acquired the status of an independent state, was represented by Musa Alami. On 7 October 1944 the Arab countries signed the Alexandria Protocol, which committed the Arab states to the defence of Palestinian national interests and, with that end in view, to helping the Palestinian people to fulfil their legitimate aspirations to independence.

At the signing of the Constituent Pact of the League of Arab States in Cairo, on 22 March 1945, the committee of the seven independent Arab states which had prepared the project stated that it sympathized as much as anyone else with the sufferings of the Jews in Europe at the hands of a few dictatorial states. The case of these Jews, however, was not to be confused with Zionism; for nothing would be more arbitrary or unjust than to seek to settle the problem of Europe's Jews by creating another injustice, whose victims would be the Arabs of Palestine, whatever their religion or denomination.[22]

On 2 April 1947 the British government requested the UN Secretary-General to convene a special session of the General Assembly and include the Palestine question on its agenda. On 28 April the assembly opened its debate on the British proposal to set up a special committee. The latter, composed of 11 members, was constituted on 15 May and was assigned the task of investigating the situation in Palestine with a view to submitting proposals for the solution of the Palestinian problem. The Arab states, questioning the neutrality of the members of the committee, rejected its membership. Their example was followed by the Arab Higher Committee of Palestine, headed by the Mufti, which boycotted the consultations of the United Nations Special Committee on Palestine (UNSCOP) and, together with the Arab countries, called for the immediate independence of Palestine, invoking the right of peoples to self-determination. Meanwhile the Zionist military and political organizations made their own case to the 11 members of the committee. On 31 August 1947 UNSCOP submitted its report, but its members were divided into two conflicting groups: the majority recommended the partition of Palestine into two states, one Jewish and one Arab, with an economic union and an international zone in Jerusalem; the minority advocated a federal state. One member of the committee remained neutral and abstained when the vote was taken. The majority Partition Plan was put to the vote in the United Nations General Assembly on 29 November 1947. The result was 33 in favour, 13 against and 10 abstentions, including Britain.

The proposed partition was very much in the Zionists' favour: the Jewish state was assigned 56.47 per cent of the total area of Palestine and the Arab state 42.88 per cent. Internationalized Jerusalem was to cover an area of 176 sq. km, i.e. 0.65 per cent of the total area, with 105,000 Arabs and 100,000 Jews. According to the Partition Plan, the Arab state was to have an area of 11,600 sq. km, with a population of 725,000 Arabs and 10,000 Jews. The Jewish state was to have an area of 15,110 sq. km, with a population of 498,000 Jews and 407,000 Arabs (see Map 5).

The Zionists accepted the Partition Plan, which gave them a state. The Palestinians and the Arab states rejected the plan, which they regarded as arbitrary and unjust. The Palestinian writer Walid Khalidi makes the following comment on the United Nations resolution:

In fact, the resolution did not say to the two principal protagonists that each party would keep what it had or most of what it had, with mutual exchanges. It told the Zionists that they were going to have eight times more than what they already had (from 7 per cent to 55 per cent of the country). But it announced to the Palestinians that they should give up 45 per cent of what they possessed, leaving one third of them to live under foreign domination as a permanent minority. In short, although the partition was much better than nothing for the Zionists, it gave the Palestinians infinitely less than their due.[23]

The fact was that, in 1947, the Jews represented 32 per cent of the total population of Palestine and possessed approximately 5.6 per cent of the country's land. Furthermore, under the Partition Plan, the Jewish state received the most fertile land in Palestine. This plan was rejected not only by the Palestinian leaders of the time—except for the Palestinian Communist Party which, like Ben-Gurion, had approved the partition—but also by the Irgun of Begin and the Lehi of Shamir.

The adoption of the Partition Resolution 181 (II) (see Appendix 1) was followed by demonstrations and a general strike throughout Palestine, involving violent clashes with the Jewish population. Extremists in both camps launched a series of raids, reprisals and acts of terrorism against each other. In short, the situation had begun to deteriorate, and the British were steadily losing control. Public services were paralysed and the mandatory authorities did nothing to restore order and security, or to intervene between the two communities so as to avoid confrontation.

In February–March 1948 a plan known as the Dalet Plan was prepared by the military-political strategists of the Zionist Haganah. It comprised 13 military operations. According to Elias Sanbar:

> It was under the Dalet Plan that 13 general operations were conducted between 1 April and 15 May 1948, of which the 8 most important took place outside the Jewish borders established by the partition, in the area theoretically allocated to the Palestinians.[24]

The purpose of the Dalet Plan was to extend as far as possible the territory allocated by the partition, on the grounds—invoked *a posteriori*—of ensuring territorial continuity, 'defendable' borders, the autonomous economic viability of the Jewish state and so-called 'security' and 'peace' for the Jewish settlements. This all took place before the withdrawal of the British and the proclamation of the Jewish state. The Dalet Plan in fact constituted a pre-determined strategy, which was designed to replace the Partition Plan approved by the United Nations, in order to defeat the purpose of that plan and bring the true intentions of the Zionist organizations to fruition. The United Nations decision on partition was regarded by these organizations as merely a way of gaining access to Palestine so as to acquire by force further territories in Palestine over which it had no recognized right of sovereignty. In fact, this was the same policy of *faits accomplis* which still prevails today.

The balance of power was heavily in favour of the Zionist organizations, which had tens of thousands of well-trained soldiers and militia at their disposal. The Palestinian forces were limited in number and in arms, on account of the restrictions imposed by the British since 1936. The leaders of their armed forces could muster only some 3,000 soldiers, under the command of 7 military political leaders (Saffuri, Saghir, Ifriqi, Zaydan, Azawi, Salama and Husseini), supported by 5,000 Arab volunteers under the command of Fawzi Qawiqji and several hundred local militia. Many Palestinian villages did not take part in the hostilities owing to lack of arms or because their population preferred to abide by the local non-aggression agreements signed between the leaders of the Jewish and Arab villages in the 1930s and 1940s—agreements which were systematically violated during the Dalet Plan operations. These accords, then, did not prevent the expulsion of the Palestinians or the destruction of their villages.

The main weakness of the Palestinians, however, lay in the lack of a properly organized political structure:[25] there was disarray owing to the voluntary exile of the nationalist leaders, bloody repression by the British, the settling of old scores, the collapse of the Palestinian economy mainly as a result of the flight of capital, insecurity, paralysis of the different public sectors and constant strikes, especially that of 1936, which lasted for six months. All these factors, which had forced the notables and members of the wealthier Palestinian classes to flee the country (as in Lebanon from 1975 to 1976 onwards), threw the Palestinian population into chaos and accelerated the disintegration of Palestinian society. This process, which lasted from 1936 to 1939, was to resume in 1947 on an even wider scale. Furthermore, the British, who wished to put down the Palestinian revolt, expelled a number of Palestinian leaders. That same policy of expelling leaders was to be adopted by Israel in the occupied Palestinian territories from 1967 onwards.

Between 1922 and 1947 two distinct Jewish and Arab economic systems were developing in Palestine. First, there was that of the Jewish Agency and the Histadrut (Confederation of Jewish Workers), which were the basis of the institutions in all fields and the infrastructure of the future Jewish state.

Britain had in fact delegated a large part of its power to the Jewish Agency, on the grounds that it thus enabled the latter to establish a 'Jewish national home'. With the acquiescence and, indeed, connivance of Britain, the Jewish Agency exerted an authority which went far beyond the official powers that had been conferred upon it: it set up a National Council composed of the leaders of the *yishuv* (Jewish settlements), which acted as a government; it collected taxes, set up a police force, organized a clandestine army (the Haganah), and controlled the Jewish National Fund, education, religious affairs, health, and so on. The Jewish Agency entrusted responsibility for economic, social and cultural affairs to the Histadrut, established in 1920, which was to control the means of production.

Second, there was the Palestinian Arab economy, which deteriorated drastically, not only on account of the above-mentioned factors but also as a result of the British government's policy, which weakened it still further by destabilizing the structures and public services of Arab Palestine. The unavowed intention of British policy was to destroy the structures and institutions of Arab Palestine so as to force the Palestinians into exile, thus raising major obstacles to the creation of a Palestinian state and reinforcing the infrastructure of the potential Jewish state.

After several clashes and skirmishes (which were neither lengthy nor widespread) between Zionists and Palestinians, it was from Jerusalem that, on 31 March 1948, the Dalet Plan was activated through its Operation Nachshon, which sought to open up a corridor between Jerusalem and Tel Aviv by attacking the strategic village of al-Quastal. The defender of the Jerusalem area, Abdel-Qader al-Husseini, cousin of the Mufti, was killed during the fighting in al-Quastal on the night of 6–7 April. The Palmach (élite commandos of the Haganah) occupied the village during the night of 7–8 April 1948. Its fall represented the first success in the execution of the Dalet Plan, which unfolded in tandem with the gradual withdrawal of the British troops. The simultaneous flight of the Palestinian leaders, leaving behind them an unarmed and defenceless civilian population, helped to facilitate the military operations scheduled in the Dalet Plan.

On the night of 9–10 April 1948 military units of Irgun and the Stern Gang captured the Palestinian village of Deir Yassin near Jerusalem, and massacred its 254 inhabitants in cold blood.[26] The village was not spared even though it had concluded a non-aggression pact with Guiva't Sha'ul, the neighbouring *yishuv*. Deir Yassin will always remain engraved in the collective memory of Palestinians and all Arabs as the Palestinian equivalent of the Nazi massacres of civilians at Oradour-sur-Glane in France and Lidice in Czechoslovakia.

On 15 April Operation Harel was launched as an extension of Operation

Nachshon. This was followed by the military operations Misparayim, Shametz, Jevussi, Mtatesh, Maccabi, Gideon, Barak, Ben Ami, Pitchfork and Shilifon, whose target was the Old City of Jerusalem. The Palestinians and the Jordanian army, however, succeeded in foiling this last operation.

To the expulsion of the Palestinian inhabitants of Lydda, Ramleh and other towns; to all the fighting; to the psychological war waged by the Zionist organizations (rumours of atrocities, epidemics and the closing of the borders with Arab countries); to the massacres, especially the one at Deir Yassin, whose memory was kept alive by the daily repetition on the *Voice of the Haganah* of the radio announcers' exhortation, 'Remember Deir Yassin!'—to all that must be added the military impotence of the forces of Husseini's al-Jihad al-Muqaddas al-Musalah (Armed Jihad) and Qawiqji's Jaysh al-Inqaz (Rescue Forces), who were unable to defend the Palestinian towns. As a result, the Palestinians were left with the desolate feeling that they had been abandoned by the United Nations, Britain, the Arab countries and their traditional leaders. All these factors induced the Palestinians to leave in droves. About 360,000 Palestinians who had been expelled or who fled the fighting left their homeland to become refugees in Arab countries.

In order to justify the forced departure of the Palestinians from their country, Israel's mendacious propaganda machine insistently attributed the responsibility for their plight to the radio stations of Arab countries, alleging that they had exhorted the Palestinians to flee, pending the entry of the Arab armies into Palestine. The British writer Erskine Childers,[27] who checked the BBC recordings of broadcasts made from the Arab region at that time, did not come across a single broadcast of that nature. He challenged the Israeli authorities to substantiate their charges, but to no avail.

Ibrahim Abu-Lughod goes even further, maintaining that, contrary to Israeli propaganda, not only were such exhortations never made, but the massive exodus of the civilian population took the Arab and Palestinian leaders by surprise.[28] The initial silence gave way to fears of the possible consequences of such a massive exodus, forcing the Arab and Palestinian leaders to take a stand and advise the Palestinians to stay put and not fall for the Zionist ploy. British, Arab, Zionist and other archives will need to be researched and checked before the truth can be established. One fact is clear: the Palestinian Communist Party, through its tracts and publications, was alone in urging the population to accept the Partition Resolution and to remain.

The Zionist military forces, which were markedly superior to their Palestinian counterparts, succeeded in taking over several regions of Palestine. They occupied Tiberias on 17 April, Haifa on 22 April, Safad on 7 May and Jaffa on 13 May 1948, as well as a number of other towns and villages, including Nazareth and Acre, in the part of Palestine that had been allotted to the Palestinian state.

The Israeli author Nathan Ghofsky writes:

> We Jewish settlers will be able to tell what really happened. We forced the Arabs to abandon their towns and villages . . . Some of them were driven out by force of arms; others were pressured into leaving by our tricks and lies . . . One need only mention the names of the cities of Jaffa, Lydda and Ramleh, . . . but there were more . . . These were a people who had lived on their own land for 1,300 years. We came and turned the native Arabs into wretched refugees. What is more, we do not feel ashamed at slandering and reviling them and defiling their good name. Instead of deeply regretting what we did . . . we attempt to justify our horrible deeds and even glory in them.[29]

Even though the targets of the Dalet Plan were not fully achieved, 200,000–300,000 more Palestinians were expelled or forced into exile. A large part of Palestine was thus occupied by means of a policy of 'emptying' captured territories of their native inhabitants in order to take over—as the Jewish slogan has it—'a land without people'.[30]

In this respect the Jewish colonization of Palestine differed from the classical colonial pattern of the nineteenth century, in which—with the exception of South Africa, whose colonizers chose the path of racial segregation—colonial settlers 'cohabited' with the native inhabitants.

Unlike the important and positive role played by the mass media in denouncing Israeli repression at the outbreak of the *intifada*, the acts of blind, savage terrorism perpetrated by the Zionist organizations, such as the Deir Yassin massacre, the expulsion and mass exodus of the Palestinians and the destruction of their villages, went almost entirely unnoticed by the Western public. Perhaps the shock of the holocaust, on which the Western public had observed a culpable silence, and the atrocities committed during the Second World War, followed in 1947 by the outbreak of the Cold War, were psychological factors that relegated the tragedy of the Palestinians to oblivion. Could this be the true explanation?

The First Arab-Israeli War

From its inception, the League of Arab States regarded the Palestinian problem as the most important cause for it to defend. On 23 March 1945, immediately after its foundation, the League adopted a decision which was annexed to its charter and which contained the following statement:

> At the end of the last war, Palestine, along with the other Arab states that were wrested from the Ottoman Empire, was freed from Ottoman rule. It became an autonomous entity, no longer dependent on any other state. The Treaty of Lausanne stipulated that its future would be decided by the interested parties. Even though Palestine did not succeed in exercising self-determination, it is none the less true that its status was defined by the Covenant of the League of Nations of 1919 on the basis of recognition of its existence as an independent nation. Accordingly, its *de jure* status as an independent international entity cannot be questioned, any more than the independence of the other Arab states.
>
> The fact that, for reasons independent of Palestine's will, its independence did not find outward expression is no obstacle to its participation in the work of the Council of the League of Arab States.[31]

The League of Arab States, which demanded immediate independence for Palestine at the London conference of September–October 1946, rejected the United Nations Partition Resolution. At its session in Sofar, Lebanon, on 16 September 1947, and in Beirut in October of the same year, the League Council decided to help the Palestinians by sending weapons and volunteers and by setting up an Arab Military High Committee to cope with the situation resulting from the departure of the British.

However, Britain had already paved the way for Palestine to be partitioned between the Jews and Jordan. Its 'option' was therefore a Jordanian one. Laurens believes that:

> the final decision was taken, on 7 February 1948 in London, at a meeting attended by Jordanian officials, Glubb Pasha and Ernest Bevin: the British would allow the Arab Legion to enter on 15 May 1948, but it would occupy only the Arab area designated in the Partition Plan, and would not enter the Jerusalem area or the Jewish state. After receiving the green light from the British, Abdallah passed on the message to the Zionist leaders. Although there was no real treaty, Jordanians and Zionists tacitly agreed that there would be no Palestinian Arab state.[32]

The proclamation of the establishment of the state of Israel on 14 May 1948 (the date of the departure of the British High Commissioner from Palestine) and the crossing of the borders of Palestine by the Arab armies the following day are two events of major importance. They resulted from the refusal of Britain, the mandatory power, to co-operate with the Security

Council in implementing the Partition Resolution. The order given by the Arab countries to their armies, on 15 May 1948, to intervene in Palestine was issued simply in accordance with the decisions already taken by the League of Arab States. At the start of the war, on 19 May 1948, the Security Council appointed Count Folke Bernadotte, the President of the International Red Cross and a member of the Swedish royal family, as its mediator in the Middle East.

Of this first Arab-Israeli War, which followed the war between the Palestinians and the Zionists, and of the role played by Jordan, Crown Prince Hassan bin Talal has written:

> The mandatory administration and British armed forces withdrew from Palestine on 14 May 1948. The mandate terminated at midnight. From that day events moved swiftly. The National Council for the Jewish state, on the same day, made a declaration of statehood at Tel Aviv . . . The Arabs, on the other hand, had declined the whole Partition Plan to which they, with the support of neighbouring and other Arab states, were bitterly opposed. As for the British, the loss of life and resources which they had sustained led them to refuse to implement the Partition Plan of 1947 against the wishes of either Jews or Arabs in Palestine, to seek the first opportunity to terminate the mandate and to remove their presence from Palestine. This they did. In a word, the British had found, after 26 years, that the policy which they were required to implement as mandatory was contradictory to a degree which rendered them incapable of implementing it, even by the use of armed force.[33]

This view—the reasons given and the intentions harboured by Britain in refusing any form of co-operation with the United Nations on the implementation of the Partition Resolution—is not commonly shared.

The Crown Prince adds:

> Within a matter of some ten hours from the Israeli declaration of statehood on 14 May 1948, the armed forces of the neighbouring Arab states, except Lebanon, at the request of the Palestine Arab inhabitants, entered what are today referred to as the occupied territories (the West Bank and Gaza). It was in response to this request that the late King Abdallah sent his forces to save the Old City of Jerusalem and these territories, which remained a coveted prize for the Israelis to secure in 1967. It should be remembered that the Israeli contention as to the presence of Arab forces cannot be substantiated. The Jordanian forces had actually withdrawn under the command of their British officers. If

the Arab Legion had been present on Palestinian soil, their presence was a part of the British security arrangements to guard vital installations in Palestine during the war and not an anti-Jewish or anti-Zionist reality. Jews and Arabs served jointly in the British-raised frontier force. With the expiry of the mandate, officers and men, Arab and Jewish respectively, joined their respective national armies.

The legend of a small armed force of Jews (David) fighting huge armed forces of some nine Arab states (Goliath) does not stand up to scrutiny. In fact, the total number of Arab armed forces which entered Palestine on and after 15 May 1948 amounted to 17,500 men: 10,000 from Egypt, 4,500 from Jordan, and 3,000 from Iraq. Lebanon sent no forces at all. Syria fought one skirmish on the Palestine border and then withdrew. Egyptian forces entered Palestine from the Sinai. The Jordanian and Iraqi forces engaged with Jewish forces already present in the areas of Palestine allotted to the Arab state under the United Nations Partition Plan of 1947, and the total number of such Jewish forces amounted to about 62,500, comprised of 3,500 Palmach regulars, 55,000 Haganah and 4,000 Irgun. The Jordanian armed forces did not enter the City of Jerusalem until 19 May, whilst from 15 to 19 May the Jewish forces were capturing the greater part of the city. It was in this situation that Jordanian forces entered the Old City and eventually held it.

Thus, apart from the fighting between Egyptian and Jewish armed forces, the fighting between the Iraqi and Jewish forces was on territory not allocated to the Jews, but territory on which Jewish fighters were already present. The fighting between Jewish and Jordanian forces was either on the same territory or in Jerusalem, allocated to neither the Jewish nor the Arab state.[34]

The region of Jenin, Kalkiliya, Nablus and Tulkarm (the Triangle) constituted the part of the territory of the Arab state of Palestine where the Iraqi units were stationed. Those units, when asked by the population why they had not intervened in the conflict, always replied: 'no orders' (in Arabic: *mako awamir*). This reply is still alive in the collective memory of Palestinians and Arabs alike.

The first phase of the Arab-Israeli War from 15 May to 11 June 1948 saw the intervention of the regular armies of six Arab countries (Yemen, the seventh Member State of the Arab League, confined itself to making a financial contribution and sending 200 soldiers). Those armed forces consisted of the following: 10,000 Egyptians, 4,500 Jordanians, 3,000 Syrians, 3,000 Iraqis, 3,000 Lebanese and 300 Saudis, together with some 15,000 Palestinian fighters. Israel countered these forces with 30,000 Israeli soldiers. (Following the proclamation of the establishment of the state of Israel, the Zionist Jews in Palestine became Israelis.)

The first truce of 11 June 1948, secured through the mediation of Count Bernadotte, created a military situation that was favourable to the Israelis. Indeed, during the truce, when relations between the Arab governments were coloured by suspicion, there was a total absence of military co-ordination, compounded by the embargo on arms sales to the Middle East adopted by Britain, on which the Arab countries of the region depended for their supplies. The embargo was the result of pressure exerted on Britain by the United States on the pretext of avoiding a dispute between the two allies and an aggravation of the conflict in the region: meanwhile, the United States continued secretly to supply arms to Israel through indirect channels. All these factors served only to increase the imbalance between the opposing forces.

During the truce, which was broken on 8 July 1948, the Israelis doubled their military strength thanks to a general mobilization and to Western volunteers. The regular Israeli army, which increased from 30,000 to more than 70,000, was composed of 60,000 soldiers from the Haganah, 5,000 from the Palmach, 2,000 fighters from the Etzel and 300 men from the Lehi. The irregular forces of the Mahal consisted of several thousand mostly non-Jewish volunteers: Americans, British, French and South Africans. These volunteers were to play an important role in the Israeli air force. With them appeared the first Israeli fighter planes.

This powerful army, which was well-trained and equipped thanks to arms supplied by the United States, Britain, France and Czechoslovakia, had overwhelming superiority over the Arab armies, whose ranks were increased by only a few thousand soldiers, from 24,000 to 35,000 men. They were poorly equipped, and only a few thousand irregular forces from the Jihad, Inqaz, and local Palestinian militia units were to join them as reinforcements.

During this second phase of the war, the Israelis occupied other territories belonging to the Palestinian state, expelling hundreds of thousands of inhabitants. The most tragic examples of this were Ramleh and Lydda, relinquished without a fight by the Jordanian army. Yitzhak Rabin seized the two Palestinian towns, and on the verbal orders of Ben-Gurion, drove out their 70,000 inhabitants, who were forced to leave their homes at two hours' notice and follow a single corridor leading to Jordan. This long march, which stretched over several days in the stifling July heat, resulted in the deaths of many women, elderly people and children. Those who did survive this horrendous ordeal found refuge in Jordan.

With a view to ending the fighting, the Security Council adopted a resolution on 15 July 1948, accompanied by immediate sanctions. A cease-fire was finally declared between the belligerents on 18 July 1948. Count Bernadotte proposed a new partition of Palestine which favoured Israel and allocated the West Bank to Jordan. He also suggested that the Palestinian refugees be allowed to return to their homes. The Arab states and Israel rejected the mediator's plan, which had been backed by the United States and Britain. In his report dated 16 September 1948, Count Bernadotte wrote:

It will be an offence against the principles of elemental justice if these innocent victims of the conflict were denied the right of return to their homes while Jewish immigrants flow into Palestine, and indeed, at least offer the threat of permanent replacement of the Arab refugees who have been rooted in the land for centuries.

Following a description of 'large-scale Zionist pillaging, and of instances of destruction of villages without apparent military necessity', he concluded:

It is, however, undeniable that no settlement can be just and complete if recognition is not accorded to the right of the Arab refugee to return to the home from which he has been dislodged. (United Nations document A.648, p.14)

The following day, Count Bernadotte was assassinated by terrorists from the Stern Gang. His aide-de-camp, the French colonel, André Sérot, died in the same attack. According to Laurens, 'the attack appears to have been planned and prepared by Yitzhak Shamir'.[35] A succession of Swedish governments have held Shamir personally responsible for the assassination of Bernadotte,[36] which accounts for the fact that Sweden continues to refuse the former Israeli Prime Minister an entry visa to this day.

The third phase of the Arab-Israeli War was launched on 15 October 1948, but this time at Israel's initiative, through its military offensive against the Egyptian army in central and southern Palestine. Nasser, who was then an officer stationed at Falouja, mounted a brilliant and heroic resistance to the attack. All attempts to seize his position failed, despite serious shortages of weaponry, especially munitions. The Israelis moved their offensive north to occupy the rest of Galilee, and east and south to Sinai. Hostilities ceased on 7 January 1949, after the British had pressured Israel into aborting its army's incursion into Egyptian territory.

During this phase of the war, the Israeli army drove out all Palestinian civilians from newly occupied settlements on the grounds that it did not want a hostile people behind its lines. This sent several hundreds of thousands of new refugees flooding into Egypt, Jordan, Syria and Lebanon. Rony Gabbay estimates the number of Palestinian refugees in 1948 at between 890,000 and 904,000, exiled to several Arab countries in the following proportions:

> In 1948, 8.2 per cent of the Palestinian people lived in Israeli-occupied territory, 30.8 per cent were in Jordan and Egypt, and 61 per cent were housed in 57 refugee camps scattered among the various Arab countries, i.e. 15 camps in Lebanon (14 per cent of refugees), 10 in Syria (9 per cent), 24 in Jordan (55 per cent) and 8 in the Gaza Strip (22 per cent).[37]

During this period, the United Nations General Assembly adopted two resolutions: Resolution 212 (II) of 19 November 1948, which set up a special emergency fund for Palestinian refugees, and Resolution 194 (III) of 11 December 1948, which resolved that 'the refugees wishing to return to their homes . . . should be permitted to do so at the earliest practicable date'.

Israel's share of responsibility in the Palestinian exodus, its policy on this problem and its rejection of the resolution dealing with the repatriation of refugees are neatly summarized in the following paragraphs by Laurens:

> Israel refuses any repatriation of refugees and is implementing a policy designed to make the expulsion of the Palestinian people irreversible. The chronology of events is significant. The exodus of the Palestinians is due to the fundamental opposition between the Zionist doctrine claiming that the Holy Land belongs exclusively to the Jewish people, and the determination of the Arab population to remain on their land.
>
> Palestinian society, already politically destabilized following the British repression of the 1930s, was poorly equipped to maintain its cohesion in the face of Zionist pressure. Naturally, it fell apart with the very first outbreaks of fighting. Beginning in April 1948, Arabs were systematically expelled. No general order or specific policy was necessary: at all levels, Zionist officials decided to do their utmost to eradicate the Arab presence from the territories under their control. To that end, Arab towns were destroyed (including 350 villages), farmland expropriated and Arab economic activity abolished. Beginning in July 1948, the Arab people showed their determination to resist, and migrations motivated by fear were less frequent and the direct use of force less prevalent. The expulsions lasted until 1950, and, in some cases, even until 1951.[38]

In Resolution 62 of 16 November 1948, the Security Council decided to invite those parties directly involved in the conflict to seek an agreement either through direct negotiations or by using the acting mediator (Ralph Bunche) in order to reach an immediate armistice. Pursuant to this resolution, Bunche organized negotiations between Israel and the Arab states beginning on 12 January 1949, with a view to drawing up an armistice agreement. These official negotiations, which were held in Rhodes, were indirect at first, and subsequently direct. Most significantly, they were bilateral, i.e. conducted separately with each Arab state. Bunche acted as mediator in these bilateral negotiations whenever problems arose, in order to bring the two sides closer to a common position. This 'Rhodes formula' put the Arab states at a disadvantage.

The formula was subsequently advocated after the June 1967 War by Gunnar Jarring, the United Nations envoy responsible for monitoring the implementation of Resolution 242, and then by US Secretary of State William Rogers in 1970. On both occasions, Israel rejected its use, and it was not applied until after the October 1973 War—at Camp David in 1978.

In laying down conditions for the holding of the peace conference of 30 October 1991, Shamir reverted to the 'Rhodes formula' (direct negotiations separately with each Arab country) and it may be asked why such a formula, initially regarded as a 'diplomatic way out' and then agreed to by all the parties as a means for each of them to save face, could not be extended to participation by the PLO.

We may be confident that, as at Rhodes, the difficulty will be surmounted as the peace process develops. The main purpose of the peace conference is to establish peace in Palestine. It is inconceivable that negotiations on this important problem, which is central to the Middle East question, should take place in the absence of the party directly concerned: the legitimate representatives of the entire Palestinian people. To allow that to happen would be to continue to deny the existence of the Palestinian people and to go back to square one (the Balfour Declaration of 1917) or to the British partition of Palestine between the Israelis and Jordanians, or to return to the Camp David Accords, which sought to determine the fate of the Palestinian people by treating them as no more than a minority. Such an outcome would merely aggravate and perpetuate their plight.

The first Arab country to negotiate with Israel on the basis of the 'Rhodes formula' was Egypt. On 24 January 1949 Ralph Bunche secured a truce between Israel and Egypt and, on 24 February 1949, after six weeks of negotiations, the head of the Egyptian military delegation, General Saffeydin, and the head of the Israeli delegation, General Walter Eytan, signed the armistice, which hinged on what was officially to be known as the 'armistice demarcation line'.

Lebanon and Israel signed similar agreements at Ras al-Naqoura, near the border with Israel, on 23 March 1949, and Jordan signed a similar armistice on 3 April 1949. Its delegation was headed by a British officer, Lieutenant-Colonel Coadde. The negotiations did not take place in Rhodes, according to J.-P. Migeon and J. Jolly, who report that, 'Officially the talks began in Rhodes, but in fact they were held in the utmost secrecy in Shouneh, King Abdallah's winter residence, and lasted four nights.'[39] Syria was the last Arab country to sign the armistice, on 20 July 1949, close by the cease-fire line at Jisr Banat-Yaacoub; Saudi Arabia, Iraq and Yemen refused to sign. The League of Arab States, having thus been unable to secure a consensus, did not ratify the armistice agreements.

The text of the agreements stresses that they constitute an armistice, not a peace treaty. It stipulates that:

> The demarcation line is by no means to be regarded as a political or territorial border: it has been drawn without prejudice to the rights, claims and positions of the two parties, at the time of the armistice, so far as the final settlement of the Palestinian question is concerned. The main purpose in tracing the armistice demarcation line is to establish a line that the armed forces of the respective parties may not cross.

The armistice prohibited the use of force, but it was not long before it was violated by Israel. True to its *fait accompli* policy, Israel attacked Egypt on 4 March 1949, and occupied the Negev all the way to the Gulf of Aqaba, on the Red Sea. The cease-fire was not restored until after Israel had completed its conquest, on 11 March 1949.

The United Nations established a Conciliation Commission composed of the United States, France and Turkey to seek a solution to the political problem of Palestine. The commission convened a conference in Lausanne, attended by the parties concerned, which began on 27 April 1949 and ended on 15 September 1949.

On 12 May 1949 the Arab countries, which had earlier rejected the Partition Resolution of 29 November 1947, 181 (II), accepted that resolution for the first time as a basis for negotiations in Lausanne with a view to reaching a political solution to the Palestine problem. In the course of the negotiations, Syria, under Hosni al-Zaim, and Hashemite Iraq agreed to receive 300,000 and 350,000 Palestinian refugees respectively and integrate them into their populations, this Syrian-Iraqi proposal being linked to the acceptance by Israel of the implementation of the Partition Resolution. Israel refused, and countered with a proposal that 45,000 Palestinians be repatriated, in addition to the 55,000 who had already returned by infiltration or through a process of family reunification. It also proposed the creation of a Palestinian state in the West Bank under Israeli control. The Arabs refused and proposed a solution predicated on the territorial continuity of the Arab world. This proposal was in turn rejected by Israel. It should be pointed out that the Palestinians were not invited by the Conciliation Commission to participate in its work.

The conference failed as a result of Israel's refusal to apply the United Nations resolutions concerning the partition of Palestine and the settlement of the Palestinian refugee problem (Resolutions 181 and 194) and the Arab countries' refusal to agree to the Israeli proposals.

The commission convened a second conference in September 1951, in Paris. This in turn came to nothing, owing to Israel's demand for 'recognition of territorial and human *faits accomplis*'—equivalent to a refusal to apply the United Nations resolutions. Since the failure of the Paris conference, none of the parties concerned has asked for the Conciliation Commission to be reconvened, despite the renewal of its mandate by the United Nations. The Paris conference was the last attempt, therefore, to settle the Palestinian problem through the agency of this commission, which Israel demanded be replaced by a United Nations good-offices committee—a proposal put forward by Israel to justify its rejection of any equitable solution.

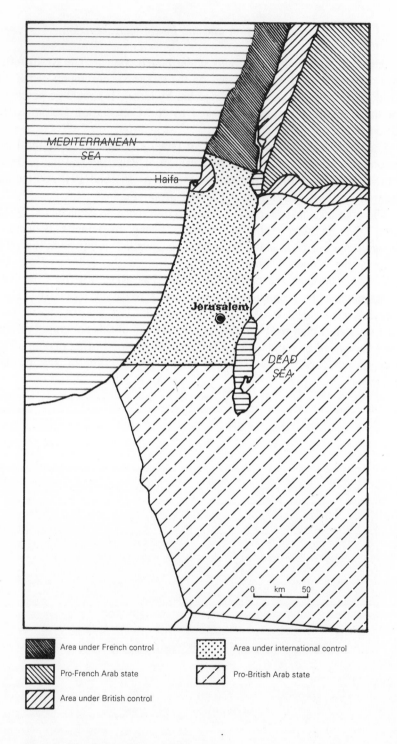

Map 3. The Sykes-Picot Agreement

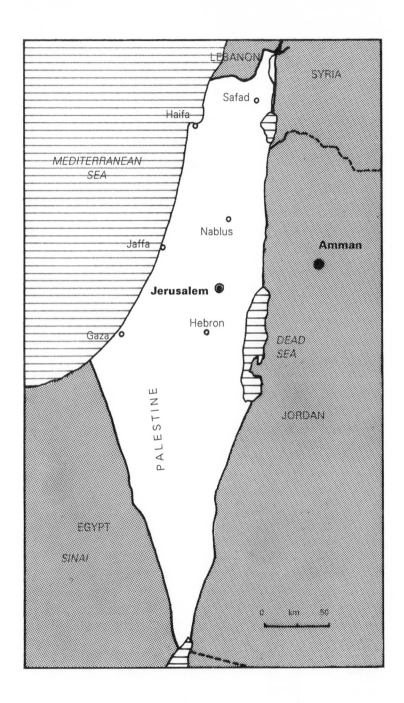

Map 4. Palestine under British Mandate

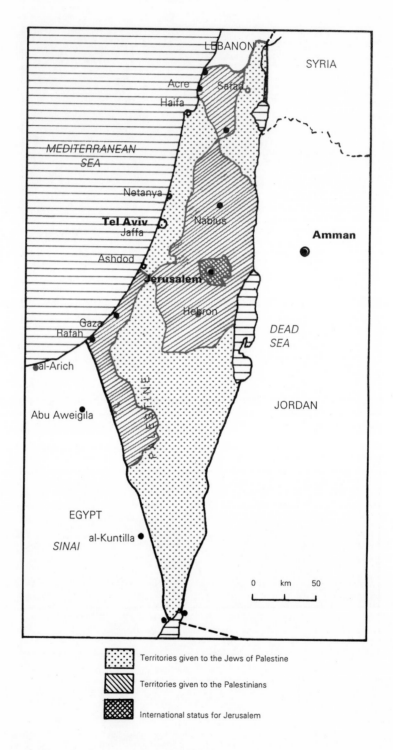

LEBANON

SYRIA

Acre

Safad

Haifa

*MEDITERRANEAN
SEA*

Netanya

Tel Aviv
Jaffa

Nablus

Amman

Ashdod

Jerusalem

Hebron

*DEAD
SEA*

Gaza
Rafah

P A L E S T I N E

JORDAN

al-Arich

Abu Aweigila

EGYPT

SINAI

al-Kuntilla

0   km   50

Territories given to the Jews of Palestine

Territories given to the Palestinians

International status for Jerusalem

Map 5. The Partition Plan (1947)

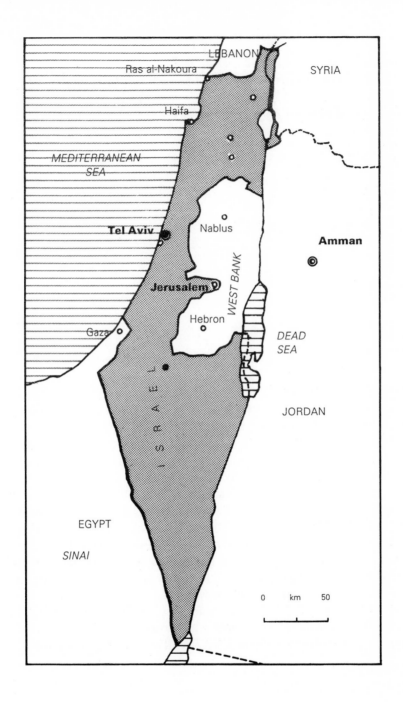

Map 6. Israel after the 1948–1949 War

6

From the 'Right of Return' to the 'Bridge of Return'

After the 1948–1949 War, dubbed the *nakba* ('disaster') by the Arabs—in which Israel conquered 77 per cent of the surface area of Palestine while destroying 416 Palestinian towns and villages—60 per cent of the Palestinian people became refugees. The name 'Palestine' was struck off the map of the world to be replaced by the designations 'Israel', 'the West Bank' and 'the Gaza Strip'. Palestinian citizenship and the Palestinian passport, which had been recognized since 1925, ceased to exist. The Palestinians' material losses were estimated by the United Nations in 1951 at around P£120 million (Palestinian pounds sterling)[1] while the Palestinians themselves assessed their losses in 1965, in terms of fixed and movable assets, industrial property and potential profits therefrom, at $300 billion. The Palestinian and UN estimates do not take account of the physical and psychological harm inflicted on the entire Palestinian people. Such estimates need to be reassessed today on the basis of present economic circumstances.

In 1948 and 1949 it was the Arab host countries, non-governmental charity organizations and the Vatican which extended relief to the Palestinian refugees before the creation of UNRWA (The United Nations Relief and Works Agency for Palestine Refugees in the Near East). It was Resolution 302 (IV) of 8 December 1949 which provided for the creation of UNRWA. Having begun operating on 1 May 1950, it established that there were 940,000 such refugees. It defines a Palestinian refugee as having lost 'both home and the means of existence'. This definition led to the creation of two further categories of refugee: exiles and displaced persons. These categories were excluded from those benefiting from UNRWA provisions and consequently deprived of relief assistance. According to Abdallah Frangi,[2] UNRWA only recognizes 52 per cent of all refugees as actually being refugees.

Palestinian refugees are also victims of exclusion twice over: they do not depend on the United Nations High Commissioner for Refugees (UNHCR), and therefore do not benefit from the legal status conferred by the Convention on the Status of Refugees. As for UNRWA, it is not authorized to accord them such status as its mission is confined to providing them with relief in kind.

The attitudes of the Arab host countries vary. Thus, in Jordan, the Palestinian refugees are allowed to benefit from Jordanian nationality, whereas in the Gaza Strip they were initially administered by an Egyptian military governor and subsequently by a civil one, and use Egyptian travel documents. Syria, for its part, has granted Palestinian refugees the same rights as those enjoyed by its nationals, with the exception of political rights; they, too, benefit from Syrian travel documents. In Lebanon, the refugees are subject to the regime applied to foreigners but with greater restrictions.[3]

Among the categories defined not as refugees but as exiles are the Palestinian bourgeoisie, or affluent classes. Such individuals managed to transfer their capital out of Palestine in time, before the war. For example, P£20 million were transferred to Amman—a figure which exceeded the total amount of Jordanian money in circulation at that time. Many Palestinians—builders, entrepreneurs, bankers, doctors, lawyers, teachers and engineers—made their fortune in Lebanon, the Gulf states and elsewhere. They participate in economic, financial and social activities in the countries of the Arab Mashreq. Palestinians are present in strength in such well-known financial institutions as the Arab Bank, Intra-Bank and the al-Mashreq. Intra-Bank's collapse in Beirut for political reasons at the start of 1967, the tragic events known as Black September in 1970, the civil war in Lebanon beginning in 1975 and the persecution of the Palestinians after the 1991 Gulf War—all these events have led these Palestinians to the firm, irreversible conviction that their economic future, and more besides, can only be secure in an independent Palestinian state, thereby allying their concerns and aspirations with those of the refugees and forming a national consensus. This accounts for the Palestinian bourgeoisie's financial and political support for the Palestinian resistance.

In the political arena, the Arab Higher Committee convened a congress in Gaza on 30 September 1948 which set up a Palestinian government-in-exile for the whole of Palestine. The congress appointed Ahmad Helmi Pasha to head this pro-Egyptian government. King Abdallah reacted to the holding of the Gaza congress by refusing to recognize Helmi Pasha's Palestinian government and by convening in his turn a congress in Amman, on 1 October 1948, of notables and traditionalists who had previously been opposed to the authority of the Arab Higher Committee. This congress was followed by another, held in Jericho on 1 December 1948. The two congresses made an appeal for Palestinian-Jordanian unity. They 'unanimously' called for union of the two banks of the River Jordan. On 11 April 1950 elections were organized to elect a parliament. On 24 April 1950 the new Jordanian Assembly 'unanimously' adopted a declaration of 'union' between the two banks. Two states recognized this 'union': Britain and Pakistan.

The Council of the League of Arab States, which had recognized Helmi Pasha's government, reacted to this 'union' by deciding that the part of Palestine attached to Jordan would be deemed provisionally entrusted to it, pending independence, when it would be returned to Palestine. Helmi Pasha's government, which was completely isolated from the Palestinian people, failed to meet any of the conditions recognized by international law for it to exist and be considered representative.

The only token of its existence was the symbolic representation of Palestine in the League of Arab States. This symbol died on 29 June 1963 with the passing of its head, Helmi Pasha. From 19 September 1963 it was Ahmad Shuqeiri who represented Palestine at the Arab League in accordance with the resolution of 23 March 1945 on Palestinian representation to the Arab League.[4] As for the Arab Higher Committee, formed in 1936, it suffered the same fate with the death of its head, Hajj Amin al-Husseini, in 1974. There still remains, however, a symbolic office of the Arab Higher Committee in Riyadh, Saudi Arabia, headed by Moussa Abu Al Saud.

After the failure of the Conciliation Commission, the international community effectively shelved the political file   Palestine, reducing the question merely to a humanitarian refugee problem. This attitude, which overlooks the existence and political rights of the Palestinian people, was mirrored in the omission of the Palestinian question from the agenda of the United Nations General Assembly (14 October–21 December 1952).[5] From 1952 until 10 December 1969 Palestine was only mentioned in the UNRWA Commissioner-General's Annual Report.

It was not until 1974 that the Palestine question was put back on the agenda of the UN General Assembly. The Clapp Fact-Finding Mission, which submitted its report to the United Nations General Assembly on 6 November 1949, recommended implementation of an economic development programme in the host countries to find jobs for the refugees. This recommendation was repeated in Resolution 393 of 2 December 1950. The Palestinians opposed this plan lest their agreement be construed as a renunciation of the right of the refugees to return to their homes in Palestine and as eliminating the substantive problem of their political rights as a people and of the preservation of their cultural and national identity.

UNRWA's activities focused on three major programmes: distribution of staple foodstuffs; preventive medical care and treatment administered in co-operation with WHO; and general education and vocational training (accounting for 45 per cent of resources) with the technical assistance of UNESCO. UNRWA again submitted several projects for Palestinian refugee integration in the host countries between 1952 and 1954, all of which foundered. Between 1953 and 1955 the US Secretary of State, John Foster Dulles, sent Eric Johnston to the region four times as President Eisenhower's special envoy in order to attempt to integrate the refugees by developing the tributaries of the River Jordan through co-operation between the Arab states and Israel. The declared aim was to safeguard the economic development of the region, but the Palestinians viewed the plan as another attempt to integrate the Palestinian refugees into the Arab host countries and thereby assimilate them. Wary of such plans, the Arab and Palestinian masses opposed them with demonstrations, telegrams of protest, petitions and events which culminated in riots in March 1955. The Americans' plans came to nothing. The last integration project with the same objectives was submitted, to no effect, by the United Nations Secretary-General, Dag Hammarskjold, on 15 June 1959.

The failure of all these plans stems from historical, socio-cultural and economic factors which may usefully be stated and explored. They can be categorized in two ways. First, the Palestinian people, as has been explained throughout their long history, have constituted a community whose components have always, notwithstanding their diversity, lived together in a society organized and cemented by their common traditions and aspirations. This people's attachment to its land and its development in freedom and independence, which have always been unifying factors, only strengthened the Palestinians' sense of belonging to a close-knit community sharing the same destiny.

Second, the political and socio-economic structures of the Arab host countries were not conducive to the integration of the Palestinians. The different level of cultural and social development between Palestinians and the indigenous population in some countries might have seriously disrupted the cohesion of their societies. Other, newly independent countries feared that the stability of their infant and fragile institutions might be jeopardized by the integration of a large number of refugees unfamiliar with structures which had been devised and set up to meet the particular needs of these host countries. If one adds to all these factors economic circumstances which hampered integration on such a scale (the effect on the employment of nationals and urban structures, for example), one can readily appreciate the severe and diverse difficulties these countries would face.

The security problems referred to in these countries, arising from the presence and movement of masses of refugees, further compounded the difficulty of resolving this problem along the lines advocated by the initiators of the unsuccessful integration projects who, wilfully or otherwise, failed to take account of such factors.

The consequences of the 1991 Gulf War for the Palestinians bear witness to these attitudes. In analysing these failures, some West Europeans and Americans sought to view them as evidence of the Arab nation's incapability of achieving union. In point of fact, these detractors forget that it was the West, especially after the dismantling of the Ottoman Empire, which introduced the Mashreq region to the notion and model of the nation state in order to prevent such union. It runs counter to one's own strategy to seek to integrate into any community of this region one or several components of another, even if they are linked by language, religion and history. In the Arab Mashreq, the failed attempts at union, still fresh in people's minds, stemmed more from imbalances in the exercise of power, especially as a result of political ambitions, than from the economic, social and cultural diversity of the peoples involved.

As far as the Palestinians were concerned, it is true to this day that the aim was not to achieve union with them but to absorb them fully, which is tantamount to the denial of their existence as a people and the destruction of their national and cultural identity. This explains the Palestinians' opposition to such integration and not their rejection of union with the other Arab peoples. The renewed questioning in Eastern Europe of abortive attempts to absorb and assimilate certain peoples or minorities confirms the accuracy and relevance of this analysis. The doomed attempts to absorb the Poles between 1772 and 1918 and the Balts in 1939 are typical examples of the futility of such an assimilationist policy, pursued for ideological or political motives. Neither pan-Arabism nor pan-Islamism will succeed in absorbing the Palestinians.

With respect to the problem of Palestinian refugees, people who have lived in camps during wartime, especially the Second World War, are well aware of the deep physical and psychological suffering endured by those confined to such camps as prisoners or refugees. The magnitude of such suffering is even greater when tens of thousands of men, women, children and the elderly, who had previously inhabited whole towns and cities, then find themselves condemned for about half a century to languish in camps of despair which the international community still tolerates on the eve of the third millennium.

Dreams and disillusionment, nostalgia and hope blend in the subconscious of the uprooted Palestinian refugees whose lives have unravelled and who withdraw into themselves to rediscover a childhood memory or to recall their home, their village, their field, their town, their freedom, even the sky of their youth. Such anguish and states of mind inspired some Palestinians to convey their feelings, pain and hopes through prose or poetry. Despite their sufferings, the Palestinian refugees considered these camps to be their homeland-in-exile, in which they would forge the resolve to resist and to free themselves from the yoke of exile. Their paramount wish was to return to Palestine. Yet this return necessitated a search for appropriate methods of achieving it. Hence they sought a strategy and an ideology on the basis of what existed in the Arab and Islamic world and upon which they relied: pan-Islamism (the Muslim Brotherhood or the Islamic liberation parties), pan-Arabism (the Baath and Arab Nationalist parties and Nasserism) or, globally, the Communist movement. The Palestinians were soon to be disabused, however, because of the failure of these parties to present a coherent and relevant political programme. They increasingly realized the need to rely on their own efforts.

Thus, after Israel occupied the Gaza Strip in 1956–57, the Palestinians developed a true political awareness of the need to move to armed struggle, inspired by that of the African, Algerian, Vietnamese, Cuban and Yemeni peoples.[6] The political means was spawned with the creation in Gaza, in 1957, of the Palestinian national liberation movement, Fatah, and, since 1959, with its publication entitled *Our Palestine*. Fatah's political programme comprised the following main objectives: achieving the renaissance of the Palestinian entity as the resistance's point of departure; relying on its own means, with the support of friends throughout the Arab world and other countries; a call for armed resistance, for a long-term popular war; and the creation of a secular, democratic state, in which Jews, Christians and Muslims would live together, to be inspired by the pluralist and tolerant history of the Palestinians. Fatah's slogan could be summed up in the words: no to tutelage, no to dependence, no to being politically hijacked by other states.

After the creation of the politico-military organization Fatah, which operated clandestinely until 1968, another important movement came into being. This was the General Union of Palestinian Students (GUPS), set up in November 1959, which brought together the various student associations from Cairo, Alexandria, Damascus, Beirut and other cities. This movement was the first autonomous Palestinian national institution.

Palestinian patriots from Arab minorities then set up in Israel itself the Palestinian movement entitled al-Ard (The Earth). This movement was created in order to demand the return of Palestinian peasants' lands confiscated by the Israeli authorities. The movement's second purpose was to make socio-economic and political demands. Israel outlawed this movement and banned its activities in 1964.

The Arab nationalists created other movements or parties, such as the Palestinian branch of the Baath, the Nasserist Arab National Union and the Arab Nationalist Movement formed by Georges Habash in 1951. To a pan-Arabist, the liberation of Palestine requires Arab unity, whereas Fatah considers that Arab unity requires the liberation of Palestine, since one cannot put the cart before the horse. These events and the evolving geopolitical situation of the Palestinians contribute to a better understanding of Palestine's modern history as it relates to the Arab world and the international environment.

7
The Palestine Liberation Organization

At the start of the 1960s, two major events vindicated the political stance of Fatah: the collapse of the union between Egypt and Syria in 1961 (United Arab Republic, 1958–61), followed by Algeria's independence in 1962. The upsurge in Palestinian nationalism was a source of concern to some regimes, who considered it to be a threat to the security and political stability of the Middle East. These regimes were seeking ways of bringing the various Palestinian political movements under their wing so as to prevent them from triggering an unprepared war with Israel. This would have placed them in a hazardous situation, given the unequal balance of forces favouring Israel, especially as Egypt had pledged—after the Suez crisis of 1956 and in exchange for Israeli withdrawal from Sinai and Gaza—'not to initiate hostilities against Israel and to prevent Palestinian attacks from its territory' for a period of ten years.[1]

At the end of 1963 Israel unilaterally proceeded to divert the waters of the Jordan to the Negev. Nasser called an Arab Summit, which convened in Cairo from 13 to 16 January 1964—the second such meeting following that held in Inshass, also in Egypt, on 27 May 1946. The Inshass Summit had met in order to take measures to deal with Jewish immigration and land confiscation, and to advocate Palestine's independence. The second summit, held in Cairo, took three decisions to confront the situation, one of which gave the Palestinians the green light to set up a political organization to enable their people to play a part in liberating Palestine and in determining their future. This organization was called upon to assert the Palestinian entity in the eyes of the international community while being placed under the auspices of the League of Arab States, which would take care of its financial needs.

The Arab Summit entrusted Ahmad Shuqeiri, as Palestine's representative to the Arab League, with the implementation of this resolution. Pursuant to his mandate, Shuqeiri drew up the texts creating this political organization, which was called the Palestine Liberation Organization. In setting up its structures, he took account of sometimes contradictory factors: bringing together in one political organization Palestinians from a diaspora which spanned several Arab countries (hence the need, in his view, to take varying sensitivities into account) and creating a political body and a conventional, albeit revolutionary, army whose structures and strategy were modelled on the Algerian National Liberation Front (FLN) and Liberation Army.

At the third Arab Summit of 5–11 September 1964, the heads of state unanimously approved the creation of the PLO as the representative of the Palestinian people. The PLO charter, drafted by an *ad hoc* group under Shuqeiri's auspices and largely inspired by pan-Arab ideology, bears the stamp of the dominant aspect of Shuqeiri's personality as an eminent lawyer more than as a politician.

From 28 May to 2 June 1964 Shuqeiri convened the first Palestinian National Congress. Saint-Prost has written in this connection:

> Four months later [i.e. after the Arab Summit] 422 Palestinians, delegated by different communities of the diaspora, met in East Jerusalem as the Palestine National Council. The PNC, inaugurated on 28 May 1964 by King Hussein of Jordan, approved without debate a Palestinian national charter and the constituent statutes of the PLO. Subsequently, Ahmad Shuqeiri was elected Chairman of the Executive Committee, whose headquarters were located in Cairo. A national fund was to finance the PLO's activities.[2]

Shuqeiri created the Palestine Liberation Army, whose contingents depended upon the Arab governments of the Mashreq.

After the June 1967 War and the Arab defeat, Shuqeiri was discredited and he resigned under pressure on 24 December 1967. The Palestine National Council (PNC), meeting for its fourth session, from 10 to 17 July 1968 in Cairo, replaced Shuqeiri by appointing Yahia Hammoudeh to head the PLO. He then amended the 1964 charter to take account of the new circumstances arising from the appearance on the political scene (after the battle of Karameh of 21 March 1968) of the then clandestine organizations of the Palestinian resistance. The amendments stemmed from the conditions set by these organizations upon their entry into the PLO, which was originally made up of Palestinian individuals who represented socio-economic rather than political currents.

It was at the fifth session of the PNC, held in Cairo from 1 to 4 February 1969, that the political and military organizations of the Palestinian resistance as such joined the PLO, whose former members have since become known as 'Independents'. At the end of the session, the PNC elected Yasser Arafat, then spokesman of Fatah, as Chairman of the PLO Executive Committee in place of Yahia Hammoudeh.

It is important to emphasize three important provisions among the amendments made to the charter, which fill a void in the first text and reflect Fatah's views. These were: the rejection of any form of intervention, patronage or dependence *vis-à-vis* the Arab countries; the assertion of the Palestinian people's sovereignty over its land and its right to self-determination; and armed struggle as a strategy to liberate Palestine.

The 1964 PLO charter has given rise to much controversy, some of it as a result of ill-intentioned attempts to present its contents as a declaration of permanent war, some indicating a failure to understand its spirit and historical, political and legal scope. One cannot appraise the charter's contents without taking into account three principal factors: the national or domestic situation of Palestine; the regional political context; and, internationally, the historic nature of the decolonization process of the 1960s.

The first factor is dominated by the Palestinians' legitimate response to Zionist ideology and strategy as defined and adopted at the Basle Congress (1897) and at Biltmore (1942), as well as to the 1917 Balfour Declaration. The Zionists' claim, based on historical and religious myth, that Palestine belonged to the Jewish descendants of the Hebrews provoked the PLO charter's legitimate response that Palestine had been inhabited for thousands of years by the Palestinians and that it was their homeland, to which they were bound by inextricable ties and inalienable rights. It is not surprising that the charter contains many provisions which, in reaffirming these rights, refute the Zionists' claims, analysed at length in Part I of this study. The charter was, therefore, more a legal response than a political one.

The domestic factor stemmed from the Palestinians' collective psychology. Arab statements have always presented Israel as an exclusive military stronghold at the service of the West, which has diverted the Palestinians' attention from the true nature of the occupiers: that of a new society with far-reaching implications and designs, which has occupied a territory after having driven out the people who lived there. Hence, the attitude of the Palestinian resistance from 1965 to 1974 was to consider each Israeli as a soldier, thus legitimizing its actions. These activities took two forms: guerrilla actions against the Israeli army and economic centres, and attacks on civilians. The most spectacular examples of the latter were aeroplane hijackings (July 1968) and the attack on Israeli athletes at the Munich Olympics (5 September 1972), which were modelled on similar terrorist attacks carried out by the Zionist organizations in Palestine in the 1930s and 1940s.

This collective psychology influenced the charter and the Palestinian resistance and, in the minds of the Palestinian people, was conveyed by a refusal to acknowledge the Israelis and by a dedication to the Palestine of the past. The Palestinians lived nostalgically for a return to their pre-1948 Palestine, to their houses (whose keys they still kept), to their towns, villages and fields, as if nothing had changed. Incidentally, the Zionist movement made use of this phenomenon of collective psychology to mislead the Jews by presenting Palestine as a land which had been empty for 2,000 years, merely awaiting their return. Thus, the Zionist charter considered Palestine to be a *terra nulliers*, a land ungoverned and uninhabited since Titus destroyed Herod's Temple in the year AD 70. It can be seen as a reaction, after an interval of some 2,000 years, to the Roman Empire.

The Palestinian charter, however, only goes back as far as 1947 and refers, on the one hand, to the prior legal situation of a territory inhabited by the Palestinian people and, on the other, to the major political event of Palestine's partition, the implications of which have been ignored. The charter is a reaction to an ideology but it fails to take account of the Israeli presence, just as the Zionist charter did not take the existence of the Palestinian people into consideration. Demanding that the Palestinian charter be declared null and void is inconceivable if the same demand is not made of the Zionist charter.

In the Arab regional environment, the charter's authors were influenced by the dominant pan-Arabism and Nasserism of the 1950s and 1960s, whose priority was to attain the unity of the Arab nation. Any other course, especially nationalism, was not only considered doomed to failure but, above all, was thought to renounce a fundamental principle, which might expose its supporters to political isolation, if not social ostracism. The military option, in a united Arab setting, was deemed to be the only way of meeting the challenge thrown down by the Zionists.

In the international arena, the accession to independence in the 1960s of many countries, as they emerged from colonial darkness after a lengthy armed struggle for liberation, also left its mark on the strategy defined by the 1964 charter. The Palestinians' attachment to the land of their forefathers and nostalgia for a past marked by glorious historical phases could not but influence the charter's philosophy. The military option was considered to be dominant at the time and was also fostered by East-West tensions.

Some people, criticizing in good faith but influenced by Israeli propaganda, admit the impact of these factors while considering that the charter did not take account of fresh events after 1948. These had transformed the political and demographic landscape of Palestine, with the settlement of a large Jewish society and the decision adopted by the United Nations General Assembly in 1947 to partition the country into two states. Such critics assert, as a consequence, that the principles and affirmations set forth in the charter are much more relevant to the situation which existed between 1917 and 1947 than to that after 1947, and that this static position of the Palestinians did not take account of prevailing realities. Yet Yasser Arafat appealed, in his speech to the United Nations General Assembly on 13 November 1974, to all Israel's Jews to agree to live together with the Palestinians in a united, democratic and secular state.

These same commentators have levelled no criticism at the Zionist charter, which quite simply denies the Palestinian people's right to exist and to live on their land. Taken to their extreme, these criticisms hold the Palestinians responsible for not wanting or not being able to seize the opportunities to turn the situation to their advantage: dialogue on the basis of the Balfour Declaration (1917), which at the time only sought to create a Jewish home in Palestine; the decision to partition Palestine into two states—one Arab, the other Jewish (1947); the Rogers Plan (1970), which proposed the implementation of Security Council Resolution 242 (1967); the 1973 Geneva conference, in which the Palestinians refused to participate; and finally the Camp David Accords (1978), in which the Palestinians had the chance to take full part as protagonists on an equal footing with the other parties.

This overlooks the fact that the Palestinians were excluded from such 'opportunities'. They are ultimately blamed for having practised an 'empty chair' policy which has only encouraged Israel's policy of expansionism to the detriment of the fundamental rights of the Palestinians, thus placing them in an increasingly unfavourable situation as time passed and each opportunity was missed. It cannot have escaped the critics' attention that the 1964 charter has not gone unaltered and that major political events have led to its updating through numerous declarations and decisions of the Palestine National Council, especially those which propounded the concept of a multi-confessional democratic state (5th session of the PNC, February 1969), the outline of the two-states-in-Palestine concept (12th session of the PNC, June 1974), and the gradual transition from a military to a political strategy to

165

resolve the Palestinian question (see Part IV).

This evolving process can also be found in the attitude taken by the Arab countries to the Palestinian problem during successive summits. It culminated in the proclamation of the state of Palestine and the adoption of its political programme at the 19th session of the PNC in Algiers (November 1988). These exceptionally important steps marked a historic turning-point in Palestinian strategy and policy. The Algiers peace initiative, enshrined in the political programme, was the beginning of an irreversible process intended to replace a 'logic of war' with a 'logic of peace', whose implementation began with the holding of the Madrid peace conference (30 October–3 November 1991).

Following this examination of the various aspects of the 1964 charter and its 1968 amendment, it would now be worth stating the various constituents of this new political factor in the Middle East, the PLO. It is an entity characterized by its political diversity. The organizations of the Palestinian resistance which form its nucleus may at times differ on the ways and means of achieving the ultimate goal, but they all agree on a common purpose: the liberation and independence of Palestine. The history of other peoples who once fought for their liberation affords many similar examples.

The main organizations of the Palestinian resistance, other than *Fatah*, are: the *Popular Front for the Liberation of Palestine* (PFLP), created in November 1967 and led by Georges Habash, a doctor (the PFLP emerged from the Arab Nationalist Movement—ANM); the *Democratic Front for the Liberation of Palestine* (DFLP), created after dissension within the PFLP in February 1969, and led by Naif Hawatmeh, a teacher; the *Popular Front for the Liberation of Palestine–General Command* (PFLP–GC), created after dissension within the PFLP in 1968, led by Ahmad Jibril, and an essentially pro-Libyan and pro-Syrian military organization; *Saiqa*, created in the autumn of 1967 by the Syrian Baath; the *Arab Liberation Front* (ALF), created in April 1969 by the Iraqi Baath; the *Palestine Liberation Front* (PLF), created in 1977 after a split within the PFLP–GC and led by a pro-Iraqi, Abul-Abbas, and a pro-Syrian, Taalat Yakub; and the *Palestinian Popular Struggle Front* (PPSF), a small organization created in 1968 and led by a pro-Syrian, Samir Ghoshy.

The control exercised by the politico-military organizations over the PLO from 1969 transformed its political image and enabled it to break free from its dependence on a number of Arab regimes, thereby becoming a political organization with its own personality, which could identify with the will and aspirations of the Palestinian people and take sovereign decisions as the

Algerian FLN had done. The Palestinian resistance's popularity among the Arab masses after their successes against Israeli enemy forces, especially the battle of Karameh in 1968, only increased the distrust and anxiety of certain Arab regimes, since they were gravely concerned that the armed conflict with Israel might spread. This radical change led to political and military crises which brought the PLO into confrontation with certain Arab host countries.

The bloody clashes in Jordan (November 1968 and September 1970) and in Lebanon (from 1969 to 1973) confirmed the correctness of the PLO's decision to revise its strategy, and led the organization to rethink its relations with the leaders of a number of Arab countries, thus causing a deep crisis. The forced departure of Palestinian fighters from Jordan (1971) and the beginning of civil war in Lebanon (1975–76) reduced their offensive capability and weakened the strategy of popular war, valiantly fought by the Palestinian *fedayeen*.

In drawing lessons from the Jordanian experience and the October 1973 War, the PLO, especially Fatah, decided to diversify its strategy by opting from 1974 for political and military action and the integration of the *fedayeen* into a conventional army. The PNC consequently decided, at its 12th session (1974), to prohibit any military action outside the occupied Palestinian territories. All subsequent terrorist actions have been carried out in violation of this decision by Palestinian dissidents, elements or organizations acting on orders from certain political regimes in the region.

The establishment of this new strategy, decided upon by the PLO in 1974, was accompanied by the creation of state structures: political, economic, social, trade union, cultural, health and military institutions (for more details, see Part IV). It is interesting to note that these Palestinian institutions of state were, to a large extent, inspired by the state structures created by the Jewish Agency in the 1930s and 1940s.

In order to foil the PLO's new strategy, which was thought to pose a serious threat to Israel's security, the Israelis invaded south Lebanon on 14 March 1978. The semi-conventional War of 1978 fought between the army of Palestinian fighters and the Israeli army lasted eight days. Israel occupied south Lebanon as far as the Litani River, thus creating an area of 5–10 km which it called a 'security zone'; its command was entrusted to Israel's factotum, Saad Haddad (replaced after his death in 1984 by Antoine Lahad). In its Resolution 425 of 19 March 1978, the Security Council denounced the Israeli agression and decided to send a UNIFIL (United Nations Interim Force in Lebanon) force to ensure that the Israeli forces withdrew.

On 10 July 1981 a second conflict broke out between the Palestinians and the Israeli army. It lasted two weeks and ended in the Palestinians' favour, as Israel failed to achieve its objectives.

In 1982 Israel launched an all-out war against the Palestinians based in Lebanon with attacks by land, sea and air. Beirut and the Palestinian military bases were subjected to an intense aerial bombardment on 4 and 5 June 1982, followed by the invasion of part of Lebanon's territory. This conflict, the longest in the region since the occupation of Palestine in 1948, lasted some three months, during which the Palestinian fighters, alone at the front, displayed exceptional courage and resistance, inflicting heavy losses on their enemy in spite of its superiority in modern weaponry. The US envoy, Philip Habib, managed to secure a cease-fire between the two belligerents on 13 August 1982. The Palestinian fighters left Beirut between 21 August and 3 September 1982.

Such heroic actions were only partially tarnished by the dissension which broke out within Fatah at the instigation of external forces and which gave rise to inter-Palestinian clashes. Having begun on 8 May 1983, this fratricidal struggle ended on 19 December 1983 with the departure from Tripoli (Lebanon) of those fighters who had remained loyal to Fatah, thanks to France and Egypt's intervention in facilitating their withdrawal. The latent conflict, interspersed with tragic episodes, which set Palestinian fighters against other forces on Lebanese soil reached its conclusion in the summer of 1991 when the Palestinians handed over their heavy armaments to the Lebanese army so that it could deploy in the south of the country, in accordance with the Taif Accords of 22 October 1989.

Thus was turned an important page in the history of Palestinian resistance to an implacable enemy, the Israeli army; a struggle rendered more arduous by a settling of scores between the Arab parties and by covert ambitions. Faced with the indifference of international decision-makers, forsaken, not to say spurned, by some erstwhile brothers, wrongly implicated in the grave events which convulsed the Gulf region in 1990 and 1991, the PLO refined its political and military strategy in order to adapt to the changing international political situation. The stated priority of the times—the peaceful settlement of all regional conflicts—was consonant with the PLO's main demand: the solution of the Palestinian question.

With the start of the Madrid peace process, at which PLO endorsement of the Palestinian negotiators from the occupied territories was essential, the organization gradually abandoned the arena of armed struggle to those who opposed the talks. In the absence of real progress towards a settlement of the conflict, however, the PLO had nothing tangible to offer the Palestinian people. This situation spawned disagreements among the various organizations of the PLO, in whose ranks three conflicting trends emerged at the Palestine Central Council meeting held in Tunis from 15 to 17 October

1992. Those favouring the unreserved continuation of Palestinian participation were represented by Mahmoud Abbas (Abu Mazen), a member of the PLO Executive Committee and of the Fatah Central Council. The second tendency was represented by Georges Habash's PFLP, Naif Hawatmeh's DFLP, the PLF and the PPSF. They demanded withdrawal from the negotiations and a reversion to the UN for a settlement of the Palestinian question, and enjoyed the support of Hamas, Ahmad Jibril's PFLP-GC, the Fatah–Abu Musa faction, Islamic Jihad in Palestine, Saiqa and the Arabi Awad Revolutionary Communist Party—most of whom had their headquarters in Damascus. Their avowed aim was to foil the plan for Palestinian autonomy since it was intended to 'consecrate the occupation, eradicate the *intifada*, settle the refugees in the Arab countries, destroy the unity of the Palestinian people and its national rights, and normalize Arab-Israeli relations while ensuring Israeli supremacy', according to a communiqué published in Damascus on 24 October 1992.

The rejectionists went on to assert that 'the Palestinian delegation does not represent the Palestinian people' and consequently 'cannot sign an agreement on its behalf'. The majority view—the realistic, critical trend represented by Arafat—supported the peace process but, while advocating continued participation in the talks for want of any viable alternative, it warned of the dangers of the Americans' exclusive position in the Middle East and called upon the Arab states to work for meaningful European involvement. The procrastination of 1992, owing to the Israeli general elections and the presidential elections in the United States, prevented any tangible progress in the peace talks and only served to enhance considerably the rise of the Islamic resistance movement in the occupied Palestinian territories.

Religious Fundamentalism

The Muslim Brotherhood, with the 're-Islamization' of Palestinian society as their prime objective outweighing the struggle against the occupation, were considered unpatriotic and devoid of political legitimacy, especially since some of their 'shock troops' had been involved in clashes with members of the secular PLO. In the eyes of many Palestinians, they were simply manipulated by the Israelis to fragment Palestinian society. Israeli leaders saw fit to turn a blind eye to the Islamists' activities in order to keep the PLO in check.

Between 1967 and 1987 the Muslim Brotherhood refrained from any anti-Israeli activity. Their Jama'a Islamiya ('Islamic Collective'), a group of nonprofit-making associations—the most important of which was created by Shaikh Ahmad Yassin in 1978—confined its aims to the social, cultural and religious fields. It was not until 14 December 1987 that the Muslim Brotherhood changed not only its name but also its aims and methods when the start of the *intifada* prompted Shaikh Yassin to found the Islamic resistance movement ('Hamas' in its abbreviated Arabic form) in Gaza.

Islamic Jihad managed to reconcile religion and patriotism by advancing the notion that Israeli occupation would thwart any attempt at re-Islamization. The way was thus opened for Islamism to secure political legitimacy. Islamic Jihad also played an important role in the process which culminated in the *intifada*. It failed, however, in its attempts to expand organizationally because of Israeli oppression on the one hand and its decision to operate in small cells on the other.

As for Shaikh Yassin, by creating Hamas through a marriage of patriotic mobilization and religious discourse, he was able to break with the quiescence of the past. As early as the summer of 1988, Hamas had become a key player in Palestinian politics and the main focus of organized opposition to the PLO. While actively resisting the occupation from the earliest days of the *intifada*, Hamas only began to experience Israeli repression in the spring of 1989. Israel finally declared it an illegal organization in September 1989.

Hamas became the vehicle of the political and religious radicalism advocated by Palestinian traditionalists close to Jordan as well as by the militant and the disgruntled. Thanks to its virtual silence over the Gulf War, Hamas retained its funding from the Gulf states and Iran. It opposed the peace talks because it considered that the whole of historical Palestine should be reunified and governed by a Sunni Muslim regime which would protect the followers of other creeds. Its strongholds were in the Gaza Strip and certain areas of the West Bank, where its rivalry with the PLO became manifest in 33 elections to professional organizations held in 1992 (it won 5 seats to the PLO's 28). Before it could join the PLO, two principal conditions had to be met: an end to Palestinian participation in the peace talks, and 40 per cent of the seats in the Palestine National Council—a price deemed exorbitant by the PLO.

Hamas accused the PLO of selling out Palestine while the PLO responded with the charge that Hamas was executing purported 'collaborators'—a practice condemned by the PLO since it divided Palestinians and debilitated the *intifada*, especially as many of those killed were the victims of mistaken identity. Fatah's differences with Hamas over the peace process brought the militants of the two sides into bloody conflict in the Gaza Strip in the spring and summer of 1992. An 'honourable truce' was eventually concluded, by which the two would resolve their differences through dialogue. Several meetings between their officials have since taken place in Sanaa, Amman, Tunis, Khartoum and the occupied territories. Logically, their increasingly frequent encounters should culminate in an agreement on the conditions governing Hamas' entry into the PLO or at least its alliance with the PLO's structures and organizations.

The *intifada* has certainly helped to confer patriotic legitimacy on Hamas and Islamic Jihad. Israel's deportation of 413 Palestinians to south Lebanon on 17 December 1992, in retaliation for Hamas' abduction and murder of an Israeli soldier four days earlier (in an attempt to secure the release of their leader, Shaikh Yassin, who had been sentenced to life imprisonment in October 1991), was a further violation of the 4th Geneva Convention of 1949. Israel's indiscriminate expulsions of intellectuals, ideologues, university academics and teachers, students, engineers, doctors and imams—the latter viewed as the brains behind the Islamists—could only inflame extremism among fundamentalists and Jews alike. If Rabin was seeking to create a spurious rift between the PLO and Hamas, the opposite actually happened. Whatever his intentions in expelling the 413 Palestinians, he contributed to Arab and international recognition of the Palestinian Islamists as a legitimate political force. This political legitimization of the Palestinian fundamentalists should facilitate the entry of Hamas and Islamic Jihad into the PLO—a necessary precondition if they are to be kept under control, especially as the Palestinian negotiators enjoy very limited leeway in the face of opponents who now have sufficient legitimacy to take over the reins if the peace process does not swiftly bear fruit.

8
Some Key Events

The political and strategic evolution of the PLO has not been dictated by international events alone. It is above all the reflection of the Palestinian people's aspirations, of its unshakeable resolve to assert its identity and national rights. It is also the consequence of painful traumas and the tragedy experienced daily by the Palestinians, both in the occupied territories and abroad.

After the turmoil of 1948, the Palestinian people underwent an unparalleled upheaval: from being a majority in its own land, it was reduced in Israel to a minority community, whose members were accorded the nebulous and ambiguous description 'Israeli Arab', with the 'nomadic' connotation given by Zionist literature to the word 'Arab'. This was intended to sever any links the Palestinians had with their homeland and soil, and to justify, sooner or later, their expulsion to an Arab country, should regional or international circumstances so permit. The description 'Israeli Arab' has spawned an army of discriminatory measures, thus creating a second class of citizens in Israel.[1]

The West Bank Palestinians were considered Jordanians and, after 1967, were treated as Palestinian Arabs in 'Judaea and Samaria' (in other words, as non-citizens under Israeli occupation, given Israel's conflation of the notions 'Arab' and 'nomad' to justify land expropriation and, subsequently, their transfer to other places once circumstances permitted). A third category comprises those Palestinians who did not manage to obtain UNRWA refugee status and who are considered as 'tolerated residents' in the Arab world.

The Palestinian people, victims of dispossession of their property, of dispersion and of physical and psychological violence, also experienced the horror of massacres perpetrated by Israel and certain Arab regimes. For the record, we shall confine ourselves to citing a few of the most significant massacres: Deir Yassin in 1948 (for details, see above); Kibya (West Bank) in 1953: a horrifying massacre committed by the Israeli army, in which some 50 houses were blown up while their occupants were still inside, killing more than 70 innocent people; Nahalin in 1954 (committed by Israel); Gaza and Khan-Younis in 1955 (committed by Israel); Kafr Kassem in 1956 (committed by Israel); Amman in 1970 (committed by the Jordanian army); Tell al-Zaatar in 1976 (committed by the Lebanese Phalangists); Sabra and Shatilla, 16–18 September 1982 (massacres perpetrated by the Lebanese Forces' militias under the indulgent eye of the Israeli military, which left 1,000 Palestinians and Lebanese dead); Sabra and Shatilla *bis* and Bourj al-Barajneh in 1985–86 and 1987, when the inhabitants of the Sabra and Shatilla camps were compelled to request the permission of religious leaders to keep themselves from starvation by eating the flesh of the corpses (massacre committed by the Shi'ite Amal movement)—as for the three refugee camps situated in the Beirut suburbs, they were quite simply razed to the ground; the Israeli bombing on 1 October 1985 of the PLO's headquarters in Tunis, intended to assassinate Chairman Yasser Arafat, as part of Israel's vicious strategy of physically eliminating Palestinian officials; the butchery on the esplanade of the al-Aqsa Mosque on 8 October 1990 (perpetrated by the Israeli police); and the pogrom of Palestinians in Kuwait in 1991, and the expulsion or exodus of some 350,000 Palestinians from the country.

Mossad (the Israeli secret service) or agents of certain Arab regimes have assassinated: Ghassan Kanafani, a writer (in Beirut, 8 July 1972); Bassel al-Kubeisi, a PFLP leader (in Paris, 6 April 1973); three Palestinian leaders, Kamal Adwan, Yusef al-Najar and Kamal Nasser (in Beirut, on the night of 9–10 April 1973); Ali Hassan Salameh, a Fatah leader (in Beirut, 22 January 1979); Zuheir Mohsen, the head of Saiqa (in Cannes, 25 July 1979); Majed Abu Sharrar, a Fatah leader (in Rome, 9 October 1981); Abdel Wahab Kayyali, the head of the ALF (in Beirut, 7 December 1981); Saad Sayel, the chief of staff of the PLA (in Lebanon, 27 September 1982); Khalil al-Wazir (Abu Jihad), the second-in-command of Fatah (in Tunis, 15 April 1988); Salah Khalaf (Abu Iyad), the deputy leader of the PLO, Hayel Abdel Hamid (Abul Hol), a Fatah leader, and Muhammad al-Omari (Abu Muhammad) (in Tunis, 14 January 1991); and Atef Bseisso, one of the principal confidants of Abu Iyad.

Other assassinated Palestinian officials represented the PLO in individual countries. These included: Hussein Abul Kheir (Nicosia), Ali Yacine (Kuwait), Said Hammami (London), Khader (Brussels), Hamshari, Kalak, Dani, Hammad and Saleh (Paris), Wael Zaiter and Kamal Youssef (Rome) and Issam Sartawi, the PLO representative to the Socialist International (assassinated in Portugal).

Other major events in the political arena have left their mark on Palestine's destiny and given Palestinians hope in their homeland's future: the Summit of Arab Heads of State in Rabat in October 1974, at which the PLO was recognized as the sole legitimate representative of the Palestinian people; Yasser Arafat's speech on 13 November 1974 to the United Nations General Assembly, preceded by the meeting between Arafat and Jean Sauvagnargues, the French Foreign Minister, on 21 October 1974 (the first meeting between a leading Western politician and the Palestinian leader); the admission of the PLO, at the same General Assembly session, as observer at the UN and its specialized agencies; the outbreak of the *intifada* on 9 December 1987; the proclamation of the state of Palestine on 15 November 1988; the launching of the PLO–US dialogue on 16 December 1988; the official visit to Paris of Yasser Arafat at the invitation of President Mitterrand in May 1989 (during this visit, the Palestinian President declared the PLO charter to be '*caduque*';[2] and the Madrid peace conference (30 October–3 November 1991).

Other events have been adversely received by the Palestinians, such as: President Sadat's visit to Jerusalem on 19 November 1977; the signing of the Camp David Accords on 17 September 1978; the Israeli law of 9 September 1985, banning any contact between an Israeli and the PLO; and the consequences of Iraq's occupation of Kuwait on 2 August 1990, followed by the Gulf War from 17 January to 28 February 1991.

The first major event of 1992 was the assassination, on 16 February, of Shaikh Abbas Moussawi, the Secretary-General of the Lebanese Hizbollah, in an Israeli air ambush in south Lebanon. One month later, on 17 March, the Israeli embassy in Buenos Aires was blown up in a bomb attack claimed by Islamic Jihad. On the night of 7–8 April, Yasser Arafat emerged unscathed from an air crash near al-Sarrah in the middle of the Libyan desert. During the 15 hours when there was no news of the whereabouts of the missing aeroplane, reactions to his supposed death underlined the true importance of Arafat's place in the maintenance and continuation of the Middle East peace process.

After 15 years of right-wing government, Yitzhak Rabin's Labour Party won the Israeli general elections to the 13th Knesset in 1992. As for the *intifada*, it resurged as a popular uprising following the hunger strike of

5,000 Palestinian inmates in 20 Israeli goals from 30 September to 15 October. The strike triggered major demonstrations of solidarity which were brutally put down by the Israeli occupying army—11 Palestinian civilians died and 300 were wounded between 1 and 18 October 1992.

In Lebanon, Rafik Hariri became Prime Minister on 31 October, following the general elections (as stipulated in the Taif Accords) held on 23 and 30 August and 6 September. Most of the Maronite population boycotted the elections. Hariri formed a government mainly comprised of technocrats; its priority was to bring about Lebanon's economic recovery.

On 3 November 1992 the Democrat candidate, Bill Clinton, was elected 47th President of the United States, taking 43 per cent of the vote compared to the outgoing President George Bush's 38 per cent and the 19 per cent obtained by the independent Texas billionaire, Ross Perot. Soon after the election, Israel expelled the 413 Palestinians to south Lebanon.

Back in Israel itself, the start of 1993 saw the Knesset's repeal, on 15 January, of the law prohibiting any contact between Israelis and Palestinians who were members of the PLO.

To complete this overview of the modern history of Palestine, we should take a brief look at the situation in occupied Palestine (the West Bank and Gaza) as well as at the policy practised by Israel as the occupying power.

9

The Occupied West Bank and Gaza

Following the June 1967 War, Israel occupied the remainder of Palestine (the West Bank and Gaza), the Syrian Golan and Egyptian Sinai. The speed of the conquest limited the population exodus to around 400,000 people, 200,000 of whom were moved to Jordan on the orders of the Israeli Governor of the West Bank, Chaim Herzog (who subsequently became President of Israel until he was replaced, in March 1993, by the Labour candidate, General Ezer Weizman). In a statement reported by AFP,[1] the Israeli President acknowledged, on 8 November 1991, that after the 1967 War he had organized, as Governor of the West Bank, the departure of 200,000 Palestinians from the occupied territories to Jordan.

In the first years of the occupation, under the Labour governments of Levi Eshkol and Golda Meir, Israeli policy in the occupied Palestinian territories was relatively liberal: reunification of families separated by the 1967 exodus, and permission for people and goods to cross the River Jordan (the Open Bridges policy), for Palestinian universities to be established and for municipal elections to be held in 1972 and 1976. This policy became more stringent as the years of occupation passed.

The Israeli Labour government called the occupied territories 'administered' to justify their refusal to apply the 1949 Geneva Convention on the Protection of Civilians in Time of War and the 1954 Hague Convention on the Protection of Cultural Property in the Event of Armed Conflict. They removed Arab place-names, replacing them with 'biblical' names which were, in fact, Canaanite, Palestinian or Graeco-Roman names[2] recorded in the Bible—in other words, they were biblical and not Hebrew. Taking advantage of the ignorance of a public not conversant with the region's geography or history, Israel obfuscated by claiming that the origin of the names Samaria and Judaea was Hebrew. In actual fact, these names were given by the Romans to two regions situated in eastern Palestine: Samaria because of the existence of a settlement of that name, and Judaea after the name (Judah) of one of the 12 Jewish tribes. Israel's choice of these names stems from its wish to 'legitimize' the colonization of these territories through a subjective reading of Palestine's history. Other examples are 'Sechem', a name of Canaanite origin given to Nablus—a town the Romans knew as Neopolis—and 'Hebron', also of Canaanite origin, the name given to the city of al-Khalil.

In his book *The Bible Came from Arabia*,[3] the Lebanese historian Kamal Salibi makes the same mistakes when analysing the origin of Canaanite place-names (regions, towns and cities) mentioned in the Bible and considering them to be biblical, in other words Hebrew. It has, in fact, been historically and scientifically established that the Canaanites originated from the Arabian peninsula. Salibi merely confirms that they came from the Red Sea coast between Hijaz and Yemen. This example more than suffices to prove that these names are tied to the history of the Canaanites, whose presence in Palestine goes back 5,000 years, well before the Bible! Salibi also overlooks an important historical factor: the words and traditions of the patriarchs (Abraham, Isaac, Jacob), which go back to the year 2000 BC, were only collated and written down some 1,000 years later. How can one accept that what had remained an oral tradition for more than a millennium could be so compiled and recorded without the patriarchs' words and deeds being altered or deformed by time, nature or man?

By persisting with its ideological place-naming, Israel may one day discover that, by revising names of towns and cities coined by the Canaanites more than 1,000 years before the Hebrews arrived in the region, it will achieve the opposite result to that intended by reawakening the Palestinians' awareness of their Canaanite origins.

As for the Zionist concept of 'Greater Israel', it bears no relation to the borders of British mandate Palestine, to the Bible or to the subjective history of the Hebrews. It is quite simply an invention of secular and nationalist Zionist ideology which interprets the Bible in this way to realize its chimerical dream. Indeed, according to the Christian and Muslim interpretations of the Bible, the biblical promise made to Abraham (see Genesis XV, 18) by the God, Yahve, was addressed to all his descendants: to his two sons, Ishmael and Isaac, and their lineage, who were not all Jews.

Furthermore, this promise could only be fulfilled by those who respected the conditions of the Covenant with Abraham, namely religious leaders and not the secularists of Likud or Labour Party. If these secularists' biblical interpretation were correct, the Covenant in question would be broken and hence rendered 'null and void'.

We have already pointed out that, historically, the Kingdom of the Hebrews, vassal of Egypt, and created by Saul (who was succeeded by David and Solomon in the years 1020–923 BC), only covered the West Bank and part of north-eastern Palestine, whereas the coastal plain, Gaza, Jaffa, Acre, Galilee and all of southern and south-west Palestine (the country of the Philistines and the Canaanites) were never part of the Kingdom of the Hebrews. Moreover, this Kingdom had no fixed borders. They fluctuated according to events, especially after the Kingdom split up into two states: the Kingdom of Israel in the north and the Kingdom of Judah in the south of the present-day West Bank. The three Hebrew Kingdoms (David's, Israel and Judah) never enjoyed independence or sovereignty, but mere autonomy (perhaps such as that mentioned in the Camp David Accords!) under, alternately, Egyptian and Mesopotamian tutelage.

By way of conclusion, one is bound to state that 'biblical geography', as recorded in Genesis XV, 18 ('In that same day the Lord made a covenant with Abram, saying, unto thy seed have I given this land, from the River of Egypt unto the great river, the River Euphrates'), has never materialized historically. The truth is that the Zionists wish to turn the Old Testament into a political manifesto and geography and history book.[4] The state of Israel, which, according to the Zionists, is the realization of God's will, was in fact created in contempt of the right of peoples to self-determination. It was built through terrorism and violence and imposed by force of arms, thus producing one of the greatest injustices of all time, since it was erected on a territory from which it had driven out a people.

Palestine is the victim of its geography, in a region where small peoples jostle for the position of great states, upon a territory whose extent cannot satisfy all the pretenders' ambitions. If one goes back to the time of the Canaanites, it was Palestine which was a great country in the region, and yet the Palestinians—the heirs to the Canaanites—do not demand their own 'Greater Palestine'. The manipulation of place-names by the Zionists for ideological purposes serves a 'legitimizing function' in order to justify after the event the establishment of Jewish settlements in the occupied territories. Labour and, later, Likud governments pursued a policy which deprived the Palestinians of their fundamental political and civil rights.

A process of economic modernization had been initiated in the pre-1948 West Bank and Gaza Strip. They had, however, both remained essentially agricultural regions, contributing about 15 per cent of the total value of Palestine's output. After 1948 the Gaza Strip, under Egyptian control, gradually became an economic 'free zone' akin to Hong Kong.

Jerusalem, which had been the political and administrative capital of Palestine, became a provincial capital of the West Bank after 1948. According to Michel Foucher:

> After 1948 the West Bank of the Jordan was severed from its adjoining westward area and joined to Transjordan, an arid Bedouin emirate, very low in population and poor in resources, less affected than the West Bank by the beginnings of modernization (education, political struggles, urban markets for agriculture) in mandated Palestine and by comparison with which, the West Bank seemed 'developed' . . . The record of 18 years is, in overall terms, one of growth in the East Bank by virtue of the transfer of resources and labour (not only the 1948 refugees) from the West Bank, which was largely confined to an admittedly dynamic function as an agricultural adjunct but which had no opportunity to diversify; conversely, the vast majority of investments were concentrated in the East Bank (industry, energy, urban development, such as at Amman, Zarqa and Irbid, and large-scale agricultural projects of the Yarmuk-Ghor system, situated exclusively east of the Jordan River). Thus, during this period, the ratios of levels of development between the two banks were reversed[5] to the extent that, in 1967, the West Bank was lagging behind economically in spite of its natural and demographic potential.[6]

Foucher writes of the 1967 economy of the occupied West Bank, which Israel had sought to integrate by forcing Israeli products upon it and by allowing Palestinian manpower to work in Israel:

> [There is a] growth in dependence: it is a contradictory outcome, therefore, since growth results from dependence and individual economic improvements contrast with collective stagnation . . . Development budgets are cut to a minimum; the modernization of public utilities (roads, electricity) involves interconnection with Israeli networks; projects are subjected to multiple authorizations which are more easily obtained by village artisanal enterprises than by industries in the urban centres; the regional banking network has been done away with and foreign exchange and insurance bureaux effect transfers to Amman but are not development banks.[7]

Since the *intifada*, however, the Palestinian economy in the West Bank and the Gaza Strip has not only been prevented from diversifying but is stifled because of an unemployment rate today approaching 60 per cent of the active population, and the pauperization of Palestinian peasants through Israeli confiscation of around 65 per cent of their land and 70 per cent of their water[8] in the occupied West Bank, and 40 per cent of their land in occupied Gaza. Israel's harsh collective reprisals and repressive measures have oppressed the population throughout the *intifada*: levying of prohibitive taxes; prolonged water, power and telephone-line cuts; destruction of harvests; uprooting of trees; extended curfews; protracted closures of educational, cultural, charity and social institutions from 1987 to 1991; and banning of trade union and press associations, among others. The arrival of fresh waves of Soviet Jewish immigrants on the one hand, and the Gulf War on the other, have wrought devastation on the Palestinian economy in the occupied territories. The population of the Gaza Strip is on the brink of famine and living in intolerable conditions.

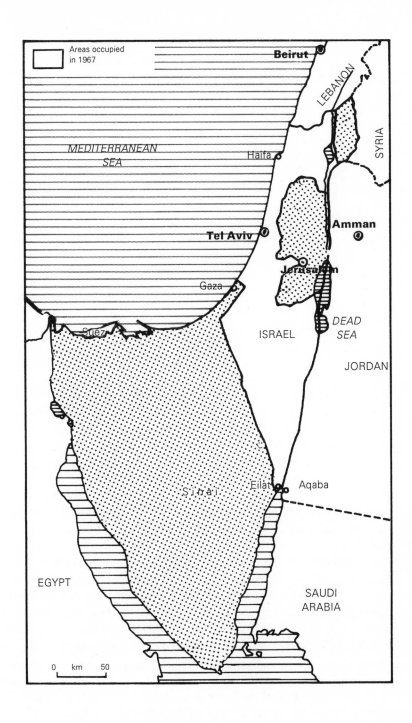

Map 7. *The Situation after the 1967 War*

10
The Settlements

The most serious feature of Israeli policy in the occupied territories, and one which marks it out from other conventional occupations resulting from armed conflicts, is the expropriation of Palestinian land and the establishment of Jewish settlements on such land, which has been confiscated on a variety of pretexts.

As early as the summer of 1967 the Israeli government had prepared a confiscation and settlement plan, called the Allon Plan after its author. This 'security-oriented' plan mainly involved the creation of buffer zones, while providing for Israeli control of a cordon some 15 km wide the length of the Jordan (Ghor), as well as the annexation of Jerusalem, Latrun and certain places near Hebron. The Allon Plan also provided for the return of inhabited Palestinian regions to Jordan or the granting of autonomy to them.

The resignation of Golda Meir, the Israeli Prime Minister, on 10 April 1974 was the result of Israeli public dissatisfaction with those responsible for the 'oversights' (*mahdal*) of the October 1973 War. Her replacement by Yitzhak Rabin (from 28 May 1974 to 7 April 1977) coincided with the cessation of the Allon Plan; Rabin followed a new settlement policy by establishing Jewish settlements in areas densely populated by Palestinians. In keeping with the Israeli policy pursued in the 1930s and 1940s of creating *faits accomplis* and developing centres of Jewish settlements, the Rabin government began by taking control of the strategic highways and then confiscating farmland.

Zionism from Herzl to Ben-Gurion had been a purely secular doctrine. The June 1967 War created fertile ground for the emergence and development of a new form of Zionism: the religious ingredient was added to political Zionism to produce a politico-religious Zionism. These Zionists, who were initially grouped together in the Gush Emunim (Bloc of the Faithful), considered the settling of Jews on the land of Palestine to be a 'religious imperative'. Unlike Golda Meir, Yitzhak Rabin did not prevent the politico-religious Zionists from establishing settlements, although they were 'illegal' from his government's standpoint.

While encouraging the proliferation of *faits accomplis* which tended towards a 'Greater Israel', Rabin, like the other Labour figures, continued to assert a policy of 'territorial compromise' with Jordan (the 'Jordanian option'). After the success of the Israeli right in the 1977 general election, Menachem Begin,[1] the Likud leader, replaced Rabin as head of the Israeli government (from 12 May 1977 to 15 September 1983). Under the first Likud government in Israel's history, Labour's ambiguous language was replaced by clear and candid statements. Begin, who had rejected the 1947 Partition Resolution, dismissed Labour's 'Jordanian option'. Faithful to his revisionist Zionism, he declared that his political programme would be predicated upon the creation of a Greater Israel throughout the land of British-mandated Palestine. Laurens sums up his policy on the occupied Palestinian territories in the following words:

Begin put forward his vaunted plan for Palestinian autonomy while at the same time guaranteeing the construction of Greater Israel by multiplying settlements and completing land appropriation. At the time of the Allon Plan, land confiscation had been carried out essentially for reasons of security. As this pretext became increasingly spurious, even for the Israeli courts, a whole array of legal subterfuges was invented. As in 1949, trusteeship of 'absenteeists'' goods was granted to Israelis, the 'absenteeists' in question being Palestinians who had fled from the 1967 invasion and who had been prohibited from returning. State land was allocated exclusively to the settlers and a large part of Palestinian property was classified as state land and confiscated, since it had not been recorded in a land register. Any pretext would do to take possession of land: urban and rural development plans were redirected to promote the transfer of property in the general interest. Pseudonyms were used to intervene in the property market and pressure of every kind was exerted on Arab landowners to sell up.[2]

Another equally worrying issue is that of seizure of water resources in the occupied territories. Indeed, when Israel annexed the Syrian Golan Heights on 14 December 1981, it was more for their water resources than for their strategic position. According to Laurens:

Since the end of the 1960s, the Israelis have been consuming all the renewable water resources of the Jewish state, or about 1,610–1,650 million cubic metres. The growth in their consumption has been made possible by the appropriation of the water of the occupied territories (West Bank: 850 million cubic metres, of which 650 million are readily exploitable; Gaza: 80 million cubic metres). At the end of the 1980s, while the Arab population of formerly mandated Palestine accounts for 41 per cent of the total population, it is only entitled to a fraction of the water resources: Israel receives 86 per cent, the Arabs of the occupied territories 8–12 per cent and the settlers 2–5 per cent.

This apportionment is only possible because of the establishment of discriminatory legislation: whereas under the mandate, water was considered to be private property, the Israeli jurisdiction extended to the occupied territories considers it collective property. The right to use it is subjected to a permit granted by the military authorities that administer the territories. Arab irrigation is severely limited and the cost of water distributed by the state grid—thanks to a subtle game of subsidies—is four times cheaper for an Israeli farmer than for an Arab one. Moreover, the Palestinians have virtually no chance of drilling new wells (there have been five authorizations since 1967), while the settlers can use very deep wells which dry up the shallow wells of the Arabs. Palestinian agriculture is, therefore, constrained by conditions which prevent its development and, in some cases, even compel it to regress, whereas the settlers have every means of 'making the desert bloom', according to the favourite theme of Zionist propaganda . . .

The water question is crucial to the future of the occupied territories. It is scarcely conceivable that Israel might accept true independence for the occupied territories when one realizes that the potential joint water supplies of Israel and the West Bank (the rains that fall on the heights of the territories and which pass into the water table shared by both areas) are 475 million cubic metres, of which 95.5 per cent is consumed by Israel. An end to Israeli supplies from the occupied territories would entail an inevitable decline in the agriculture and industry of the Jewish state.[3]

Water has become a complex geo-political issue;[4] hence the importance attached by the Palestinians to the third phase of the Middle East peace conference, dealing with multilateral questions, including water problems.

From Begin to Shamir

After the massacre, from 16 to 18 September 1982, of some 1,000 Palestinians and Lebanese Shi'ites in the Palestinian refugee camps of Sabra and Shatilla, perpetrated by the Lebanese Forces militias under Elie Hobeika's leadership with the consent of the Israeli army surrounding the camps, and following the March 1983 Kahane Report which implicated Ariel Sharon in these massacres, Begin resigned as Prime Minister on 15 September 1983, under the pressure of Israeli public opinion, for 'personal' reasons. On 11 October he was replaced by Yitzhak Shamir, whose government fell on 19 March 1984. The July 1984 general election allowed neither Labour nor Likud to form a government in coalition with the small Israeli political parties.

On 13 September 1984 an agreement between Likud and Labour established an 'alternating system' of government leadership: two years for Shimon Peres as Prime Minister (1985–86) to be followed by two further years for Yitzhak Shamir from 20 October 1986. This Labour-Likud government agreement stalled Israeli policy on a political solution in the Middle East.

The 1988 Israeli general election results forced Likud and Labour to form a new government of 'national unity'. Yitzhak Shamir became leader of this government on 22 December 1988. In 1990 Shimon Peres triggered a ministerial crisis by trying to form a government which would accept the Baker Plan, but failed. Subsequently, Shamir managed to form a government on 11 June 1990 which encompassed the extreme right, the religious parties and Likud. The departure from Shamir's government of Tehiya and Moledet, two extreme right-wing parties, on 19 January 1992 triggered the dissolution of the Knesset on 4 February, early general elections on 23 June and the formation of a new Labour government, headed by Yitzhak Rabin, on 13 July.

The political evolution in Israel towards intransigence and extremism, not to mention fanaticism, was the consequence of the accession to power of the right and of ultra-nationalist politico-religious Zionism. This drastic shift from Labour pragmatism to the Likud dogmatism of a chauvinistic and expansionist ideological doctrine strengthened and accelerated the archaic practice of settlement. The Shamir government allowed the Jewish settlements in the occupied Palestinian territories to benefit from unprecedentedly favourable treatment: tax privileges, exceptional, generous loans and special subsidies. In a report submitted to the American Congress on 20 March 1991, during a debate on foreign aid, the State Department affirmed that more than 200,000 Jewish settlers were already established in the occupied territories and more than 90,000 settlers were living in 150 settlements in the West Bank, where Israel had already seized half of the land. These figures showed an increase of 9,000–10,000 settlers compared to the previous year and 40,000 settlers more than in 1984.

The US report also gave the following figures: in East Jerusalem and its Palestinian suburbs, about 120,000 settlers had been installed in 12 new districts; in the Gaza Strip, the Israeli occupation authorities had already confiscated 30 per cent of the land and 3,000 Jewish settlers had moved into 18 settlements; and in the Golan, 12,000 settlers had moved into 30 settlements. Thirteen per cent of the population of the occupied territories were now Jewish settlers, of whom 4 per cent were Soviet immigrants.[5]

Between the publication of this report and the end of December 1991, the Israeli government created a further three settlements on the occupied Palestinian territories. At the same time, the government continued to implement a programme of extending and developing existing settlements. Ariel Sharon, the Israeli Housing Minister, also continued a settlement programme known as the 'Seven Stars', which involved the establishment of new settlements on the 1949 armistice line.[6] The aim of this programme was to secure, by *faits accomplis*, the shifting of Israel's pre-1967 borders into the West Bank.

To understand more fully what is at stake, it may be useful to recall a few figures. The surface area of the West Bank is 5,450 sq. km and its population is estimated at approximately 990,600, of whom 375,000 are refugees (18.2 per cent of the total population of the Palestinian people of 5,431,000).[7] The surface area of the Gaza Strip is 362 sq. km and its population is estimated at approximately 564,100, of whom 435,000 are refugees (10.4 per cent of the total population of the Palestinian people). The Palestinian Arab minority in Israel (633,000 people) accounts for 12.2 per cent of the total Palestinian population. According to these statistics, the Palestinians in the territories occupied in 1967 account for only 28.6 per cent of the total population of the Palestinian people. As for the occupied Palestinian territories (Gaza and the West Bank) themselves, they amount to only 21.2 per cent of the total surface area of British-mandated Palestine.

The population of Jerusalem, which at the start of the century was one-third Muslim, one-third Jewish and one-third Christian, only includes 120,000 Palestinians today, of whom 10,000 are Christian. The Jewish population of Jerusalem stands at half a million, however, of whom 5,000 live in the Jewish quarter of the occupied Old City. In a statement on 13

October 1991[8] to settlers who had recently seized houses in the Silwan district of East Jerusalem, Ariel Sharon asserted that the Israeli government's policy was to 'Judaize' Jerusalem by increasing the Jewish settlers in the city. On 8 December 1991 the Israeli government officially approved the establishment of those Jewish settlers in houses of the Palestinian Silwan district of Jerusalem.[9] Thus, 'universal Jerusalem' is becoming a universal city only in memory.

The non-Palestinian Christian population of the city has plummeted: the French, Italian, Greek and Russian communities have virtually ceased to exist. The strong German colony, which was established in Jerusalem as far back as 1873, was deported to Australia in 1941 by the British. The Maghreb district was demolished in 1967. The British have also left Jerusalem. Around 50,000 Palestinian Christians from Jerusalem and its suburbs have emigrated since 1967. The acceleration of the *fait accompli* policy of the Israeli occupation authorities is destroying Jerusalem's soul, and its unique global character as a city three times holy and with a universal calling.

The Soviet Jews

Until 1989 the advocates of a Greater Israel did not possess the demographic means to carry through their policy, and a statement such as that made by Shamir to the Knesset at the inauguration of his government in 1986—'settlement throughout Eretz Israel is one of the supreme values of Zionism'[10]—was not taken seriously as a demographic proposition. It is interesting in this connection to recall General de Gaulle's words to the Lebanese President, Charles Helou:

> The demographic and political situation in Israel will depend a great deal upon the Soviet authorities. It is in Russia that the main source of Jewish immigrants is to be found. The USSR will determine whether or not it will assist overpopulation in Israel.[11]

It is regrettable that neither the Arabs nor the Palestinians took de Gaulle's words seriously. Camille Aboussouan, in his study, quotes the following writings of General de Gaulle about Israel:

> From a human point of view, I feel satisfaction that it should rediscover a national home and I see this as an outcome which would compensate for so much suffering endured down the ages and taken to its extreme at

the time of the massacres perpetrated by Hitler's Germany. But if Israel's existence seems to me very justified, I feel that it should be very prudent with the Arabs. They are its neighbours, and will remain so for ever. It is at their expense and upon their lands that it has just been sovereignly established. Thereby it has wounded them in all that is most sensitive to their religion and their pride. That is why, when Ben-Gurion tells me of his plan to settle 4 or 5 million Jews in Israel, which could not accommodate them in its present form, and when his words reveal to me his intention to extend the borders as soon as the chance arises, I call upon him not to do it. 'France', I tell him, 'will help you tomorrow, as it helped you yesterday, to stand your ground, whatever happens. But it is not ready to provide you with the means to conquer new territories. You have pulled off a *tour de force*. Don't overdo it now! Suppress pride which, as Aeschylus said, 'is the son of happiness who devours his father'.[12]

De Gaulle's vision, which had also foreseen the 1967 War, was subsequently confirmed by the mass immigration of Soviet Jews. This new wave of Soviet Jewish immigration, starting in 1989, stemmed from a key factor in Soviet politics: *perestroika*, which culminated in economic collapse in the Soviet Union and the birth of a xenophobic, extreme right-wing tendency, together with freedom for Soviet Jews to emigrate. The Soviet Jews had no choice of host country. The United States limited the number of Jewish immigrants authorized to settle in the country to 50,000 a year and the borders of Western Europe became increasingly impervious to such an exodus.

According to official estimates, the number of Soviet Jewish immigrants is approaching 400,000 out of the 1 million Jews which Israeli forecasts expect to arrive in the next three to five years. Still according to these estimates, the number of Jews in the former USSR varies from 1.5 to 2 million. It is estimated that 30 per cent of the arrivals are actually non-Jews, which presents the Israeli authorities with the problem of revising the 'law of return'.

This mass immigration cannot fail to have both demographic and political consequences in Israel and in the occupied Palestinian territories.[13] The same is true regionally and internationally. Israel's Jewish population has been bolstered by the arrival of these immigrants, who have increased its ranks by 10 per cent in a country inhabited by 30 per cent of the world's Jews.

The success of the policy of Soviet Jewish immigration was a very important card which Likud intended to play in fighting Labour, which had always stated that, in time, the demographic factor would work against

Israel. Likud thus expected to realize its dream of a Greater Israel. For the Palestinians, who had always denounced the policy of Jewish immigration, the arrival of the Soviet Jews constituted a real threat to their personal security, as well as to that of their property, while jeopardizing the fulfilment of their national rights. For the Arab countries, this immigration was of a piece with Israel's expansionist policy and would sooner or later provoke a new Arab-Israeli conflict, as had been the case ever since 1948 whenever the Israeli population was augmented by Jews from abroad. Lastly, in international terms, the new situation created by this mass immigration could not fail to concern certain powers which were worried by the potential risks of instability in the Middle East region.

From Shamir to Rabin

The Labour Party's victory over Likud at the general elections of 23 June 1992 was a clear indication of the extent of US influence over the Israeli electorate. By denying Shamir the loan guarantees he was seeking, the Bush administration had ensured that his Labour rival, Yitzhak Rabin, would win. Immediately after his government was sworn in, Rabin suspended the construction of 6,681 housing units planned by Likud, while at the same time authorizing the continued building of 10,467 others.

In justifying this partial halt to settlements, Rabin invoked the distinction between 'political' and 'security' (or 'strategic') settlements. It was a flimsy distinction. According to Rabin's classification, the Jerusalem area, the 1949 demarcation lines and Israel's borders with Egypt and Jordan were encompassed in the zone of 'security settlements', which covered 2,800 sq. km, or 51 per cent of the occupied territories. In the view of Meron Benvenisti,[14] the former deputy Mayor of West Jerusalem:

> This region, at the start of 1992, comprised 76 Jewish localities inhabited by 71,000 people, compared to 51 localities inhabited by 24,000 people in the settlements termed 'political'. More than 400,000 Palestinians live within the Rabin lines and are divided among 149 localities.

Rabin's conception of 'political' and 'strategic' settlements was based on that adopted by the Haganah in the Palestine of the 1930s and 1940s, whereby Jewish settlements were viewed as an essential device for securing the future borders of the Jewish state since they were intended to establish continuity in the pattern of the Jewish population. For Israel, the notion of 'demographic continuity' was synonymous with that of 'security'; it could only be achieved by dismembering Palestinian society. Rabin thus aimed to make any continuity of Palestinian population impossible and thereby preclude the creation of a Palestinian state. His geostrategic approach was based on the 1970 Allon Plan and on its extensive implementation by his first government of 1974–77. During that period, he modified the plan by building an additional 36 Jewish settlements and expanding the limits of Jerusalem and its suburbs. Put simply, Rabin's conception was that the term 'political' applied to those settlements which were located in areas which the Labour Party did not intend to retain, whereas the 'strategic' settlements were intended to remain under Israeli sovereignty.

This approach would make only 35 per cent of the West Bank negotiable, with 28 per cent reserved for 'strategic settlements' and authority over the remaining 37 per cent to be shared between the Palestinians and the Israelis as communal land.

It is estimated that there are now 105,000 settlers in the occupied West Bank, 4,000 in the Gaza Strip, 135,000 in occupied East Jerusalem and a further 15,000 in the Golan. Settlements are estimated to number between 200 and 210. Their proliferation is out of all proportion to the surface area of the Palestinian land which has been confiscated. Moreover, since Israel continues to publish incomplete statistics, it is impossible to arrive at precise figures for settlers and settlements. This problem is compounded by the myriad Israeli services responsible for the colonization process, all operating separately and issuing different statistics: the cabinet of the Prime Minister, the Housing Ministry, the Agriculture Ministry, the Intergovernmental Committee for Settlements' Affairs, the World Jewish Congress, the Jewish Agency and a variety of religious and extremist organizations. It is also impossible to keep track of private building.

The Palestinians are also the victims of the acts of brutality and terrorism perpetrated by Jewish settlers who not only make their own law but then proceed to consider themselves above it: Palestinian civilians are murdered, attacked by gangs, harassed in all manner of ways, and their homes and property are vandalized and ransacked. In its 1992 report, Betselem recalled that of the 39 settlers who had committed murders since the start of the *intifada*, only 3 had been brought to trial. The severest penalty so far handed down was a three-year prison sentence on a Shilo settler convicted of murder who was subsequently released after having served a third of his term.

Al-Haq, a Palestinian human rights association in the occupied territories, states that two different jurisdictions exist side-by-side, thus creating a *de facto* situation of apartheid in the occupied Palestinian territories. Indeed, the Palestinians are placed under military jurisdiction whereas a military order of March 1981 granted the Jewish settlements and their inhabitants the status of juridical extra-territoriality, allowing them alone to benefit from Israeli civilian law. Furthermore, the settlers have privileges denied other Israelis: low rents, low-interest housing loans, income tax rebates, cheap land and water in the occupied territories, ready access to weapons, free transport, and so on. They also enjoy the tacit support of the Israeli political establishment. The peace negotiations placed the settlers before a dilemma: could they countenance the notion that these privileges and immunities might be challenged?

Rabin, like Shamir before him, would not dismantle any of the existing 200–210 settlements. Indeed, both men preferred to approach the Palestinian problem as though it were an internal Israeli conflict. They opposed Palestinian national self-determination, negotiations with the PLO and the establishment of an independent Palestinian state, and were both considered to be 'hawks' on 'security' issues. Yitzhak Shamir told the Israeli daily *Maariv* on 3 July 1992 that he had intended to 'stall the Arab-Israeli negotiations for at least ten years until the number of Jews living in the territories was such that Israeli control would be irreversible'. According to Louis-Jean Duclos:

[Shamir] has never hesitated to state loud and clear that there was never any question of envisaging the slightest territorial withdrawal, or restrictions on settlements, whatever the cost in American pressure and retaliation. The incoming candidate [Rabin], however, has exuded ambiguity and complexity: the PLO would continue to be kept out of the negotiations, though not its supporters so long as they were residents of the occupied territories, or even of Jerusalem; there would be a withdrawal from the most densely populated Arab areas but control of them would only be handed over to a reliable successor, for example Jordan; short of the annexation of the remainder, 'strategic' settlements would be developed there instead of the so-called 'political' ones which would simply be 'frozen'; lastly, the 'autonomy' of the Palestinians would be less personal than under Likud but more certainly provisional.[15]

Duclos adds:

The main difference between Labour's approach and that of Likud was less a matter of substance than of degree, in terms of the extent of the concessions and, above all, of the amount of imagination devoted to obfuscating concepts and to minimizing their scope.[16]

In Duclos' view, the composition of the new parliamentary majority (62 members), and the consultations which preceded its formation, visibly failed to shed any light on the political direction of the new government. The ambiguities of the Labour manifesto were now to be exacerbated by the confusion stemming from the 'cohabitation' within the same cabinet of proven 'liberals', cold pragmatists and the purportedly non-Zionist 'religious' groups, not to mention the overtures made to convinced annexationists.[17]

The Rabin government (44 Labour members, 12 Meretz 'liberals' and 6 members from the religious Shas Party) retained virtually the same diplomatic options as the Shamir administration in preserving the Madrid framework, maintaining the restrictions on the criteria governing the composition of the Palestinian delegation and scarcely changing the four Israeli delegations (the only head of delegation to be replaced being Yossi Ben Aharon, Shamir's former right-hand man, who gave way to Itamar Rabinovitch, close to Shimon Peres).

Rabin, whose ideas had provided the basis for the 1989 Shamir Plan, stated that he intended to implement the Camp David Accords and Resolutions 242 and 338 of the Security Council—a commitment to which Shamir had paid no more than lip-service. To the Palestinians none the less, Rabin was a military man, bereft of political vision, who was responsible for the expulsion of the inhabitants of Ramleh and Lydda in 1948 and for the Six-Day War in 1967. In their eyes, he was the architect of the 'iron fist' policy, the 'bone-breaker' during the *intifada* from 1988 to 1990, and the man responsible for the expulsion of the 413 Palestinians to south Lebanon at the end of 1992. Those who know Rabin endorse the Palestinians' assessment of him and see him as a military man who takes decisions on the strength of army and security service reports and seldom on the basis of an acute political appraisal of the situation.

Likud, for its part, was ideologically wedded to the Zionist principle of the 'uniqueness of the land' in support of the dogma of a Greater Israel, whereas the Labour Party was more preoccupied with its own dogma predicated on the 'uniqueness of the Jewish people'. In Labour's view, it was demographic trends not moral considerations which prevented any annexationist designs, since their aim was to uphold the Jewish character of the Hebrew state and annexation would be tantamount to *de jure* formalization of the apartheid regime which already existed *de facto*.

Any close examination of the political manifestos of Likud and Labour would lead one to be wary of the instinctive sense of optimism that prevailed in 1991 and 1992. If any glimmer of hope still lingered, it was to be faintly discerned in the emergence within the younger ranks of the Labour Party of a veritable pacifist fringe, calling for dialogue with the PLO and recognition of the principle of an independent Palestinian state. An Israeli opinion poll reported in *Le Figaro* in early 1993[18] gave 47 per cent of Israelis as being in favour of a direct dialogue with the PLO to break the deadlock at the peace talks.

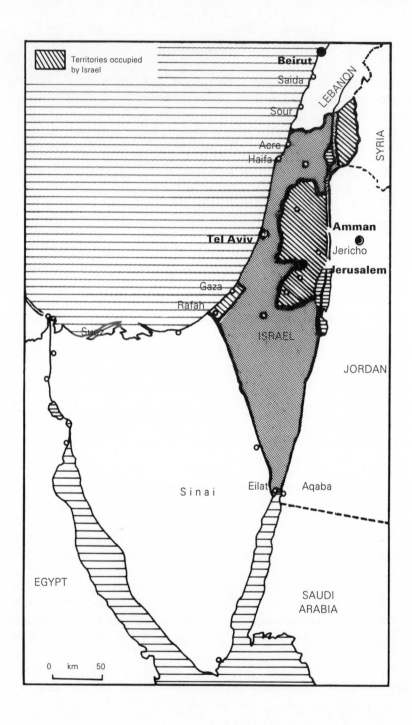

Map 8. Israel and the Occupied Territories (1992)

11
The Intifada
and its Consequences

The date 9 December 1978 marked the beginning of the popular uprising in the occupied Palestinian territories: the consequence of a policy which denied the Palestinian people their national rights and the start of a process of widespread popular resistance which would have political repercussions.

As had been the case with the First World War—whose outbreak was provoked by the assassination in Sarajevo of Archduke Franz-Ferdinand, the heir to the throne of Austro-Hungary, on 29 June 1914—the *intifada*'s immediate cause was an event which sparked a broader fire. Two days prior to the uprising, a traffic accident (according to the Israeli version), or the fact that (according to the Palestinians) an Israeli[1] lorry deliberately rammed a Palestinian collective taxi in the Gaza Strip, left four dead and nine injured. We shall return to the true origins of this popular uprising later.

The first clashes took place in the Jabaliya Palestinian refugee camp. In a matter of days, this violent but unarmed revolt had overshadowed all other uprisings since 1967—these had been limited in time and space and were related to circumstantial events affecting the Palestinian people inside or outside the occupied Palestinian territories. The *intifada* encompassed the entire population, young and old, men and women, refugees and intellectuals, schoolchildren and labourers, traders and peasants. All the built-up areas also participated spontaneously in this 'Revolt of the Stones': refugee camps, towns and villages.

The spontaneous action soon became organized, thanks to the clandestine infrastructure of the Palestinian resistance organizations (Fatah, the PFLP, the DFLP, the Palestinian Communist Party and the Islamic movement). The first communiqué of the United Patriotic Leadership of the *intifada* was published on 4 January 1988. The Islamic fundamentalist movement, Hamas, refused to join the clandestine United Leadership. The fundamentalists had been tolerated by the Israeli occupation authorities in the 1970s and at the start of the 1980s since they were rivals, not to say enemies, of the secular PLO. These activists attack symbols of modern society (cinema, theatre and dance, for example) and their retrogressive social project is the 're-Islamization' of Palestinian society by authoritarian means. Their political project is the forcible establishment of an Islamic state over the whole of Palestine. Their concept of Islam is somewhat outdated: it takes account neither of Islam with a cultural dimension (*hadari* Islam—civilized Islam compared to bedouin, or primary, Islam) nor of the socio-cultural evolution of Muslim societies through 15 centuries of history.

To gather support, the Islamic fundamentalist movements have exploited the frustrations, despair and intolerable plight of the Palestinian population under Israeli occupation. Since 1986 these movements have, to some extent, become the spearhead of the fight against the Israeli occupiers. Hamas, like the PLO in its beginnings, refuses to recognize the international dimension of the Palestinian question. It has failed, however, in its attempt to compete with the secular movements of the PLO, whose sympathizers are grouped in the United Patriotic Leadership, which remains the main inspiration and organizer of the uprising.

The Palestinian population began to organize in the local popular committees which enforce compliance with directives from the United Leadership: large-scale demonstrations and strikes; boycotting Israeli products while replacing them, where possible, with Palestinian goods; refusal to pay Israeli taxes and other forms of civil disobedience. These local committees are dedicated to enabling the Palestinians to run their own daily lives by catering for their needs: supplies for poor families or families under curfew, first aid, legal and cultural assistance, and organization of home-based teaching to alleviate the consequences of the closure of schools and universities by Israeli military order.

Great solidarity is displayed among the Palestinian population, especially during clashes with the soldiers of the occupying army or during curfews. A radical change in traditionalist values can be observed (abolition of the marriage dowry, sexual equality, and so on), in short, the affirmation of the values of a modern society in the family (father–mother–child) and in social relationships. The process of dismantling Israel's network of informers has given rise to certain abuses and personal score-settling. This practice of 'eliminating collaborators' has been denounced by the PLO, especially as Israel has capitalized on this practice to infiltrate its agents into the ranks of militant Palestinians in order physically to eliminate members or leaders of the *intifada*. According to the annual report of the Israeli humanitarian organization, Betselem, a third of all Palestinians killed in 1991 were murdered by Israeli soldiers masquerading as Palestinians. The report further states that torture is practised in a routine and systematic way during interrogations of Palestinians.[2]

Israel responded to the *intifada* by decreeing a State of Emergency to 'crush the uprising by all possible means',[3] according to a statement by Yitzhak Rabin, the then Minister of Defence. Rabin had ordered his soldiers to break the bones of demonstrators, an order which was followed to the letter. Two images shocked international public opinion: a CBS television film showing Israeli soldiers in the Nablus area breaking the arms of two young Palestinians, and another showing four Palestinians from Salem who emerged after apparently being buried alive by a bulldozer.[4]

The statistics in a book by Ibrahim Souss[5] give a precise idea of the scale of Israel's repressive measures after four years of the uprising: after one year, the excessive use of firearms by the Israeli army caused some 300–400 dead and 20,000 wounded on the Palestinian side, to which should be added 6,000 imprisoned (out of 20,000 arrested) and several dozen expulsions.[6]

Laurens has commented on the spontaneous nature of the uprising: 'The *intifada* is totally spontaneous in origin. The Israeli policy of multiple pressure has passed beyond the point of equilibrium, where the fear of repression no longer offsets despair about the future.'[7] Several factors provoked this collective human explosion, however. The 'collision' was only the spark igniting the powder keg. There was an accumulation of inhuman practices by the Israeli occupier: confiscation of land (65 per cent of land in the West Bank and 45 per cent in Gaza); appropriation of 70 per cent of Palestinian water sources; systematic establishment of Jewish settlements, largely in the occupied Palestinian territories, in order to carry out the subsequent transfer of Palestinians across the River Jordan; Palestinians considered as 'foreigners' on their own land; and so on. This constant humiliation inflicted on Palestinian national feelings was exacerbated by 60 per cent unemployment among the active population and by the measures of harassment and repression mentioned earlier.

The political situation in 1987 played a catalytic role in the outbreak of the *intifada*. First, there was the restored national unity in the Palestine National Council in Algiers in April 1987, following the PLO's 'crossing of the wilderness' after its forced departure from Beirut and Lebanon in 1982–83. Then there was the disappointment caused by the Amman Arab

Summit in November 1987, which relegated the Palestinian question to the background for the first time since the creation of the League of Arab States—a decision very poorly received by the Palestinian people. The Palestinians of the occupied territories understood that they could no longer count on the outside world to save their souls, and that the time had come to fight against injustice and for the dignity of the Palestinian people by relying on their own strength. They set themselves goals which prompted the PLO to spell out its programme for peace in November 1988.

The first consequence of the *intifada* was the ending in Lebanon of the 'War of the Camps' waged by the pro-Syrians against the Palestinians in the refugee camps which supported the PLO. The second was the reappearance of the 1949 armistice lines separating Israel from the occupied Palestinian territories, including Jerusalem—which once more became West and East, Israeli and Palestinian.

The *intifada* overturned Israel's image in the West as the purported 'victim' and thus revealed its true face as an occupying power, as well as showing the sorry position of the Palestinians as the true victims and not the aggressors in the Middle East since 9 December 1917, when General Allenby occupied Jerusalem. The reversal took place not only in the media. It was a political reversal as well, since Israel was now the rejectionist camp, with Likud playing the role once filled by the Arab countries. This unarmed Palestinian revolt disturbed Jewish communities throughout the world. It contributed to their realization of the existence of the Palestinian people as a national entity and not as refugees, and of the realities of the repressive Israeli occupation which had dispossessed them.

The Israeli army's brutal repression of the 'Revolt of the Stones' traumatized Israel's Palestinian community (Israeli Arabs). On 21 December 1987 they were already displaying solidarity with their brothers and sisters in the occupied territories by observing a general strike in Israel. The peaceful *intifada* strengthened, on the one hand, the ultra-nationalist and religious advocates of a Greater Israel, who supported the forcible suppression of the *intifada*, and, on the other hand, the peace camp, especially among the Israel army and the intellectuals. The soldiers of Yesh-Gvul ('There is a limit') and Generals for Peace attracted more than 1,000 reservist officers and joined forces with intellectuals who had adopted the slogan, 'Free Israel from the Territories'. To these groups should be added the Peace Now movement. They all called for a negotiated political solution, ranging from the 'Jordanian option' to direct negotiations with the PLO.

Likud and Labour did not translate this political evolution into their election manifestos, however. Thus, the general election results of 1 November 1988 did not reflect any change: the Israeli electorate left Labour and Likud at level-pegging, thereby strengthening the religious parties and tilting Israel to the right. This new political configuration paralysed the Israeli government still further. It was motivated by the rationale of force, whereby peace can only be founded on domination, and security on power.

This rationale has spawned an attitude among Israelis of contempt for the Arabs. Its advocates have adopted as their slogan the notion that 'the Arabs only understand force'. One of their spokesmen, Rafael Eitan—leader of the extreme right-wing Tsomet Party with 8 seats in the Knesset—conveyed this racial prejudice and hatred of the Arabs, as well as his extreme chauvinism, when he proclaimed:

> We openly state that the Arabs have no right to settle on even a single centimetre of Eretz Israel . . . Force is the only thing the Arabs understand and will ever understand. We will use extreme force until the Palestinians come grovelling to our feet.[8]

General Eitan, the former Israeli army Chief-of-Staff, was a member of Shamir's coalition government until the end of December 1991. He once described the Palestinians as 'cockroaches'.

The *intifada* also had a negative effect on Israel's economy. The occupation of the West Bank and Gaza, which had been profitable for Israel, now became a major burden. Estimates indicate that it was costing Israel between $1 and $2 billion a year.

Jordan recognized the *intifada* by officially announcing, on 31 July 1988, its decision to 'sever legal and administrative ties' with the West Bank. In August 1988 Jordan decided to sever its economic links as well, creating a legal void which was promptly filled by the proclamation of the Palestinian state (on 15 November 1988 in Algiers). Indeed, the Palestine National Council meeting from 12 to 15 November 1988 marked a historic turning-point in the PLO's political direction by virtue of its strategic choice to make the major concession of recognizing Israel's right to exist and to security, thereby opting for a two-state solution for the territories of British-mandated Palestine. The PLO's political programme, including the Palestinian peace initiative, adopted by the PNC and confirmed in Arafat's speech to the UN General Assembly's session on the Palestinian question in Geneva (13–16 December 1988), marked the start of a second PLO diplomatic offensive, following that of 1974. Both offensives were waged by Arafat, but whereas the civil war in Lebanon in 1975–76 had frozen the first, the second was severely affected by the 1991 Gulf War. Both political overtures were historic landmarks in the evolution of the Palestinian national movement.

The first result of the 1988 Palestinian peace offensive was the opening of the US-PLO dialogue on 16 December 1988, which was to be conducted through the American Embassy in Tunis. On 5 January 1989 France raised the PLO's Paris bureau to the rank of Delegation-General of Palestine. Italy and other European Community countries did likewise. On 14 March 1989 the US Secretary of State, James Baker, asked Israel to begin talks with the PLO. One hundred and twenty-seven countries recognized the Palestinian state proclaimed in Algiers (see Part IV).

Lastly, the *intifada* of the Palestinian people brought the Middle East conflict back to its true roots: in other words, it is essentially an Israeli-Palestinian conflict, and only secondarily an Arab-Israeli one. On 9 December 1991 the *intifada* entered its sixth year. Israel has learnt no lessons from it. On the contrary, repression and destruction in the occupied Palestinian territories are increasing each day. The words of a French Ambassador, Pierre Hunt, are sufficient comment:

We know about the arbitrary arrests, the houses razed, the daily resort to intimidation and violence, the discrimination against the Palestinian economy, the closed universities and the incessant curfews which make supplies and health care ever more haphazard. By a sinister reversal of history, has Gaza not become a veritable ghetto? . . . Curiously, Western public opinion, so prompt to flare up over more distant misfortunes, remains silent. One becomes accustomed to reading, on the inside pages of *Le Monde*, in small type, about children being killed by bullets or prisoners being crammed into goals. How can one explain this docility, not to say complaisance, towards Israel? Is it contempt for the Arabs, fear of the Jewish movements among the electorate, or perhaps guilt born of the atrocities of the Shoah [holocaust]? . . . But what link can there be between a strictly European, historical tragedy and the wretched plight the Jewish state has reserved for the Arab people of Palestine, even if the wars endured or undertaken in their time have developed their own nefarious logic?[9]

According to the Israeli daily *Hadashot* of 24 February 1992, it was Dany Brinker, the commander of the Israeli police in the occupied territories, who set up a special investigative unit in 1991 which has systematically resorted to torture in order to extract confessions from Palestinian detainees. The newspaper quoted from the eye-witness account of an Israeli policeman:

In the morning, the interrogation room located in a wing of the Hebron military administration looks like a battlefield—the floor is strewn with broken sticks and blood-stained ropes. The detainees, their clothes in tatters, can scarcely crawl at the end of the interrogation.

Betselem has condemned in particular 'the absence of any proportion between the intensity of the interrogation and the alleged crime'. The International Committee of the Red Cross has urged 'the Israeli government to put an immediate end to the ill-treatment meted out to Palestinian detainees from the occupied territories during interrogation' and to prohibit the 'pressure exerted on the prisoners to force them to collaborate'.[10]

On 16 March 1992 the Israeli Knesset passed a law authorizing Israeli soldiers to shoot at fleeing stone-throwers. It effectively legalized the crimes of the Israeli army's 'special units', which comprised agents of the Shin Bet (from Shirut Betahonin—'security services') disguised as Palestinians. These 'death squads' carried out summary executions of Palestinians deemed by these 'special units' to be activists intead of arresting and trying them. The units were described as 'assassins' by the distinguished Israeli professor, Leibowitz. Between January 1989 and December 1991 they killed 69 Palestinians in cold blood, including 20 below the age of 15.

According to several first-hand reports, the bloody repression only worsened after Rabin came to power. Yizhar Beer, the Director of Betselem, stated on 7 February 1993 that 'there are more deaths under Rabin than under Shamir'. He added, 'In Gaza, every family has had at least one of its members killed, wounded or exiled.'[11] Indeed, Rabin had declared on Israeli television on 11 October 1992 that '80,000 Palestinians have been arrested since the start of the *intifada*'. He said that 'every Palestinian family has had at least one of its members in prison at one time or another'.[12]

Betselem's most recent statistics, which are considered authoritative in Israel, indicate that 23 Palestinians were killed in December 1992, 15 in January 1993 and 26 in February 1993. The number of children killed was on the increase, rising from 10 per cent of all fatalities in the last six months under Shamir to 20 per cent in the first six months under Rabin.

Patrice Claude, *Le Monde*'s special correspondent, wrote on 2 February 1993 that since the start of the *intifada* '111 Israelis, civilians and military, have been killed by Palestinians . . . In the same period, 10 times as many Palestinians have fallen to Israeli bullets.' He described the new form of collective punishment devised by Rabin's army: the demolition of the houses of suspects' families by anti-tank missiles.

Since last July [1992], 16 such operations have been carried out in Gaza: 29 houses were attacked and usually reduced to rubble. In most cases, as the families concerned scarcely had 3 minutes to take out their personal effects and escape with their lives, they lost everything: furniture, household appliances, books, mementoes, clothes. Everything was burnt, everything was shot up. In only 6 houses did the army act on reliable information and wanted men were actually inside: 7 were arrested and 2 killed.

In his report dated 10 February 1993, the Israeli police controller, Avraham Adan, deplored the fact that Israeli policemen displayed 'brutality' and always lied to conceal their abuses. The report established that '64 per cent of policemen involved in physical exactions between February 1989 and May 1991 have been promoted'.[13]

It is paradoxical that since Labour has returned to power in Israel, except for the partial freeze on settlements, nothing has changed: confiscations of Palestinian land, violations of human rights, murders by 'death squads', house demolitions and vandalism by settlers taking the law into their own hands all continue. The number of Palestinian adults and children killed is actually higher than under Shamir. Both under Shamir and now under Rabin, reason and moderation have been cast to the winds—replaced by work stoppages, hunger strikes, demonstrations, confrontations, clashes, skirmishes, increasing violence, deaths, injuries, expulsions, air raids, excesses, blunders, bloodshed, murder, riots, gun law, arrests, shootings, stabbings and bomb blasts, not only in the occupied territories but in Israel itself.

As the toll of deaths and woundings rises so does the scale of violence and injustice, while the negotiations merely mark time—all contributing to a serious deterioration in the plight of Palestinians in the occupied territories and transforming the *intifada* from an unarmed popular uprising into a veritable urban guerrilla war. Such a transformation may well be exploited by the Israeli extreme right, sowing chaos and launching 'reprisal' raids against Palestinians in Israel proper—a development which would be tantamount to a civil war in Israel itself.

History may record that the *intifada* is in the process of neutralizing the ideological dimension of the Arab/Palestinian-Israeli conflict. Notwithstanding the suffering of an entire people, the *intifada* will have been the decisive factor in alerting the world to the gravity of the situation and in triggering a negotiating process conducive to a just and lasting settlement of the Palestinian question. Any other outcome could only aggravate the destabilizing factors in the region and encourage political or religious extremists. The already precarious balance in the Middle East would be dangerously affected and it would be no surprise to discover tomorrow that the activists in the streets were holding sway. Let us hope that President

Bush's message was received when, on the eve of the Madrid peace conference, he expressed the wish that the belligerents might lay aside the past and look instead to the future.

Part III
Jerusalem

12
Uru-Salem/ Yerushalayim/Jerusalem/ al-Quds

Jerusalem's strategic position, geography and history have made it a focal point for some of the most ancient sources and memorial sites. It is a place where people seek their personal roots and which contains some of the most fundamental symbols of the cultural identity and perhaps even of the destiny of individual Jews, Christians and Muslims, each one of whom cherishes an image of Jerusalem deep in their heart. Jerusalem is therefore unique, continuing to live intensely after several thousand years of convulsions and destruction, which would have destroyed any other city. It is the Holy City of all the children of Abraham—Jews, Christians and Muslims—and the symbol of their unity in faith.

Its mission as peacemaker throughout thousands of years has transformed the elements which charactize its fragility into a source of durability, since it has always listened to the voice of its prophets, who exhorted it to become the city of human fellowship and of harmony among peoples. This longevity is based not on military, economic or political might but on the force of the spiritual and intellectual influence emanating from the diverse passions that it inspires in the world's consciousness as the thrice-holy city. This city, by virtue of its geographical location and the human endeavour invested in its development, was predestined to become the symbol of the reconciliation and unity of mankind in all its diversity through faith, and of the mutual understanding of peoples, whatever their roots or cultural identity.

The Canaanites were the first to become aware of this mission: hence the name Uru-Salem, meaning city of peace. The word Salem, the name of the Canaanite god of peace, gave rise to *salam* in Arabic and *shalom* in Hebrew, both meaning peace.

The city developed in the fourth millennium BC. The tablets of Ebla, Ras Shamra and Tell al-Amarna and the Egyptian Execration Texts dating from about 2000 BC contain a description of Uru-Salem and several names of Canaanite Kings: Kaddum-Salem, Ammu, Yaker, Melki-Sadeq, Aduni-Sadeq, Aduni-Bazeq, Abdu-Heba and others. The Hebrew Bible also mentions the names of several Canaanite Kings of Uru-Salem.

It was at Uru-Salem that the Canaanite religion and 'Bible', the basis and source of inspiration of the three monotheistic religions, were developed. The Canaanite notion of religious sacrifice has been incorporated into Jewish, Christian and Muslim tradition, according to which the sacrifice of Ibrahim (Abraham) took place in Jerusalem. The Christian feast of Christmas replaced the Canaanite celebration of the birth of their gods Saher and Salem, both of whom were born on 25 December of two different goddesses and of the same father, the god El. Easter was also the Canaanite feast to celebrate the coming of spring, prior to the harvest. For the Canaanites it was the festival of renewal, during which they ate unleavened bread, that is to say bread that did not draw on the previous harvest. The Jews and Christians replaced this festival by their religious feasts (Passover and Easter), whereas the Palestinian peasants, following the Canaanite tradition, continue to celebrate the feast as a spring festival.

The Canaanite city was built in honour of Salem, god of the evening star, and of peace. The Canaanite temple is said to have been built on the rock that became the site of the Mosque of the Dome of the Rock. Our knowledge of the Canaanite city is very limited because archaeological excavations that might have uncovered its secrets have not taken place. The reasons for this are political and theological. According to the Israeli writer Amos Elon:

> The same rock is said to have been the Jebusite Araunah's threshing floor, which David bought for 50 shekels but found barely large enough for his little shrine, 'the ground around it being precipitous and steep'.[1] David's son, Solomon, walled up the eastern side towards the ravine to make more ground available for the first Hebrew temple.[2]

This assertion regarding the exact site of the Temple is at variance with the scientific facts, since no document dating from the time of its construction, said to be 1000 BC, bears out the event, which is reported only by Jews (Tanaa'im) living long afterwards, in the first century of the Christian era. The inaccurate description of the Temple given by Josephus

Flavius, a Romanized Jewish historian writing in Greek, also dates from the first century AD. Professor Kaufman of the Hebrew University of Jerusalem backs up this view regarding the site of the Temple when he writes:

> The exact site of the Temple is not recorded in any text . . . It has also been definitively established that no trace of it remains today. The latest statement to this effect is that of Kathleen Kenyon, who only recently has written, 'There is absolutely nothing left of the Temple built by Herod recalled by Josephus Flavius.'[3]

For the Canaanites, the construction of the Canaanite Temple imbued the city of Uru-Salem with its sacred character, which endured during the history of the Palestinian people, the city thus becoming successively the Jewish Yerushalayim, the Christian Jerusalem and the Muslim al-Quds.

Elon writes about the reverberations of Jerusalem's transcendent divinity:

> A priest-king of Salem called Melchizedek (King of Righteousness) meets Abraham with bread and wine, and blesses him in the name of El-Elyon (most high God), 'possessor of heaven and earth'.[4] David renamed the city Zion and took for himself the old priest-king's emblems of earthly and divine sovereignty. The memory of the ancient priest-king Melchizedek continued to hang mysteriously over the city; it entered Christian and Muslim lore as well. In Psalm 110, Melchizedek is at God's right hand and presides over the Last Judgement. In another account, Melchizedek was Shem, Noah's firstborn, who founded Jerusalem after the flood and reigned there as king and high priest.[5]

With regard to the arrival of Abraham (in Arabic, Ibrahim al-Khalil) in Uru-Salem in 2000 BC, Dajani writes:

> Coming from Ur in Iraq, Ibrahim al-Khalil the Aramaean (Syrian) arrived in the region of Jerusalem and was welcomed by the 'Banu Hath', to whom the land belonged. And the father of the prophets chose Palestine as his homeland. Al-Hanbali, writing about Abraham's immigration in his book *al-Uns al-Jalil,* says that Abraham left his native country for the love of God. God commanded him to go to Hebron and he went. On entering the cave of Hebron not long afterwards, he heard a voice enjoining him: 'O Ibrahim, honour the bones of thy father Adam.' Other historians hold that the voice was heard in Uru-Salem.
>
> [With regard to Ibrahim, Dajani adds:] When Hagar gave him a boy, he called him Ismail, which means 'obedient to Allah'. Ibrahim

established a firm link between Palestine and the Hijaz on the one hand and between Jerusalem and Mecca on the other. Ismail married his daughter to his nephew al-Iss, the son of Isaac. After Sarah's death, preceded by that of Hagar, Ibrahim al-Khalil, the friend of God, married a Canaanite, who gave him 6 children: Yaqshan, Zamran, Medan, Madian, Yashq and Sharkh. He then married another woman, who gave him 5 boys. Abraham had 13 sons, including Ismail and Isaac. Ismail was the eldest. We also find this idea in al-Masudi and among all the children of Palestine, who consider Abraham one of their ancestors.[6]

In Judaism, Abraham was preparing to sacrifice his son Isaac at Jerusalem, while the Muslims say that the sacrifice of Ismail was to take place in Mecca and that it was therefore neither Isaac nor Jerusalem that was involved. As for Yerushalayim, the Hebrews' behaviour towards it varied with the nature of historical events. According to Ezekiel, 'Thy birth and thy nativity is of the land of Canaan; thy father was an Amorite, and thy mother an Hittite.'[7] Amos Elon writes that, 'In the Hebrew Bible, Jerusalem was seen both "as a widow"[8] and as a "harlot".'[9, 10]

At another period in their history the Hebrew notables exiled in Babylon expressed their attachment to Jerusalem in the following words: 'If I forget thee, O Jerusalem, let my right hand forget her cunning.'[11] Spiritually, Jerusalem is a Holy City for the Jews. During prayers they turn towards Jerusalem. According to Jewish tradition the city is the dwelling place of God: 'God is in the midst of her.'[12] And the celestial Jerusalem is a replica of the earthly Jerusalem.

The first Temple of Yahweh was built in Jerusalem by King Solomon in the tenth century BC; the second, built by Zorobabel, was renovated or rather rebuilt and expanded by Herod 1,000 years after the first. Its exact site remains unknown. The Temple was destroyed twice: in 587 BC and in AD 70. For Orthodox Jews, it will not be raised a third time until the coming of the Messiah. According to the Halakha (rabbinical law), one may not set foot in the Temple before having completed all the purificatory rites. Fanatical Jewish fundamentalists such as Gush Emunim (Bloc of the Faithful) and Christian fundamentalists, especially Protestants, believe that the third Temple must be built before the coming of the Messiah.

Christian fundamentalists and millennarians believe that when the Jews have built their Temple it will be destroyed for a third time and all the Jews will become Christians. According to the Evangelists, the millennium, the second coming of Christ and the end of the world will occur only after all the Jews have gathered together in Palestine and converted to Christianity immediately after the destruction of their Temple. This is why Evangelical,

Charismatic and Pentecostal Christians—mainly Americans—are helping the Zionist movement, especially the Jewish fundamentalists, to build the third Temple.

The Holy Places of Judaism in Jerusalem are: the tombs of King David, Absalom and Rachel, the Wailing Wall and several synagogues dating from the eighteenth and nineteenth centuries. The Wailing Wall, which the Muslims call Buraq and which is next to the al-Aqsa Mosque, is definitely not a remnant of the Temple of Solomon. Israeli archaeologists maintain that it is a vestige of the Temple of Herod the Great, who built it around the year 20 BC. In their view, several sections date from Herod, since the architecture is typically Roman; the rest is of Ottoman origin. In the Muslim tradition it is the place where the Prophet Muhammad tethered his steed (Buraq) before ascending to heaven (Miiraj).[13] The archaeological excavations carried out by the Israeli Ministry of Religious Affairs have uncovered no trace of the Temple of King Solomon, the prototype of Canaanite temples, which was built by Canaanite architects and masons.

The Zionist movement has added a political dimension to the religious attachment of Jews to Jerusalem. Tovia Preschel summarizes that view in the following words:

> Throughout centuries of exile, Jerusalem remained alive in the hearts of Jews everywhere as the Holy City and spiritual centre of their lives. They never ceased to mourn its destruction and to pray and hope for its restoration as their national and religious capital.[14]

To consider, as some do—by associating it with King David—that the 'Tower of David' is a Jewish monument is the result of confusion: the Muslim version of the name David (Daoud) is sometimes used by Muslims who name their children after the prophets of the revealed religions. Muslims consider David and Solomon to be prophets as well as kings. Of the Tower of David, Amos Elon writes, 'In reality, it is the seventeenth-century minaret of a Turkish military-garrison mosque. Nevertheless, the tower became the main emblem of the nascent Zionist movement in the nineteenth century.'[15] Jews and Christians also believe that God will enter by the Gate of Pity (Golden Gate) to judge us.

Thus it is religion which legitimates the attachment to Jerusalem of the three monotheistic communities. It is the conflation of religion and politics, and not their beliefs, which lies at the origin of the antagonism throughout history between the children of the single faith of Abraham.

For Christians, Jerusalem is the city where Jesus Christ preached, revealed himself, was arrested, condemned to death and crucified, and rose again. The Church was created and developed in Jerusalem, and in the New Testament Jerusalem is described as a 'bride' (Revelation XXI, 2). Some of the most important Christian Holy Places in Jerusalem are: the Church of the Holy Sepulchre, the Church of Saint Anne, the Tomb of the Virgin, the Cenacle, Gethsemane and the Church of the Ascension. There are 35 Christian churches in Jerusalem today (Catholic, Orthodox, Protestant and Monophysite) and 3 patriarchs (Greek, Latin and Armenian).

The Church of the Holy Sepulchre was built on the site of the Altar of Aphrodite and the Church of the Nativity on that of the Temple of Adonis. In the Christian tradition, the Church of the Holy Sepulchre is the site of Adam's tomb, the centre of the earth, the sacrifice of Abraham, the Mount of Calvary, the stone of the anointing, Christ's tomb and the place where the risen Christ met Mary Magdalene. This holy church is shared today by Orthodox Christians (Greeks and Armenians), who own 70 per cent of it, Latins, Copts, Assyrians and Ethiopians.

Other sites in Jerusalem are also venerated by Christians, and some by Jews, Christians and Muslims alike. These sites include Mount Zion (a word of Canaanite origin meaning 'arid desert'). On this hill the Canaanites built a temple to worship their god Ba'al, which was surrounded by a fortress to defend the city of Uru-Salem. When David took the fortress he gave its name to the entire city, which he called Zion.

On Mount Zion there stands a building which is venerated by the Jews as the Tomb of David and by the Christians as the site of the Last Supper. Christ was brought to the Mount after his arrest and it was there that Peter denied him three times. The Muslims, who consider the tomb to be an Islamic holy place, also built a mosque on the site, which was confiscated and converted into a synagogue by the Israelis after the 1948 War.

Many religious sites in Jerusalem owe their identity more to faith than to science; neither their authenticity nor their location has ever been scientifically determined. Such sites include: the Temple of Solomon, which was rebuilt by Herod some 10 centuries after its destruction; the Tomb of David, which was built by the Crusaders some 2,000 years after his death; and the Tomb of Absalom, which was erected about 1,000 years after his death. Certain scientists have cast doubt on the authenticity of Herod's family tomb and the Tomb of the Virgin Mary.

Jerusalem, which is called al-Quds ('the Holy City') in Arabic, is a hallowed and blessed place for Muslims. It was in fact from al-Quds, and more specifically from the Rock, that the Prophet ascended to heaven: the al-Aqsa Mosque is mentioned by name in the first verse of the Quranic chapter known as 'The Night Journey' (*al-Israa wal-Miiraj*). It was also at al-Quds, on the esplanade of the al-Haram al-Sharif (al-Aqsa) Mosque, that

Muhammad led the Prophets of the revealed religions in prayer.

In the early days of Islam, Muslims faced Jerusalem (the first *qibla*) when praying, and the Holy City was an integral part of the pilgrimage route, which also included Mecca and Medina. Jerusalem ceased to be a place of pilgrimage following two major historical events: the Crusades; and the conflict between the Wahhabis and the Hashemites, which was instigated by the British.

In the two compendia of authenticated *hadiths* (the authoritative sayings of the Prophet Muhammad which rank immediately after the Quran), compiled by Boukhari and by Muslim, it is reported that Muhammad restricted the pilgrimage to three sanctuaries: his own mosque in Medina, the al-Haram Mosque in Mecca and the al-Aqsa Mosque in Jerusalem. In another *hadith*, Ibn Maja reports the following dialogue:

We asked the Prophet to speak to us about the significance of the Mosque of Jerusalem in Islam. This was his reply: 'It is the place where all will gather for the Last Judgement. Go there and pray. One prayer said there is equal to 1,000 prayers said elsewhere.'

This could account for the fervent wish expressed by King Faisal of Saudi Arabia, in a conversation with Henry Kissinger after the October 1973 War, that he might pray at the al-Aqsa Mosque.

The Rock is also of great religious significance to Muslims. In his scholarly treatise entitled *Aalam al-Masajid* (p. 286), al-Zarkashi writes that 'the Mosque of Jerusalem is dear to Paradise because the Rock it shelters comes from Paradise and is the naval of the world'. Among the great Islamic theological treatises in which the religious importance of Jerusalem has been stressed are Ibn Farkah's *Ba'ath al-Nufus ila Ziyarat al-Quds al-Mahrus* (On Encouraging the Faithful to Visit Jerusalem, the Protected City), Hibat Allah al-Shaffi's *al-Uns fi Fadhail al-Quds* (On Delighting in the Blessings of Jerusalem) and Ibn al-Jawzi's *Fadhail al-Quds* (On the Blessings of Jerusalem). The following *hadiths* of the Prophet are mentioned in these works:

. . . on the day of the Last Judgement, God will transport the Kaaba to Jerusalem and bring it to rest on Mount Zion.

. . . to die in Jerusalem is to die in Paradise.

. . . an evil deed in Jerusalem is more reprehensible than 1,000 evil deeds elsewhere; and a virtuous deed in Jerusalem is equivalent to 1,000 virtuous deeds outside the Holy City.

In his book, *Muthir al-Gharam fi Fadhail al-Quds wal-Sham* (Calling forth Delight in the Blessings of Jerusalem and Syria), Ibn Surur al-Maqdissi, the great tenth-century Palestinian geographer and theologian, wrote that on the day of the Last Judgement, God would transport to Jerusalem all that was precious in Mecca and Medina.

In his book, *al-Jami al-Mustaqsa fi Fadhail al-Masjid al-Aqsa* (Compendium of the Blessings of the al-Aqsa Mosque), Ibn Assaker, the twelfth-century Arab historian, defined happiness as eating fruit in the shadow of the Dome of the Rock after praying in that holy mosque.

Another major religious and historical event illustrates the important place occupied by Jerusalem in the hearts of all Muslims. In 638, contrary to his usual practice (as attested by numerous examples of his refusal), the Caliph Omar ibn al-Khattab agreed to enter the Holy City in person in order to receive its keys from the hands of the Patriarch Sophronios. At Sophronios' request, Omar recounted to him the basic tenets of Islam, which the Patriarch found to be similar to those of Christianity. He then invited Omar to pray in the Church of the Holy Sepulchre, but Omar declined on the grounds that if the Muslims found out that he had prayed there, they might appropriate the church.

Jerusalem is sacred to Muslims not only because it is the site of the *miiraj*, the Dome of the Rock and the al-Aqsa Mosque, but also because it is regarded by them as the city of Abraham, Solomon and Jesus, who are recognized as prophets by Islam.

The Muslims' deep attachment to the Holy City draws its strength from religious roots, but it also has a politically mobilizing dimension. For example, when in 1229 the Ayyubid Sultan of Egypt, Palestine and Syria, al-Malik al-Kamil, surrendered Jerusalem to the German Emperor, Frederick II, in a peace treaty signed by the two men in Jaffa, the peasants of Palestine revolted, and the Muslims, in their grief, gave violent expression to the anger they felt against their 'capitulationist' Sultan. Their revolt, which was supported by all Muslims, continued until the Holy City was restored to its inhabitants in 1244.

More recently, the arson which damaged the al-Aqsa Mosque on 21 August 1969 prompted the establishment of the Organization of the Islamic Conference and of the al-Quds Committee, whose purpose was to put an end to the Israeli occupation of East Jerusalem. The fire, started by one Denis Michael Rohan, a member of a millennarian Protestant sect, was not the only act of aggression, or attempted aggression, against a Muslim holy place; in April 1982 an Israeli soldier named Alan Harry Goodman fired his automatic M-16 rifle at Muslims gathered for prayer at the Dome of the Rock, killing one man and wounding some ten other people.

In early 1984, 16 members of a Jewish Kabbalist sect stockpiled explosives with which to blow up the two Muslim mosques, the Dome of the Rock and al-Aqsa. Several months later, 28 armed students of a *yeshiva* (Jewish rabbinical school) were stopped before they could enter a tunnel leading to the al-Aqsa Mosque. About one year later, a 28-member terrorist group belonging to a clandestine organization of Jewish settlers in the occupied West Bank were arrested on the eve of their attempt to dynamite the Dome of the Rock.

On 8 October 1990, 22 Palestinians were killed and hundreds of others were wounded by live rounds of ammunition fired by members of the Israeli occupying forces following a peaceful Palestinian protest against the attempts by a group of fanatical Jewish extremists to profane the esplanade of the Haram al-Sharif.

These provocations and attacks against the al-Aqsa Mosque could have had irreparable consequences. It was a miracle (and perhaps also because the human injury and material damage were limited) that a confrontation was averted between the Muslim and Jewish communities.

No one can predict the domestic and international consequences of the destruction of the two sacred mosques of Jerusalem, but they would be extremely serious. It would not be possible to contain the legitimate reaction of the Muslim community, and the blame would fall exclusively on Israel as long as it continued to occupy East Jerusalem.

The many different names given to Jerusalem testify to its eventful history and unique nature. When its Canaanite founders, the ancestors of the Palestinians, built it on such arid, craggy terrain, did they not intend it to be a religious site alone? This landscape, described by Ernest Renan as the 'Fifth Gospel', was chosen by the Canaanites as the site of the city they founded to worship their god of peace and prosperity, Salem. The Canaanite divinity is surely the source of its peaceful calling.

It is not known when Uru-Salem became Jebus—a word derived from the Canaanite Jebusites who lived there at the time. In the Old Testament, we also find the name of Zion, which initially designated a part of the city of Jebus on which stood a fortress seized by David when he took the city from the Jebusites, and which ultimately came to be the name of the whole city. The Hebrews, using a corrupt form of the Canaanite name of the city, called it Yerushalem—transformed by the Jews of today into Yerushalayim. Saint Matthew, in the New Testament, called it Hagia Polis ('Holy City'). But the Christian name of Uru-Salem, which is also a distortion of its Canaanite name, became Jerusalem. The Roman Emperor Hadrian (Aelius Hadrianus) gave the city the name Aelia Capitolina.

To the Muslims, the city was known as Bait al-Maqdis ('the Holy House'). There were subsequently to be several variants of this name, including Bait al-Quds, al-Quds, al-Quds al-Sharif and al-Madina al-Muqadassa. The Islamo-Christian Arabic name is al-Quds. The Holy City has also been variously called Dar al-Salam, Madinat al-Salam and Qaryrat al-Salam, among others. All these names confirm the sacred character of the city.

The Palestinians regard Jerusalem, both geographically and historically, as the beating heart of Palestine and its natural capital. Jerusalem and the Palestinian people are inseparable, by virtue of their common history and destiny. The culture which finds expression in its monuments bears witness to this. And its stones and streets live only through the people who are their moving spirit and who hear the voice of the history that dwells within them.

To the Palestinians, Jerusalem is the centre where their past lives on and which holds the seeds of their future; hence it is in Jerusalem that they perceive the roots of their present. They feel sublimely and mystically united with the city, to the extent that, over the centuries, they have drawn from it all their metaphorical and symbolic concepts, and indeed the very meaning of their tolerant, pluralistic humanism.

To separate the Palestinian people from Jerusalem and deny them the right to exercise sovereignty over it is to deprive them of the expression of this pluralistic and humanistic identity, to cut them off from their source of inspiration, from their collective values, and leave them with no alternative to the lure of nationalism and chauvinism. To the collective Palestinian mind, it would be an unforgivable crime to violate history and geography in this way, to sever a nation and a people from their capital which symbolizes their identity and the landmarks of their community.

Palestinian Jerusalem is the meeting-point of so many cultures and civilizations. For in Jerusalem, geographical theology adds its weight to historical theology; it is a place where all monotheists have perceived a meeting of God and the human race. For in Jerusalem, God is revealed and delivers His message.

The Palestinians regard the unilateral occupation and annexation of East Jerusalem by the Israeli government as illegal and as motivated by the desire to exercise sole control over the Holy City, leading ultimately to its Judaization or at least to the imposition by force of the supremacy of the Jewish religion and its privileges over the other religions. This policy is perceived by the Palestinians as a prejudicial attempt to end the ecumenical and universal character of the occupied Holy City.

No sooner had Jerusalem been annexed for the purpose of turning it into a Jewish city or 'eternal capital of Israel' than the Israeli authorities took a series of flagrantly unjust measures, evicting Palestinians from certain quarters of the Old City, demolishing their houses, settling fanatical Jews in the heart of the Muslim and Christian quarters, building a dozen Jewish quarters on the land confiscated from the Palestinians, carrying out illegal raids and establishing a 'Jewish belt' around the city. This policy of annexation, deliberately implemented in violation of the Security Council's decisions, is aimed at 'Israelizing' Jerusalem, which belongs spiritually to the three revealed monotheistic religions, and, politically, has always been an integral part of Palestine.

To mislead international opinion and compound the confusion, Israel invokes the need to 'reunify' the city, possibly in an allusion to the case of Berlin. The situation of Jerusalem is totally different from that of Berlin, however: in the latter case, there has been a reversion to a previous historically, politically and legally normal order, whereas in the case of Jerusalem, the western part is inhabited by Israelis and the eastern part by Palestinians—quite apart from other considerations which we have mentioned elsewhere.

'Reunification' is justifiable only if there is an agreement between Palestinians and Israelis to make it the capital of a united, secular and democratic Palestine in which undivided sovereignty is exercised. By annexing East Jerusalem, however, Israel has acted unilaterally in bringing this part of the city under its sole sovereignty. Israel is thus depriving Jerusalem of its cohesion, its integrity and its harmony, by continuing to encroach upon the Old City, house by house, and by striving to make life impossible for its inhabitants, the custodians of its stones and its memory.

Israel's exclusive hold over the city (which is political and ideological, not spiritual, in nature) seeks to turn Christian and Muslim Jerusalem into a mere collection of artistic and historic monuments, an archaeological museum, a pleasantly developed tourist site—in short, Israel is in the process of turning Jerusalem into a modern tourist city, like so many other cities elsewhere in the world. Yet Jerusalem is a site of exceptional universal value which is now endangered. It is a city which, in terms of its role and significance through the ages, is unique in the world, but it is a city whose authenticity is today in jeopardy. Jerusalem is also a population, devoted to the cohesion of its city and to peace in its everyday life; but it is a population today saddened and oppressed, suffering with every passing day, and against its will, the consequences of exclusivity, and in danger of falling prey to the horrors of exclusion.

As evidence of Israel's discriminatory and annexationist policies, Elon mentions certain measures and practices engaged in by the occupying power:

> In the former Jewish quarter of the Old City, Arabs were evicted from houses occupied by Jews before 1948. But Arabs in the united city were not allowed to repossess property across the former dividing lines that they had been forced to abandon in 1948.[16]

Elon also writes:

> In Jerusalem after 1967, form did not follow function; it followed ideology and politics. The politics of town planning and of housing in this period were the politics of demography and annexation . . . The new suburbs—intended exclusively for the growing Jewish population—were heavily subsidized by the central government and built on expropriated Arab land. Little public housing was made available to the Arab population, which grew at almost the same rate. [He adds that there was a] disproportionate appropriation of public funds.[17]

As a rider to these quotations, it should be mentioned that the expropriation of property belonging to Arabs and to the Islamic Waqf in what was known as the Jewish quarter was an arbitrary act. Indeed, although most of the inhabitants of the Jewish quarter were Jews, it is none the less true that Arabs occupied the district before 1948 and that they and the Islamic Waqf had legitimate rights to property, which should have been respected by the occupying Israeli power. Moreover, Israeli law prohibits non-Jews from buying or renting property in the Jewish quarter.

In an article published in its official newspaper *L'Osservatore Romano* in 1971, the Vatican expressed its disapproval and its condemnation of the Israeli policy of *faits accomplis:*

> A very grave state of affairs is being created against legality, on the basis of the logic of *faits accomplis*. The measures of expropriation suffice to give an idea of the radical manner in which a character not conforming to its historical and religious nature and to its universal vocation is being imposed on the city. In January 1968, 300 acres of land were confiscated in the Mount Scopus area and are already largely built up with Jewish residential quarters. In August 1970 another 1,200 acres have been confiscated in the Arab zone of Jerusalem and around the city, in order to implement the 'Greater Jerusalem' plans. Another project is under study for the Old City of Jerusalem, according to which about 6,000 Arabs will be displaced and several buildings consficated. It is impossible

to avoid experiencing a profound apprehension in the face of such grave changes. Even in Israel itself these plans have provoked well-founded criticisms and not just from an urbanistic point of view.[18]

On his various fact-finding missions over the past 20 years, the personal representative of the Director-General of UNESCO has emphasized in his successive reports, which have been presented to UNESCO's Executive Board and General Conference, the extent of the modifications and the serious violations of the Hague Convention of 1954 and of UNESCO's decisions and resolutions. Those reports describe in great detail, on the basis of personal observation by the Director-General's representative and information supplied by both Palestinian and Israeli authorities, all the demolitions and archaeological excavations conducted since 1967; these have caused serious damage to the Islamic and Christian cultural heritage, particularly around the al-Aqsa Mosque. Even Muslim cemeteries have not escaped destruction.

The new buildings in the city have completely transformed its historical architectural appearance. The gravity of this situation warranted the inclusion by UNESCO of the Old City of Jerusalem in the World Heritage List, in accordance with the 1972 Convention for the Protection of the World Cultural and Natural Heritage.[19] It can only be deeply regretted that although all the reports submitted to UNESCO have been studied carefully by the appropriate UNESCO bodies and have given rise to important decisions, the occupying Israeli authorities have taken no action on them.

As early as 1947, the United Nations started to take an interest in Jerusalem, as part of Palestine, when Britain informed that organization of its decision to relinquish its mandate over Palestine. The General Assembly of the United Nations, in its Resolution 181 (II) of 29 November 1947 on the partition of Palestine into two states, also defined the status of Jerusalem. The resolution stipulated that:

> The City of Jerusalem shall be established as a corpus separatum under a special international regime and shall be administered by the United Nations . . . The Trusteeship Council shall . . . elaborate and approve a detailed Statute of the City.

It has never been possible to apply the statute, as Israel and Jordan were opposed to it. On the other hand, the *de facto* partition of Jerusalem after the 1948 War between Israel and Jordan was confirmed by the cease-fire agreement between the two belligerent states on 30 November 1948. It became official under the armistice agreement signed on 3 April 1949. These two agreements were concluded thanks to the efforts of a mediator appointed by the United Nations General Assembly.

In Resolution 194 (III) of 11 December 1948, the General Assembly reaffirmed the resolution on the partition of Palestine and the international status of Jerusalem. As we have already seen, it established a Conciliation Commission for Palestine (CCP). The CCP set up a special committee for Jerusalem, whose recommendations Israel rejected. After rejecting the resolution, Israel decided to place West Jerusalem, which it had occupied in 1948, under its jurisdiction.

In September 1948 Israel installed its Supreme Court in West Jerusalem, and the Knesset met there in February 1949. On 23 January 1950 the Knesset proclaimed West Jerusalem 'capital of Israel', and in 1951 the Israeli government was in turn installed in the western part of Jerusalem (the New City); Jordan, for its part, decided to extend its jurisdiction to the Old City.

On 4 April 1950 the Trusteeship Council approved a statute for Jerusalem. Israel rejected that statute and declared that it would accept an international regime only for the Holy Places in the Old City, which was not under its jurisdiction. Jordan was not yet a member of the United Nations. On 12 July 1953 the Israeli government transferred its Ministry of Foreign Affairs from Tel Aviv to West Jerusalem. This transfer caused protests from the permanent members of the Security Council and from the entire international community. States that had embassies in Israel refused to move them from Tel Aviv to West Jerusalem.

The armistice agreement struck between Israel and Jordan included the principle of freedom of access to the Holy Places, but its implementation was linked to the issue of the return of the Palestinian refugees. From 1948 to 1967 Jerusalem was divided between two hostile states. The Israelis did not have access to the Jewish Holy Places in the Old City, owing to the continuing state of war between Israel and Jordan. Amos Elon sums up this situation as follows:

Pious Jews gazed from their rooftops, across minefields, towards the lost stones where they could no longer worship. Arabs, likewise, stared across in the opposite direction at the old homes in West Jerusalem they had been forced to abandon during the fighting, which were now occupied by new Jewish immigrants.[20]

On 5 June 1967 war broke out between Israel and the neighbouring Arab countries. From 7 June onwards, the eastern part of Jerusalem was occupied by the Israeli army. On 27 June 1967 the Israeli Knesset adopted the following text: 'State law, jurisdiction and administration shall apply to all parts of Eretz Israel [what was mandatory Palestine] which the government shall determine by decree.' The next day the Israeli government published a decree extending 'state law, jurisdiction and administration' to the occupied eastern part of Jerusalem. This position was also strengthened by more tangible measures such as the demolition of the historic Maghreb quarter.

On 5 July 1967 the General Assembly of the United Nations adopted Resolution 2253 (ES-V), in which it called upon Israel 'to rescind all measures already taken and to desist forthwith from taking any action which would alter the status of Jerusalem'. On 14 July 1967 the General Assembly adopted Resolution 2254 (ES-V), deploring the failure of Israel to implement General Assembly Resolution 2253 (ES-V). Both those resolutions were ignored by Israel, which even transferred the Israeli High Court to occupied East Jerusalem.

The United Nations Security Council also condemned Israel and demanded the annulment of the measures affecting the status of the city. In addition to the famous Resolution 242 of 22 November 1967, emphasizing the inadmissibility of the acquisition of territory by war, the Security Council adopted several resolutions concerning Palestinian East Jerusalem. On 21 May 1968 it adopted Resolution 252, paragraph 2 of which reads:

> Considers that all legislative and administrative measures and actions taken by Israel, including expropriation of land and properties thereon, which tend to change the legal status of Jerusalem are invalid and cannot change that status.

In Resolution 267 of 3 July 1969, the Security Council reaffirmed its previous resolution and once more urgently called upon Israel 'to rescind forthwith all measures taken by it which may tend to change the status of the City of Jerusalem, and in future to refrain from all actions likely to have such an effect'.

Following the extensive damage caused by arson to the al-Aqsa Mosque on 21 August 1969, the Security Council adopted Resolution 271 of 15 September 1969, which:

> Condemns the failure of Israel to comply with the aforementioned resolutions and calls upon it to implement forthwith the provisions of these resolutions.
>
> [It also calls upon Israel] scrupulously to observe the provisions of the Geneva Conventions and international law governing military occupation and to refrain from causing any hindrance to the discharge of the established functions of the Muslim Supreme Council of Jerusalem,

including any co-operation that council may desire from countries with predominantly Muslim population and from Muslim communities in relation to its plans for the maintenance and repair of the Islamic Holy Places in Jerusalem.

Security Council Resolution 298 of 25 September 1971:

Confirms in the clearest possible terms that all legislative and administrative actions taken by Israel to change the status of the City of Jerusalem, including expropriation of land and properties, transfer of populations and legislation aimed at the incorporation of the occupied section, are totally invalid and cannot change that status.

Israel refused to comply with that resolution or to recognize the applicability to East Jerusalem of the 4th Geneva Convention relative to the Protection of Civilian Persons in Time of War, of 12 August 1949.

Resolution 465 of 1 March 1980 reaffirms the foregoing resolutions concerning the character and status of the city. Resolution 476 of 30 June 1980 expresses the grave concern of the international community at 'the legislative steps initiated in the Israeli Knesset with the aim of changing the character and status of the Holy City of Jerusalem'.

Lastly, following the enactment by the Israeli Knesset of a 'basic law' proclaiming a change in the character and status of the Holy City of Jerusalem, the Security Council adopted Resolution 478 of 20 August 1980, in which it:

Affirms that the enactment of the 'basic law' by Israel constitutes a violation of international law and does not affect the continued application of the Geneva Convention relative to the Protection of Civilian Persons in Time of War, of 12 August 1949, in the Palestinian and other Arab territories occupied since June 1967, including Jerusalem;

Determines that all legislative and administrative measures and actions taken by Israel, the occupying Power, which have altered or purport to alter the character and status of the Holy City of Jerusalem, and in particular the recent 'basic law' on Jerusalem, are *null and void* and must be rescinded forthwith;

Decides not to recognize the 'basic law' and such other actions by Israel that, as a result of this law, seek to alter the character and status of Jerusalem and calls upon:

(a) All Member States to accept this decision;

(b) Those States that have established diplomatic missions at Jerusalem to withdraw such missions from the Holy City.

Israel's reaction to this decision by the Security Council was identical to that adopted towards the other decisions and resolutions of the United Nations concerning East Jerusalem:

> The Israeli government considers that there is no justification for the question of Jerusalem being brought before the Security Council, nor for the resolution adopted in that connection . . . Israeli policy with regard to Jerusalem will not be altered.

Since then, the Security Council and the General Assembly of the United Nations have adopted several decisions and resolutions condemning the repeated Israeli violations of international conventions and Israel's persistent refusal to respect the resolutions. From 1948 to the present day, therefore, the positions have remained unchanged: on the one hand, the perseverance of the United Nations in its resolutions and, on the other, the continuing refusal by Israel to comply with those resolutions and decisions.[21]

Since the occupation and annexation of Palestinian Jerusalem, the Holy City has been more divided than ever, contrary to what Israeli propaganda says about its 'reunification'. The city lives in a state of permanent tension, with an increasing number of ghettos and enclaves. For the Israeli occupiers dream of a Jerusalem populated solely by Jews in which the Christian and Muslim Holy Places would be museums open to Christian and Muslim pilgrims.

Amos Elon confirms this statement when he says that the 'reunification' is not genuine, that each part of the city has its own separate economic, social, political and cultural structures. In reality, there are two cities, which have been artificially 'reunited for ideological and political purposes'. He describes the situation as follows:

> There are two distinctly separate downtown areas—that is, two business-and-entertainment centres—one Palestinian and one Israeli. Welfare policies in the two sectors are governed by different criteria. Each community is still served by its own fire department, hospitals, and medical emergency crews. Schools are entirely separate. There are two urban and inter-urban transportation systems, often serving the same routes; two electric power grids (administered, respectively, by an Israeli and a Palestinian company); and two price scales for real estate. Jews will not use Arab electricity if they can avoid it, and Arabs, if they can help it, will not put their money into an Israeli-owned bank. The new

Jewish suburbs across the old demarcation line are often isolated, high-density enclaves encircled by low-density, semi-rural areas inhabited by Palestinians. An ingenious new road network enables Israelis in the new suburbs to travel back and forth almost without seeing an Arab.[22]

The occupiers pretend not to understand that a city consists first and foremost of men and women who have a history, traditions and a culture and who, through their presence, make that city live. A city unique in its history and vocation, such as Jerusalem, can never be reduced to its monuments, houses, streets and squares or transformed into a modern town like any other. Hence it is a question not simply of providing access to the Holy Places but also of safeguarding the character and homogeneity of Jerusalem in its historical, social, cultural and religious dimensions as a unique and thrice-holy city.

Israel's exclusive control, as occupying power, over East Jerusalem has meant that one religion has enjoyed supremacy and privileges over the others. This exclusive control must be replaced by an ecumenical approach; this can come about only with the ending of the Israeli occupation and the granting of guarantees by the Palestinian state, which would have sovereignty over the eastern part of the city, to ensure respect for its universal character and unimpeded access to its religious buildings. An interreligious council could be created by decision of the Security Council to supervise the observance of these guarantees by the Palestinian national authorities.

In conclusion, we may recall the appeal made by Pope John Paul II, who declared, 'My hope is that a common monotheistic tradition may help to promote harmony between all those who invoke the name of God.'[23] Let us also remember the question asked by Father Lelong ('War or peace in Jerusalem?'), the reply to which depends principally, of course, on political, economic and military factors. But it also depends—to a far greater extent than is usually realized—on how believers live their faith in their respective communities. To take up the distinction proposed by Bergson in *The Two Sources*, will that faith be 'closed' or 'open'? Jews, Christians and Muslims must now make a choice. 'Will they manage to be themselves while also respecting others? Will they realize that God belongs to no one and that He calls on all of us to seek peace?'[24]

Throughout the millennia of its history, from Uru-Salem to al-Quds, from the god Salem to the One God (Elohim, God, Allah), from Canaan to Arafat, Jerusalem has built up its attributes as a 'house of peace', an ecumenical city, a thrice-holy city and, above all, a city of altruism. If the Israelis have unilaterally made its western half their capital, its eastern half is, will remain and can only be the capital of the sovereign state of Palestine. But Jerusalem is also, and must remain, the shrine or capital of the monotheistic religions.

For it is the eternal, essential vocation of Jerusalem to promote peace and understanding between human beings in accordance with its philosophical, ethical and religious values: fundamental values for more than 2 billion people on all continents. Aware of the importance the international community attaches to Jerusalem because of its calling and its role in reconciling peoples, Yasser Arafat has always affirmed that, 'The war started in Jerusalem, and it is there that peace will be revived.'

CHRISTIAN

QUARTER

MUSLIM

QUARTER

Dome of
the Rock

JEWISH

al-Aqsa
Mosque

ARMENIAN

QUARTER

QUARTER

0   50 100 150 m

Map 9. The Old City of Jerusalem

Part IV
The State of Palestine: a Legal Study

13
The Formation of the State of Palestine

1. The state of Palestine was proclaimed by the Palestine National Council meeting in Algiers on 15 November 1988. The proclamation was a turning-point in the modern history of Palestine, the 'land of God's revelations to humanity'. Since that date, 92 countries[1] have recognized the new state and established diplomatic relations with it. The United Nations General Assembly adopted a resolution[2] on 15 December 1988 which 'acknowledges' the proclamation of the state of Palestine and decides that the designation 'Palestine' should be used in the United Nations system in place of the designation 'Palestine Liberation Organization'.

The question of the existence of the state of Palestine from the point of view of international law can no longer be evaded and leads to another question regarding the admission to international organizations of the state thus proclaimed. It is a question that has quite rightly been raised by Palestine, whose President applied in spring 1989 for admission to a number of international organizations with a universal vocation.

The present study has been compiled in order to help answer these questions. It confines itself strictly to legal considerations and seeks to take the heat out of a debate that has all too often been clouded by the prejudices, misunderstandings and hatred generated by several thousand years of history and exacerbated by over 40 years of armed conflict, of blood and tears.

2. The state of Palestine was not created out of nothing but is the product

of a long, gradual process of maturing. Any attempt to provide a detailed historical record of this process, even beginning in the twentieth century, would take us beyond the scope of this study. This has in any case already been done, memorably, by the United Nations.[3] It might nevertheless be helpful to give a broad outline of the recent history of the Palestinian people, which led to the decision to found its own state in 1988.

1917–1947: Palestine, a Nation on a Dependent Territory

3. The formation of states in the Arab Middle East is a recent phenomenon. The emergence of these states, facilitated by the development of the Arab Nationalist Movement, resulted from the detachment of the various territories from the Ottoman Empire at the end of the First World War. Initially, the League of Nations placed the former Ottoman provinces of Arab culture under mandate to the Western powers which had emerged victorious from the 1914–18 War. Article 22 of the Covenant of the League of Nations states that:

> Certain communities formerly belonging to the Turkish Empire have reached a stage of development where their existence as independent nations can be provisionally recognized subject to the rendering of administrative advice and assistance by a Mandatory until such time as they are able to stand alone. The wishes of these communities must be a principal consideration in the selection of the Mandatory.

As noted by a distinguished writer, 'They were really states in the full sense of the term . . . whose accession to independence had been provisionally deferred.'[4]

4. Palestine (formally distinguished from Transjordan in 1922) was placed under British mandate—without its population being consulted—together with Transjordan and Iraq, while Syria and Lebanon were placed under French mandate.

The communities of the mandated territories rapidly forged national identities in the struggle against the mandatory powers to obtain independence. When the United Nations came into being in 1945, all these communities, except Palestine, had achieved the status of sovereign states. Syria, Lebanon and Iraq became founding members of the United Nations. Transjordan joined them later.

5. Palestine was different because of the provision[5] in the mandate imposed on it whereby the mandatory power was to implement the Balfour Declaration issued on 2 November 1917 by the British government in favour of 'the establishment in Palestine of a national home for the Jewish people . . . it being understood that nothing shall be done which may prejudice the civil and religious rights of existing non-Jewish communities in Palestine'. In 1922 the population of Palestine was 750,000, of whom less than 10 per cent were Jews and over 90 per cent Arabs.[6] Moreover, according to the correspondence between Sir Henry McMahon and Sherif Hussein, Britain had promised independence to the Arab countries, including Palestine, as soon as the war was over.[7]

The validity of the Balfour Declaration in terms of international law is more than questionable, and one may ponder the inherent contradiction in the terms of the mandate as well as its compatibility with the principles stated by US President Woodrow Wilson regarding the right of peoples to self-determination. Many studies of this subject have been written.[8] Suffice it to say that these contradictory proclamations, together with emigration and Arab resistance to it, were bound to lead to prolonged disorder and bloody conflict on Palestinian soil.

6. A British Royal Commission headed by Lord Peel, set up to inquire into the disturbances in 1937, submitted a report[9] which, while standing by the Balfour Declaration, recognized the justice of the Palestinian people's demands for independence and acknowledged that Britain's dual obligations were not reconcilable. The report concluded that the partition of Palestine into two states seemed to offer a chance of peace. Further to this report, Britain published a White Paper[10] in which it stated that the aspirations of the Arabs and Jews could not be satisfied under the terms of the mandate and that partition was the best solution. The Arabs would obtain their national independence and the Jews their 'national home'. Under the White Paper plan, one-third of the area of Palestine was to be allotted to the Jews.

However, the plan proved difficult to implement and was abandoned. On the basis of a study by a new technical commission, the British government declared in 1938[11] that further examination had shown that the political, administrative and financial difficulties involved in the proposal to create two independent states—one Arab and one Jewish—inside Palestine were so great that this solution was impracticable.

In 1939 Britain published another White Paper[12] in which it stated that those who drafted the mandate could not have intended that Palestine should one day become a Jewish state against the will of the Arab population of the country. That would be contrary to Britain's obligations under the mandate and to the assurances that had been given to the Arab people in the past. The solution envisaged was the establishment within ten years of an independent Palestinian state in which power would be shared between Arabs and Jews. But the outbreak of war in 1939 led to the shelving of attempts to solve a Palestinian problem created artificially by the mandatory power.

7. Several points of great legal significance may be deduced from this brief overview:

(a) The Covenant of the League of Nations viewed the population of the mandated territories, including the population of Palestine, as a nation whose independence was provisionally suspended.

(b) As observed later by the International Court of Justice,[13] the terms of the mandate did not involve any cession of territory or transfer of sovereignty to the mandatory power, which was to exercise an international administrative function with the object of promoting the well-being and development of the inhabitants.

(c) Arab aspirations towards an independent Palestinian state were recognized as legitimate by the mandatory power while it was exercising its mandate, but the British government's policy on the matter was extremely erratic.

(d) Without reference to the irreconcilable terms of the Palestine mandate and Britain's inconsistent policy before and after the institution of the mandate, the Arab Palestinian identity asserted itself in the following ways: in the struggle against the Zionists, who were trying to settle in greater numbers in Palestine, and in the struggle against the British, who were effectively depriving the country's Arab population of rights that they had recognized in theory. These rights were based not on abstract claims but on actual physical presence on the land throughout the colonial period, not to mention that preceding it. Under law, that presence constituted the very criterion for determining whether a people was entitled to self-determination.[14]

(e) During the period of the mandate, this awareness of a Palestinian identity was reinforced by the activities of a variety of Palestinian institutions in the political, economic and cultural fields.

(f) At the end of the mandate period, the Arab population of Palestine still constituted a comfortable majority (67 per cent) despite the artificial demographic changes brought about by the mass immigration of Jews into the country in the interwar period. In 1939 Arabs owned 94 per cent of the total territory of Palestine.

The Formation of the State of Palestine

1947–1949: Two States in Palestine?

8. Britain, having been unable to implement the contradictory terms of the Palestine mandate (creation of a Jewish national home and safeguarding of Arab rights), offloaded responsibility for solving the Palestinian problem onto the United Nations in February 1947.

The United Nations General Assembly, after considering various possibilities, finally adopted Resolution 181(II) on 29 November 1947, which provided for a Plan of Partition of Palestine into a Jewish state and an Arab state, with international status for Jerusalem. The Arab Palestinians initially resisted the Partition Plan, which established an unjust link between the persecution of the Jews in Europe—for which the Palestinians bore no responsibility—and the amputation of their territory.

9. The Arab view was not upheld by the General Assembly, and the Arab proposal that the International Court of Justice be asked to deliver an advisory opinion on the competence of the United Nations to decide on the partition of Palestine was also rejected, causing a resurgence of strife.

On 14 May 1948, several months before the deadline set by Resolution 181(II), the Jews proclaimed the creation of the state of Israel. This proclamation[15] invokes the 'natural right' of the Jews to return to the land of their ancestors, the Balfour Declaration, the persecution of the Jews in Europe and United Nations Resolution 181(II) concerning the partition of Palestine. This policy of *fait accompli* spurred the Arab states to military intervention on behalf of the Palestinians. This was the first Arab-Israeli War, which ended with Israel occupying more Palestinian land than it had been assigned under the Partition Plan. Only the West Bank of the Jordan and the Gaza Strip escaped occupation by Israel. Hundreds of thousands of Palestinians joined an exodus and became refugees in the territories that had not been occupied or in neighbouring Arab countries.

10. The United Nations was now deeply involved in the Palestinian question, which thus became the core issue of the broader Middle East question. Among the resolutions adopted by the United Nations, Resolution 194(III) of 11 December 1948 is of special importance since it stated that Palestinian refugees wishing to return to their homes and live at peace with their neighbours had a right to do so and provided for compensation to be paid, in accordance with the provisions of international law, to those choosing not to return.

Some months later, between February and July 1949, armistice agreements were concluded between Israel and the Arab states under the auspices of the United Nations. The agreements specified that they had been dictated by military, and not political, considerations, that they did not prejudice the positions of any of the parties and that no political advantage could be gained from them. Hence, they gave Israel no legal right to the territories occupied during the hostilities, beyond the lines specified in the Partition Resolution.

On 12 May 1949 Israel was admitted to the United Nations by Resolution 273(III). The representative of Israel had previously undertaken before the Special Political Committee to apply the United Nations resolutions, in particular Resolution 181(II) of 29 November 1947 on partition, and Resolution 194(III) of 11 December 1948 on the return of refugees. The admission resolution recalls this undertaking on the part of Israel in paragraph 3.

11. As for the Arab Palestinian state provided for under the Partition Plan, it did not materialize and remained, for the time being, a latent state. Resolution 181(II), which is still in force, confers on it, in advance, full international legitimacy; and Israel's undertaking to implement that resolution is legally enforceable if only because:

It is well recognized that declarations made by way of unilateral acts, concerning legal or factual situations, may have the effect of creating legal obligations . . . When it is the intention of the state making the declaration that it should become bound according to its terms, that intention confers on the declaration the character of a legal undertaking, the state being thenceforth legally required to follow a course of conduct consistent with the declaration. An undertaking of this kind, if given publicly, and with an intent to be bound, even though not made within the context of international negotiations, is binding.[16]

That is the conclusion that may be drawn from this decisive period in the history of Palestine.

1950–1973: The Gestation of the State of Palestine

12. Although the 'Arab state' which the United Nations decided to create in 1947 existed more in theory than in practice, the Palestinians, who made up the population of this state, did not vanish into thin air. They maintained their Palestinian identity, refused to be integrated into the surrounding Arab states, and never gave up hope of returning to their homes, in accordance

with the resolutions of the United Nations. Although living as refugees in tents and temporary encampments, they never lost sight of the idea of setting up a state of their own. They worked hard to preserve their identity, in particular by strengthening collective structures. The period from 1950 to 1973 was a period of organic gestation of a state which was one day to be born.

13. Throughout this period, the Palestinians suffered more hardship (in the 1967 War) and made further sacrifices in their, albeit sporadic, armed struggle against the occupying power. At the same time, they built up an organic structure which was to be the basis of the national movement which would seek to create a state in the future. A political and military organization, the PLO, came into being in 1964. It was the PLO which henceforth took on responsibility for co-ordinating Palestinian activities in every domain, with the aim of actually creating a Palestinian state and securing international recognition for the legitimacy of this objective.

There were several milestones in the long march of the Palestinians during this period. The first was the 1967 War, which resulted in the military occupation of what remained of Palestinian territory and a fresh exodus of refugees. There followed the 1973 War, whose initial stages boosted Arab morale and whose consequences for the status of the PLO and international action would be felt after 1974.

14. As far as international recognition was concerned, several important texts were adopted during this period, including:

(a) Security Council Resolution 242 of 22 November 1967, which emphasized, in particular, the inadmissibility of the acquisition of territory by war, and requested the withdrawal of Israel from the territories occupied in 1967;

(b) General Assembly Resolution 2535 (XXIV) of 10 December 1969, which referred for the first time to 'the inalienable rights of the people of Palestine';

(c) Resolution 2672 (XXV) of 10 December 1970, which recognized that the Palestinian people were entitled to self-determination, in accordance with the charter of the United Nations;

(d) Resolutions 2787 (XXVI) and 2963 (XXVII), which reasserted the right to self-determination; and

(e) Resolution 3070 (XXVIII), which reaffirmed the right of peoples under colonial and foreign domination to self-determination, freedom and independence, and also reaffirmed the legitimacy of the struggle for liberation by all available means, including armed struggle, and condemned governments which did not recognize the right to self-determination and independence of peoples.[17]

15. Here it is only possible briefly to outline the structural organization adopted by the Palestinian people. A more detailed account can be found in studies[18] devoted to this aspect of the Palestinians' efforts to obtain recognition as a state.

The PLO has a quasi-governmental structure. The Palestine National Council, which acts as a parliament, includes representatives from all sections of the Palestinian people in exile and within Palestine. This council elects the Executive Committee and a Central Council which supervises the implementation of the guidelines of the National Council. The Executive Committee acts as a government and has the following departments—foreign affairs, the occupied territories, education, health, information, social matters, culture, defence and 'popular organizations'. This last department co-ordinates the activities of a large number of professional organizations, some of which, such as the General Union of Palestinian Workers or the General Union of Palestinian Students, existed long before the creation of the PLO. Others were created over the years, such as the General Union of Palestinian Women (1963), and the unions of teachers (1969), artists (1969), lawyers (1971), writers (1972), engineers (1973) and farmers (1975). These organizations have hundreds of thousands of members. The General Union of Palestinian Workers alone has 100,000 members, and the teachers' union has more than 50,000. Also attached to the PLO are:

(a) the Palestine Red Crescent Society (1969), which monitors the health of the population and has a large number of hospitals and medical centres;

(b) the Palestine National Fund, which administers the organization's finances;

(c) Samed (1970), in charge of vocational training for young people and administering a large number of economic enterprises;

(d) the Palestine Research Centre, which has hundreds of publications to its credit;

(e) the Wafa Press Agency, the Bureau of Information; and, last but not least,

(f) the Armed Forces of the Palestinian Revolution.

This brief outline shows that solid foundations were being prepared for the future state.

1974-1987: The Consolidation of the Incipient State

16. This period constituted a particularly important phase in the development of the Palestinian national movement in its efforts to form an independent state. The growth of quasi-governmental Palestinian institutions, and the solemn recognition by the United Nations of the inalienable rights of the Palestinian people, had given it more confidence; this enabled the movement to take up a number of challenges and gradually to strengthen its position in the international arena at all levels. This period was thus the prelude to the 'formal' creation of a Palestinian state.

17. As regards the PLO's political strategy, the chief argument put forward by Israel and its friends against the establishment of a Palestinian state in international organizations and other fora was that the aim of the proposed state, according to the PLO's own charter, was the destruction of Israel, a member state of the United Nations, since the charter provided for the institution of a secular state throughout Palestine. This argument is of no legal relevance. However, in response to it, and in deference to internal, regional and international considerations (analysis of which would go beyond the scope of this study), the PLO has gradually modified its position, especially since 1974. This is apparent from the political programmes and declarations of the various meetings of the Palestine National Council, which is responsible for the PLO's political orientation.

Thus, in the ten-point programme approved by the 12th Palestine National Council in Cairo in June 1974, the second point includes a declaration of intent to build up a national authority on every single part of liberated Palestinian land. This is a step away from the aim of liberating the whole of Palestine in order to establish a united, democratic, secular state. It is true that the 12th Council's programme is somewhat ambiguous in that point 4 mentions moves towards a democratic state and point 1 rejects Security Council Resolution 242. However, the reason for this rejection had nothing to do with the fact that the resolution implied recognition of Israel, but rather that it did not explicitly recognize Palestinian rights. Moreover, the programme mentions a national authority on liberated Palestinian soil but not a mini-state alongside Israel.

The 15-point programme of the 13th Palestine National Council, held in Cairo in March 1977, takes another step in the same direction, as point 11 expresses the wish to construct a national state in the liberated part of Palestine. However, the ambiguity remains, because point 9 refuses to recognize Israel.

The 14th Palestine National Council, held in Damascus in 1979, was dominated by opposition to the Camp David Accords rather than by the strategic orientation of the state to be established.

The 15th Palestine National Council, held in Damascus in 1980, again took up the aim of creating a Palestinian state on part of the territory of Palestine while, in the same year, declarations by the PLO President clarified the development of the organization's strategy. Indeed, following the Kreisky-Arafat meeting, Arafat stated that the PLO did not seek the destruction of Israel, but the creation of an independent state on every inch of Palestinian land from which the Israelis withdrew. [19]

The 16th Palestine National Council, held in Algiers in February 1983, agreed to a plan drawn up at the 1982 Arab Summit in Fez—which contained a clause in paragraph 7 concerning the provision by the Security Council of guarantees for peace between all the states in the region, including the independent state of Palestine.

It is interesting to follow this slow but sure evolution of the Palestinian national movement towards the position adopted in the solemn proclamation of the state of Palestine on 15 November 1988. Nevertheless, there was still an element of deliberate vagueness in all these stands, owing to understandable psychological considerations and to the desire to preserve consensus within the movement.

18. Alongside this development in the PLO's position, reflected in the texts adopted at successive sessions of the Palestine National Council, contacts were made at various levels—although they were not always officially recognized[20]—between PLO officials and leading Israeli figures between 1975 and 1987.

The armed struggle to achieve the PLO's objectives—even if only as a form of self-defence—has never been completely abandoned. However, international credibility and a strictly legal approach to the planned Palestinian state were bolstered by the diplomatic activity of the legitimate representatives of the Palestinian people, who began to place progressively more emphasis on peaceful means (support for the peace conference).

19. On a bilateral level, the PLO opened information bureaux and diplomatic missions in a large number of Asian and African countries as well as in Europe and America, some of them enjoying full diplomatic status. This is the case, in the heart of Europe, for those established in Vienna and Athens. By the beginning of the 1980s the PLO was represented in more than 100 countries and enjoyed wider diplomatic recognition than the state of Israel itself.[21] Intense diplomatic activity accompanied the establishment of these missions. Many official and semi-official visits took place, as well

as meetings between PLO officials and heads of state or foreign ministers in various countries worldwide, and not just in the Third World states or East European countries which traditionally supported the PLO.

20. On the regional level, the summit meeting of Arab Heads of State in Rabat (October 1974) recognized the PLO as the sole legitimate representative of the Palestinian people. It also asserted the right of this people to establish an independent national authority on its soil. Subsequent summit conferences of Arab Heads of State in Fez (1982), Casablanca (1985), Amman (1987) and Algiers (1988) confirmed this support for the PLO and the institution of a Palestinian state.

Throughout this period, other regional organizations affirmed the right of the Palestinian refugees to return to their land, the rights of the Palestinian people to self-determination, independence and sovereignty, and their right to establish a state, under the leadership of the PLO. Such action, for example,[22] was taken by the Islamic Conference, the Non-Aligned Movement, the Organization of African Unity, the Arab-African Conference and the Warsaw Pact.

Represented by the PLO, Palestine is also a full member of the League of Arab States, the Islamic Conference, the Non-Aligned Movement and the Group of 77.

The organization which, in relative terms, was most reticent in its attitude to the PLO was the European Community. However, it is interesting to note that as early as 1977 the EC's representative made the following statement to the United Nations General Assembly:

The Nine . . . continue to believe that a solution to the conflict will be possible only if the legitimate right of the Palestinian people to give effective expression to its national identity is translated into fact. This would take into account, of course, the need for a homeland for the Palestinian people. (United Nations document A/32/PV 7, para. 51)

Later, the declaration by the European Community in Venice, on 13 June 1980, affirmed its support for two universally accepted principles: the right to exist of all states in the region, including Israel, and justice for all peoples, which implies recognition of the legitimate rights of the Palestinian people. The PLO, the declaration says, 'must participate in the negotiations towards the solution of the conflict'. It adds, 'a just solution should at last be found for the Palestinian problem, which is not simply a refugee problem'. Subsequent declarations by the European Community took a similar line.

21. During this period, the PLO achieved significant success in international organizations with worldwide membership, particularly the United Nations.

First of all, from 1974 onwards—for the first time since 1952—the Palestinian question had a separate place from the Middle East question on the General Assembly's agenda. Moreover, since 1974, all United Nations General Assembly resolutions concerning the Palestinian question have contained an affirmation of the right of the Palestinian people to independence and sovereignty, in addition to the affirmation of inalienable rights and the right to self-determination which was included between 1969 and 1973. Since 1980 UN resolutions have added the right of the Palestinian people to establish its own state.[23] There are a large number of such resolutions.[24] Most of them specify that the PLO is the sole legitimate representative of the Palestinian people and that the rights of the Palestinian people must be exercised under the leadership of the PLO. This is specified in Resolutions 35/169 and 207, 36/266, 37/123, 38/180, 39/146, 40/168, 41/162, and it is an important point (see Chapter 14).

Furthermore, certain resolutions ratifying recommendations made by the Committee on the Exercise of the Inalienable Rights of the Palestinian People (for instance, Resolution 35/169) specified that the territories evacuated by Israel and taken over by the United Nations would be handed over to the PLO as the representative of the Palestinian people.

Special mention must be made of the General Assembly's decision to accord observer status to the PLO. Resolution 3237 (XXIX) of 22 November 1974 invites the PLO to participate not only in the proceedings of the 29th General Assembly, as Resolution 3210 (XXIX) had already done, but also to participate on a permanent basis in all General Assembly sessions and all conferences held under the auspices of the General Assembly and other United Nations organs. Observer status was also granted to the PLO by the Economic and Social Council and its subsidiary organs.

A novel development took place at the Economic and Social Commission for Western Asia (ESCWA), where the PLO, having first obtained observer status in May 1975, gained full member status from April 1977—confirmed by the Economic and Social Council in July 1977.[25]

The situation in the Security Council is even more remarkable. Rule 39 of the Council's Rules of Procedure allows it to invite any person it deems competent to provide information or assistance. Rule 37 states that any member of the United Nations which is not a member of the Security Council may be invited to participate, without the right to vote, in the discussion of any question brought before the Security Council when the Council considers that the interests of that member are specially affected.

Rule 38 states that the member (which is not a member of the Security Council) may submit proposals and draft resolutions which may be put to a vote at the request of a representative on the Council. Therefore the right to take part in Council debates in accordance with Rule 39 and those reserved for United Nations members in accordance with Rule 37 are in principle quite different.

Yet on 30 November 1975 the serving President of the Security Council told a meeting of the Council that the PLO representative would be invited to take part in debates on the Palestinian question in January 1976. This statement was contested by some members of the Security Council but was not put to a vote. At the meeting of 4 December 1975 the President of the Council said he had received a request to invite the PLO representative, although he did not specify whether it was an invitation under Rule 39 or Rule 37 of the Rules of Procedure. He added that if the invitation were approved by the Council, the PLO representative would have the same rights as a member state of the United Nations which was not a member of the Council, in accordance with Rule 37. The British delegate objected that this right could not be given to an entity which was not a member of the United Nations and which did not itself claim to be a state or government. Although two permanent Council members voted against, the invitation was approved because it was regarded as a procedural issue.

Some writers[26] have affirmed that although the invitation extended to the PLO was a matter of procedure, the fact that it was granted the same rights as a state which is not a member of the Council in accordance with Rule 37 was a constitutional matter of great importance. None the less, from January 1976 onwards the PLO was invited to take part in Security Council debates concerning Palestine with the same rights as United Nations member states which did not belong to the Security Council, thus creating a precedent within the United Nations in favour of the PLO.[27]

Equally exceptional was the granting to an observer of the right of reply in the General Assembly. At the 29th session of the Assembly, the President allowed the PLO representative to exercise this right. This set a precedent, and the procedure was repeated at the 32nd and 33rd sessions. Several states objected in writing to the granting of this right.[28] Here again, a precedent had been created in favour of the PLO, even though Rule 73 of the Assembly's Rules of Procedure specifies that this right is the prerogative of member states.

The right to speak at plenary meetings of the Assembly was granted to the PLO President in 1974 by General Assembly Resolution 3210 (XXIX). Previously, only member states had had this right;[29] an observer could only take the floor at meetings of subsidiary organs. This privilege has been freely applied since 1974.

The PLO is allowed to attend all conferences convened under the auspices of United Nations organs, whereas other observers only attend conferences in which they have a particular interest.

The PLO's permanent and very wide-ranging participation in international activities has made it necessary to set up permanent PLO missions in New York and Geneva, with all that this implies for the granting of privileges and diplomatic immunity, on which we need not dwell here.[30]

In fact, the PLO participated as an observer in the work of other organizations in the United Nations system, and of conferences convened under the auspices of the United Nations itself, even before obtaining the status of permanent observer at the General Assembly on 22 November 1974.

It attended, for example, the Plenipotentiary Conference of the International Telecommunication Union (September–October 1973), the World Health Assembly (May 1974), the Universal Postal Congress (May–July 1974), the World Population Conference (August 1974), the General Conference of UNESCO (October 1974) and the World Food Conference (5–16 November 1974). After 22 November 1974, when United Nations General Assembly Resolution 3237 (XXIX) was adopted, the PLO was present at almost all international gatherings.

22. It may be concluded from all this that, thanks to United Nations resolutions and practices adopted on a continuous basis which crystallized as customary rules in the law of international organizations, the PLO acquired permanent observer status with much wider prerogatives than those traditionally granted to an observer which is not a state. This may be considered as the prelude to full member status, which should, however, be acquired as laid down in the constitutions of these organizations.

The precedents set by regional organizations (Arab League, Islamic Conference, Non-Aligned Movement) or the United Nations Economic and Social Commission for Western Asia where the PLO has full member status, are new and irreversible developments.

Therefore, even before the declaration of the Palestinian state, the PLO was a subject of international law representing a potential or emergent state. The criticisms of certain writers[31] cannot alter the course of this development, which is well established in international law.

The distinction put forward by Professor Virally[32] between 'political rights'—which the PLO would here be recognized as having—and 'legal rights' is not a compelling one because the law, however it is qualified, remains the law, and is inspired in essence by political considerations and

242

decreed by political authorities.

International law is no exception to this general rule: it is always created by 'political' organs, states or international organizations, just as domestic law is created by a political organ, a parliament. The flexibility which is characteristic of international law and the alterations that international organizations impose on it are acknowledged by the highest legal authority, the International Court of Justice.[33] In 1949 it had already recognized that the United Nations had implicit powers not included in its charter.[34] It also took a bold stand on the case of South-West Africa. As the United Nations Secretary-General said in the introduction to his 1960–61 report, the United Nations must not be 'a static conference machinery' but a 'dynamic instrument', using appropriate means in accordance with the 'principles and purposes' of the charter.

23. In conclusion, it may be said that the Palestinian state declared on 15 November 1988 had been in preparation for a long time, in suffering and in exaltation, in the armed struggle as in internal structuring, and in diplomatic activity at bilateral, regional and world levels. It has been said that the PLO was a government in all but name: it might be added that Palestine itself had all the characteristics of a state and that only its official proclamation was wanting—an omission put right on 15 November 1988.

14
Legal Aspects of the Existence of the State of Palestine

24. The transition from a nation to a hypothetical state, and then through a period of gestation to a potential state, was a slow process but a sure one. Every conceivable obstacle delayed the long-advocated and long-awaited proclamation of independence, to the point that two authors from opposite camps,[1] both of whom were in favour of the establishment of a Palestinian state, referred to the possibility of its advent in one case as 'thinking the unthinkable' and in the other as 'the art of the impossible'. However, the unthinkable became possible and the state of Palestine is now a reality from the legal standpoint, even though Israel's stubbornness prevents it from enjoying all the powers conferred upon a state by international law.

The Proclamation of the State of Palestine

25. The existence of the state is a fact. A state does not need outside assistance to come into being. In December 1988, subsequent to the proclamation of the Palestinian state, the Israeli delegate to the General Assembly disputed the validity of the proclamation, claiming that it was a unilateral act which had not been negotiated or approved (in other words, negotiated with Israel or approved by Israel). However the right to existence, or in legal parlance, the right to self-determination, cannot as such be the subject of negotiation. To cite one writer,[2] it is altogether possible to

negotiate on the subject of frontiers or relations with neighbours, but not on the right to self-determination. This right is a peremptory norm of general international law that must therefore be acknowledged by all states that recognize *jus cogens*.

In the words of the President of the state of Palestine,[3] the proclamation of that state was a constitutive and at the same time constitutional act, which is to say that it had a legal basis. The attitude of third parties to the state may depend upon their perception of that legal basis.

Legal grounds for the proclamation

Historical rights

26. The proclamation invokes the historical rights of the Palestinians, who are characterized as being rooted in their land and by the 'organic, indissoluble . . . relationship between the people and their land and history'.[4] The ownership and occupation of Palestine by the Palestinians was indeed unbroken and, by the mandate it gave to the British, the League of Nations recognized the Palestinian nation's vocation to establish itself as a state. Although the Palestinians were forcibly expelled and dispossessed in 1948 and in 1967, they could not be deprived of their historical rights, for they never at any time renounced their identity. On the contrary, whether as refugees in neighbouring states or in their own land under occupation, they strengthened their attachment to their national identity, thanks to sound organization and structures.[5]

The durability of a people's rights to its land despite such phenomena as colonization and foreign occupation, which today have been clearly condemned by international law, entails the right to self-determination. This is the second legal basis for the proclamation.

The right to self-determination

27. This right was one of the principles proclaimed by the American President Woodrow Wilson at the close of the First World War—hence the mandates system (Article 22 of the Covenant of the League of Nations), which was to prepare the inhabitants of the territories occupied by the Allied Powers of the First World War for independence, at least in the case of 'A' mandates, to which category Palestine belonged.

The charter of the United Nations asserted the right of peoples to self-determination in Article 1, paragraph 2, and in Article 55. Several resolutions adopted subsequently confirmed this right, in particular Resolution 1514 (XV) concerning the Declaration on the Granting of Independence to Colonial Countries and Peoples (1960), and Resolution 2625 (XXV) concerning the Declaration on Principles of International Law concerning Friendly Relations and Co-operation among States in accordance with the charter of the United Nations (1970). The principle of the right of peoples to self-determination is also covered by the first article of both the two international covenants on human rights, which were adopted by the General Assembly in 1966 and entered into force in 1976.

28. More specifically, the right of the Palestinian people to self-determination has been asserted in many of the resolutions mentioned in Part I of this study.[6] The assertion of this right became increasingly explicit in 1969, 1974 and 1980, when the rights of the Palestinian people to independence, national sovereignty and the establishment of its own state in Palestine were specified. Without getting caught up in the doctrinal controversy concerning the binding nature of General Assembly resolutions or their role in the development of international law,[7] suffice it so say that the charter of the United Nations, which proclaims the right of peoples to self-determination, is necessarily binding on all member states, and its provisions prevail over any conflicting rights or obligations (Article 103).

Furthermore, the literature on the subject regards normative resolutions interpreting or applying the principles of the charter as mandatory. This is the case for the resolutions on self-determination, especially as the International Law Commission considered that the right to self-determination was peremptory and came under *jus cogens*.[8] It follows that this right prevails over all other rights, including of course the right, or more precisely the power, that Israel may derive as an occupying power from the rules of traditional international law with respect to the law of war.[9]

Judge Tanaka wrote in this respect:

The appearance of organizations such as the League of Nations and the United Nations . . . is bound to influence the mode of generation of customary international law. A state, instead of pronouncing its view to a few states directly concerned, has the opportunity, through the medium of an organization, to declare its position to all members of the organization . . . In former days, practice, repetition and *opinio juris sive necessitatis*, which are the ingredients of customary law, might be combined together in a very long and slow process extending over centuries. In the contemporary age of highly developed techniques of communication and information, the formation of a custom through the medium of international organizations is greatly facilitated and accelerated; the establishment of such a custom would require no more than one generation or even far less than that.[10]

He continued as follows:

> Of course, we cannot admit that individual resolutions, declarations, . . . etc. have binding force upon the members of the organization. What is required for customary . . . law is the repetition of the same practice; accordingly, in this case, resolutions, declarations, etc. on the same matter in the same . . . organization must take place repeatedly. Parallel with such repetition, each resolution, declaration, etc. being considered as the manifestation of the collective will of individual participant states, the will of the international community can certainly be formulated more quickly and more accurately as compared with the traditional method . . . This collective, cumulative and organic process of custom-generation . . . can be seen to have an important role from the viewpoint of the development of international law.[11]

In a similar vein, Professor Higgins wrote that with the development of international organizations, the votes and views of states had acquired legal significance as an expression of customary law. If collective acts by states were repeated with sufficient frequency and accepted by a sufficiently large number of them, they would in the end become law. He added that 17 years of United Nations activity had given the world a new and important source of customary international law.[12]

The resolutions on the right of the Palestinian people to self-determination, which were reiterated with such frequency from 1969 to 1991, thus have undoubted legal significance and may be invoked against all members of the organization.

Apart from their repetition, a further factor may be noted in connection with these resolutions: the ever-increasing number of votes in their favour. As Professor Pellet[13] has remarked, a large number of votes in the affirmative attenuates the fact that the resolutions of international organizations are unilateral acts. According to Pellet, it was difficult to believe that the representatives of states would devote so much time and energy to drawing up these instruments if they were to be regarded as scraps of paper. They were intended to have legal effect, and they had legal effect.

Resolution 181 (II)

29. The third legal tenet underpinning the proclamation of the establishment of the Palestinian state is Resolution 181(II) of 1947 concerning the partition of Palestine into two states, one Jewish and the other Arab. Everyone is familiar with the circumstances under which this resolution was adopted.[14] At that time, the Arab Palestinians rejected the

resolution on the grounds that it did not take into account their aspirations as the majority of the inhabitants of Palestine.

Today the situation is different, since the Jewish state has been established and has been consolidated by the immigration of hundreds of thousands of Jews from all over the world, in addition to which Israel has obtained rights that now have the status of 'acquired' rights. Reference was also made to this resolution in Israel's Declaration of Independence, in which it was invoked to provide a legal basis for the existence of that state.[15]

However, only part of the resolution has been implemented. The fact that no action was taken to implement the provisions of the other part, concerning the establishment of the 'Arab state', does not in itself invalidate the resolution. Israel is obliged to accept it in its entirety. It cannot lay claim to rights for itself under the resolution and object to the obligations ensuing from it. In any case, it formally undertook to implement the resolution when it was admitted to membership of the United Nations. General Assembly Resolution 273(III), admitting Israel to membership of the United Nations, refers to this undertaking. At the time, the representative of the Jewish Agency declared at the United Nations that:

> Unlike other General Assembly resolutions, which were mere recommendations without any binding force, this resolution was different in as much as it concerned the future of a territory under international mandate. Only the United Nations in its entirety was competent to decide about the future of that territory and consequently its decision was binding.[16]

Regardless of any discussion on the legal status of General Assembly resolutions (see para. 28 above), it clearly follows from that declaration that Resolution 181(II), which the Israeli representatives accepted and have used to their advantage on many occasions, may be invoked against Israel.[17]

The International Court of Justice subsequently affirmed that the United Nations was responsible for the former mandated territories that had not been turned into trust territories (cases on South-West Africa). Even more striking is the fact that Resolution 43/176 of the General Assembly of the United Nations, adopted on 15 December 1988, states that the proclamation of the state of Palestine was in line with General Assembly Resolution 181(II) of 29 November 1947. As for Resolution 43/177, which was also adopted on 15 December 1988, it states that the Partition Plan still holds, affirming the principle of 'guaranteeing arrangements for security of all states in the region, including those named in Resolution 181(II) of 29 November 1947, within secure and internationally recognized boundaries'. This is of course a reference to the Jewish state and to the Arab state.

The PLO's competence to proclaim the establishment of the Palestinian state

30. Repeated United Nations resolutions affirming the right of the Palestinian people to set up its own state have also asserted that this right would be exercised under the leadership of the PLO, the legitimate representative of the Palestinian people. The General Assembly endorsed recommendations of the Committee on the Exercise of the Inalienable Rights of the Palestinian People, which specified that once the territories occupied by Israel had been evacuated, they should be taken over by the United Nations, which would hand them over to the PLO. The 1976 report of this same committee (United Nations document A/31/35) states that it is up to the Palestinian people to decide when and how to express its national independence and that the PLO is a guardian of the inalienable rights of the Palestinian people.

The League of Arab States, as well as several regional bodies, have also recognized the PLO's representativeness, and it should be noted that the European Parliament resolution adopted on 15 December 1988 requests member states of the EC to grant the PLO recognition as the Palestinian government in exile.[18] Internally, the representativeness of the PLO and its National Council is not in doubt.[19]

The significance and effects of the proclamation of the Palestinian state

31. The legal bases for the proclamation are undoubtedly important. Equally important from the political point of view is the fact that the proclamation implicitly recognizes the state of Israel by accepting Resolution 181(II) and by condemning the use of force against the territorial integrity of Palestine and of 'other states'. Internationally, what matters most, however, is the new situation created by the proclamation.

What it did was to oblige all the world's states to face up to their responsibilities and take a stand with regard to this new development. Their response was not long in coming. Within the week following the proclamation, that is to say by 21 November 1988, some 50 states had extended recognition to the new Palestinian state; a month later 90 had done so.[20]

Thus, as far as the great majority of the members of the international community are concerned, Palestine is a *de jure* state. In the eyes of the majority of the remaining states, it is a *de facto* state (witness the semi-official welcome extended to Yasser Arafat in France in May 1989, the dialogue between the Americans and Palestinians which lasted from December 1988 to June 1990, and the meeting in March 1991 between the United States Secretary of State and a Palestinian delegation mandated by the PLO). As for the states that voted for the many resolutions asserting the right of the Palestinian people to establish its own state under the leadership of the PLO but that have not yet recognized the state established in accordance with these resolutions, they would be highly inconsistent if they were to refuse to recognize the Palestinian state.

32. Finally, Resolution 43/177, which acknowledged the proclamation and was adopted virtually unanimously (two votes against and two abstentions), deserves special mention.

Admittedly, this resolution, in which it was decided to use the designation Palestine in place of the designation PLO, adds 'without prejudice to the observer status and functions of the Palestine Liberation Organization within the United Nations system'. However, this does not mean that the organization does not recognize Palestine's statehood: non-member states also have observer status, in some cases inferior to that of the PLO. Some of the rights granted to the PLO—and hence to Palestine—have not been conferred upon non-member states (right of reply in plenary meetings, right of participation in the Security Council, rights of a full member of ESCWA, etc.). The words 'without prejudice' mean that the resolution does not affect the rights already acquired by the PLO. As for the admission of the Palestinian state to membership of the United Nations, it should be in line with the procedure provided for in Article 4 of the charter (see Chapter 15).

33. Furthermore, the proclamation and the widespread recognition to which it gave rise mean that the PLO has been given legal status by the international community, its legitimacy having already been recognized in the UN's previous resolutions. The fact that Palestine has acquired legality means that it can exercise the rights of a state, but also that it must perform the obligations incumbent upon a state with respect to those states that have recognized it.

Finally, it should be noted that all the states that have recognized Palestine did so without showing concern, or at least not overtly, for the legal basis of the proclamation, or for what are known as the constitutive elements of a state. They simply exercised their discretionary power in such matters. However, having exercised such power, Palestine's existence as a state may be invoked against them and they are legally bound to treat it as they would any other state.

Palestine and the 'Constituent Elements' of the State

34. The prevailing view is that the creation or birth of a state is not an event in law.[21] It is a fact which, although it has legal consequences, lies outside the scope of the law. Consequently, the opinion of other states regarding the existence—or non-existence—of a particular entity as a state is of no particular relevance, a principle expressed by jurists when they assert that the recognition of a state has declaratory but not constituent value.[22]

On the other hand, any state, since it is sovereign, may decide in a given context whether or not an entity may be termed a state. Its decision needs follow no fixed criteria. If the given entity does not, in reality, possess the characteristics of a state, it will not be any more a state because it has received what is called 'premature' recognition. Conversely, nothing may be inferred from the refusal by one state to recognize another.

In actual fact, international practice varies considerably. Thus, a large number of states have been refused recognition of their statehood by other states at one time or another in their history, especially at the time of their admission into international organizations. However, they have subsequently been recognized, or admitted to international organizations, without acquiring new characteristics or satisfying any particular criterion any more than had previously been the case. Guinea-Bissau, declared independent on 26 September 1973, was recognized by 40 states in the closing months of the same year, at a time when it was still fighting the Portuguese forces and no Guinean party had undisputed control over all Guinean territory.[23] Guinea-Bissau was admitted to the OAU on 20 September 1974, a year before Portugal effectively withdrew from its territory.[24]

Similarly, the provisional government of the Republic of Algeria was recognized by 36 states before the referendum on self-determination of 1 July 1962, and 25 states had even recognized the provisional government of the Republic of Algeria before the Evian Agreements had been concluded.[25]

Thus, neither occupation of territory nor the failure to draw final borders has, historically, been an obstacle to recognition of an entity as a state.[26]

Although the French Minister of Foreign Affairs declared, on 16 November 1988, that it is contrary to French legal precedent to recognize a state without a defined territory,[27] this declaration expresses only the individual opinion of France. States are free to take into consideration such criteria as they consider appropriate for the recognition of states and to decide whether they have been satisfied in each individual case. France nevertheless recognized the American Declaration of Independence which, like Israel's, contains no mention of territorial limits.

Furthermore, in connection with the French declaration, Professor Charvin[28] has observed that Britain denounced the recognition of the United States by France in 1778 at a time when the territory of the new state was still subject to Britain, which even declared war on France because of this premature recognition. Professor Charvin gives other examples of states that were recognized, in Latin America for example, before their borders had been clearly set, or when their territories were still occupied (Belgium in 1831, Albania in 1913, etc.).

These examples show clearly that, in practice, states are not deterred by the theoretical importance of largely academic criteria. Recent and not-so-recent history provide sufficient proof of this. Moreover, Israel is recognized by far fewer states than recognize Palestine; the prevailing view is nevertheless that it is a state.

The practice of international organizations and their constitutions are just as unclear, and this includes the charter of the United Nations, which provides no definition of a state, despite the fact that at the San Francisco conference certain delegations (Venezuela, Brazil and Bolivia) requested that the concept of statehood be defined. This seemed all the more necessary in that preparations were being made to admit as original members the Ukraine and Byelorussia, which did not exercise sovereignty under international law, together with the Philippines and India, whose status as sovereign states had not yet been established.

This question, left unanswered when the UN charter was drawn up, was re-examined at the first session of the International Law Commission in the spring of 1949. Leading jurists such as G. Scelle and M. Alfaro discussed at length the difficulties involved in defining a state. Georges Scelle, the then chairman of the commission, declared before the latter, on 22 June 1950, that he had been studying international law for 50 years and still did not know what a state was, and would probably die in ignorance.[29] Thus, when the Declaration of the Rights and Duties of States was adopted, the International Law Commission came to the conclusion that efforts to provide a definition of a state were futile.[30]

It is also interesting to note that neither the Permanent Court of International Justice, nor the International Court of Justice, nor the Permanent Court of Arbitration nor the Arbitral Tribunal have ever hazarded either a definition of a state or a definition of a nation, or any criterion for distinguishing between the two concepts.

The lack of a definition has occasionally created considerable confusion, especially concerning referral to certain United Nations organs. Article 34 of the Statutes of the Court stipulates that 'Only States may be parties in cases before the Court.' And Article 93, paragraph 2, of the charter of the United Nations provides for the possibility of non-member states becoming parties before the International Court of Justice. But how does one know if a non-member state is actually a state? The question is not purely academic, having been raised in the case of Liechtenstein, and settled by a ruling that it was a state. This 'state', which has no army of its own and has requested its neighbour Switzerland to manage its foreign affairs, customs, currency, post and telecommunications, had come before the court. The Security Council and the General Assembly subsequently acknowledged Liechtenstein's statehood.

This example emphasizes the difficulty of providing a legal definition of a state. What does emerge is that the acknowledgement of an entity's statehood by other states or international organizations is dependent on political rather than legal factors.

35. Legal opinion is also divided as to the definition of a state. Nevertheless, many authors, drawing upon the Declaration of Montevideo, adopted on 27 December 1933 by the seventh Inter-American Conference, uphold the theory of the 'constituent elements' of the state, according to which, in the terms of the third 'restatement' of international law prepared by the United States State Department, according to international law, a state is an entity which has a defined territory and a permanent population, under the control of its own government and which enters into relations with other entities displaying the same characteristics or has the capacity to do so.[31]

Although this theory is not universally accepted and, as has been seen, has little effect upon international practice, these traditional criteria of statehood should be examined in the light of historical precedents and then applied to the specific situation of Palestine.

Population

36. The Palestinian people numbers about 5.5 million. Some 665,000 live in Israel, and 1,600,000 in the occupied territories of the West Bank of the Jordan and Gaza; the rest of the population lives in exile, usually with refugee status (see Part II).

37. This exile population, whose right of return has been repeatedly affirmed by the United Nations, starting with Resolution 194(III) in 1948 and up to Resolution 45/73 of 11 December 1990, has never lost its identity. The PLO offers it efficient structures and Part I of this study has shown how these structures are organized.[32]

Furthermore, the Palestinian people is not the first to have been forced by the vicissitudes of history to live in a diaspora. The representatives of the state of Israel today would be ill-placed to accuse Palestine of not satisfying the criterion of being a permanently settled population. This is a cynical way of exploiting the fact that the Palestinian people is prevented from reforming in its own territory.

38. So far as the internal population is concerned, the structures are less visible, precisely because of the Israeli occupation. This population has nevertheless constantly displayed its allegiance to the PLO. The popular uprising, the *intifada*, which has continued since December 1987 despite repression by the occupying authorities, proves how attached the population is to its identity.[33]

This population is supposed to be protected by the 4th Geneva Convention of 1949, to which Israel is a party, and by The Hague Convention of 1907, the provisions of which have become customary international law. These two conventions are thus binding upon the Israeli government. It nevertheless disregards them in practice, which has led to its condemnation in numerous General Assembly resolutions, adopted after examination of the reports of the Special Committee to Investigate Israeli Practices Affecting the Human Rights of the Palestinian People and Other Arabs of the Occupied Territories,[34] or when the Middle East question is raised.[35]

Similarly, when Israel has been condemned by the Security Council, the United States—Israel's traditional defender—has either supported the motion or abstained.[36]

39. Thus, it is a proven fact that the Israeli occupation is effecting demographic, geographical, historical and cultural changes in the occupied territories, expropriating land and water resources, and subjecting the inhabitants of these territories to expulsion, administrative internment and torture. To quote just a few examples, Security Council Resolution 446 (1979) determines that the policy and practices of Israel in establishing settlements in the occupied territories have no legal validity and calls upon Israel, as the occupying power, to abide by the 4th Geneva Convention of 1949 and to rescind its previous measures; Resolution 465 (1980) considers that the measures taken by Israel to change the physical character, demographic composition and institutional structure of the occupied territories have no legal validity and constitute a flagrant violation of the 4th Geneva Convention relative to the Protection of Civilian Persons in Time of War; Resolution 476 affirms that measures taken by Israel are null and

void; Resolution 478 decides not to recognize the Israeli 'basic law' on Jerusalem. The same terms are to be found in other resolutions.[37]

The legal validity of these resolutions derives not only from the binding nature of Security Council resolutions in respect of all members of the United Nations, by virtue of Article 25 of its charter, but also from international law, both customary and contractual.[38]

It is interesting, in this respect, to recall that Israel, at the beginning of the 1967 occupation, accepted that the 1949 Geneva Conventions were applicable, but changed its position in later military orders. This change of position—which the Israeli Supreme Court itself condemned[39]—is illegal: the 4th Geneva Convention overrides Israeli domestic law. Furthermore, the 'military necessity' argument, provided for in the convention and invoked by Israel, cannot counter the detailed provisions of the convention or the humanitarian spirit which inspired its creation and which is evident in the very title of the convention, 'Protection of Civilians'. Moreover, the first article lays down that the convention shall be applicable 'in all circumstances'.[40]

40. It is apparent from the texts to which we have referred that the population of the Palestinian state, whose rights are flouted by Israel and upheld by the United Nations, exists both from the human and from the legal point of view.

This conclusion is supported by the wide range of historical factors which have already been mentioned—recognition by the League of Nations of a Palestinian nation destined to become a state, Resolution 181(II) of the General Assembly creating an Arab state in Palestine, and repeated proclamations by the United Nations of the Palestinian people's right to self-determination, etc.

The territory

41. Resolution 181(II) of 1947, on the partition of Palestine, allocated a clearly defined territory to the Arabs. This territory was occupied by Israel in two stages, in 1948–49 and in 1967. Israel has in fact annexed the parts occupied in 1948, but has not dared officially to annex the parts occupied in 1967 (the West Bank and Gaza), except for Jerusalem. According to international law, the status of these territories is that of occupied territories, and sovereignty over them is the sole prerogative of the Palestinian people.

Clearly, military occupation of a territory by force in no way deprives the people who originally occupied it of its rights over that territory, especially if that people never cease to protest, thereby ensuring that validity cannot be conferred—as would be the case for an occupation that had become peaceful and continuing. Moreover, in this case, the occupation has been broadly condemned, in particular by Security Council Resolution 242. In any event, traditional principles of international law do not allow sovereignty to be derived from military occupation. Previously, in 1934, the Permanent Court of International Justice had upheld this principle in the Franco-Greek lighthouse case.[41] The same principle was confirmed by the Geneva Conventions of 1949 and by the 1977 Protocol.[42]

42. So far as the West Bank is concerned, its annexation by Jordan in 1950 was to have been temporary, pending a definitive solution to the Palestinian problem. The terms of the official act uniting the two banks[43] made clear that it was not to affect the rights of the Palestinians. In 1979 King Hussein declared before the General Assembly of the United Nations that Jordan, in bringing about union in 1950, continued to support the historic rights of the Palestinian people, and that these rights would be exercised once the Palestinian question had been definitively resolved. He also asserted the right of the Palestinians to set up their independent state if they so wished.[44]

On 31 July 1988 Jordan decided upon its legal and administrative withdrawal from the Palestinian territories occupied by Israel and declared that the independent Palestinian state must be established on Palestinian lands.[45]

43. So far as the borders of Palestinian territory—once established—are concerned, the fact that they have not been definitively fixed, pending agreements at the Middle East peace conference, does not constitute a hindrance to recognition of Palestinian statehood. There are instructive historical precedents here.

In 1917 Poland was recognized by the Supreme Council of Allied and Associated Powers before its definitive eastern borders had been fixed. The same applied to Czechoslovakia in 1918.[46] If matters had been otherwise, Israel would have had no justification either—and for the same reasons as those it advances with regard to Palestine—for being regarded as a state: the borders of both entities are inextricably linked.

The government

44. In a letter dated 9 December 1988,[47] the permanent observer from Palestine transmitted to the Office of the Secretary-General of the United Nations the decision of the Palestine National Council, adopted on

15 November 1988, to entrust the Executive Committee of the PLO with the powers and responsibilities of the provisional government until the government is formed.

In the political declaration adopted on the same day as the Proclamation of Independence, the Palestine National Council decided, pending the establishment of a provisional Palestinian government, to entrust the Executive Committee with these functions. Yasser Arafat was designated President of the state of Palestine, and Farouq Kaddoumi Minister of Foreign Affairs.

45. Relations between the PLO and the leadership of the *intifada* reflect one aspect of the way in which the PLO exercises its authority within occupied Palestinian territory. It is significant that the memorandum presented by the Palestinian delegation to the US Secretary of State, James Baker, on 12 March 1991 should contain the words:

> The PLO is our sole legitimate leadership and interlocutor, embodying the national identity and expressing the will of the Palestinian people everywhere. As such, it is empowered to represent us in all political negotiations and endeavours, having the overwhelming support of its constituency.[48]

There are other examples of the authority of the PLO over its people. Thus public strike orders given by the PLO are widely followed; in the municipal elections in the occupied territories in 1972 and in 1976, PLO candidates were elected to the municipal councils and to the post of mayor.[49] More than 80 per cent of the votes went to these candidates.[50] Furthermore, even before the proclamation of the state of Palestine, the PLO had acquired a quasi-governmental structure in all spheres of activity.[51] However, while the PLO's authority over Palestinian territory is not exercised overtly—due, obviously, to the Israeli occupation—this is no hindrance to recognition of the representativeness of the PLO as the executive authority of the Palestinian state. It is paradoxical that Israel should invoke the lack of legal authority of the PLO in Palestine, when the impossibility of complete effectiveness is due to an illegal state of affairs—the prolonged military occupation—created by the party invoking this argument.

Nemo auditur propriam turpitudinem allegans . . .

Immediacy

46. The fourth 'element' that is said to be a 'constituent' of

statehood—what the American 'Restatement' terms the capacity to enter into relations with other states[52]—overlaps, to a considerable extent, with the concept of immediacy, familiar to experts on international law, by virtue of which states are direct subjects of international law,[53] assuming the obligations and enjoying the rights that this entails. This implies, in particular, that the state is able to enter into diplomatic relations, conclude treaties, etc. Even here one may query whether this is a consequence rather than a criterion of statehood.

47. In any event, it is clear in the case of Palestine that this fourth condition, if it is a condition, has been met. Ninety-two states (about two-thirds of the members of the international community) have recognized the state of Palestine and have consequently established diplomatic relations with Palestine, which is the most tangible proof of this ability to enter into relations with other countries.

Likewise, Palestine has concluded a large number of international agreements, and is a full member of the League of Arab States, the Non-Aligned Movement, the Organization of the Islamic Conference, etc., which implies that Palestine can be—and in fact is—party to the constitutions of these institutions. Palestine also receives assistance from several international non-governmental and inter-governmental organizations, and the European Community regards the occupied territories as an 'economic entity', distinct from Israel, whose commercial relations with the EC are governed by different rules.

There is, consequently, no doubt that Palestine has immediate, direct access to international law. Not only does it have the ability to maintain relations with other states; it actually uses it, both bilaterally and within the framework of worldwide or regional international organizations.

48. In conclusion, it seems clear that there is incontrovertible proof of the existence of perfectly adequate arguments to justify the recognition of Palestinian statehood. Furthermore, it can never be repeated too often that no proof is required by a state which wishes to recognize another state as having this status. This is a matter for the discretionary power of the state carrying out this essentially political act, which has legal implications for relations between the states concerned. This is a very important point when determining upon what conditions Palestine may be admitted to the United Nations and to its Specialized Agencies and granted the status of a full member.

15
The Admission of Palestine to International Organizations

49. After the proclamation of the state of Palestine, its leaders decided to request that it be admitted to a number of international organizations with worldwide membership and to the Geneva Conventions of 12 August 1949. However, for reasons of political expediency, Palestine has, until now, not requested admission to the United Nations.

From a legal point of view, however, it is not possible to draw a hard and fast line between admission to the United Nations and admission to one or other of its Specialized Agencies. In fact, given the links between various international organizations (which explain the frequent use of the expression 'family of the United Nations'), membership of one of them can automatically lead to membership of another. There is such a link between the United Nations and UNESCO, for example: Article II.1 of the constitution of UNESCO stipulates: 'Membership of the United Nations Organization shall carry with it the right to membership of the United Nations Educational, Scientific and Cultural Organization.' The admission to the United Nations of an applicant such as Palestine would thus lead *ipso facto* to its admission to UNESCO.

This would logically require the question of the conditions governing Palestine's admission to the principal organization to be considered first. But that is no reason why reflection should not begin on the specific problem of admission to the Specialized Agencies, which can be an issue in itself.

Towards the Long-Promised Peace

The Admission of Palestine to the United Nations

50. In principle, the admission of Palestine to the United Nations—like the admission of any applicant state—poses no problems from the legal point of view, but can create political problems stemming from the procedure laid down in the charter for the admission of new members.

As in every international organization, the principles governing the right to admission to the United Nations are laid down in its charter. XArticle 4, paragraph 1, of the charter lays down five basic conditions, and paragraph 2 specifies the procedure to be followed. The candidate requesting admission must fulfil the following conditions: be a state; be a peace-loving state; accept the obligations contained in the charter; be able to carry them out; and be willing to do so.

The candidate is under no obligation to provide proof that it fulfils these conditions. A proposal to this effect was made during discussions on the question, but it was not adopted.[1]

51. The third condition is self-evident: a state which desires to become a party to an international treaty accepts *ipso facto* the obligations laid down in that treaty. Palestine has already declared in its proclamation of independence that it accepts the obligations of the United Nations charter,[2] which means that it also satisfies the fifth condition.

With regard to the first condition, Palestine has considered itself to be a state since 15 November 1988, with some justification, as is demonstrated in Part II of this study.[3] Indeed, just under 100 of the member states of the United Nations formally consider it as such. This means that most of the members of the General Assembly have already made up their minds on the subject.

Fulfilment of conditions 2 and 4 is left to the judgement of the members of the organization. The Proclamation of Independence states that the state of Palestine believes 'in the solution of international and regional problems by peaceful means' and 'rejects the threat or use of force, violence and intimidation against its territorial integrity . . . or [that] of any other state'. This declaration—which is binding upon the state of Palestine—as well as the increasingly moderate positions adopted by the PLO from 1974 to 1992,[4] should dispel any doubts on this subject.

Palestine is already taking an active part, as mentioned above, in the work of the United Nations. All it really lacks is the right to vote. Israel's fear of admitting as a member a state which might try to destroy another member state should be assuaged by the fact that the PLO has recognized Israel.

Member states have no reason to wait for withdrawal from the occupied territories or for the drawing of the respective borders of Palestine and Israel at the peace conference to admit the state of Palestine to United Nations membership. Admission should not be conditional on these events, however important they may be. Quite the contrary: Palestine's admission would make them easier to accomplish.

But this should not prevent member states from forming their own opinion concerning fulfilment of these conditions. To be sure, as stated by the International Court of Justice in its Advisory Opinion of 28 May 1948, concerning the Conditions of Admission of a State to Membership in the United Nations, 'political considerations' should not be superimposed upon the five basic conditions laid down in Article 4 'and prevent the admission of an applicant which fulfils them',[5] but 'it does not, however, follow from the exhaustive character of paragraph 1 of Article 4 that an appreciation is precluded of such circumstances of fact as would enable the existence of the requisite conditions to be verified'.[6] This explains the great importance of the procedural conditions established in paragraph 2 of Article 4.

52. This provision stipulates that 'the admission of any . . . state [meeting these conditions] to membership in the United Nations will be effected by a decision of the General Assembly upon the recommendation of the Security Council'.

The logical conclusion to be drawn from the attitude of the General Assembly at its 43rd session, during which it adopted Resolutions 43/176 and 43/177, and from its attitude during the preceding sessions when resolutions were adopted asserting the right of the Palestinian people to establish its independent state, is that it is in favour of the admission of Palestine.

Thus, Resolution 43/176 acknowledges the proclamation of the state of Palestine and decides that the designation 'Palestine' should be used in place of the designation 'Palestine Liberation Organization' in the United Nations system (142 of the states present voted for the resolution, two states—Israel and the United States—voted against, and two states abstained). Resolution 43/177 welcomes the outcome of the 19th Extraordinary Session of the Palestine National Council as a positive contribution towards a peaceful settlement of the conflict in the region.

The real criterion which should guide the General Assembly with respect to the admission of new members is whether or not the admission would serve the purposes of the organization, especially as concerns the maintenance of of peace.

This is a particularly opportune time for obtaining a positive vote from the General Assembly, given the climate of *détente* which now reigns throughout the world and, above all, the enthusiasm and speed with which many states recognized the state of Palestine immediately after its Proclamation of Independence. This enthusiasm was also manifest in the almost unanimous vote of the members of the General Assembly in favour of the resolution which acknowledged the proclamation.

53. The situation is likely to differ in the Security Council. Its decision on a matter such as admission, which is not a procedural matter, must be made by an affirmative vote of nine members, including the concurring votes of the permanent members of the Security Council (Article 27). In United Nations practice, the abstention of one permanent member does not necessarily invalidate the decisions made by a majority of nine members. If the request for the admission of Palestine is submitted to the Security Council, the members of the Security Council may well argue that one or more of the basic conditions have not been fulfilled. Even so, there are many precedents where arguments of this kind have not prevented admission from being ultimately granted.

The 'Repertory of Practice of United Nations Organs', with its five supplements from 1945 to 1980, gives many examples of requests for admission which were opposed on the grounds that the applicant states were lacking in one or the other of the constituent elements of a state (clearly defined territory and fixed borders, independent authority, etc.). However, these states were ultimately granted membership without any change having taken place in the elements said to be lacking. About 30 countries have had their requests for admission challenged or rejected, including: Mauritania, Jordan, Nepal, Bahrain, Japan, Kuwait, Israel, Oman, Congo, Burundi, Rwanda, Italy, Austria, Vietnam, Bulgaria, Sri Lanka, Romania, Finland, Hungary, Portugal, Albania, Libyan Arab Jamahiriya, Laos, Cambodia, Federal Republic of Germany, German Democratic Republic, Belize, Angola, Luxembourg and Mongolia.[7]

Moreover, like the members of the General Assembly, the members of the Security Council do not need to justify their vote. They are guided by their personal judgement or, to be more precise, by their attitude towards the state seeking admission—an admittedly broad interpretation of the notion of 'discretionary power'[8] but one which corresponds to the consistent practice of the council.

54. What we know of the United States' present political attitude hardly allows us to assume that the US will either vote for the admission of Palestine or abstain.

Four permanent members of the Security Council—China, France, Britain and the United States—have admittedly declared themselves willing, or 'even committed themselves' to refrain from using their vote when the Security Council is called upon to make decisions on recommendations of this nature,[9] and the question of abstention was even raised in the American Congress. According to the Vandenberg Resolution of 11 June 1948 (Resolution 239, 80th session, 2nd session),[10] the United States, a permanent member of the Security Council, should abstain if it is not in favour of the admission of a state.

In principle, when such a pledge is made publicly and with the intention of committing oneself, it becomes binding.[11] Yet it was made in very different international circumstances from those of today and one wonders if a state can forego a privilege which is granted to it by the charter.

Even if nothing, from a legal standpoint, would seem to prevent it from doing so (this is a 'personal' privilege of the five permanent members which is not granted to them in the general interest of the organization), it would be rash to conclude that the United States will feel bound by its previous promise to do no more than abstain—which would not constitute an obstacle to the Security Council recommending the admission of Palestine.

55. All the indications are that the US would block the admission of Palestine by using its veto.

The International Court of Justice, in its opinion of 3 March 1950, stated that the recommendation of the Security Council (not opposed by any permanent member) was indispensable. The court was categorical and kept to the letter of the charter.[12] After several requests for admission had been blocked by the use of the veto, the General Assembly, by its Resolution 296K (IV) of 22 November 1949, requested the members of the Security Council to abstain when recommendations were submitted concerning admission; but, although this resolution is in keeping with the spirit of universality of the United Nations, it is not binding on the permanent members of the Security Council.

If we assume that there is still a danger of the veto being used against the admission of Palestine, is there any way of overcoming this obstacle? The American Professor Francis Boyle envisages a procedure making this possible.[13] If a request for admission is made on behalf of Palestine and the United States exercises its right to veto during the examination of this request, United Nations member states might consider this veto as a violation of Article 80, paragraph 1, of the charter (binding on the United States), which is aimed at safeguarding the rights of mandated peoples, including the right to independence laid down in Article 22 of the Covenant of the League of Nations. This would lead to a dispute between the United States and these member states, who would accuse the United States of violating the charter.

If this happened, the Security Council would have to settle the dispute within the framework of Chapter VI on the Pacific Settlement of Disputes, in keeping with Article 35 of the charter.

Article 36, paragraph 1, of the charter stipulates that the Security Council may recommend appropriate procedures or methods of adjustment. A member of the Security Council might therefore propose a solution for the admission of Palestine to the United Nations. The United States, a party to the dispute, would then have to abstain during the voting on this proposal, in keeping with Article 27, paragraph 3. Even if the United States voted against, the President of the Security Council would have to consider its vote invalid.

A recommendation by the Security Council on the admission of Palestine would thus be adopted despite the objection of the United States. However, the recommendation of the Security Council would be made pursuant to Article 36, paragraph 1, concerning the settlement of disputes and not pursuant to Article 4 on admission. The General Assembly could then decide to grant admission on the strength of this recommendation.

56. Doubts may be entertained about the chances of success, if not the legal merits, of this scenario. As admission would not solve the problem of the withdrawal of Israel from the occupied territories and as it is uncertain whether the scenario devised by Professor Boyle would succeed, he proposes that the General Assembly have recourse to the 1950 'Uniting for Peace' Resolution to overcome any veto which the United States might use to prevent the sanctions provided for in Chapter VII being applied against Israel.

The chances of success of this second scenario seem greater than those of the first, and it would help to 'force the hand' of Israel and the United States. It is also proposed by another American professor, John Quingley, in an article entitled 'The Palestine Question in International Law'.[14]

Be that as it may, it seems that if a request for the admission of Palestine to the United Nations were to be vetoed by the United States (in the past, many requests have been so vetoed) while being approved by the General Assembly, this might have positive effects. The position of Palestine as a state, albeit a non-member, would be strengthened and withdrawal from the occupied territories facilitated, Israel appearing more clearly than ever as the occupant without title of the territory of another state.

57. In any event, a refusal of admission cannot have adverse legal effects

for Palestine, given that the Security Council, which has 15 members and whose primary responsibility is to safeguard peace, is not empowered to take the status of a state away from, or to confer it on, any given entity. All it can do is to play a part in granting membership of the organization, with the ensuing rights and duties.

Voting in the General Assembly, which is composed of almost all the members of the international community, is a different matter. Its recognition of the status of 'state', or its refusal to grant such recognition, is far more important, from the political point of view at least.

The Admission of Palestine to the Specialized Agencies: the Cases of UNESCO and WHO

The case of UNESCO

The admission of Palestine to UNESCO in theory

58. In principle, the admission of Palestine to UNESCO should not encounter any difficulties. It would be an open and shut case if Palestine had been admitted to the United Nations because Article II, paragraph 1, of the UNESCO constitution provides that member states of the United Nations have the right to membership in UNESCO. However, in strictly legal terms, the fact that it has not been so admitted should not make matters any more difficult.

Indeed, paragraph 2 of the same article provides that:

> States not members of the United Nations Organization may be admitted to membership of the Organization, upon recommendation of the Executive Board, by a two-thirds majority vote of the General Conference.

The UNESCO constitution gives no definition of a 'state' and contains no other provision governing the admission of new members. The admission of Palestine cannot and should not be made subject to any condition other than that contained in the above-mentioned article. The opinion of the International Court of Justice of 24 May 1948 on the admission of new members to the United Nations was categorical in this regard.[15] This opinion is applicable to UNESCO. No state may make its vote in support of a state applying for membership of an organization contingent upon a condition which is not stipulated in that organization's constitution; the recommendation of the General Assembly of the United Nations, which was once a condition for the admission of new members to UNESCO, is no longer required.

59. As the great majority of the members of UNESCO (over two-thirds) have recognized Palestine as a state, it follows that those members should vote for its admission to the organization.

While it is true that recognition and admission to an international organization are two different acts and are not necessarily related to each other, this only means that the admission of a state to the organization is not followed automatically by the bilateral recognition of the new member by all the old members. The organization cannot oblige its members to recognize a state against their will.

While this seems obvious with respect to members which may have voted against admission, it holds equally true for those members which may support admission but refuse to recognize the new member. The Secretary-General of the United Nations has cited several examples illustrating this situation in a memorandum on the legal aspects of representation at the United Nations.[16]

A similar, though not identical, situation occurred when the members of the United Nations which voted in favour of General Assembly Resolutions 43/176 and 43/177 (acknowledging the proclamation of the independence of Palestine, and describing that proclamation as a positive contribution towards a peaceful settlement of the Middle East conflict) included a number of states which had not recognized the state of Palestine.

Normally, however, the obverse should not occur. Countries which have recognized Palestine as a state should not vote against its admission to UNESCO, where the candidate's statehood is the sole condition for admission. Recognition affects the legal relationship between the recognizing state and the entity whose statehood has been recognized, and this should be reflected in the vote on membership. The situation would be different if the candidate's statehood were not a sufficient condition in itself.

60. In any case, the argument which has been used by Israel,[17] according to which the admission of Palestine to a technical organization such as UNESCO would constitute an unacceptable politicization of the organization, is ill-founded. It is the refusal to admit a candidate on political grounds that should be so considered and condemned.[18]

Moreover, as Professor Rosalyn Higgins[19] has pointed out, in an organization of a technical or humanitarian nature such as UNESCO, the term 'state'—which is replaced in other Specialized Agency constitutions by the terms 'nation' (FAO), 'country' (IBRD, IMF, ITU, UPU) and 'territories' (WMO)—has a much looser meaning than at the United Nations.

Several entities whose statehood was contested at the United Nations—and which were refused membership in that organization because certain members considered that they lacked an important element of statehood, such as being independent, actually existing, or having stable and defined borders—have, nevertheless, been admitted to UNESCO and WHO. Those entities include Kuwait, Austria, Japan, Jordan, Vietnam, Korea, the Federal Republic of Germany and the German Democratic Republic. All these states were admitted to certain Specialized Agencies before they were admitted to the United Nations.

This is readily explained by the non-political but technical and/or humanitarian nature of the Specialized Agencies. As Dr Togba,[20] delegate of Liberia to WHO, said in a debate on the admission of South Korea, 'disease recognizes no borders'. The same is true of backwardness in education, science and culture.

61. It is still true, however, that the constitutions of international organizations afford their member states the broadest latitude in assessing the qualifications of candidates for admission. No theory (such as that of the constituent elements of the state), no organ of the organization, no Secretary-General or Director-General, no Executive Board, Legal Committee or other body can dictate the attitude of member states or their vote on the admission of new members. Any organ that did would be exceeding its authority in the matter.

Among the constitutions of international organizations, only the charter of the United Nations contains a veto provision (in the Security Council) which can be used to obstruct the will of the majority of its members to admit a candidate to membership of their organization. At UNESCO, however, the admission of a new member depends entirely on the will of the majority of the organization's members, and they must be guided only by consideration of the objectives of that organization.

In the specific case of Palestine, over two-thirds of the members of UNESCO are in favour of admitting it to membership of the organization. Moreover, UNESCO's unstinting efforts to deal with the educational problems of the Palestinian people and to promote the preservation of its cultural identity are common knowledge.[21]

Consequently, Palestine should be assured of admission to UNESCO. In fact, however, its application for admission has not had the expected results. Let us take a look at what happened.

The admission of Palestine to UNESCO in practice

62. In a letter to the Director-General of UNESCO on 27 April 1989, Yasser Arafat requested that the state of Palestine be admitted to membership of UNESCO.[22] This letter was transmitted by the Director-General to the Chairman of the Executive Board in order for it to be followed up in 'the most appropriate manner'.

On 12 May 1989 an explanatory note was submitted by seven African and Asian member states supporting the admission of Palestine.[23] On 21 May Israel submitted a document in which it set out certain arguments against admission[24] and, on 8 June, the seven authors of the explanatory note submitted an addendum to their note rebutting the arguments of the representative of Israel.[25]

63. It was only on 19 June, after long negotiations behind the scenes of the Executive Board in the weeks preceding the discussion of the issue, that the board debated the admission of Palestine.

The Chairman of the Executive Board then stated that after lengthy and delicate negotiations on the item, the parties concerned had reached a consensus and had requested him to present a draft decision on their behalf, in the hope that it would be approved without debate, and with the understanding that, following approval, only two speakers—the observer of Palestine and the permanent delegate of Israel—would take the floor. He then asked the board to approve the draft decision by consensus. It was so decided.[26]

Among other provisions, the text which was adopted as the Executive Board's decision states that the board:

> 6. Stressing the importance of continuing to examine this question in a spirit of mutual understanding and constructive co-operation with a view to achieving a consensus . . .
>
> 7. Considering the need to involve the Palestinian people more closely with activities that belong in UNESCO's fields of competence . . .
>
> 8. Decides to propose that the General Conference provide for the closest possible participation of Palestine in the action of UNESCO . . :
>
> (a) Invites the Director-General to study all possible approaches and to propose appropriate ways and means of giving effect to this decision . . .;
>
> (b) Decides to reconsider this matter at its 132nd session with a view to formulating, in a spirit of consensus and with due regard to the higher interests of the organization, the recommendation to be transmitted to the General Conference;

9. Decides to include in the provisional agenda of the 25th session of the General Conference the following item:
Request for the admission of Palestine to UNESCO.[27]

This text evades the main issue—a decision to propose to the General Conference the admission of Palestine—and replaces it with a decision proposing that the General Conference provide for the closest possible participation of Palestine in the action of UNESCO.

The Executive Board also decided to reconsider the matter of admission at its 132nd session but, at the same time, included it on the agenda of the 25th session of the General Conference which was held after the 132nd session.

It is worth noting that the text mentions the importance of consensus and refers to the higher interests of the organization.

It is possible to understand why no consensus was achieved. Yet one may still ask why a consensus was called for in order to admit a new member when what was required was a constitutional majority of two-thirds. Moreover, how would 'the higher interests of the organization' be affected by the admission of a new state?

64. The statements of the representatives of Palestine and Israel shed light on certain points. In the statement by the observer of Palestine[28] we note:

that the request for admission will be included in the agenda of the General Conference and remain there until the organization agrees to admit Palestine and that this position will be defended without any ambiguity, hesitation, retreat or bargaining (para. 3.4);

that the admission or non-admission of Palestine brings it no further recognition and does not affect its status as a state in terms of international law (para. 3.5);

that Jordan's withdrawal from the occupied West Bank creates a legal vacuum which could be filled by the admission of Palestine to UNESCO (para. 3.6); and

that the state of Palestine, which is concerned not to be the cause of a new crisis for UNESCO, has sought to avoid a confrontation, for some would consider a vote to be a confrontation although they know perfectly well that the majority of voters support the Palestinian request both on the Executive Board and at the General Conference (para. 3.8).

The representative of Palestine added that he hoped that the admission of Palestine to UNESCO would be adopted enthusiastically and unanimously at the next session of the Executive Board. Palestine did not wish to become a member of an organization whose purpose was co-operation in an atmosphere of tension and confrontation, but neither would it accept the rejection of its membership.

It is worth noting the Palestinian representative's observation that 'the tragedy of the Palestinian people has given it maturity and wisdom, teaching it that history advances slowly and that it must arm itself with patience and perseverance in the struggle for its legitimate rights'.

In the brief statement by the delegate of Israel[29] we note:

that UNESCO has, in the recent past, strayed far from the path which leads to the aims for which it was created, which is why several member states have left the organization. These very important states have given to understand on several occasions that they might be willing to reconsider their position if the organization under Mr Mayor's leadership returned to the path traced out for it by its founding fathers; . . .

that paragraph 9 of the decision [concerning the inclusion of the request for the admission of Palestine on the agenda of the 25th session of the General Conference] by no means eliminates the scourge of politicization which has affected the organization;

that the content of paragraph 9 is a pretext for continuing to lay claim to the status of member state which would be contrary to the interest of the organization.

It emerges from these extensive quotations from the only two speeches made on the issue of the admission of Palestine that the text eventually adopted was hammered out behind the scenes. The Palestinians and their friends once more proved very accommodating even though it was quite clear, as the representative of Palestine said, that admission would obtain the required majority in the Executive Board and at the General Conference.

In applying pressure, Palestine's adversaries adduced a number of arguments, starting with the point that, if Palestine was admitted, the United States would not return to the organization, which would exacerbate UNESCO's financial crisis and affect its programme.

65. Certain promises were made in view of the moderation demonstrated by the Palestinians on the issue of their country's admission to the organization: it was agreed that Palestine would receive greater assistance from UNESCO, and the Director-General was asked to study the ways and means of providing this increased aid. But even if the effect is beneficial, it is rather paradoxical to provide increased aid to a state which, for obscure

reasons, is refused admission.

The Director-General did, in fact, submit a document to that effect to the 132nd session of the Executive Board.[30] The document is disappointing, however. Apart from some tens of thousands of dollars, most of the promised aid was to depend on extra-budgetary funds (paras. 13, 16, 20, 21, 27, 29, 32 and 33), funds which were probably to be supplied by the Arab states. The aid would be provided if additional resources were approved (para. 27) or if additional funding were found (para. 19).

It is noteworthy that the Director-General's proposals for strengthening Palestine's participation in UNESCO do not call for any modification in the constitution or the main statutory provisions of the organization, as stated in paragraph 35 of the report.

While abiding by the terms of the 'consolation' decision adopted by the Executive Board, Professor Alain Pellet, the specialist in international law consulted by the Director-General regarding ways of increasing UNESCO's assistance, makes more wide-ranging proposals. Although his report has not been published for 'reasons of economy', it has been made available to the members of the Executive Board.[31] It states that the admission of Palestine as a member could constitute a means of involving it in the closest possible way in the action of the organization. If admission could not be considered, however, Pellet took the view that the General Conference was free to adjust the rights and obligations of Palestine *vis-à-vis* UNESCO and that, even if Palestine were not admitted to membership of the organization, UNESCO was not limited by the terms of the current observer status, however broadly it were defined. These proposals were not examined, as a special envoy of the government of the United States (a non-member state of UNESCO) was sent to Paris to prevent them from being considered.

66. In spite of the Palestinian representative's hope that the request for the admission of his country would be unanimously approved by the Executive Board, the situation remained unchanged and the request for the admission of Palestine was set aside for a further two years.

At its 26th session, the UNESCO General Conference adopted Resolution 26C/062 on 15 October 1991. This again deferred Palestine's admission to UNESCO for two years, while inviting the Director-General to increase Palestine's participation in the programmes and activities which UNESCO implemented or in which it collaborated.

It would be difficult to conclude these remarks without observing that the Palestinians have been rewarded for their 'spirit of sacrifice' and for 'arming themselves with patience' with vacuous and unfulfilled promises. Nothing has been gained to date in terms of respect for international law, the policy of co-operation or the universality of UNESCO.

The case of WHO

67. Conditions for the admission of new members to WHO are simpler than those for admission to the United Nations or even UNESCO. Article 3 of the WHO constitution states that 'Membership in the organization shall be open to all states.' This proclamation of the principle of universality, which is not stated in the same way in the two other organizations considered above, is dictated by the supremely humanitarian nature of WHO. In fact, the introduction to the constitution of this organization declares that 'the enjoyment of the highest attainable standard of health is one of the fundamental rights of every human being', and that 'the health of all peoples . . . is dependent upon the fullest co-operation of individuals and states'. The emphasis is therefore placed on individuals over and above states and peoples, as if to underline further the humanitarian spirit which prompted the creation of WHO.

Article 6 of the WHO constitution stipulates that states which are not members of the United Nations 'may apply to become members [of WHO] and shall be admitted as members when their application has been approved by a simple majority vote of the World Health Assembly'.

This is in contrast to the condition of a two-thirds majority required by UNESCO and the United Nations. Furthermore, the United Nations demands a recommendation from the Security Council, where a contrary vote by only one state, if that state is one of the five permanent members of the council, can block admission. At UNESCO, a recommendation from the Executive Board must precede the General Conference vote on the admission of new members.

The memorandum from the German Democratic Republic,[32] when it requested admission to WHO in 1972, highlighted the distinctive nature of the organization's admissions procedure. It pointed up the fact that it displays significant openness towards non-members of the United Nations. In consequence, a state cannot be refused admission for political reasons which have nothing to do with the fundamental objectives of WHO. The memorandum also recalled that the organization's objective is in line with Article 25 of the Universal Declaration of Human Rights of 10 December 1948 concerning the right to health.

Finally, it should be pointed out that, as in the case of other international organizations, the WHO constitution contains no definition of a 'state' for admission purposes, that it is taken for granted that members are free to appraise the eligibility of candidates as they see fit, and that they must be guided in their judgement solely by the objectives of the organization.

68. For all these reasons, Palestine had every chance of being admitted to WHO, especially bearing in mind that more than 90 members of the organization had recognized Palestine as a state when it submitted its membership application on 1 April 1989.

Therefore, a vote in favour by a majority of the members could be regarded as a foregone conclusion, because, as Turkey's representative said later, approval of admission is a natural consequence of recognition.[33] However, things turned out differently in practice.

69. A brief examination of what happened at the WHO World Health Assembly between 6 and 12 May 1989 is instructive, since it shows how procedural artifice can misdirect situations that are legally straightforward.

Palestine's request for admission to WHO was made known to all the organization's member states. On 28 April the United States sent its comments[34] on that request, stating, 'It is not for a specialized, technical body such as the World Health Assembly to undertake political and legal steps . . . ' and 'If the application comes to a vote at the World Health Assembly, the United States will vote against it and will urge friends of WHO to do the same.' However, the United States added, 'We believe it is in the best interests of all of us to find a way to avoid having this issue placed before the Assembly for a vote. A deferral of action will work to the benefit of the entire WHO membership.'

The delegate of the Libyan Arab Jamahiriya said during a debate on the admission issue, on 12 May 1989, that some states had threatened to withdraw their financial contributions to the organization if Palestine were admitted.[35]

Of course, nothing in the WHO constitution allows the refusal of admission of a new member to be made a condition for the payment of contributions, to the detriment of the interests of all members of the organization.[36]

The WHO Director-General informed the meeting of 12 May that he had had contacts with Washington and with delegates in Geneva in order to reach a compromise on the issue of Palestine's admission.[37] That compromise was aimed at postponing discussion of admission until the following year, in exchange for an increase in WHO's aid to the Palestinian people. The Director-General added that the World Health Assembly should do nothing 'to jeopardize the future of the organization'. Twice during the same speech, he stated to members of the Assembly, 'The future is in your hands.'

During the same session, the delegate of the Libyan Arab Jamahiriya said

that the Director-General had contravened Article 37 of the WHO constitution on the relations between the Director-General and member states.[38]
The legal adviser added that he had no comment to make on that subject.[39]

70. However, at the start of the session, the delegate of Tonga spoke in
defence of a draft resolution that he and a few other states had submitted,
following the submission of another draft resolution by the Arab states
supporting the admission of Palestine to WHO.[40]

Tonga's proposal comprises several sections. In this draft resolution, the
Assembly:

1. Expresses the hope that the Palestinian people will be fully represented within the World Health Organization by their legitimate
representatives;
2. Requests the Director-General:
(1) to pursue his studies on the application of Palestine . . . and its
implications for the work of WHO;
(2) to report on the outcome of his studies to the Forty-third World
Health Assembly for its decision;
(3) to undertake immediately . . . further assistance to improve the
health conditions of the Palestinian people in the occupied territories;
(4) to enter into discussion with all parties concerned with a view to
ensuring extensive assistance in the field of health to the Palestinian
people in the occupied territories.[41]

This proposal had priority in the debate since it was furthest removed in
substance from the purpose of the item on the agenda.

The delegate of Algeria said that the proposal was wholly irrelevant,
since it dealt essentially with possible WHO aid to the Palestinian people,
whereas the basic issue of the agenda item under discussion was the
admission of Palestine to WHO.[42]

The delegate of the Libyan Arab Jamahiriya[43] said that paragraph 2 of the
draft resolution (concerning the studies to be prepared) did not fall within the
competence of either the Director-General or WHO. Article 2 of the
constitution made no provision for the organization to examine states'
capacities or their legitimacy. As for the other paragraphs of the draft
resolution, they dealt with another item on the agenda, namely item 29,
concerning the health situation of the Palestinian people in the occupied
territories.

The delegate of the Libyan Arab Jamahiriya added that the issue was
plain: there was a request for admission and a draft proposal to accept that

admission. States should assume their responsibilities and vote, by roll-call, for or against admission. Any departure from this structure would be inacceptable.

None the less, some states supported Tonga's proposal and called for a vote on it, in order to avoid voting on the admission issue. Nicaragua then put forward[44] amendments to Tonga's proposal by introducing a paragraph indicating approval of Palestine's admission instead of the paragraph on the studies to be prepared by the Director-General. Consequently, some states asked to discuss and vote on Nicaragua's amendment before voting on Tonga's proposal, as required by Rule 67 of WHO's Rules of Procedure. The Assembly President agreed that Nicaragua's amendment, although introduced belatedly, should nevertheless be discussed, in accordance with Rule 52 of the Rules of Procedure.

At that juncture, Britain put forward a proposal that the Assembly should not consider any amendment to Tonga's proposal and should go on to vote on Tonga's proposal, in its original form, assuming the British proposal were accepted. The representative of Britain requested that his proposal be voted on first, despite objections by several delegates to the use of this procedure to avoid a vote on the request for admission.

The proposal by Britain and the draft submitted by Tonga were accepted after the organization's legal adviser had indicated what, in his opinion, was the correct order of voting. However, this order is questionable, in the light of the Rules of Procedure. Moreover, one might draw attention to several constitutional irregularities here. In addition to the fact, mentioned above, that Tonga's proposal that the Director-General should prepare studies on Palestine's request exceeds the competence of the Director-General and of WHO, the amendment submitted by Nicaragua should have been put to the vote before the proposal by Britain. Furthermore, the British proposal was not submitted in writing and circulated as stipulated in Rule 52 of the Rules of Procedure of the Assembly. This proposal to consider no amendment to Tonga's initial draft resolution also has no basis in the Rules of Procedure. In point of fact, it should be possible to amend any proposal, and the Assembly should express its agreement or disagreement with the amendment by voting, especially since the President of the Assembly had accepted that Nicaragua's amendment should be considered and circulated in keeping with Rule 52 of the Rules of Procedure. Giving priority to the vote on Nicaragua's amendment would be consistent with Rule 68 of the Rules.

It was a highly questionable ploy to revert by a tortuous route to Tonga's draft while refusing to consider Nicaragua's amendment without a vote being taken on it, and at the same time voting on the proposal by Britain. None the less, a majority of the member states accepted this procedure with the thought at the back of their minds that it would preserve 'the future of our organization', to quote the words of the Director-General, with regard to the withholding of contributions mentioned in the speech by the delegate of the Libyan Arab Jamahiriya.

Consequently, Article 6 of the constitution of WHO was applied in a manner inconsistent with its real purpose. If a legal study were to be carried out, it should not be on the political and legal aspects of the admission of Palestine to WHO but on the 'right' of a state to make its contribution conditional on a vote and contingent upon whether that vote is in line with its wishes or political ideas.[45]

71. It is interesting in this connection to look at a number of explanations for votes that were given before the Assembly went on to consider another agenda item.

The Nigerian delegate stated[46] that his country had recognized Palestine and thought that the latter should become a member of WHO. That admission should not, however, disturb the work of the organization, since WHO had a mission which concerned the health of hundreds of millions of people throughout the world. Since the matter had not been amicably settled, Nigeria had abstained from voting.

The representative of Senegal stated[47] that the Organization of African Unity had expressed the wish that Palestine become a member of WHO, but he pointed out that WHO must be able to continue its essential tasks since no one wished to see this organization 'set out on the slippery slope of a financial crisis which might end up by wiping out almost four decades of effort'.

The representative of Iran stated:

All we had was references to different rules of procedure; what was forgotten was the issue itself . . . we should be dismayed that [faced with] an issue of such grave significance and importance, . . . we have been . . . watching a chess game which has been played based on the Rule of Procedure. . . . Is this what they expect of us?[48]

The delegate of the Libyan Arab Jamahiriya stated[49] that the adopted draft was an attack on the constitution of WHO. Article 6 of that constitution, straightforward and clear as it was concerning the admission of members, had thus been circumvented by procedural artifice.

It should be added that many states' fears of a financial crisis, fears which were also apparent in their preference for voting by secret ballot, perverted the use of the legal rules and the constitution of WHO.

If one takes into account the fact that UNESCO, which has lost certain contributions, and the United Nations, whose contributions were frozen for a certain period of time, nevertheless overcame their crises, one realizes that the attitude of the states in WHO was justified neither by the constitution nor by actual experience. A universal international organization cannot go under as a result of a crisis. Respect for the law and the courageous will of the majority must constitute a reliable lifeline. One might ask if the lesson has been learnt for the future.

Conclusion

By the end of 1991, the year of the Madrid peace conference, the dove of peace had, here and there, found a home. Would it subsequently be welcomed, with the same spirit and with the same hospitality, in the 'Land of Peace'? As the great Palestinian poet, Mahmoud Darwish once said, 'Ah! If only the doves could grow in the Ministries of Defence!'[1] There is no doubt that, out of the peace conference in Madrid, Washington, Moscow or elsewhere, some flickerings of hope can be discerned; after all, despite the turmoil between them this century, the Arabs and Jews have coexisted for more than 3,000 years and lived side by side in tolerance and friendship. The era of peace, mutual understanding and co-operation which is increasingly taking root across the globe cannot fail to extend its virtues to the Middle East. This is the dearest wish we can now express, so that the children of the region may enjoy a future of peace, security, concord and prosperity in a climate of solidarity and co-operation.

Speaking on television on his birthday long before the Madrid conference, Yasser Arafat movingly conveyed the following message to his enemies: 'I hold out my hand to the Israelis. It is now for them to hold out theirs so that we may truly make peace.' Leaving his hand outstretched to the viewers, he added, 'May they make with us the "Peace of the Brave" of which de Gaulle spoke!'[2] His message of peace was not heeded by the Israeli government of Yitzhak Shamir, which wished to delay the moment of truth by every possible means. Yet Arafat believed he was answering a 'message'

278

from Shamir who, a few days earlier, on 29 July 1991, had stated that his country did not intend to 'live with its sabre for ever drawn' and that he would choose the 'royal road, which is that of renewal'[3]—without, however, making clear what the nature of that road was.

On the eve of the Madrid conference, this was the situation that made the intervention of a mediator essential, in the absence of any understanding with the inflexible Israeli Prime Minister.

This book does not pretend to bring home to Israel the Palestinian message of peace, nor does it expect to establish ties or substitute acceptance for rejection. To achieve that, one must first refute the conflation of mythology, religion and history which has been used as an ideology of justification and an instrument of nationalist, expansionist policy. We may derive an impetus from the past to gain insight into the future.

Throughout its long history, Palestine has too often been the victim of conflict and conquest, be it geopolitical or geoideological. The invasions which most marked the collective memory were the eight Crusades, from the twelfth to the thirteenth centuries, and the seven waves of Zionist immigration of the nineteenth and twentieth. In both cases, there was a refusal to be integrated into the region. The crusader Kingdom of Jerusalem, and the state of Israel, were both viewed by the Arabs as appendages of the West, as enclaves and colonialist bridge-heads.

The collapse of the East European Communist regimes, and especially the break-up of the USSR, will radically alter Israel's strategic importance to the West in the Arab region. If Israel is not to 'live with its sabre for ever drawn', to use Shamir's words, 'the royal road' of Israel's 'renewal' can no longer remain the course it has chosen to follow since its creation, in its intoxication with blind power. The true path is that of political, economic and cultural integration in the Near and Middle East. First and foremost, such a renewal, for Israel, makes a shift from the rationale of force to one of the imperative of peace, involving its withdrawal from the Arab territories occupied in 1967, including East Jerusalem and south Lebanon, its recognition of the Palestinian people's existence and rights, and its acknowledgement of the wrongs it inflicted on this people in 1948. Israel must declare its readiness to contribute to putting right these wrongs, since its legitimacy and psychological acceptance by the Palestinians and Arabs will, to a large extent, hinge on such a gesture in order to reconcile Palestinian and Israeli rights. The question of the refugees and Palestinian property in Israel and the problem of Jerusalem will then be resolved in a climate of confidence.

Israel cannot keep its Palestinian minority in Galilee, the Triangle and the Negev under surveillance for ever, deny it the right to freedom of speech in seeking to preserve its Palestinian identity, and deprive it of the other rights which international law recognizes for minorities, especially the right to autonomy. Israel's integration in the region, in the context of the country's renewal, will entail a more active role for its Sephardim since it is not they who are responsible for the Palestinian people's tragedy. Moreover, their Middle Eastern culture may provide a bridge with the Arab world. The time has come to admit that the historical Zionist project for a Jewish state stretching from the Nile to the Euphrates and accommodating all the world's Jews, which Herzl described in his diary,[4] has failed. Israel has relinquished Sinai; and the Litani River has not actually become Israel's northern border, despite its invasion of southern Lebanon in 1982. Israel only accounts for a third of the world's Jewish population and the Israelis today are just one more minority in the Middle East. It is time that Israel agreed to become a country like any other, and considered itself to be a multi-ethnic state in the process of becoming bi-national, instead of remaining wedded to its cloistered conception of being a purely Jewish state beset by a ghetto mentality.

Now that the United Nations has repealed (on 16 December 1991) the resolution of 10 November 1975 equating Zionism with racism and racial discrimination, Israel has become morally duty-bound, if it wishes to choose the path of peace and integration in the region, to envisage reconstituting Zionism as a cultural, religious but apolitical concept, while jettisoning fantasies of a Greater Israel—a notion which has no biblical roots since the Bible never mentioned Eretz Israel ('land of Israel') as a state or political entity. In this connection, *aliya* (Jewish immigration into Israel) must be regulated; it cannot go on indefinitely. Israel must opt for the future, not hanker after the past. Its fundamental laws need to be amended, as does any exclusive or discriminatory legislation. The institutions born of political Zionism—the World Jewish Congress, the Jewish Agency, Keren Kayemet (the Jewish National Fund), Keren Hayessud (the Reconstruction Fund)—should revise their charters and activities. By way of example, according to the Jewish National Fund, any land it has 'saved' becomes 'Jewish' land: it cannot be sold or let to a 'non-Jew', or even be worked on by a 'non-Jew'. Such discrimination must be abolished.

The law on the lands of 'absentees' (meaning Palestinians expelled or forced into exile) should be repealed, since the Palestinians will not countenance the idea that they are to be considered as permanent 'absentees'. The 'emergency laws' passed by the British against the Jews in 1945, and since applied by Israel exclusively to the Palestinians, should also be annulled. The 'law of return' and the law on 'nationality' also need amendment, since the Palestinians are excluded from the benefits of the former and are reduced to second-class status by the latter, simply because they are not Jews. Here it is essential to replace the category of 'Jewish nationals' by one of 'Israeli nationals', so that Israel may become the state of all its citizens. Israel's school textbooks are the object of grave ideological manipulation: they incite Israeli children to hate Arabs and distrust them. Textbooks should be an instrument of peace and understanding, not a vehicle for hatred and war, and should advocate the noble principle of harmony and coexistence. 'Since wars begin in the minds of men, it is in the minds of men that the defences of peace must be constructed,' proclaims the UNESCO constitution.

These changes and corrections should be reciprocated by the Arabs and Palestinians, who are also called upon to adopt confidence-building measures. The Palestinians, too, must strive to overcome the great shortcomings of narrow-minded political nationalism and religious sectarianism, by reverting to the centuries-old calling of Palestine, a country of pluralism, tolerance and peace. Nationalism, as a justifying ideology, with its romantic exaltation of an idealized past, has been legitimized by an occupation by usurpers, but it is possible that it will only prolong the Palestinian people's suffering and, in today's world, hinder Palestine's liberation. The trap of anti-semitism should also be eschewed, and no credence should be attached to the 'Protocols of the Elders of Zion', fabricated in 1897 by von Plehve and reproduced, incidentally, from a pamphlet written in 1864 by Maurice Joly attacking Napoleon III. The Palestinians, too, must therefore foreswear some of their geopolitical dreams: the restoration of the *status quo ante* of 1948 Palestine is unrealistic. Israel is a fact of life, recognized by the international community.

History in the region is inextricably bound up with religion. However, to manipulate them both for political or ideological purposes is to play with fire. It will inevitably lead to a theologizing of the conflict: an incitement, among people on all sides, to Holy War.

The greatest disservice that could be done to monotheism, to Abraham's faith and to the three revealed religions of Judaism, Christianity and Islam would be to diminish the Bible and the Quran by translating them into political manifestos. The rule, 'Love thy neighbour as thyself' is cardinal in the Bible, and Numbers (XV, 16) states, 'One law and one manner shall be for you and for the stranger that sojourneth with you.' The Quran says, 'God has ordained for you the faith . . . enjoined to Abraham, Moses and Jesus . . . and which we have revealed to you, and be not divided therein' (sura XLII, verse 13).

Palestine cannot remain an island of despair, injustice, conflict and denial of the rights of peoples and individuals. The twentieth century has witnessed the break-up of the great empires of the tsars, Ottomans, Nazis, colonialists and Communists. The end of the century has been marked, for the greater good of mankind, by the settlement of grave regional conflicts. The era of ideologies is a thing of the past. Sooner or later, Zionism will go the same way. Force is now circumscribed by international law, whose noble principles have, with time, ultimately won the day. These principles, which are above all rooted in justice and fraternity, should inspire any settlement which is to be applied in the region. There can be no good principles for one and bad principles for the other. Otherwise, one would perpetuate a situation which was dangerous to Middle East peace, stability and security, and whose repercussions might affect other regions in new ways.

Finally, if the children of Abraham's faith are to live in peace on this Holy Land, where their common forefathers were born, the imperative of equality between the region's peoples demands the creation of an independent Palestinian state, which may join Israel and the other states of the region in their own commonwealth of independent states, economic community or Benelux-like institution. This is the spirit with which we would like to see the peace conference imbued, so that true peace, leading to the progress, well-being and fraternity of Palestinians and Israelis, Arab and Jews, might at last be established. Any outcome to the peace conference which does not grant the Palestinians a state, affording them refuge, security, protection and an end to their persecution and suffering, will not be a credible or enduring settlement.

Long ago, in Descartes' time, man said, 'I think, therefore I am.' Today, the oppressed man says, 'I fight, therefore I am.' One can only wish that, tomorrow, man may say, 'I love, therefore I am,' and that we may at last taste of what Shakespeare called 'the milk of human tenderness'.

Appendix 1.
UN General Assembly
Resolution 181 (II), 29 November 1947

Future Government of Palestine

A

The General Assembly,

Having met in special session at the request of the mandatory Power to constitute and instruct a special committee to prepare for the consideration of the question of the future government of Palestine at the second regular session;

Having constituted a Special Committee and instructed it to investigate all questions and issues relevant to the problem of Palestine, and to prepare proposals for the solution of the problem, and

Having received and examined the report of the Special Committee (document A/364) including a number of unanimous recommendations and a plan of partition with economic union approved by the majority of the Special Committee,

Considers that the present situation in Palestine is one which is likely to impair the general welfare and friendly relations among nations;

Takes note of the declaration by the mandatory Power that it plans to complete its evacuation of Palestine by 1 August 1948;

Recommends to the United Kingdom, as the mandatory Power for Palestine, and to all other Members of the United Nations the adoption and implementation, with regard to the future government of Palestine, of the Plan of Partition with Economic Union set out below;

Requests that

(a)   The Security Council take the necessary measures as provided for in the plan for its implementation;

(b)   The Security Council consider, if circumstances during the transitional period require such consideration, whether the situation in Palestine constitutes a threat to the peace. If it decides that such a threat exists, and in order to maintain international peace and security, the Security Council should supplement the authorization of the General Assembly by taking measures, under Articles 39 and 41 of the Charter, to empower the United Nations Commission, as provided in this resolution, to exercise in Palestine the functions which are assigned to it by this resolution;

(c)   The Security Council determine as a threat to the peace, breach of the peace or act of aggression, in accordance with Article 39 of the Charter, any attempt to alter by force the settlement envisaged by this resolution;

(d)   The Trusteeship Council be informed of the responsibilities envisaged for it in this plan;

Calls upon the inhabitants of Palestine to take such steps as may be necessary on their part to put this plan into effect;

Appeals to all Governments and all peoples to refrain from taking any action which might hamper or delay the carrying out of these recommendations, and

Authorizes the Secretary-General to reimburse travel and subsistence expenses of the members of the Commission referred to in Part I, Section B, paragraph 1 below, on such basis and in such form as he may determine most appropriate in the circumstances, and to provide the Commission with the necessary staff to assist in carrying out the functions assigned to the Commission by the General Assembly.

Appendix 2.
UN General Assembly Resolution 181 (III) (City of Jerusalem), 29 November 1947

A. SPECIAL REGIME

The City of Jerusalem shall be established as a *corpus separatum* under a special international regime and shall be administered by the United Nations. The Trusteeship Council shall be designated to discharge the responsibilities of the Administering Authority on behalf of the United Nations.

B. BOUNDARIES OF THE CITY

The City of Jerusalem shall include the present municipality of Jerusalem plus the surrounding villages and towns, the most eastern of which shall be Abu Dis; the most southern, Bethlehem; the most western, Ein Karim (including also the built-up area of Motsa); and the most northern Shu'fat.

C. STATUTE OF THE CITY

The Trusteeship Council shall, within five months of the approval of the present plan, elaborate and approve a detailed Statute of the City which shall contain *inter alia* the substance of the following provisions:

1. *Government machinery; special objectives.* The Administering Authority in discharging its administrative obligations shall pursue the following special objectives:

   (a)   To protect and to preserve the unique spiritual and religious interests located in the city of the three great monotheistic faiths throughout the world, Christian, Jewish and Moslem; to this end to ensure that order and peace, and especially religious peace, reign in Jerusalem;

   (b)   To foster co-operation among all the inhabitants of the city in their own interests as well as in order to encourage and support the peaceful development of the mutual relations between the two Palestinian peoples throughout the Holy Land; to promote the security, well-being and any constructive measures of development of the residents, having regard to the special circumstances and customs of the various peoples and communities.

2. *Governor and administrative staff.* A Governor of the City of Jerusalem shall be appointed by the Trusteeship Council and shall be responsible to it. He shall be selected on the basis of special qualifications and without regard to nationality. He shall not, however, be a citizen of either State in Palestine.

   The Governor shall represent the United Nations in the City and shall exercise on their behalf all powers of administration, including the conduct of external affairs. He shall be assisted by an administrative staff classed as international officers in the meaning of Article 100 of the Charter and chosen whenever practicable from the residents of the city and of the rest of Palestine on a non-discriminatory basis. A detailed plan for the organization of the administration of the city shall be submitted by the Governor to the Trusteeship Council and duly approved by it.

3. *Local autonomy*. (a) The existing local autonomous units in the territory of the city (villages, townships and municipalities) shall enjoy wide powers of local government and administration.

(b) The Governor shall study and submit for the consideration and decision of the Trusteeship Council a plan for the establishment of special town units consisting, respectively, of the Jewish and Arab sections of new Jerusalem. The new town units shall continue to form part of the present minicipality of Jerusalem.

4. *Security measures*. (a) The City of Jerusalem shall be demilitarized; its neutrality shall be declared and preserved, and no paramilitary formations, exercises or activities shall be permitted within its borders.

(b) Should the administration of the City of Jerusalem be seriously obstructed or prevented by the non-co-operation or interference of one or more sections of the population, the Governor shall have authority to take such measures as may be necessary to restore the effective functioning of the administration.

(c) To assist in the maintenance of internal law and order and especially for the protection of the Holy Places and religious buildings and sites in the city, the Governor shall organize a special police force of adequate strength, the members of which shall be recruited outside of Palestine. The Governor shall be empowered to direct such budgetary provision as may be necessary for the maintenance of this force.

5. *Legislative organization*. A Legislative Council, elected by adult residents of the city irrespective of nationality on the basis of universal and secret suffrage and proportional representation, shall have powers of legislation and taxation. No legislative measures shall, however, conflict or interfere with the provisions which will be set forth in the Statute of the City, nor shall any law, regulation, or official action prevail over them. The Statute shall grant to the Governor a right of vetoing bills inconsistent with the provisions referred to in the preceding sentence. It shall also empower him to promulgate temporary ordinances in case the Council fails to adopt in time a bill deemed essential to the normal functioning of the administration.

6. *Administration of justice*. The Statute shall provide for the establishment of an independent judiciary system, including a court of appeal. All the inhabitants of the City shall be subject to it.

7. *Economic union and economic regime*. The City of Jerusalem shall be included in the Economic Union of Palestine and be bound by all stipulations of

the undertaking and of any treaties issued therefrom, as well as by the decisions of the Joint Economic Board. The headquarters of the Economic Board shall be established in the territory of the City.

The Statute shall provide for the regulation of economic matters not falling within the regime of the Economic Union, on the basis of equal treatment and non-discrimination for all Members of the United Nations and their nationals.

8. *Freedom of transit and visit; control of residents.* Subject to considerations of security, and of economic welfare as determined by the Governor under the directions of the Trusteeship Council, freedom of entry into, and residence within, the borders of the City shall be guaranteed for the residents or citizens of the Arab and Jewish States. Immigration into, and residence within, the borders of the city for nationals of other States shall be controlled by the Governor under the directions of the Trusteeship Council.

9. *Relations with the Arab and Jewish States.* Representatives of the Arab and Jewish States shall be accredited to the Governor of the City and charged with the protection of the interests of their States and nationals in connexion with the international administration of the City.

10. *Offical languages.* Arabic and Hebrew shall be the official languages of the city. This will not preclude the adoption of one or more additional working languages, as may be required.

11. *Citizenship.* All the residents shall become *ipso facto* citizens of the City of Jerusalem unless they opt for citizenship of the State of which they have been citizens or, if Arabs or Jews, have filed notice of intention to become citizens of the Arab or Jewish State respectively, according to part I, section B, paragraph 9, of this plan.

The Trusteeship Council shall make arrangements for consular protection of the citizens of the City outside its territory.

12. *Freedoms of citizens.* (a) Subject only to the requirements of public order and morals, the inhabitants of the City shall be ensured the enjoyment of human rights and fundamental freedoms, including freedom of conscience, religion and worship, language, education, speech and Press, assembly and association, and petition.

(b)   No discrimination of any kind shall be made between the inhabitants on the grounds of race, religion, language or sex.

(c)   All persons within the City shall be entitled to equal protection of the laws.

(d)   The family law and personal status of the various persons and communities and their religious interests, including endowments, shall be respected.

(e)   Except as may be required for the maintenance of public order and good government, no measure shall be taken to obstruct or interfere with the enterprise of religious or charitable bodies of all faiths or to discriminate against any representative or member of these bodies on the ground of his religion or nationality.

(f) The City shall ensure adequate primary and secondary education for the Arab and Jewish communities respectively, in their own languages and in accordance with their cultural traditions.

The right of each community to maintain its own schools for the education of its own members in its own language, while conforming to such educational requirements of a general nature as the City may impose, shall not be denied or impaired. Foreign educational establishments shall continue their activity on the basis of their existing rights.

(g)   No restriction shall be imposed on the free use by any inhabitant of the City of any language in private intercourse, in commerce, in religion, in the Press or in publications of any kind, or at public meetings.

13.   *Holy Places*. (a) Existing rights in respect of Holy Places and religious buildings or sites shall not be denied or impaired.

(b)   Free access to the Holy Places and religious buildings or sites and the free exercise of worship shall be secured in conformity with existing rights and subject to the requirements of public order and decorum.

(c)   Holy Places and religious buildings or sites shall be preserved. No act shall be permitted which may in any way impair their sacred character. If at any time it appears to the Governor that any particular Holy Place, religious building or site is in need of urgent repair, the Governor may call upon the community or communities concerned to carry out such repair. The Governor may carry it out himself at the expense of the community or communities concerned if no action is taken within a reasonable time.

(d)   No taxation shall be levied in respect of any Holy Place, religious building or site which was exempt from taxation on the date of the creation of the City. No change in the incidence of such taxation shall be made which would either discriminate between the owners or occupiers of Holy Places, religious buildings or sites, or would place such owners or occupiers in a position less favourable in relation to the general incidence of taxation than existed at the time of the adoption of the Assembly's recommendations.

14.   *Special powers of the Governor in respect of the Holy Places, religious buildings and sites in the City and in any part of Palestine*. (a) The protection of the Holy Places, religious buildings and sites located in the City of Jerusalem shall be a special concern of the Governor.

(b)   With relation to such places, buildings and sites in Palestine outside the city, the Governor shall determine, on the ground of powers granted to him by the Constitutions of both States, whether the provisions of the Constitutions of the Arab and Jewish States in Palestine dealing therewith and the religious rights appertaining thereto are being properly applied and respected.

(c)   The Governor shall also be empowered to make decisions on the basis of existing rights in cases of disputes which may arise between the different religious communities or the rites of a religious community in respect of the Holy Places, religious buildings and sites in any part of Palestine.

In this task he may be assisted by a consultative council of representatives of different denominations acting in an advisory capacity.

D. DURATION OF THE SPECIAL REGIME

The Statute elaborated by the Trusteeship Council on the aforementioned principles shall come into force not later than 1 October 1948. It shall remain in force in the first instance for a period of ten years, unless the Trusteeship Council finds it necessary to undertake a re-examination of these provisions at an earlier date. After the expiration of this period the whole scheme shall be subject to re-examination by the Trusteeship Council in the light of the experience acquired with its functioning. The residents of the City shall be then free to express by means of a referendum their wishes as to possible modifications of the City.

PART IV
CAPITULATIONS

States whose nationals have in the past enjoyed in Palestine the privileges and immunities of foreigners, including the benefits of consular jurisdiction and protection, as formerly enjoyed by capitulation or usage in the Ottoman Empire, are invited to renounce any right pertaining to them to the re-establishment of such privileges and immunities in the proposed Arab and Jewish States and the City of Jerusalem.

Appendix 3.
UN General Assembly Resolution 194 (III), 11 December 1948

Palestine—progress report of the United Nations Mediator

The General Assembly,

Having considered further the situation in Palestine,

1.   *Expresses* its deep appreciation of the progress achieved through the good offices of the late United Nations Mediator in promoting a peaceful adjustment of the future situation of Palestine, for which cause he sacrificed his life; and

Extends its thanks to the Acting Mediator and his staff for their continued efforts and devotion to duty in Palestine;

2.   *Establishes* a Conciliation Commission consisting of three States Members of the United Nations which shall have the following functions:

(a)   To assume, in so far as it considers necessary in existing circumstances, the functions given to the United Nations Mediator on Palestine by resolution 186 (S-2) of the General Assembly of 14 May 1948;

(b)   To carry out the specific functions and directives given to it by the present resolution and such additional functions and directives as may be given to it by the General Assembly or by the Security Council;

(c)   To undertake, upon the request of the Security Council, any of the functions now assigned to the United Nations Mediator on Palestine or to the United Nations Truce Commission by resolutions of the Security Council; upon such request to the Conciliation Commission by the Security Council with respect to all the remaining functions of the United Nations Mediator on Palestine under Security Council resolutions, the office of the Mediator shall be terminated;

3.   *Decides* that a Committee of the Assembly, consisting of China, France, the Union of Soviet Socialist Republics, the United Kingdom and the United States of America, shall present, before the end of the first part of the present session of the General Assembly, for the approval of the Assembly, a proposal concerning the names of the three States which will constitute the Conciliation Commission;

4.   *Requests* the Commission to begin its functions at once, with a view to the establishment of contact between the parties themselves and the Commission at the earliest possible date;

5.   *Calls upon* the Governments and authorities concerned to extend the scope of the negotiations provided for in the Security Council's resolution of 16 November 1948 and to seek agreement by negotiations conducted either with the

Conciliation Commission or directly, with a view to the final settlement of all questions outstanding between them;

6.   *Instructs* the Conciliation Commission to take steps to assess the Governments and authorities concerned to achieve a final settlement of all questions outstanding between them;

7.   *Resolves* that the Holy Places—including Nazareth—religious buildings and sites in Palestine should be protected and free access to them assured, in accordance with existing rights and historical practice; that arrangements to this end should be under effective United Nations supervision; that the United Nations Conciliation Commission, in presenting to the fourth regular session of the General Assembly its detailed proposals for a permanent international regime for the territory of Jerusalem, should include recommendations concerning the Holy Places in that territory; that with regard to the Holy Places in the rest of Palestine the Commission should call upon the political authorities of the areas concerned to give appropriate formal guarantees as to the protection of the Holy Places and access to them; and that these undertakings should be presented to the General Assembly for approval;

8.   *Resolves* that, in view of its association with three world religions, the Jerusalem area, including the present municipality of Jerusalem *plus* the surrounding villages and towns, the most eastern of which shall be Abu Dis; the most southern, Bethlehem; the most western, Ein Karim (including also the built-up area of Motsa); and the most northern, Shu'fat, should be accorded special and separate treatment from the rest of Palestine and should be placed under effective United Nations control;

Requests the Security Council to take further steps to ensure the de-militarization of Jerusalem at the earliest possible date;

Instructs the Conciliation Commission to present to the fourth regular session of the General Assembly detailed proposals for a permanent international regime for the Jerusalem area which will provide for the maximum local autonomy for distinctive groups consistent with the special international status of the Jerusalem area;

The Conciliation Commission is authorized to appoint a United Nations representative, who shall co-operate with the local authorities with respect to the interim administration of the Jerusalem area;

9.   *Resolves* that, pending agreement on more detailed arrangements among the Governments and authorities concerned, the freest possible access to Jerusalem by road, rail or air should be accorded to all inhabitants of Palestine;

Instructs the Conciliation Commission to report immediately to the Security Council, for appropriate action by that organ, any attempt by any party to impede such access;

10.   *Instructs* the Conciliation Commission to seek arrangements among the Governments and authorities concerned which will facilitate the economic

development of the area, including arrangements for access to ports and airfields and the use of transportation and communication facilities;

11.   *Resolves* that the refugees wishing to return to their homes and live at peace with their neighbours should be permitted to do so at the earliest practicable date, and that compensation should be paid for the property of those choosing not to return and for loss of or damage to property which, under principles of international law or in equity, should be made good by the Governments or authorities responsible;

Instructs the Conciliation Commission to facilitate the repatriation, resettlement and economic and social rehabilitation of the refugees and the payment of compensation, and to maintain close relations with the Director of the United Nations Relief for Palestine Refugees and, through him, with the appropriate organs and agencies of the United Nations;

12.   *Authorizes* the Conciliation Commission to appoint such subsidiary bodies and to employ such technical experts, acting under its authority, as it may find necessary for the effective discharge of its functions and responsibilities under the present resolution;

The Conciliation Commission will have its official headquarters at Jerusalem. The authorities responsible for maintaining order in Jerusalem will be responsible for taking all measures necessary to ensure the security of the Commission. The Secretary-General will provide a limited number of guards for the protection of the staff and premises of the Commission;

13.   *Instructs* the Conciliation Commission to render progress reports periodically to the Secretary-General for transmission to the Security Council and to the Members of the United Nations;

14.   *Calls upon* all Governments and authorities concerned to co-operate with the Conciliation Commission and to take all possible steps to assist in the implementation of the present resolution;

15.   *Requests* the Secretary-General to provide the necessary staff and facilities and to make appropriate arrangements to provide the necessary funds required in carrying out the terms of the present resolution.

Hundred and eighty-sixth plenary meeting,
11 December 1948

At the 186th plenary meeting on 11 December 1948, a committee of the Assembly consisting of the five States designated in paragraph 3 of the above resolution proposed that the following three States should constitute the Conciliation Commission: FRANCE, TURKEY, UNITED STATES OF AMERICA.

The proposal of the Committee having been adopted by the General Assembly at the same meeting, the Conciliation Commission is therefore composed of the above-mentioned three States.

Appendix 4.
UN Security Council Resolution 242,
22 November 1967

The Security Council,

Expressing its continuing concern with the grave situation in the Middle East,

Emphasizing the inadmissibility of the acquisition of territory by war and the need to work for a just and lasting peace in which every State in the area can live in security,

Emphasizing further that all Member States in their acceptance of the Charter of the United Nations have undertaken a commitment to act in accordance with Article 2 of the Charter,

1.   *Affirms* that the fulfilment of Charter principles requires the establishment of a just and lasting peace in the Middle East which should include the application of both the following principles:

(i)   Withdrawal of Israel armed forces from territories occupied in the recent conflict;

(ii)   Termination of all claims or states of belligerency and respect for and acknowledgement of the sovereignty, territorial integrity and political independence of every State in the area and their right to live in peace within secure and recognized boundaries free from threats or acts of force;

2.   *Affirms further* the necessity

(a)   For guaranteeing freedom of navigation through international waterways in the area;

(b)   For achieving a just settlement of the refugee problem;

(c)   For guaranteeing the territorial inviolability and political independence of every State in the area, through measures including the establishment of demilitarized zones;

3.   *Requests* the Secretary-General to designate a Special Representative to proceed to the Middle East to establish and maintain contacts with the States concerned in order to promote agreement and assist efforts to achieve a peaceful and accepted settlement in accordance with the provisions and principles in this resolution;

4.   *Requests* the Secretary-General to report to the Security Council on the progress of the efforts of the Special Representative as soon as possible.

Adopted unanimously at the 1382nd meeting.

Appendix 5.
The Begin Plan for Administrative Autonomy in the West Bank and Gaza, December 1977

1. The administration of the military government in Judea, Samaria and the Gaza district will be abolished.

2. In Judea, Samaria and the Gaza district administrative autonomy of the residents, by and for them, will be established.

3. The residents of Judea, Samaria and the Gaza district will elect an Administrative Council composed of 11 members. The Administrative Council will operate in accordance with the principles laid down in this paper.

4. Any resident 18 years old or over, without distinction of citizenship, including stateless residents, is entitled to vote in the elections to the Administrative Council.

5. Any resident whose name is included in the list of candidates for the Administrative Council and who, on the day the list is submitted, is 25 years old or over, is eligible to be elected to the council.

6. The Administrative Council will be elected by general, direct, personal, equal, and secret ballot.

7. The period of office of the Administrative Council will be four years from the day of its election.

8. The Administrative Council will sit in Bethlehem.

9. All the administrative affairs relating to the Arab residents of the areas of Judea, Samaria and the Gaza district will be under the direction and within the competence of the Administrative Council.

10. The Administrative Council will operate the following departments: education; religious affairs; finance; transportation; construction and housing; industry, commerce, and tourism; agriculture; health; labour and social welfare; rehabilitation of refugees; and the department for the administration of justice and the supervision of the local police forces. It will also promulgate regulations relating to the operation of these departments.

11. Security and public order in the areas of Judea, Samaria and the Gaza district will be the responsibility of the Israeli authorities.

12. The Administrative Council will elect its own chairman.

13. The first session of the Administrative Council will be convened 30 days after the publication of the election results.

14. Residents of Judea, Samaria and the Gaza district, without distinction of citizenship, including stateless residents, will be granted free choice of either Israeli or Jordanian citizenship.

15. A resident of the areas of Judea, Samaria and the Gaza district who requests Israeli citizenship will be granted such citizenship in accordance with

the citizenship law of the state.

16.   Residents of Judea, Samaria and the Gaza district who, in accordance with the right of free option, choose Israeli citizenship, will be entitled to vote for, and be elected to, the Knesset in accordance with the election law.

17.   Residents of Judea, Samaria and the Gaza district who are citizens of Jordan or who, in accordance with the right of free option, become citizens of Jordan, will elect and be eligible for election to the parliament of the Hashemite Kingdom of Jordan in accordance with the election law of that country.

18.   Questions arising from the vote to the Jordanian Parliament by residents of Judea, Samaria and the Gaza district will be clarified in negotiations between Israel and Jordan.

19.   A committee will be established of representatives of Israel, Jordan and the Administrative Council to examine existing legislation in Judea, Samaria and the Gaza district; and to determine which legislation will continue in force, which will be abolished, and what will be the competence of the Administrative Council to promulgate regulations. The rulings of the committee will be adopted by unanimous decision.

20.   Residents of Israel will be entitled to acquire land and settle in the areas of Judea, Samaria and the Gaza district. Arabs, residents of Judea, Samaria and the Gaza district, who, in accordance with the free option granted them, become Israeli citizens, will be entitled to acquire land and settle in Israel.

21.   A committee will be established of representatives of Israel, Jordan and the Administrative Council to determine norms of immigration to the areas of Judea, Samaria and the Gaza district. The committee will determine the norms whereby Arab refugees residing outside Judea, Samaria and the Gaza district will be permitted to immigrate to these areas in reasonable numbers. The rulings of the committee will be adopted by unanimous decision.

22.   Residents of Israel and residents of Judea, Samaria and the Gaza district will be assured freedom of movement and freedom of economic activity in Israel, Judea, Samaria and the Gaza district.

23.   The Administrative Council will appoint one of its members to represent the council before the government of Israel for deliberation on matters of common interest, and one of its members to represent the council before the government of Jordan for deliberation of matters of common interest.

24.   Israel stands by its rights and its claim of sovereignty to Judea, Samaria and the Gaza district. In the knowledge that other claims exist, it proposes, for the sake of the agreement and the peace, that the question of sovereignty in these areas be left open.

25.   With regard to the administration of the holy places of the three religions in Jerusalem, a special proposal will be drawn up and submitted that will include the guarantee of freedom of access to members of all faiths to the shrines holy to them.

26.   These principles will be subject to review after a five-year period.

Appendix 6.
The Camp David Accords, September 1978

1. Egypt, Israel, Jordan and the representatives of the Palestinian people should participate in negotiations on the resolution of the Palestinian problem in all its aspects. To achieve that objective, negotiations relating to the West Bank and Gaza should proceed in three stages:

(a) Egypt and Israel agree that, in order to ensure a peaceful and orderly transfer of authority, and taking into account the security concerns of all the parties, there should be transitional arrangements for the West Bank and Gaza for a period not exceeding five years. In order to provide full autonomy to the inhabitants, under these arrangements the Israeli military government and its civilian administration will be withdrawn as soon as a self-governing authority has been freely elected by the inhabitants of these areas to replace the existing military government. To negotiate the details of a transitional arrangement, the Government of Jordan will be invited to join the negotiations on the basis of this framework. These new arrangements should give due consideration both to the principle of self-government by the inhabitants of these territories and to the legitimate security concerns of the parties involved.

(b) Egypt, Israel and Jordan will agree on the modalities for establishing the elected self-governing authority in the West Bank and Gaza. The delegations of Egypt and Jordan may include Palestinians from the West Bank and Gaza or other Palestinians as mutually agreed. The parties will negotiate an agreement which will define the powers and responsibilities of the self-governing authority to be exercised in the West Bank and Gaza. A withdrawal of Israeli armed forces will take place and there will be a redeployment of the remaining Israeli forces into specified security locations. The agreement will also include arrangements for assuring internal and external security and public order. A strong local police force will be established, which may include Jordanian citizens. In addition, Israeli and Jordanian forces will participate in joint patrols and in the manning of control posts to assure the security of the borders.

(c) When the self-governing authority (administrative council) in the West Bank and Gaza is established and inaugurated, the transitional period of five years will begin. As soon as possible, but not later than the third year after the beginning of the transitional period, negotiations will take place to determine the final status of the West Bank and Gaza and its relationship with its neighbours, and to conclude a peace treaty between Israel and Jordan by the end of the transitional period. These negotiations will be conducted among Egypt, Israel, Jordan, and the elected representatives of the inhabitants of the West Bank and

Gaza. Two separate but related committees will be convened, one committee, consisting of representatives of the four parties which will negotiate and agree on the final status of the West Bank and Gaza, and its relationship with its neighbours, and the second committee, consisting of representatives of Israel and representatives of Jordan to be joined by the elected representatives of the inhabitants of the West Bank and Gaza, to negotiate the peace treaty between Israel and Jordan, taking into account the agreement reached on the final status of the West Bank and Gaza. The negotiations shall be based on all the provisions and principles of UN Security Council Resolution 242. The negotiations will resolve, among other matters, the location of the boundaries and the nature of the security arrangements. The solution from the negotiations must also recognize the legitimate rights of the Palestinian people and their just requirements. In this way, the Palestinians will participate in the determination of their own future through:

1) The negotiations among Egypt, Israel, Jordan and the representatives of the inhabitants of the West Bank and Gaza to agree on the final status of the West Bank and Gaza and other outstanding issues by the end of the transitional period.

2) Submitting their agreement to a vote by the elected representatives of the inhabitants of the West Bank and Gaza.

3) Providing for the elected representatives of the inhabitants of the West Bank and Gaza to decide how they shall govern themselves consistent with the provisions of their agreement.

4) Participating as stated above in the work of the committee negotiating the peace treaty between Israel and Jordan.

2. All necessary measures will be taken and provisions made to assure the security of Israel and its neighbours during the transitional period and beyond. To assist in providing such security, a strong local police force will be constituted by the self-governing authority. It will be composed of inhabitants of the West Bank and Gaza. The police will maintain continuing liaison on internal security matters with the designated Israeli, Jordanian and Egyptian officers.

3. During the transitional period, representatives of Egypt, Israel, Jordan and the self-governing authority will constitute a continuing committee to decide by agreement on the modalities of admission of persons displaced from the West Bank and Gaza in 1967, together with necessary measures to prevent disruption and disorder. Other matters of common concern may also be dealt with by this committee.

4. Egypt and Israel will work with each other and with other interested parties to establish agreed procedures for a prompt, just and permanent

implementation of the resolution of the refugee problem.

(In one of ten letters of clarification, President Carter wrote to Menachem Begin on 22 September, acknowledging that he had been informed that the Israeli government construed and understood the expressions 'Palestinians' or 'Palestinian People' as 'Palestinian Arabs', and 'West Bank' as 'Judea and Samaria'.)

Appendix 7.
The Reagan Plan,
1 September 1982

1. As outlined in the Camp David accords, there must be a period of time during which the Palestinian inhabitants of the West Bank and Gaza will have full autonomy over their own affairs. Due consideration must be given to the principle of self-government by the inhabitants of the territories and to the legitimate security concerns of the parties involved.

The purpose of the five-year period of transition which would begin after free elections for a self-governing Palestinian authority is to prove to the Palestinians that they can run their own affairs, and that such Palestinian autonomy poses no threat to Israel's security.

2. The United States will not support the use of any additional land for the purpose of settlements during the transition period. Indeed, the immediate adoption of a settlement freeze by Israel, more than any other action, could create the confidence needed for wider participation in these talks. Further settlement activity is in no way necessary for the security of Israel and only diminishes the confidence of the Arabs that a final outcome can be freely and fairly negotiated.

The purpose of this transition period is the peaceful and orderly transfer of domestic authority from Israel to the Palestinian inhabitants of the West Bank and Gaza. At the same time, such a transfer must not interfere with Israel's security requirements.

3. Beyond the transition period, peace cannot be achieved by the formation of an independent Palestinian state in those territories. Nor is it achievable on the basis of Israeli sovereignty or permanent control over the West Bank and Gaza.

It is the firm view of the United States that self-government by the Palestinians of the West Bank and Gaza in association with Jordan offers the best chance for a durable, just and lasting peace.

4. The Arab-Israeli conflict should be resolved through negotiations involving an exchange of territory for peace. It is the United States' position that—in return for peace—the withdrawal provision of Resolution 242 applies to all fronts, including the West Bank and Gaza.

5. Jerusalem must remain undivided, but its final status should be decided through negotiations.

Appendix 8.
The Arab Peace Plan Adopted at Fez, 9 September 1982

1. Israel's withdrawal from all the territories it occupied in 1967, including Jerusalem.

2. Dismantling of the settlements built by Israel in the Arab territories after 1967.

3. Safeguarding freedom of worship for all religions in the Holy Places.

4. Reaffirmation of the Palestinian people's right to self-determination and to exercise its inalienable national rights under the leadership of the Palestine Liberation Organization, its sole legitimate representative, as well as to compensation in the case of those not wishing to return.

5. The West Bank and the Gaza Strip to be placed under United Nations trusteeship for a transitional period not exceeding a few months.

6. Creation of an independent Palestinian state with Jerusalem as its capital.

7. The UN Security Council to guarantee peace between all the states of the region, including the independent Palestinian state.

8. The UN Security Council to guarantee compliance with these principles.

Appendix 9.
The Mubarak Plan,
August 1989

1.   An undertaking by Israel to accept the results of elections to be held in the occupied West Bank and Gaza. These elections shall be free and democratic.

2.   The elections shall be conducted under the supervision of Western observers.

3.   The Israeli army shall withdraw in advance from the areas in which these elections are to take place.

4.   On the day of voting, access to the Occupied Territories will be forbidden for Israeli nationals.

5.   The Palestinian inhabitants of East Jerusalem will be entitled to vote in the elections.

6.   The candidates in the elections will enjoy complete freedom of speech.

7.   The elected individuals shall be protected by a form of immunity in order to shelter them from any judicial prosecution.

8.   Israel shall pledge to commence negotiations on the final status of the Occupied Territories convening a time-frame of 3 to 5 years. This time-frame is an interim period.

9.   Israeli settlements in the Occupied Territories shall be suspended.

10.   Israel shall accept the principle of 'land for peace' as an integral part of any final settlement.

Appendix 10.
The Letters Exchanged between
the PLO and Israel,
9 September 1993

From Mr Arafat to Mr Rabin

Mr Prime Minister,

The signing of the Declaration of Principles marks a new era in the history of the Middle East. In firm conviction thereof, I would like to confirm the following PLO commitments:

The PLO recognizes the right of the State of Israel to exist in peace and security.

The PLO accepts United Nations Security Council Resolutions 242 and 338.

The PLO commits itself to the Middle East peace process, and to a peaceful resolution of the conflict between the two sides and declares that all outstanding issues relating to permanent status will be resolved through negotiations.

The PLO considers that the signing of the Declaration of Principles constitutes a historic event, inaugurating a new epoch of peaceful coexistence, free from violence and all other acts which endanger peace and stability. Accordingly, the PLO renounces the use of terrorism and other acts of violence and will assume responsibility over all PLO elements and personnel in order to assure their compliance, prevent violations and discipline violators.

In view of the promise of a new era and the signing of the Declaration of Principles and based on Palestinian acceptance of Security Council Resolutions 242 and 338, the PLO affirms that those articles of the Palestinian Covenant which deny Israel's right to exist, and the provisions of the Covenant which are inconsistent with the commitments of this letter, are now inoperative and no longer valid. Consequently, the PLO undertakes to submit to the Palestinian National Council for formal approval the necessary changes in regard to the Palestinian Covenant.

Sincerely,

Yasser Arafat, Chairman, The Palestine Liberation Organization

From Mr Rabin to Mr Arafat

Mr Chairman,

In response to your letter of 9 September 1993, I wish to confirm to you that, in light of the PLO commitments included in your letter, the Government of Israel has decided to recognize the PLO as the representative of the Palestinian people and commence negotiations with the PLO within the Middle East peace process.

Yitzhak Rabin, Prime Minister of Israel

Appendix 11.
Declaration of Principles on Interim Self-Government Arrangements, 13 September 1993

The government of the state of Israel and the PLO team (in the Jordanian-Palestinian delegation to the Middle East Peace Conference) (the 'Palestinian delegation'), representing the Palestinian people, agree that it is time to put an end to decades of confrontation and conflict, recognize their mutual legitimate and political rights, and strive to live in peaceful coexistence and mutual dignity and security and achieve a just, lasting and comprehensive peace settlement and historic reconciliation through the agreed political process. Accordingly, the two sides agree the following principles:

Article I: Aim of the Negotiations
The aim of the Israeli-Palestinian negotiations within the current Middle East peace process is, among other things, to establish a Palestinian interim self-government authority, the elected Council (the 'Council'), for the Palestinian people in the West Bank and the Gaza Strip, for a transitional period not exceeding five years, leading to a permanent settlement based on Security Council Resolutions 242 and 338.

It is understood that the interim arrangements are an integral part of the whole peace process and that the negotiations on the permanent status will lead to the implementation of Security Council Resolutions 242 and 338.

Article II: Framework for the Interim Period
The agreed framework for the interim period is set forth in this Declaration of Principles.

Article III: Elections
1. In order that the Palestinian people in the West Bank and Gaza Strip may govern themselves according to democratic principles, direct, free and general political elections will be held for the Council under agreed supervision and international observation, while the Palestinian police will ensure public order.

2. An agreement will be concluded on the exact mode and conditions of the elections in accordance with the protocol attached in Annex I, with the goal of holding the elections not later than nine months after the entry into force of this Declaration of Principles.

3. These elections will constitute a significant interim preparatory step towards the realization of the legitimate rights of the Palestinian people and their just requirements.

Article IV: Jurisdiction
Jurisdiction of the Council will cover the West Bank and Gaza Strip territory, except for issues that will be negotiated in the permanent status negotiations. The two sides view the West Bank and the Gaza Strip as a single territorial unit, whose integrity will be preserved during the interim period.

Article V: Transitional Period and Permanent Status Negotiations
    1. The five-year transitional period will begin upon the withdrawal from the Gaza Strip and Jericho area.
    2. Permanent status negotiations will commence as soon as possible, but not later than the beginning of the third year of the interim period, between the government of Israel and the Palestinian people's representatives.
    3. It is understood that these negotiations shall cover remaining issues, including: Jerusalem, refugees, settlements, security arrangements, borders, relations and co-operation with other neighbours, and other issues of common interest.
    4. The two parties agree that the outcome of the permanent status negotiations should not be prejudiced or preempted by agreements reached for the interim period.

Article VI: Preparatory Transfer of Powers and Responsibilities
    1. Upon the entry into force of this Declaration of Principles and the withdrawal from the Gaza Strip and the Jericho area, a transfer of authority from the Israeli military government and its civil administration to the authorized Palestinians for this task, as detailed herein, will commence. This transfer of authority will be of preparatory nature until the inauguration of the Council.
    2. Immediately after the entry into force of this Declaration of Principles and the withdrawal from the Gaza Strip and Jericho area, with the view to promoting economic development in the West Bank and Gaza Strip, authority will be transferred to the Palestinians on the following spheres: education and culture, health, social welfare, direct taxation, and tourism. The Palestinian side will commence in building the Palestinian police force, as agreed upon. Pending the inauguration of the Council, the two parties may negotiate the transfer of additional powers and responsibilities, as agreed upon.

Article VII: Interim Agreement
    1. The Israeli and Palestinian delegations will negotiate an agreement on the interim period (the 'Interim Agreement').
    2. The Interim Agreement shall specify, among other things, the structure of the Council, the number of its members, and the transfer of powers and responsibilities from the Israeli military government and its civil administration to the Council. The Interim Agreement shall also specify the Council's executive

authority, legislative authority in accordance with Article IX below, and the independent Palestinian judicial organs.

3. The Interim Agreement shall include arrangements, to be implemented upon the inauguration of the Council, for the assumption by the Council of all of the powers and responsibilities transferred previously in accordance with Article IV above.

4. In order to enable the Council to promote economic growth, upon its inauguration, the Council will establish, among other things, a Palestinian Electricity Authority, a Gaza Sea Port Authority, a Palestinian Development Bank, a Palestinian Export Promotion Board, a Palestinian Environmental Authority, a Palestinian Land Authority and a Palestinian Water Administration Authority, and any other authorities agreed upon, in accordance with the Interim Agreement that will specify their powers and responsibilities.

5. After the inauguration of the Council, the Civil Administration will be dissolved, and the Israeli Military Government will be withdrawn.

Article VIII: Public Order and Security
In order to guarantee public order and internal security for the Palestinians of the West Bank and the Gaza Strip, the Council will establish a strong police force, while Israel will continue to carry the responsibility for defending against external threats, as well as the responsibility for overall security of Israelis for the purpose of safeguarding their internal security and public order.

Article IX: Laws and Military Orders
1. The Council will be empowered to legislate, in accordance with the Interim Agreement, within all authorities transferred to it.

2. Both parties will review jointly laws and military orders presently in force in remaining spheres.

Article X: Joint Israeli-Palestinian Liaison Committee
In order to provide for a smooth implementation of this Declaration of Principles and any subsequent agreements pertaining to the interim period, upon the entry into force of this Declaration of Principles, a Joint Israeli-Palestinian Liaison Committee will be established in order to deal with issues requiring co-ordination, other issues of common interest, and disputes.

Article XI: Israeli-Palestinian Co-operation in Economic Fields
Recognizing the mutual benefit of co-operation in promoting the development of the West Bank, the Gaza Strip and Israel, upon the entry into force of this Declaration of Principles, an Israeli-Palestinian Economic Co-operation Committee will be established in order to develop and implement in a cooperative manner the programmes identified in the protocols attached as Annex III and Annex IV.

Article XII: Liaison and Co-operation with Jordan and Egypt
The two parties will invite the governments of Jordan and Egypt to participate in establishing further liaison and co-operation agreements between the government of Israel and the Palestinian representatives, on one hand, and the governments of Jordan and Egypt, on the other hand, to promote co-operation between them. These arrangements will include the constitution of a continuing committee that will decide by agreement on the modalities of admission of persons displaced from the West Bank and Gaza Strip in 1967, together with necessary measures to prevent disruption and disorder. Other matters of common concern will be dealt with by this committee.

Article XIII: Redeployment of Israeli Forces
1. After the entry into force of this Declaration of Principles, and not later than the eve of elections for the Council, a redeployment of Israeli military forces in the West Bank and the Gaza Strip will take place, in addition to withdrawal of Israeli forces carried out in accordance with Article XIV.
2. In redeploying its military forces, Israel will be guided by the principle that its military forces should be redeployed outside populated areas.
3. Further redeployments to specified locations will be gradually implemented commensurate with the assumption of responsibility for public order and internal security by the Palestinian police force pursuant to Article VIII above.

Article XIV: Israeli Withdrawal from the Gaza Strip and Jericho Area
Israel will withdraw from the Gaza Strip and Jericho area, as detailed in the protocol attached as Annex II.

Article XV: Resolution of Disputes
1. Disputes arising from the application or interpretation of this Declaration of Principles, or any subsequent agreements pertaining to the Interim Period, shall be resolved by negotiations through the Joint Liaison Committee to be established pursuant to Article X above.
2. Disputes which cannot be settled by negotiations may be resolved by a mechanism of conciliation to be agreed upon by the parties.
3. The parties may agree to submit to arbitration disputes relating to the Interim Period, which cannot be settled through conciliation. To this end, upon the agreement of both parties, the parties will establish an arbitration committee.

Article XVI: Israeli-Palestinian Co-operation Concerning Regional Programmes
Both parties view the multilateral working groups as an appropriate instrument for promoting a 'Marshall Plan', the regional programmes and other programmes, including special programmes for the West Bank and Gaza Strip, as indicated in the protocol attached as Annex IV.

Article XVII: Miscellaneous Provisions

1. This Declaration of Principles will enter into force one month after its signing.

2. All protocols annexed to this Declaration of Principles and agreed minutes pertaining thereto shall be regarded as an integral part hereof.

Done at Washington DC, this 13th day of September 1993.

For the Government of Israel   For the PLO

Witnessed by:
The United States of America   The Russian Federation

Annex I: Protocol on the Mode and Conditions of Elections

1. Palestinians of Jerusalem who live there will have the right to participate in the election process, according to an agreement between the two sides.

2. In addition, the election agreement should cover, among other things, the following issues:

   a. The system of elections.

   b. The mode of the agreed supervision and international observation and their personal composition; and

   c. Rules and regulations regarding the election campaign, including agreed arrangements for the organizing of mass media, and the possibility of licensing a broadcasting and TV station.

3. The future status of displaced Palestinians who were registered on 4 June 1967 will not be prejudiced because they are unable to participate in the election process due to practical reasons.

Annex II: Protocol on Withdrawal of Israeli Forces from the Gaza Strip and Jericho Area

1. The two sides will conclude and sign within two months from the date of entry into force of this Declaration of Principles, an agreement on the withdrawal of Israeli military forces from the Gaza Strip and Jericho area. This agreement will include comprehensive arrangements to apply in the Gaza Strip and the Jericho area subsequent to the Israeli withdrawal.

2. Israel will implement an accelerated and scheduled withdrawal of Israeli military forces from the Gaza Strip and Jericho area, beginning immediately with the signing of the agreement on the Gaza Strip and Jericho area and to be completed within a period not exceeding four months after the signing of this agreement.

3. The above agreement will include, among other things:

a. Arrangements for a smooth and peaceful transfer of authority from the Israeli military government and its civil administration to the Palestinian representatives.

b. Structure, powers and responsibilities of the Palestinian authority in these areas, except: external security, settlements, foreign relations, and other mutually agreed matters.

c. Arrangements for the assumption of internal security and public order by the Palestinian police force (consisting of police officers recruited locally and from abroad holding Jordanian passports and Palestinian documents issued by Egypt). Those who will participate in the Palestinian police force coming from abroad should be trained as police and police officers.

d. A temporary international or foreign presence, as agreed upon.

e. Establishment of a joint Palestinian-Israeli Co-ordination and Co-operation Committee for mutual security purposes.

f. An economic development and stabilization programme, including the establishment of an emergency fund, to encourage foreign investment, and financial and economic support. Both sides will co-ordinate and cooperate jointly and unilaterally with regional and international parties to support these aims.

g. Arrangements for a safe passage for persons and transportation between the Gaza Strip and Jericho area.

4. The above agreement will include arrangements for co-ordination between both parties regarding passages:

a. Gaza–Egypt; and

b. Jericho–Jordan

5. The offices responsible for carrying out the powers and responsibilities of the Palestinian authority under this Annex II and Article IV of the Declaration of Principles will be located in the Gaza Strip and in the Jericho area pending the inauguration of the Council.

6. Other than these agreed arrangements, the status of the Gaza Strip and Jericho area will continue to be an integral part of the West Bank and Gaza Strip, and will not be changed in the Interim Period.

Annex III: Protocol on Israeli-Palestinian Co-operation in Economic and Development Programmes

The two sides agree to establish an Israeli-Palestinian Continuing Committee for Economic Co-operation, focusing, among other things, on the following:

1. Co-operation in the field of water, including a water development programme prepared by experts from both sides, which will also specify the mode of co-operation in the management of water resources in the West Bank and Gaza Strip, and will include proposals for studies and plans on water rights of each party, as well as on the equitable utilization of joint water resources for

implementation in and beyond the Interim Period.

2.   Co-operation in the field of electricity, including an electricity development programme, which will also specify the mode of co-operation for the production, maintenance, purchase and sale of electricity resources.

3.   Co-operation in the field of energy, including an energy development programme, which will provide for the exploitation of oil and gas for industrial purposes, particularly in the Gaza Strip and in the Negev, and will encourage further joint exploitation of other energy resources. This programme may also provide for the construction of a petrochemical industrial complex in the Gaza Strip and the construction of oil and gas pipelines.

4.   Co-operation in the field of finance, including a financial development and action programme for the encouragement of international investment in the West Bank and the Gaza Strip, and in Israel, as well as the establishment of a Palestinian Development Bank.

5.   Co-operation in the field of transport and communications, including a programme which will define guidelines for the establishment of a Gaza Sea Port area, and will provide for the establishing of transport and communications lines to and from the West Bank and the Gaza Strip to Israel and to other countries. In addition, this programme will provide for carrying out the necessary construction of roads, railways, communications lines, etc.

6.   Co-operation in the field of trade, including studies, and trade promotion programmes, which will encourage local, regional and inter-regional trade, as well as a feasibility study of creating free trade zones in the Gaza Strip and in Israel, mutual access to these zones, and co-operation in other areas related to trade and commerce.

7.   Co-operation in the field of industry, including industrial development programmes, which will provide for the establishment of joint Israeli-Palestinian industrial research and development centres, will promote Palestinian-Israeli joint ventures, and provide guidelines for co-operation in the textile, food, pharmaceutical, electronics, diamonds, computer and science-based industries.

8.   A programme for co-operation in, and regulation of, labour relations and co-operation in social welfare issues.

9.   A human resources development and co-operation plan, providing for joint Israeli-Palestinian workshops and seminars, and for the establishment of joint vocational training centres, research institutes and data banks.

10.   An environmental protection plan, providing for joint and/or co-ordinated measures in this sphere.

11.   A programme for developing co-ordination and co-operation in the field of communications and media.

12.   Any other programmes of mutual interest.

Annex IV: Protocol on Israeli-Palestinian Co-operation Concerning Regional Development Programmes

1. The two sides will cooperate in the context of the multilateral peace efforts in promoting a development programme for the region, including the West Bank and the Gaza Strip, to be initiated by the G-7. The parties will request the G-7 to seek the participation in this programme of other interested states, such as members of the Organization for Economic Co-operation and Development, regional Arab states and institutions, as well as members of the private sector.

2. The development programme will consist of two elements:

a. An economic development programme for the West Bank and the Gaza Strip.

b. A regional economic development programme.

a. The economic development programme for the West Bank and the Gaza Strip will consist of the following elements:

(1) A social rehabilitation programme, including a housing and construction programme.

(2) A small and medium business development plan.

(3) An infrastructure development programme (water, electricity, transportation and communications, etc).

(4) A human resources plan.

(5) Other programmes.

b. The regional economic development programme may consist of the following elements:

(1) The establishment of a Middle East development fund, as a first step, and a Middle East Development Bank, as a second step.

(2) The development of a joint Israeli-Palestinian-Jordanian plan for co-ordinated exploitation of the Dead Sea area.

(3) The Mediterranean Sea (Gaza) – the Dead Sea Canal.

(4) Regional desalinization and other water development projects.

(5) A regional plan for agricultural development, including a co-ordinated regional effort for the prevention of desertification.

(6) Interconnection of electricity grids.

(7) Regional co-operation for the transfer, distribution and industrial exploitation of gas, oil and other energy resources.

(8) A regional tourism, transportation and telecommunications development plan.

(9) Regional co-operation in other spheres.

3. The two sides will encourage the multilateral working groups, and will co-ordinate towards its success. The two parties will encourage intersessional activities, as well as pre-feasibility and feasibility studies, within the various multilateral working groups.

Appendices

AGREED MINUTES TO THE DECLARATION OF PRINCIPLES ON INTERIM SELF-GOVERNMENT ARRANGEMENTS

A. General Understandings and Agreements

Any powers and responsibilities transferred to the Palestinians pursuant to the Declaration of Principles prior to the inauguration of the Council will be subject to the same principles pertaining to Article IV, as set out in these agreed minutes below.

B. Specific Understandings and Agreements

Article IV. It is understood that:

1. Jurisdiction of the Council will cover West Bank and Gaza Strip territory, except for issues that will be negotiated in the permanent status negotiations: Jerusalem, settlements, military locations, and Israelis.

2. The Council's jurisdiction will apply with regard to the agreed powers, responsibilities, spheres and authorities transferred to it.

Article VI (2). It is agreed that the transfer of authority will be as follows:

1. The Palestinian side will inform the Israeli side of the names of the authorized Palestinians who will assume the powers, authorities and responsibilities that will be transferred to the Palestinians according to the Declaration of Principles in the following fields: education and culture, health, social welfare, direct taxation, tourism, and any other authorities agreed upon.

2. It is understood that the rights and obligations of these offices will not be affected.

3. Each of the spheres described above will continue to enjoy existing budgetary allocations in accordance with arrangements to be mutually agreed upon. These arrangements will also provide for the necessary adjustments required in order to take into account the taxes collected by the direct taxation office.

4. Upon the execution of the Declaration of Principles, the Israeli and Palestinian delegations will immediately commence negotiations on a detailed plan for the transfer of authority on the above offices in accordance with the above understandings.

Article VII (2). The Interim Agreement will also include arrangements for co-ordination and co-operation.

Article VII (5). The withdrawal of the military government will not prevent Israel from exercising the powers and responsibilities not transferred to the Council.

Article VIII. It is understood that the Interim Agreement will include arrangements for co-operation and co-ordination between the two parties in this regard. It is also agreed that the transfer of powers and responsibilities to the Palestinian police will be accomplished in a phased manner, as agreed in the Interim Agreement.

Article X. It is agreed that, upon the entry into force of the Declaration of Principles, the Israeli and Palestinian delegations will exchange the names of the individuals designated by them as members of the Joint Israeli-Palestinian Liaison Committee.

It is further agreed that each side will have an equal number of members in the Joint Committee. The Joint Committee will reach decisions by agreement. The Joint Committee may add other technicians and experts, as necessary. The Joint Committee will decide on the frequency and place or places of its meetings.

Annex II. It is understood that, subsequent to the Israeli withdrawal, Israel will continue to be responsible for external security, and for internal security and public order of settlements and Israelis. Israeli military forces and civilians may continue to use roads freely within the Gaza Strip and the Jericho area.

Notes

Doing the Unthinkable

(1) The bulk of this book was written before the historic Washington agreement of September 1993. The present chapter was added specially to take account of this startling new departure in the Middle East peace process.

(2) Ninth session: 27 April–13 May 1993. Tenth session: 15 June–1 July. Eleventh session: 31 August–9 September.

(3) A regional economic organization comprising Turkey, Iran, Pakistan, Afghanistan and the Asian states of the former Soviet Union.

PART I. THE MIDDLE EAST PEACE CONFERENCE

1. Madrid: The Launch of the Peace Process

(1) Michel Jobert, *Gulf Diary (August 1990–August 1991)*, Paris, Albin Michel, 1991, p. 331.

(2) *Ramses 92: Le Monde et son Evolution*, Paris, IFRI-Dunod, 1991, p. 131.

(3) See James G. McDonald, *My Mission to Israel*, New York, Simon and Schuster, 1951, pp. 181-182.

(4) *The Arab-Israeli Conflict*, Princeton, New Jersey, Princeton University Press, 1974, vol. III, pp. 64-68.

(5) See George W. Ball, *Error and Betrayal in Lebanon*, Washington, DC, Foundation for Middle East Peace, 1984.

(6) *The Times*, 25 June 1969.

(7) Reproduced in the magazine *Eurabia, France-Pays Arabes*, Paris, no. 178, December 1991, p. 16.

(8) See M.K. Shahib, *The United States and the Palestinians*, London, Croom Helm, 1981, p. 252.

(9) W.B. Quandt, *Decade of Decisions: American Policy towards the Arab-Israeli Conflict 1967–1976*, Berkeley, University of California Press, 1977, p. 313.

(10) Henry Laurens, *Le Grand Jeu. Orient Arabe et Rivalité Internationale*, Paris, Armand Colin, 1991, p. 299.

(11) Xavier Baron, *Les Palestiniens, un Peuple*, Paris, Le Sycomore, 1984, p. 411.

(12) George Corm, *Le Proche-Orient Eclaté, 1956–1991*, Paris, Gallimard, Coll. 'Folio-Histoire', 1991, pp. 256-257.

(13) Alain Gresh, *The PLO, The Struggle Within*, London, Zed Books, 1988,

p. 29.

(14) See Omar Massalha, 'Pour en Finir avec les Ambiguités', *L'Humanité*, 26 March 1991, p. 15.

(15) See Basma Kodmani-Darwich and Mary Chartouni-Dubarry, *Golfe et Moyen-Orient, les Conflits,* Paris, IFRI-Dunod, 1991, pp. 81-86.

(16) *Rapport Annuel Mondial sur le Système Economique et les Stratégies.*

(17) *Ramses 92: Le Monde et son Evolution*, p. 127.

2. The US Initiative

(1) See *Washington Post*, 7 March 1991.

(2) *Le Monde*, 13 April 1991, p. 3.

(3) 'Proche-Orient: De la Guerre à la Paix?', *Le Monde*, special issue, November 1991, p. 108.

(4) Israel refers to the English version (withdrawal 'from territories' and not 'from the territories'). It claims to have implemented Resolution 242 by withdrawing from '90 per cent of occupied territories'. By means of this cynical attitude, Israel seeks to dupe public opinion since, on the one hand, Resolution 242 deals with different territories belonging to three countries (Palestine, Egypt and Syria) and, on the other, 90 per cent of liberated territory is Egyptian desert. The West Bank, Gaza and the Golan, according to Israel, are 'disputed' and not 'occupied' territories. They are thus to be negotiated upon the basis of this tendentious interpretation. In the opinion of the Arab countries, the actual text of Resolution 242 makes a non-negotiable demand for withdrawal from all the occupied territories. Resolution 338, however, mentions the word 'negotiations'.

(5) See report of the Jafee Center for Strategic Studies, Tel Aviv University, Israel, 14 April 1991.

(6) *Le Monde*, 24 May 1991, p. 4.

(7) *Eurabia, France-Pays Arabes*, Paris, no. 177, November 1991, p. 7.

(8) *Le Monde*, 1 November 1991, p. 4.

(9) Ibid., 2 November 1991, p. 4.

(10) Ibid.

(11) Ibid., 3-4 November 1991, p. 3.

(12) Ibid., 28 November 1991, p. 6.

3. The Process Itself Becomes the Main Issue

(1) 1st session: 3–4 November 1991; 2nd session: 10–18 December 1991; 3rd session: 13–16 January 1992; 4th session: 24 February–4 March 1992; 5th session: 27–30 April 1992; 6th session: 24 August–24 September 1992; 7th session: 21 October–19 November 1992; 8th session: 7–17 December 1992.

(2) *Revue d'Etudes Palestiniennes*, Paris, no. 46, 1992, p. 164.

(3) See *Eurabia, France-Pays Arabes*, Paris, no. 188, December 1992–January 1993, pp. 14-15, from *Haaretz*, 17 July 1992.

(4) *Le Monde*, 28 January 1993, p. 26.

(5) Ibid., 29 January 1993, p. 5.

(6) See WARBURTON, CEE report, Brussels, February 1993.

(7) *Le Monde*, 14-15 March 1993, p. 5.

(8) On 18 April the Arab League Foreign Ministers met in the Egyptian capital for the League's 99th session.

PART II. HISTORICAL OVERVIEW

4. *Palestine from its Origins to the Nineteenth Century*

(1) Paul Valéry, *Regard sur le Monde Actuel*, Paris, La Pléiade, Gallimard, vol. 2, p. 935. (Quoted by Roger Garaudy, *Palestine, Terre des Messages Divins*, Paris, Albatros, 1986, p. 345.)

(2) Qafzeh is the name of the mountain of Nazareth.

(3) Francis Hours, 'Le Proche-Orient Préhistorique: l'Occupation du Proche-Orient au Paléolithique', *Le Grand Atlas Universalis de l'Archéologie, Encyclopaedia Universalis*, France, 1985, p. 164.

(4) Jacques Cauvin, 'La Naissance de l'Agriculture', *Encyclopaedia Universalis,* p. 166.

(5) Martin Noth, *History of Israel: Biblical History*, 2nd edn, New York, Harper and Row, 1960.

(6) E.M. Laperrousaz, 'Palestine', *Encyclopaedia Universalis*, 1980, vol. 12, p. 429.

(7) Ibid.

(8) H.E. Del Medico, *La Bible Cananéenne Découverte dans les Textes de Ras Shamra*, Paris, Payot, 1950, p. 15.

(9) A.H. Gardiner, *Notes on the Story of Sinuhé*, 1916. (Quoted by Garaudy, *Palestine . . . ,* p. 30.)

(10) Hadad, god of storms; El, the solitary god; Ba'al, son of El who came back to life and multiplied; Anath, goddess of fertility, ever-virgin sister of Ba'al; Salem, god of prosperity and peace; Saher, the moon god; Aliyan, god of springs; Dagon, the corn god; Yamm, the sea god; Mot, the god of drought.

(11) Garaudy, *Palestine . . . ,* p. 33.

(12) Fr. Decret, *Cartage ou l'Empire de la Mer?*, Paris, Seuil, 1977, p. 11.

(13) See Garaudy, *Palestine . . . ,* p. 40.

(14) *Les Religions du Proche-Orient, Textes Sacrés Babyloniens, Ougaritiques, Hittites* (introduced by Labat, Caquot, Sznycer, Vieyra), Paris, Fayard, Denoël (Collection: 'Le Trésor Spirituel de l'Humanité'), 1970, p. 375. (Quoted by Garaudy, *Palestine . . . ,* p. 40.)

(15) For further details, see e.g., R. Dussaud, *Les Origines Cananéennes du Sacrifice Israélite*, Paris, Leroux, 1921. (Quoted by Garaudy, *Palestine . . . ,* p. 38.)

(16) See Henry Laurens, *Le Grand Jeu. Orient Arabe et Rivalité Internationale*, Paris, Armand Colin, 1991.

(17) Laperrousaz, 'Palestine', p. 429.

(18) R. de Vaux (O.P.), *The Early History of Israel*, London, John Knox, 1978.

(19) Kathleen Kenyon, *Amorites and Canaanites. The Sweich Lectures of the British Academy (1963)*, Oxford, Oxford University Press, 1966, p. 5.

(20) W.F. Albright, *From the Stone Age to Christianity—Monotheism and the Historical Process*, Baltimore, Johns Hopkins Press, 1946.

(21) Garaudy, *Palestine . . . ,* p. 41.

(22) Ibid., p. 69.

(23) André Neher, *L'Essence du Prophétisme,* Paris, Calmann-Lévy, p. 177. (Quoted by Garaudy, *Palestine . . . ,* p. 69.)

(24) Quoted by Garaudy, *Palestine . . . ,* p. 73.

(25) We base our summary of this historical period mainly on two major works which have dealt scientifically and objectively with many aspects of this problem with respect to both ancient and modern history: Roger Garaudy, *Palestine, Terre des Messages Divins* and Henry Laurens, *Le Grand Jeu. Orient Arabe et Rivalité Internationale.*

(26) Angelo S. Rappoport, *Histoire de la Palestine*, Paris, Payot, 1932, p. 160. (Quoted by Garaudy, *Palestine . . . ,* p. 93.)

(27) See *L'Encyclopaedia Palestina*, Beirut, 1990, vol. 2.

(28) See Amin Maalouf, *The Crusades through Arab Eyes*, London, Al Saqi Books, 1984.

(29) Al-Hanbali, *Uns al-Jalil biTarikh al-Qudsi wal Khalil.*

(30) Agreement signed by Britain, Austria, Prussia and Russia, in London on 15 July 1840. Source: Adel Ismaïl, *Documents Diplomatiques et Consulaires*, Beirut, Edition des Oeuvres Politiques et Historiques, 1980, vol. 24, pp. 313-321.

(31) Robert Mantran, 'Palestine (la Palestine Ottomane)', *Encyclopaedia Universalis,* vol. 12, p. 439.

(32) Burhan Ghalioun, *Le Malaise Arabe, l'Etat contre la Nation*, Paris, La Découverte, 1991, p. 27.

(33) See Henry Cattan, *The Palestine Question*, London, Croom Helm, 1988, pp. 3-9.

(34) Michel Mourre, *Dictionnaire Encyclopédique d'Histoire*, Paris, Bordas, 1986, vol. 6, p. 3,482.

(35) Laurens, *Le Grand Jeu . . . ,* p. 55.

(36) Nadia Benjelloun-Ollivier, *Yasser Arafat: La Question Palestinienne*, Paris, Fayard, 1991, p. 156.

(37) Theodor Herzl, *The Jewish State*, 1896.

(38) Laurens, *Le Grand Jeu . . . ,* p. 56.

(39) Walter Laqueur, 'Zionism and its Liberal Critics, 1896–1948', *Journal of Contemporary History*, 6/4, 1971, p. 180. (Quoted by G.E. Irani, *The Papacy and the Middle East: The Role of the Holy See in the Arab-Israeli Conflict—1962–1984*, Princeton, University of Notre Dame Press, 1986, p. 20.)

(40) Ralph Schoenmann, *The Hidden History of Zionism*, Santa Barbara, Calif., Veritas Press, 1988, p. 47.

(41) Ibid., p. 71.

(42) For details, see: Garaudy, *Palestine* . . ., p. 236; David Yisraeli, *The Palestine Question in German Policy from 1889 to 1945*, Ramat-Gan, Israel, Bar-Ilan University, 1974.

5. Zionism in Action and the Palestinian Reaction

(1) 'Israel, Les Arabes', *Les Dossiers de l'Histoire*, Aubervilliers, France, no. 75, April 1991, p. 22.

(2) Ibid., p. 24.

(3) Quoted from Henry Cattan, *The Palestine Question*, London, Croom Helm, 1988, p. 10.

(4) George Corm, *Fragmentation of the Middle East: From Suez to the Invasion of Lebanon*, Hutchinson, London, 1988.

(5) Ibid.

(6) Ralph Schoenmann, *The Hidden History of Zionism,* Santa Barbara, Calif., Veritas Press, 1988, p. 29.

(7) Neville Mandel, 'Turks, Arabs and the Jewish Immigration into Palestine, 1882–1914', unpublished doctoral thesis, Saint Antony's College, Oxford, 1965, p. 32. (Quoted by A.W. Kayyali, *Palestine: A Modern History*, London, Croom Helm, 1978, p. 16.)

(8) Clayton to Sykes, 15 December 1917, Clayton Papers, Durham University, 141/I.

(9) Ormsby-Gore to Balfour, 19 April 1918, Foreign Office [henceforth FO] 371/3395, London.

(10) See FO 371/3398, 22 April 1918, London.

(11) 'Future of Palestine', FO 371/3383, May 1918, London.

(12) Weizmann to Balfour, FO 371/3395, 30 May 1918, London.

(13) FO 371/3386, 16 November 1918, London.

(14) FO 371/4153, 19 February 1919, London.

(15) On this period of Palestinian history see Ibrahim Abu-Lughod (ed.), *The Transformation of Palestine*, Illinois, 1971.

(16) Ghazi Mabrouk, *La Palestine Assassinée*, Tunis, Distribution: Demeter, pp. 68-69.

(17) Quoted by G.E. Irani, *The Papacy and the Middle East: The Role of the Holy See in the Arab-Israeli Conflict—1962–1984,* Princeton, University of Notre Dame Press, 1986, p. 36.

(18) Jean-Pierre Migeon and Jean Jolly, *A Qui la Palestine?*, Paris, Publications Premières, 1970, p. 59.

(19) For details see Elias Sanbar, 'Palestine 1948, the Expulsion', *Revue d'Etudes Palestiniennes*, Paris, 1984, pp. 115-122.

(20) 'The Strategic Importance of Syria to the British Empire, General Staff, War Office', FO 371/4178, 9 December 1918. (Quoted by Kayyali, *Palestine . . .* , p. 61.)

(21) Henry Laurens, *Le Grand Jeu. Orient Arabe et Rivalité Internationale*, Paris, Armand Colin, 1991, p. 70.

(22) League of Arab States, archives. Decisions concerning Palestine in the Annex to the Alexandria Protocol, 1944, Cairo, Egypt.

(23) Walid Khalidi, 'La Question Palestinienne après la Guerre du Golfe', *Revue d'Etudes Palestiniennes*, Paris, no. 40 (summer 1991), pp. 32-33.

(24) Sanbar, 'Palestine 1948 . . . ', p. 164.

(25) On political structures in Palestine see Bayane al-Hout, *The Leaders and the Palestinian Institutions 1917–1948*, Beirut, 1981 (in Arabic).

(26) See the accounts published in the Israeli daily *Yediot Aharonot* of 4 and 29 April 1972. See also Jacques de Reynier, *A Jérusalem un Drapeau Flottait sur la Ligne de Feu*, Neuchâtel, 1950, pp. 69-79. The two accounts are summarized and commented on by Sanbar, 'Palestine 1948 . . . ', pp. 167-176.

(27) See Erskine Childers, 'The Other Exodus', *Spectator*, London, 12 May 1961.

(28) See Abu-Lughod (ed.), *Transformation of Palestine . . .* , pp. 165-201.

(29) Nathan Ghofsky, in *Jewish News Letter,* 9 February 1959. (Quoted by Mabrouk, *Palestine Assassinée . . .* , p. 80.)

(30) Sanbar, 'Palestine 1948 . . . ', p. 186.

(31) Marcel Colombe, 'Le Problème de l'"Entité Palestinienne" dans les Relations Inter-Arabes', *Orient*, no. 29, 1964, p. 58. (Quoted by Laurens, *Le Grand Jeu . . . ,* p. 194.)

(32) Laurens, *Le Grand Jeu . . . ,* p. 74.

(33) Hassan bin Talal, Crown Prince of Jordan, *Palestinian Self-Determination. A Study of the West Bank and Gaza Strip*, London, Quartet, 1981, pp. 35-36.

(34) Ibid., pp. 36-37.

(35) Laurens, *Le Grand Jeu . . . ,* p. 85.

(36) On the assassination of Bernadotte and Sérot, see Simon Jargy, *Guerre et Paix en Palestine*, Neuchâtel, Switzerland, Editions de la Baconnière, 1968.

(37) Rony Gabbay, *A Political Study of the Arab-Jewish Conflict, the Arab Refugee Problem (A Case Study)*, Geneva, 1959, pp. 165-183. (Quoted by Sanbar, 'Palestine 1948 . . . ', p. 202.)

(38) Laurens, *Le Grand Jeu . . . ,* p. 87.

(39) Migeon and Jolly, *A Qui la Palestine?,* p. 87.

6. From the 'Right of Return' to the 'Bridge of Return'

(1) See Sami Hadawi, *Palestinian Rights and Losses in 1948*, London, Saqi Books, 1988, p. 121.

(2) Abdallah Frangi, *The PLO and Palestine*, London, Zed Books, 1983, p. 91.

(3) On the situation of the Palestinian refugees in the Arab countries see Channing Richardson, *The Palestinian Arab Refugee*, London, Ithaca, Cornell University Press, 1955.

(4) Decision of the Council of the League of Arab States on the Palestinian Question (1st–50th session, League of Arab States, Cairo, p. 21).

(5) George Tomeh, 'Why the UN Dropped the Palestinian Question', *Journal of Palestine Studies*, vol. IV, no. 1, 1974, p. 19.

(6) See Edward W. Said, *The Question of Palestine*, New York, Times Books, 1979; and Xavier Baron, *Les Palestiniens, un Peuple*, Paris, Le Sycomore, 1984.

7. The Palestine Liberation Organization

(1) Rémi Favret, *Arafat, un Destin pour la Palestine*, Renaudot et Cie, 1990, p. 52.

(2) Charles Saint-Prost, *Yasser Arafat, Biographie et Entretiens*, Paris, Jean Picollec, 1990, p. 91.

8. Some Key Events

(1) For full details of the discriminatory nature of these measures in the socio-economic, cultural, educational fields, etc. in Israel, see Sabri Jiryis, *The Arabs in Israel*, Beirut, Palestine Research Centre, 1968.

(2) Arafat was speaking in English at a press conference and used this French word meaning 'null and void' to indicate that the charter had been overtaken by events.

9. The Occupied West Bank and Gaza

(1) See *Le Monde*, 10-11 November 1991.

(2) See T.L. Thompson, F.J. Gonçalves and J.M. Van Cangh, *Toponymie Palestinienne*, Louvain-la-Neuve, Institut Orientaliste de l'Université Catholique de Louvain, Ed. Peters, 1988.

(3) Kamal Salibi, *The Bible Came from Arabia,* London, Jonathan Cape, 1985.

(4) See Y. Aharoni and M. Avi-Yonah, *La Bible par les Cartes*, Paris, Brepols, 1991.

(5) In 1967 the value added of the industrial sector of the East Bank was treble that of the West Bank: the reverse of the situation in 1948. In 1967 per capita GNP was 50 per cent higher in the East; the reverse was true in 1950.

Source: Meron Benvenisti, *The West Bank Data Project, A Survey of Israeli Policy*, Washington DC, 1984.

(6) Michel Foucher, *Fronts et Frontières, un Tour du Monde Géopolitique*, Paris, Fayard, 1988, p. 337.

(7) Ibid., p. 339.

(8) If the Palestinians were to recover the water resources that Israel has confiscated from them, Israel would be compelled to scale down its agricultural production and later to depend on agricultural imports.

10. The Settlements

(1) Begin died in Tel Aviv from a heart attack on 9 March 1992.

(2) Henry Laurens, *Le Grand Jeu. Orient Arabe et Rivalité Internationale*, Paris, Armand Colin, 1991, pp. 376-377.

(3) Ibid., p. 377.

(4) See Michel Foucher, *Fronts et Frontières, un Tour du Monde Geopolitique,* Paris, Fayard, 1988, pp. 342-344; and 'Proche-Orient: De la Guerre à la Paix?', *Le Monde,* special issue, November 1991, pp. 126-128.

(5) *Majallat al-Dirasat al-Filastiniyah/Revue d'Etudes Palestiniennes*, Beirut, no. 7, summer 1991, pp. 68-74.

(6) The Israelis call this demarcation line 'the Green Line', which means, according to their propaganda, that everything to the west of this line is green since it is Israeli, and everything beyond the line is desert since it is Arab!

(7) Of the Palestinians, 26.8 per cent live in Jordan (1,458,400); 5.1 per cent in Syria (276,800); 7.9 per cent in Lebanon (427,500); and 9 per cent in the Gulf states (before the Gulf War, the percentage was 14.2 per cent). There are a further 64,200 in Egypt; 27,000 in Iraq; 32,100 in Libya; 59,000 in the other Arab states; 120,000 in the US, and the remaining 10.4 per cent live elsewhere in the world. Source: UNESCO, *Studies on the Educational and Training Needs of the Palestinian People*, Paris, March 1990.

(8) *Le Monde*, 15 October 1991, p. 5.

(9) Ibid., 10 December 1991.

(10) Rémi Favret, *Arafat, un Destin pour la Palestine,* Renaudot et Cie, 1990, p. 283.

(11) Camille Aboussouan, *Les Lourds Devoirs de la Liberté, De Gaulle en son Siècle*, Paris, Institut Charles de Gaulle, F. 297, p. 9.

(12) Ibid., p. 9; see also *Mémoires d'Espoir*, Paris, Plon, 1970, vol. I, pp. 278-279.

(13) For more details, see Joost R. Hiltermann, 'L'Immigration Soviétique et la Mainmise sur Jérusalem', *Revue d'Etudes Palestiniennes*, no. 40, summer 1991, pp. 61-76.

(14) *Haaretz*, 2 July 1992.

(15) Louis-Jean Duclos, 'Peace Put to the Test at the Polls', *Les Cahiers de*

l'Orient, Paris, no. 28, 4th quarter, 1992, p. 22.
  (16) Ibid., p. 30.
  (17) Ibid., p. 33.
  (18) *Le Figaro*, 21 January 1993, p. 24.

11. The Intifada *and its Consequences*
  (1) On 6 March 1992 the Israeli lorry-driver was cleared of manslaughter charges.
  (2) *Le Monde*, 10 December 1991, p. 7.
  (3) *Universalia*, 1989, *Encyclopaedia Universalis*, p. 288.
  (4) Ibid., pp. 288-291.
  (5) Ibrahim Souss, *De la Paix en Général et des Palestiniens en Particulier*, Paris, Belfond-Le Pré aux Clercs, 1991, pp. 98-137.
  (6) *Universalia*, 1989, *Encyclopaedia Universalis,* p. 288.
  (7) Henry Laurens, *Le Grand Jeu. Orient Arabe et Rivalité Internationale,* Paris, Armand Colin, 1991, p. 382.
  (8) Gad Becker, in *Yediot Aharonot*, 13 April 1983.
  (9) Pierre Hunt, 'Israèl en Défi de Paix', *Le Monde*, 1 November 1991, p. 2.
  (10) *Revue d'Etudes Palestiniennes*, no. 45, 1992, p. 164.
  (11) *Libération*, 8 February 1993, p. 19.
  (12) *Le Monde*, 10 October 1992, p. 6.
  (13) Ibid., 12 February 1993, p. 5.

PART III. JERUSALEM

12. Uru-Salem/Yerushalayim/Jerusalem/al-Quds
  (1) Flavius Josephus, *The Jewish War*. (Quoted by Amos Elon, *Jerusalem, City of Mirrors*, Boston, Mass., Little, Brown and Co., 1989, p. 15.)
  (2) Elon, *Jerusalem, City of Mirrors*, p. 15.
  (3) Asher S. Kaufman, 'Dans l'Ombre du Temple', *Autrement*, Paris, no. 4, October 1983, p. 27.
  (4) Genesis XIV, 19.
  (5) Elon, *Jerusalem, City of Mirrors,* p. 23.
  (6) Ahmad S. Dajani, 'Le Peuple de Palestine et Jérusalem, Histoire et Futur', study submitted to the international seminar on Jerusalem, organized by the Organization of the Islamic Conference, Paris, 1-2 December 1980, pp. 16-17.
  (7) Ezekiel XVI, 3.
  (8) Lamentations I, 1.
  (9) Ezekiel XVI, 35.
  (10) Elon, *Jerusalem, City of Mirrors*, p. 31.
  (11) Psalm 137, verse 5.

(12) Psalm 46, verse 5.

(13) See 'Jérusalem', *Autrement*, special issue, no. 4, October 1983.

(14) Tovia Preschel, 'Jerusalem', in *Encyclopaedia of Zionism and Israel*, New York, Herzl Press, McGraw Hill, 1971, vol. I, pp. 604-606.

(15) Elon, *Jerusalem, City of Mirrors*, p. 51.

(16) Ibid., p. 41.

(17) Ibid., pp. 43-44.

(18) *L'Osservatore Romano*, 22-23 March 1971. (Quoted by G.E. Irani, *The Papacy and the Middle East: The Role of the Holy See in the Arab-Israeli Conflict—1962-1984*, Indiana, University of Notre Dame Press, 1986, pp. 81-82.

(19) Further detailed information can be found in the report entitled, 'Synoptic Report on Developments in the Safeguarding of the Monumental Heritage of Jerusalem from 1971 to 1987' (24 C/15, Annex V), and the report dated 20 August 1991 entitled, 'Report on the State of the Cultural and Religious Heritage of Jerusalem and on the Needs to be Met to Ensure its Preservation and Restoration' (26 C/14).

(20) Elon, *Jerusalem, City of Mirrors*, p. 39.

(21) See in this connection the compilation of resolutions and decisions adopted by the General Assembly and the Security Council on the question of Palestine from 1947 to 1990. Chronological compilation (A/AC.183/L.2/Add.2 to 10).

(22) Elon, *Jerusalem, City of Mirrors,* pp. 47-48.

(23) Quoted by Michel Lelong in *Guerre ou Paix à Jérusalem*, Paris, Albin Michel, 1982, pp. 180-181.

(24) Ibid., pp. 181-182.

PART IV. THE STATE OF PALESTINE: A LEGAL STUDY

13. The Formation of the State of Palestine

(1) See UNESCO document 131 EX/43, 1989, Annex II.

(2) United Nations, General Assembly, Resolution 43/177.

(3) *The Origins and Evolution of the Palestine Problem*: part I: *1917-1947*, UN publ., sales no. 78.1.19; part II: *1947-1977*, UN publ., sales no. 78.1.19; part III: *1978-1983*, UN publ., sales no. 84.1.13.

(4) C. Rousseau, *Droit International Public*, vol. II, 'Les Sujets', Paris, Sirey, 1974, p. 382.

(5) Preamble to the Mandate for Palestine, 24 July 1922.

(6) Great Britain: General Statement of Census of 1922, p. 3.

(7) British Parliamentary Papers, Cmd. 5954 and 5957.

(8) See for example: Abu-Lughod, *The Transformation of Palestine*, 1971; H. Cattan, *Palestine and International Law*, 1973; the United Nations publication

quoted in note 3 above; W.T. and S.V. Mallison, *The Palestine Problem in International and World Order*, 1986; Quingley, 'Palestine Question in International Law. A Historical Perspective', *Arab Studies Quarterly*, vol. 10, no. 1, 1987.

(9) 'Command Paper', Cmd. 5479. This summary of the situation for the period 1937–1939 is based on an analysis of the United Nations publication quoted in note 3 above.

(10) Cmd. 5854.

(11) Cmd. 5893.

(12) Cmd. 6019.

(13) ICJ Advisory Opinion of 11 July 1950, International Status of South-West Africa, Reports of Judgements, Advisory Opinions and Orders, p. 132.

(14) V. Nguyen Quol Dinh, P. Daillier and A. Pellet, *Droit International Public*, LGDJ, 3rd edn, 1987, p. 462.

(15) See text of the proclamation in *La Revue de Droit International Public*, 1989, pp. 409-411.

(16) ICJ, Judgement of 20 December 1974, Nuclear Tests, Record, 1974, p. 270.

(17) See *United Nations Resolutions on Palestine and Arab-Israeli Conflict*, Washington, DC, Institute for Palestine Studies, vol. I: 1975, vols. II and III: 1988.

(18) Abu Kydyab, *Social and Educational Institutions of the PLO*, fifth United Nations Seminar on the Question of Palestine, 1982; L. Brand, *Palestinians in the Arab World. Institution Building and the Search for State*, 1988; X. Baron, *Les Palestiniens, un Peuple*, 1984; H. Cohen, *The PLO. People, Power and Politics*, 1984; A. Gresh, *The PLO, The Struggle Within*, 1988; R. Hamid, 'What is the PLO?', *Journal of Palestine Studies*, 1975; Rubenberg, *The PLO as Institutional Infrastructure*, 1983; E. Said, *The Question of Palestine*, 1978; Zebrowski, *Active Role of the PLO in Creating State and Social Structure*, eighth United Nations Seminar on the Question of Palestine, 1985.

(19) *Le Monde*, 27 March 1980.

(20) P. Boyle, 'On Secret Israeli-Palestinian Relations' in Alain Gresh, *The PLO, The Struggle Within*, London, Zed Books, 1983.

(21) See in this connection: Abraham, 'The Development and Transformation of the Palestine National Movement' in Nasser Aruri (ed.), *Occupation, Israel over Palestine*, 1984, pp. 391-423; Gresh, *The PLO . . .* , pp. 147 *et seq.*

(22) For the documents of regional organizations concerning Palestine, see: K.P. Sauvant and Jan Kowitsh, *The Third World without Super-Powers* (collected documents), 1978, 4 vols; K.P. Sauvant and J.W. Müller, *The Group of 77* (collected documents), 2 vols; 'Action Taken by Intergovernmental Organizations' in *Report of the Committee on the Exercise of the Inalienable*

Rights of the Palestinian People, A/43/35, 1988, pp. 24-26.

(23) The first reference to the right of the Palestinian people to set up its own state occurred in the resolution of the Commission on Human Rights in February 1980, several months before the adoption of resolution ES7/2 of the General Assembly.

(24) Relevant General Assembly resolutions include: Resolutions 3236 (XXIX) 22 November 1974; 3376 (XXX) 10 November 1975; 31/20 (24 November 1976); 32/14 (7 November 1977); 33/28 (7 December 1978); 34/65 (12 December 1979); ES7/2 (21 July 1980); 35/169 (15 December 1980); 35/207 (16 December 1980); 36/120 (10 December 1981); 37/86 (10 December 1982); 38/58 (13 December 1983); 38/180 (19 December 1983); 39/49 (11 December 1984); 39/146 (14 December 1984); 40/96 (12 December 1985); 41/43 (2 December 1986); 42/66 (2 December 1987); 43/54 (6 December 1988); 43/176 (15 December 1988); 44/42 (6 December 1990); 45/83 (13 December 1990).

For the text and analysis of United Nations resolutions on Palestine, and for the number of votes obtained for each resolution, see: *The United Nations Resolutions on Palestine and the Arab-Israeli Conflict*, 3 vols. (covering the period 1947–1986), Washington, DC, Institute for Palestine Studies, 1979–1988; *The Origins and Evolution of the Palestine Problem*, UN Doc. ST/SG/SER.F/1, 1979; *An International Law Analysis of the Major United Nations Resolutions Concerning the Palestine Question*, UN Doc. ST/SG/SER.F/4, 1979; *United Nations Initiatives on the Question of Palestine*, UN Doc. A/Conf. 114/10, 1983; *United Nations Resolutions on Palestine 1947–1983*, A/AC183/L2 + add.

(25) The legal validity of this decision has been questioned. See: R.G. Sybesma-Khol, *The Status of Observers in the United Nations*, 1981, p. 440; E. Suy, 'The Status of Observers in International Organizations', *Collected Courses of The Hague Academy of International Law*, vol. 60, 1978.

(26) L. Gross, 'Voting in the Security Council and the PLO', *American Journal of International Law*, 1976, pp. 470-491.

(27) Sybesma-Khol, *Status of Observers . . .* , p. 39.

(28) For the impact of this practice, see H. Mzioudet, 'La Participation des Mouvements de Libération Nationale à la Diplomatie: Cas de l'OLP', *Etudes Internationales*, Tunis, 1988.

(29) An exception had been made for the Pope.

(30) In 1988 the ICJ had been called upon to give an advisory opinion about certain difficulties arising from the refusal of the United States to respect these privileges and immunities; see Advisory Opinion of 26 April 1988, 'Applicability of the Obligation to Arbitrate under Section 21 of the United Nations Headquarters Agreement of 26 June 1947', Reports, 1988, p. 125.

(31) For example, C. Lazarus, 'Le Statut des Mouvements de Libération Nationale à l'Organisation des Nations Unies', *Annuaire Français de Droit*

International, 1974, pp. 198-199.

(32) M. Virally, 'L'ONU et le Droit', *Journal de Droit International*, 1972, pp. 501-533.

(33) The Court's interpretation 'cannot remain unaffected by the subsequent development of law, through the Charter of the United Nations and by way of customary law', ICJ, Advisory Opinion of 21 June 1971, Namibia, Reports, 1971, p. 31; see also Advisory Opinion of 16 October 1975.

(34) ICJ, Advisory Opinion of 11 April 1949, 'Reparations for Injuries Suffered in the Service of the United Nations', Reports, 1949, pp. 178-180.

14. Legal Aspects of the Existence of the State of Palestine

(1) W. Khalidi, 'Thinking the Unthinkable. A Sovereign Palestinian State', *Foreign Affairs*, July 1978; J.H. Weiler, 'Israel and the Creation of a Palestinian State: The Art of the Impossible and the Possible', *Texas International Law Journal*, summer 1982, pp. 287-387. See also F.A. Boyle, 'Create the State of Palestine!', *Scandinavian Journal of Development Alternatives*, June-Sept. 1988, pp. 25-58.

(2) M. Klarin, 'The Palestinian State', *Review of International Affairs*, Belgrade, no. 932, 1989, p .6.

(3) Y. Arafat, 'Significance of the Proclamation of the Palestinian State', *Review of International Affairs*, Belgrade, no. 939, May 1989, p. 9.

(4) For the text of the declaration, see UNESCO document 131 EX/43. J.M. Segal's article, originally published in the *Washington Post* of 27 May 1988 and reproduced in the *Journal of Palestine Studies*. M. Flory, 'Naissance d'un Etat Palestinien', *Revue Générale de Droit International Public*, 1989, no. 2, pp. 385-415.

(5) See numbered points 12–15 above.

(6) See numbered point 21 above.

(7) A plentiful literature exists on this subject. See in particular: M. Bedjaoui, *Towards a New International Order*, UNESCO, 1979; J. Castaneda, 'Legal Status of United Nations Resolutions', *Collected Courses of The Hague Academy of International Law*, 1970, vol. 129; L. Di Qual, *Les Effets des Résolutions des Nations Unies*, 1967; R.J. Dupuy, 'Droit Déclaratoire et Droit Programmatoire. De la Coutume Sauvage à la "Soft Law"', Colloque de la Société Française de Droit International, 1974; R.A. Falk, 'On the Quasi-legislative Competence of the General Assembly', *American Journal of International Law*, 1966; G. Fitzmaurice, 'Statute of the Resolutions of the United Nations', *British Yearbook of International Law*, 1958; M. Garibaldi, 'The Legal Statute of General Assembly Resolutions', *American Society of International Law*, Proceedings, 1979; R. Higgins, *The Development of International Law through the Political Organs of the United Nations*, 1963; Institute of International Law, 'United Nations General Assembly Resolutions', *Institute Yearbook,* 1985 and Cairo

session, 1987; Graduate Institute of International Studies, Geneva, symposium on resolutions in the creation of international development law, 1971; Johnson, 'The Effects of the Resolutions of the General Assembly', *British Yearbook of International Law*, 1955–1956; J.G. Kim, 'La Validité des Resolutions des Nations Unies', *Revue Générale de Droit International Public*, 1979; A. Pellet, *Droit International du Développement*, 1987; Proceedings of the American Society of International Law, 1979, 'The Effects of United Nations General Assembly on Customary International Law', etc; K. Skubizewski, *A New Source of Law of Nations: Resolutions of International Organs*, Mélanges Guggenheim, 1968; B. Sloan, 'The Binding Force of Recommendations of the General Assembly', *British Yearbook of International Law*, 1948; A.J.P. Tammes, 'Decision of International Organs as a Source of International Law', *Collected Courses of The Hague International Law Academy*, 1958, vol. 94; H. Thierry, 'Les Résolutions des Organes Internationaux dans la Jurisprudence de la Cour Internationale de Justice', *Collected Courses of The Hague International Law Academy*, 1980, vol. 167; M. Virally, 'La Valeur Juridique des Recommandations des Organisations Internationales', *Annuaire Français de Droit International*, 1956; M. Virally, 'A Propos de la Lex Ferenda', Mélanges Reuter, 1980; P. De Visscher, 'Observations sur les Résolutions Déclaratives de Droit Adoptées au Sein de l'Assemblée Générale des Nations Unies', *Mélanges Bindschedler*, 1980; P. Weil, 'Vers une Normativité Relative en Droit International Public', *Revue Générale de Droit International Public*, 1982.

(8) *Yearbook of the International Law Commission*, 1966, vol. II, p. 270.

(9) J.H. Weiler, 'Israel and the Creation of a Palestinian State: The Art of the Impossible and the Possible', *Texas International Law Journal*, summer 1982, pp. 316–323; A. Pellet, 'La Destruction de Troie n'Aura pas Lieu', *Pal. Yb.I.L.*, 1987–1988, pp. 44–84; A. Roberts, 'Prolonged Military Occupation: The Israeli-Occupied Territories since 1967', *AJIL*, 1990, no. 1, pp. 44–103.

(10) ICJ, *Reports*, 1966, p. 291.

(11) Ibid., p. 297.

(12) R. Higgins, 'Seventeen Years' Work by the United Nations has Provided us with an Important New Source of Customary International Law', 1963, p. 10.

(13) A. Pellet, 'Le "Bon Droit" et l'Ivraie—Plaidoyer pour l'Ivraie', in *Le Droit des Peuples à Disposer d'Eux-mêmes, Mélanges Offerts à Charles Chaumont*, 1984, pp. 389–390.

(14) For a more detailed analysis of this resolution see W.T. and S.V. Malisson, *An International Law Analysis of the Major United Nations Resolutions Concerning the Palestine Question*, UN Doc. ST/SG/SER.F/4, 1979, pp. 9–27.

(15) The text of the declaration in the *Revue Générale de Droit International Public*, 1989, p. 410.

(16) See United Nations document A/C.1/SR 127 of 27 April 1948, p. 108, statement by Mr Shertok, representative of the Jewish Agency.

(17) This is confirmed by consistent international legal precedents, cf. PCIJ, 1931, *Railway Traffic between Lithunia and Poland* (series A/B, fac.42), p.116 or ICJ, 1948, *Corfu Channel*, ICJ Report, 1948, p. 26.

(18) See M. Flory, 'Naissance d'un Etat Palestinien', *Revue Générale de Droit International Public,* 1989, no. 2, p. 403.

(19) See numbered point 22 above.

(20) See note 1.

(21) Cf. C. Rousseau, *Droit International Public,* vol. III, 1977, p. 514.

(22) Cf. V. Nguyen Quoc Dinh, P. Daillier and A. Pellet, *Droit International Public,* LGDJ, 3rd edn, 1987, pp. 492-493.

(23) Cf. Rousseau, *Droit International Public,* vol. III, p. 541.

(24) M. Bedjaoui, 'L'Admission d'un Nouveau Membre à l'OUA', in *Mélanges Offerts à Charles Chaumont,* 1984, pp. 51-52.

(25) Rousseau, *Droit International Public,* p. 542.

(26) See also the chapter devoted to the concept of statehood in the practice of the United Nations in Higgins, 'Seventeen Years' Work . . . ', pp. 17-34.

(27) *Revue Générale de Droit International Public,* 1989, p. 453.

(28) R. Charvin, 'L'Intifada, de l'Affirmation d'un Peuple à la Naissance d'un Etat', *Palestine et Droit,* 1989, no. 3, p. 23.

(29) Ref. ILC.

(30) Ibid.

(31) Restatement of the Law Third, *The Foreign Relations Law of the United States,* vol. I, American Law Institute Publishers, 1987, pp. 72- 77.

(32) See numbered point 15 above.

(33) Charvin, 'L'Intifada . . . ', pp. 6-25.

(34) See for example Resolutions 31/106, 32/91, 33/113, 34/90, 35/122, 36/147, 37/88, 38/79, 39/95, 40/161, 41/63, 42/160, 43/21, 44/2, 44/48 or 45/74.

(35) See for example Resolutions 36/226, 37/123, 38/180, 39/146, 40/168, 41/162, 42/209, 43/54, 44/40, or 45/83 and D. Weissbrecht, 'The Role of International Organizations in the Implementation of Human Rights and Humanitarian Law in Situations of Armed Conflict', *Vanderbilt Journal of Transnational Law,* vol. 21, 1988, p. 330.

(36) See also Resolutions of the Security Council Nos: 446 (1979), 465, 468, 471, 476, 478 (1980), 497 (1981), 582 (1986), 605 (1987), 608 (1988), 636, 641 (1989), 672, 673 (1990), 726 (1992).

(37) W. Olson, 'United Nations Security Council Resolutions Regarding Deportations from Israeli Administrated Territories. The Applicability of the Fourth Geneva Convention Relative to the Protection of Civilian Persons in Time of War', *Stanford Journal of International Law,* vol. 24, no. 2, 1988, pp. 611-636.

(38) See especially Roberts, 'Prolonged Military Occupation . . . ', and

Pellet, 'La Destruction de Troie . . . '

(39) Cf. decision Beth/El Bekavoth of 13 March 1979.

(40) See especially: K. Shehadeh, *Occupier's Law: Israel and the West Bank*, rev. edn, 1988, p. XI; International Association of Democratic Lawyers Mission to the Territories Occupied by Israel, 12–20 October 1980, 'Introductory Report and Legal Conclusions', 1981 (mineographed); A. Gersson, *Israel, the West Bank and the International Law*, 1978; E. Nakhleh, *The West Bank and Gaza. Toward the Making of a Palestinian State*, 1979; International Commission of Jurists, *The West Bank and the Role of Law*, 1980 and *The Administration of Occupied Territories = the West Bank*, 1991.

(41) PCIJ, Series A/B, facsimile no. 62.

(42) This is also accepted by certain Israeli writers. See, for example, Y. Dinstein, 'The International Law of Belligerent Occupation and Human Rights', *Israeli Yearbook of Human Rights*, 1978, p. 105.

(43) *The Legal Status of the West Bank and Gaza*, United Nations Publication, New York, 1982, p. 7.

(44) Ibid., p. 9.

(45) Charvin, 'L'Intifada . . . ', p. 11.

(46) Cf. Rousseau, *Droit International Public*, vol. III, p. 609.

(47) United Nations document A/43/928.

(48) The complete text of the memorandum is reproduced in *Revue d'Etudes Palestiniennes*, no. 40, 1991, pp. 106-108.

(49) *The Legal Status of West Bank and Gaza,* United Nations, 1982, p. 30.

(50) Alain Gresh, *The PLO, The Struggle Within,* London, Zed Books, 1988, p. 203.

(51) See numbered point 15 above.

(52) See numbered point 35 above.

(53) ICJ, Advisory Opinion of 11 April 1949, 'Reparations for Injuries Suffered in the Service of the United Nations', Reports, 1949, p. 178.

15. The Admission of Palestine to International Organizations

(1) *Repertory of Practice of United Nations Organs*, vol. I, p. 200, para. 54.

(2) See UNESCO document 131 EX/43, 1989.

(3) Contra: F.L.J. Kirgis, 'Admission of Palestine as a Member of a Specialized Agency Witholding the Payment of Assessment in Response', *American Journal of International Law*, 1990, no. 1, pp. 218-230.

(4) See especially numbered points 17 and 18 above.

(5) ICJ, *Reports*, 1948, p. 62.

(6) Ibid., p. 63.

(7) *Repertory of Practice of United Nations Organs*, vol. I, table, pp. 214-235, and supplement 1, pp. 1,398; R. Higgins, *The Development of International Law through the Political Organs of the United Nations,* 1963, pp. 11-49.

(8) See numbered point 51 above.

(9) *Repertory of Practice of United Nations Organs*, vol. 1, p. 216, para. 87.

(10) Quoted by G. Feuer, in J.P. Cot and A. Pellet (eds), *La Charte des Nations Unies* (commentary article par article), 2nd edn, 1991, p. 173.

(11) See numbered point 11 above.

(12) ICJ, 'Competence of the General Assembly for the Admission of a State to the United Nations', *Reports*, 1950, pp. 8-10.

(13) F.A. Boyle, 'Create the State of Palestine!', *Scandinavian Journal of Development Alternatives,* June-Sept. 1988, pp. 25-58.

(14) Published in *Arab Studies Quarterly*, 1987, vol. 10, no. 1, p. 56.

(15) See note 5 above.

(16) Quoted in UNESCO document 131 EX/43, p. 10.

(17) Cf. UNESCO document 132 EX/SR.25.

(18) See numbered point 25 above.

(19) R. Higgins, 'Seventeen Years' Work by the United Nations has Provided us with an Important Source of Customary International Law', 1963, p. 43.

(20) WHO official documents, second World Health Assembly, 10th meeting, p. 123.

(21) Cf. United Nations document A Conf./140/13, *Review of the Activities of the United Nations System of Organizations to Assist the Palestinian People*, 1983, pp. 38-42; and, more recently, UNESCO document 132 EX/31 of 25 September 1989. The texts of UNESCO resolutions in favour of Palestine are reproduced in *United Nations Resolutions on Palestine and the Arab-Israel Conflict 1947–1986*, 3 vols, Washington, DC, Institute of Palestine Studies, 1979–1988.

(22) UNESCO document 131 EX/45

(23) UNESCO document 131 EX/43.

(24) UNESCO document 131 EX/INF.7.

(25) UNESCO document 131 EX/43 Add.

(26) UNESCO document 131 EX/SR.1-31, p. 421.

(27) UNESCO document 131 EX/Dec., 9.4.

(28) UNESCO document 131 EX/SR.1-31, pp. 424-426.

(29) Ibid., p. 426.

(30) UNESCO document 132 EX/131.

(31) Ibid., internal doc.

(32) Memorandum of the Ministry of Health of the German Democratic Republic to the Member States of the World Health Organization, 1972.

(33) WHO document A42/VR/10, p. 38.

(34) WHO document CL9, 1989 (in A/42/INF.DOC./3).

(35) WHO document A42/VR/10, p. 8.

(36) The article by Kirgis cited in note 3 above is pertinent in this respect. However, the author is opposed to the principle of admitting Palestine to the

Specialized Agencies.

(37) WHO document A42/VR/10, p. 9.

(38) Ibid., p. 12.

(39) Ibid., p. 13.

(40) Proposal by Tongan delegate (WHO document A42/VR/10).

(41) Serial number of the Tongan proposal (WHO document A42/VR/10).

(42) Ibid., p. 4.

(43) Ibid., p. 8.

(44) WHO document A42/INF.DOC./3 Add.

(45) See Kirgis, 'Admission of Palestine . . . '

(46) WHO document A42/VR/10.

(47) Ibid., p. 37.

(48) Ibid., pp. 39-40.

(49) Ibid., p. 35.

Conclusion

(1) *Rien qu'une Autre Année*, Paris, Ed. Minuit, 1983.

(2) 'La Marche du Siècle' (The March of the Century), FR3 (French television), 3 August 1991.

(3) *Le Monde*, 31 July 1991, p. 22.

(4) Theodor Herzl, *Diaries*, vol. II, 1904, p. 711.

Index